MW01089212

Just about everyone knows that large numbers of people—especially younger and more educated people—are dropping out of church. To stop this trend, some focus on hot music or cool graphics or casual dress or catering to what people want politically. But more and more of us are coming to the conclusion that many people are leaving because they see deep and significant problems in what most Christians believe and preach. This book could help tens of thousands of churches and pastors imagine a better way forward...real-life sermons from the fresh and needed perspective of open, relational, and process theology. Enthusiastically recommended!

—**Brian D. McLaren**, author of *Do I Stay Christian?*

Anyone who ventures behind a pulpit is taking a risk, wagering there's good news left in our ancient texts. Too often, the goodness of God is hidden under the bushel of Almighty dogma and a controlling tradition. In this timely and needed volume, you hear from a staggeringly diverse collection of proclaimers who haven't escaped the call to preach, but insist the goodness of God should not be compromised because the power of God is love. I'm thrilled to have a preaching book to recommend without hesitation!

—**Tripp Fuller**, host of Homebrewed Christianity

For far too long, classic Christianity has held to a view of God as unchanging and the nature of God's interaction with the world as controlling. Scripture presents God as creative and responsive, however, intentional, initiating, and influenceable—a God who works in partnership with humans. This book demonstrates through the preaching of Scripture that God's good, loving, dynamic power operates *in process* with the freedom of others. God takes risks that may lead to evil and suffering, as well as to the righteous work of cooperative partners.

—**Karen Strand Winslow**, author of *Imagining Equity: The Gifts of Christian Feminist Theology*

Preaching the Uncontrolling Love of God

Sermons, Essays, and Worship Elements from the Perspective of Open, Relational, and Process Theology

Jeff Wells, Vikki Randall, Nichole Torbitzky, Thomas Jay Oord, EDITORS

FOREWORD BY John B. Cobb Jr.

Print: 978-1-958670-32-3
Ebook: 978-1-958670-31-6

Printed in the United States of America

Library of Congress Cataloguing-in-Publication Data

Preaching the Uncontrolling Love of God: Sermons, Essays, and Worship Elements from the Perspective of Open, Relational, and Process Theology / Editors: Jeff Wells, Vikki Randall, Nichole Torbitzky, Thomas Jay Oord

Table of Contents

Essays on Preaching, Teaching, and Practicing Open, Relational, and Process Theologies

Worship Elements Expressing Open, Relational, and Process Theologies

Foreword

JOHN B. COBB, JR.

Process and Faith

It is just possible that this book will mark a new stage in American Protestantism. Mainstream Protestantism in the United States is deeply influenced by Luther and Calvin, who encouraged Christians to give priority to Biblical teaching rather than to what the church derived from its Greek and Roman origins. However, some beliefs were carried over into the new churches with little critical reflection and then projected onto the Bible. For example, most Protestants thought they were supposed to think that God is omnipotent, even though the stories that are brought together in the Bible imply humans are responsible for their decisions and often work against God's hopes for the world. At the same time, the decisions of Christians are often affected by their sense of God's call. Divine and human actions interact.

The Bible tells us many stories that are woven together into one overarching one. It invites us to find the unfinished stories to which we can contribute new chapters. For Christians, the Bible's most important stories are about Jesus, and Jesus invites us to be his disciples.

Some of us see all this as process thinking and feel called to continue in that tradition. Of course, there are many features of the world that remain unchanged for millions of years. We are not proposing that we ignore the science that focuses on these. To ignore the changeless makes no sense. But the tendency to identify the sacred with the changeless and to worship that does not appeal to me or seem biblical. We process theologians think that since we cannot change the changeless, it is wise to attend most to the changing world. This was also the decision of the ancient Hebrews as well.

To those of us in the process tradition, the Bible and its innumerable stories are congenial. Some religious teachings, considered primary in some traditions, are about the changeless features of reality. Some people seek such timeless truths in the Bible, and of course, they can find some. But we, in the process tradition celebrate the biblical prioritizing of process.

We think that, at last, scientists are discovering that the world is not made up ultimately of changeless atoms moving in changeless patterns. The world is made up of ever new events in ever-changing patterns. The question is how so much of the present can, nevertheless, be seen to have been the inevitable consequence of the past. Thus, a great deal of prediction is possible, as well. Much cosmology seemed, until recently, endlessly repetitive. Much theology was a matter of locating God's actions in Jesus in a context that was otherwise ultimately predetermined. But many of us now think that we should locate the stories of Jesus, as the Bible does, in the context of the entire history of Israel and its neighbors. We should ask what is happening in God's world, how does that look in light of what we have learned from Jesus, and what being a disciple of Jesus now requires of us.

Because of the importance of the Bible in Protestant churches, stories play an important role. Some of us were delighted to find that the most creative thinking in science was moving toward process thought and that it was evoking, also, some process philosophy. It seemed possible to bring Christian thought and creative philosophy together.

We organized "Process and Faith" to promote this. It has played a role at the margins of "liberal" Protestantism since the 1960s. Sometimes that role has been quite significant, sometimes barely visible. Like many organizations, it has had ups and downs, but in recent years, mostly downs. For some time now, the organization has not been able to give leadership.

However, we rejoice that communities of process Christians have emerged who are pursuing the work of integration independently and sharing what they have learned. The vision for this book arose out of the work of one of those communities, the Church of the Village, led by its pastor, Jeff Wells. Clearly, the many contributors are in fact part of the wider community concerned with "process and faith," whether any of them have ever been associated with the organization to which we gave that name. I hope this book will help in the revival of that organization and will, in turn, be helpful in promoting it.

Many now know that they live in a world of deeply interconnected events without knowing that this recognition locates one in a new metaphysical vision. What is humanly and theologically important is that we live and think that way, not how we label it. Many of us have derived this understanding from the Bible without getting involved in philosophy. The fact that others emphasize the philosophical importance of this way of experiencing ourselves and our world has allowed still other Christians to dismiss process thought as just another philosophy that does not really make any difference in ordinary human life. If we point out that relational living differs from treating everything as independent from everything else, some easily agree. But they don't see the need to involve philosophy. They feel that the connectedness of things is already fully expressed in the Christian emphasis on love.

On the other hand, currently, there is more chance than ever before that process thinking will play a real role in the mainstream of what is left of liberal Protestantism. This is because it is difficult for Protestant leadership to think that simply continuing what they have been doing in the recent past is promising for the future. This book calls attention to another possibility and invites its serious consideration. It shows that this other possibility has already been widely and richly developed. This book is a great achievement.

Perhaps the main immediate reason, currently, for giving special attention to this possibility for faith is that the broader movement of process thought is now not simply marginal. For a long time, those who view matters somewhat historically have recognized that there are serious problems with "modern" science, "modern" spirituality, and "modern" thought generally. But for most people, the "modern" world was still the way ahead for them personally and for the United States as a whole. To critique it and offer an alternative, as process thought did, was at best eccentric.

If "modern" is simply used to mean whatever is currently dominant, its critique will simply express the critical spirit. This is always needed, but it does not offer an alternative expression of Christianity. History has given the word a different role. We speak of "modern" history as beginning in Europe in the seventeenth century. "Modern" came to mean that type of thinking and social life that was gaining control in that century and becoming foundational to European thought and action most clearly in the eighteenth century. It understood the world as made up of self-contained individual entities. It provided the assumptions of the natural sciences and the technology associated with them. More and more, it dominated education.

Of course, most people continued premodern patterns in some parts of their lives. These often included their religious thought and practice. But most of those who were considered in the lead saw this clinging to past patterns as resistance to progress. In the nineteenth century, the goal of universal education was that everyone should be exposed to modern thought presented as the way ahead for individuals and society.

In addition to the enormous resistance from custom and habit, there were always a few intellectuals who clung to the old ways and defended them by appealing to the great thinkers they had produced, such as Thomas Aquinas. The Catholic church gave this kind of resistance support. But it tried to do so without disrupting the victory of modern science and technology.

"Modernity" was a movement to which many thinkers contributed. It always included a variety of specific beliefs. A course in "modern philosophy" studies the main thinkers from the seventeenth century on. In that period, there were many who continued the Medieval preference for Aristotle, but the defense of the past did not attract the quality of originality and creativity that went into the development of new alternatives. Obviously, "modern" thinkers do not all agree. Nevertheless, there is widespread agreement that René Descartes played the largest role in shifting the intellectual assumptions of Europe in the seventeenth century away from the Aristotelian basis of medieval thought.

When we think of Descartes as providing the basic metaphysics for the modern period, we do not mean that everyone adopted it. Nevertheless, most people took for granted that mind and matter were fundamental, that both existed, and that they differed greatly from each other. There were ways to write about additions and subtractions and multiplications, either of mental or physical entities. But how were mental entities related to physical ones?

The duality of mind and matter was a major problem. The two obvious alternatives were materialism and idealism. It might be that the ultimate reality is matter and that mental entities, if they exist at all, have no influence on what happens. Or maybe materiality is simply a mental idea imposed on some data of experience. But few people followed either of these extremes. There seemed to be two kinds of entities. Most moderns think in such dualistic ways. However, because of the problems with dualism, many philosophers work hard to avoid it.

In the twentieth century, some realized that if we shifted from thinking of "things" to thinking of events, we could deal more directly with the actual world and understand it without dualism. For "process thinkers," the world is made up of interrelated events. Events happen and then constitute the past. The past contributes itself to the present, which then becomes the past for what is next to come. The present is always deeply affected by the past, but it always also plays some role, however minor, in its own self-determination, which, in turn, affects the future. This picture of a dramatically interdependent world is now widely acceptable as an alternative to the modern tendency to see a multiplicity of fundamentally independent entities. Process thought gets some credit for having led in the focus on relationships.

For process thinkers, instead of locating entities in either the mental or the physical world of "things," "things," in the common modern sense, are understood to emerge in the world of events. They are not the entities of which everything is composed. More fundamental are happenings, occurrences, "occasions of experience." More fundamental than electrons and protons, it seems, are quantum events that are happenings rather than simply mental or physical things. Thus, the world is made of events, and there are both mental and physical aspects in every event. Since avoiding dualism is, today, often taken as a gain, process thought is sometimes approved for having taken this step long ago.

Thus, although most people do not identify themselves as process thinkers, process thought is now broadly influential without being offensive. Christians may acknowledge process ideas as a major source of their thought. They may also point out that process thought is closer to biblical thought than is the modern thought it offers to replace. Many people will listen without offense. They have begun to recognize the problems of much "modern" Christian thinking and more Christians are ready to take different proposals seriously. Process theology may be the best developed alternative. It already deals with what some consider new issues.

For example, process theology has worked out the relation between human beings and other animals credibly. The topic is important today as other species are going extinct, and most Christian thought leaders have very little to say. Process thinkers have at least been aware of the urgency of thinking this through. Finally, it seems Western civilization is ready to acknowledge the problem. This is a truly new situation with radical possibilities.

More broadly, many Christians realize that theology that does not guide us toward the avoidance of ecological disaster is inadequate. Many also realize that in this area process thought was often in the lead. This realization opens many doors.

For these reasons, publication of this book is an important moment in the history of American Protestant theology. It offers the opportunity to see how thinkers, specifically preachers, who are truly committed to process theology seek to influence the life of the churches where they work. People new to this discussion will get a feel of what it would be like to be part of a Christian community guided by process theology.

Some ask whether acceptance of process thinking can be helpful to persons today who are no longer comfortable with their membership in churches that seem committed to outdated ideas. I point to the work of Tripp Fuller and Tom Oord. I have the greatest appreciation and admiration for these two men. They understand how there are many deeply committed Christians who feel themselves pressured to believe things they cannot truly believe and to act in ways that do not seem genuinely Christian. They have offered to those who are in this position an opportunity to be authentically convinced of central Christian beliefs and liberated from pressure to believe what makes little sense or seems untrue when examined in today's world. Many of them become better disciples of Jesus and more wholistic and authentic in their personal lives.

I rejoice that both Tripp Fuller and Tom Oord are themselves process theologians. They address especially those in conservative churches who really understand the truth and saving power of the gospel but can no longer affirm much that conservatives associate with it. They find that many are helped by learning that what most attracts them and challenges them in the Christian tradition is consistent with a cutting-edge science and philosophy.

Perhaps there is a complementary possibility for liberals who realize that they have unwisely given up much of what distinguishes discipleship to Jesus. They find it is modernity and not "reason" that has made them think they must abandon some important Biblical and traditional teaching. This has sometimes made their modern Christianity more modern than Christian.

Perhaps process theology could check the wide collapse of liberal Protestantism. I want to explore this possibility with you. To do so, we must ask what is the reason for the dramatic decline of liberal Protestantism? The full answer, of course, would require a serious study of hundreds of individual cases. What I offer instead is a few impressions that may be worth considering.

In the early decades after World War II, tens of millions of Americans looked to liberal Protestantism to help them maintain moral standards and raise their families. It could also give them a sense that they and their nation were on the right track. They thought they could do this best if they avoided theological controversy, and the best way of avoiding controversy was to avoid controversial topics. Liberal Protestant churches certainly communicated values, but they were usually the values held by the people who came to them. Few came to learn new "Christian" values.

I am not condemning this. The liberal churches helped millions of people. What they communicated was valuable. Their teachings and practices rarely did harm to those involved. There were discussions of important questions at their seminaries that went beyond what was elsewhere available. My experience, insofar as I fit in, was fine. My four sons had good experiences growing up in a fine liberal church.

They did not need any great "liberation" from the church. The church gave them complete freedom to continue participation or not. None continued, but they do not resist attending with their parents when they are near their childhood church. In general, they do not think their children need what they got from church or that they will profit from being active in a church.

In my process view, a disciple of Jesus will be likely to act in distinctive ways. But the experience of most liberal Protestants did not make many of them think that becoming a liberal Protestant would change the behavior of a new member significantly. In short, the strategy of being noncontroversial and continuous with the surrounding culture did not communicate that there is something quite distinctive about being a Christian or a member of the church.

Now, I do not favor an attempt to persuade people that although being a Christian makes little difference in the here and now, it will make the difference between heaven and hell after death. But if we take Jesus seriously, there will be highly distinctive features of our lives. For example, Jesus' strong emphasis on the love of enemies would differentiate our decisions on both personal and socio-political matters from the dominant culture. The question of how Christians differ from others, and therefore the importance of the decision to be a disciple, would be more apparent.

My experience of the church as an adolescent included a strong social gospel emphasis. It did not lift up love of enemy, but it communicated to me that faith in God called on me to strive for justice. I believe that the development of the social gospel by the liberal churches was a major contribution to American history. It made possible the New Deal of President Roosevelt. By counting on serious leaders of the social gospel to help him, he could implement some of what they had called for.

My negative point about the liberal church after World War II is that there was no comparable leadership in the church. Certainly, during this period, the liberal churches have supported many good movements, but I am not aware that any of these movements are thought of as having been prepared for, or initiated by, the churches. Political and social progressives hope they can count on liberal churches for support, but rarely do they look to them for guidance.

Process theology encourages us to be disciples of Jesus, adjusting radically to the enormous historical differences of our times from his. Other aspects of process thought will facilitate that. We can formulate a discipleship that is both costly and fulfilling. As we move into what may be civilization's last days, disciples of Jesus may have the most promising and healing of messages. At least, liberal Protestants who find great help in process thought, can, and I think should, work on projects of this kind.

I encourage you, as you read the sermons and essays collected here, to ask whether you are being called to something distinctive, something lacking in the secular world, but not intellectually dubious or inferior. I think discipleship to Jesus places one in a unique relation to a history whose prospects are currently threatened.

I have given special attention to love of enemy because Jesus seems to have thought that was both distinctive of his vision and intellectually credible. My judgment is that unless we transform our enemies into partners, we will continue to devote more of our resources to opposing them than to joining them in saving the habitability of the planet.

But there are other necessary changes. We must also transform our understanding of how we are related to the nonhuman creatures with which we share this planet. We need greater clarity about our responsibility for the condition of our planet. We need to appreciate much more deeply how our lives are bound up with that of other people, both neighbors and at a great distance. The sermons and essays in this book will make clear that there are many differences introduced by a faith richly informed by process thought.

I believe process thought can help us appreciate the wisdom of Jesus and truly serve him. I believe that if Protestant churches widely taught discipleship to Jesus, they would lose some of their current members, but others, who have left, would consider returning, and some, who have experienced the shallowness of so much contemporary secular life, would again turn to the church. They might save the church while the church saved them.

You will gather that, in my case, acceptance of process thinking opens me to fuller discipleship to Jesus, something that modernity, at least in most of its forms, works against. Process theology is a form of postmodern theology. It emphasizes how it responds to the limitations and negative consequences of most forms of modernity. It is as a Christian believer, not as a philosopher, that I commend process thought as a liberating pathway toward becoming a better disciple of Jesus.

Introduction

JEFF WELLS

This book presents a collection of sermons, essays, and worship elements that portray and highlight the experience of preaching and practicing open, relational, and process theologies—primarily in Christian and Unitarian Universalist congregations.

While there is plenty of deeply meaningful and transformative theology contained in these pages, this is not a book of theology. It is a book about how to put specific theological perspectives into practice. You might call it a "how-to" manual. This book is intended as a resource for those who are already bringing process, relational, and open theologies into local church worship, preaching, and teaching. It is also for those who are new to open, relational, and process theologies and want to learn how others have introduced them to their congregations. The book's audience in local congregations will be clergy, ministers of worship arts, worship planning teams, music leaders, and lay persons with a passion for theological understanding. Importantly, this book will be a valuable resource in preaching, worship, and practical theology classes at seminaries and theological schools.

When I found my way back to the church after a 20-year sojourn in atheism and left-wing political activism, I immediately gravitated to those who called themselves "progressive Christians." In the United Methodist Church in New York, I became active in anti-racism work, the struggle for LGBTQ+ inclusion, activism around immigration, and more. My progressive faith was focused on social justice work and Martin Luther King Jr.'s vision of beloved community. But my Christian faith and practice had a very weak and amorphous theological foundation—a potpourri of social gospel, feminist, liberation, and Wesleyan perspectives lacking an overarching framework. It was full of holes and left many questions about God and God's relationship with the world unexplored or unanswered.

I had heard about process-relational theology since the early 2000s, when I first entered seminary, aspiring to become a second-career ordained minister. But I had not given it a serious study. By 2016, the worship planning team at the Church of the Village—where the regional bishop had recently appointed me—considered process theology as a live option in our discernment. However, it was not yet a dominant theological framework for us. In addition to an assistant pastor and me, that team included the Minister of Worship Arts and the Chair of Worship, who had both studied process theology. I began to take it seriously in early 2017, when I ordered C. Robert Mesle's book, *Process Theology: A Basic Introduction* (1993). Then, in the spring of 2020, I embarked on an intensive and ongoing study. Through the late summer and fall of 2020, Church of the Village worship featured many sermons from a process-relational perspective preached by me and others.

When I began to grasp the breadth and deep significance of process-relational and open and relational theology, it was a revelation to me. Process theology gave me a systematic theological framework with a sound metaphysical and philosophical grounding. I realized that I had been preaching process-aligned theological concepts for years before I knew what that was. I have discovered that many clergy unconsciously preach open, relational, and process ideas. Also, it is clear to me that process, open, and relational concepts have been incorporated into the thinking and practice of many Christian denominations and congregations, even though they are not always recognized explicitly as such.

Moreover, many clergy preach from process, open, relational perspectives but do so without using the theological terminology associated with them. Some do that intentionally to avoid alienating church members. You will find examples of such sermons in this book. In each case, we asked the authors to include an introductory paragraph showing how process-relational or open and relational theological ideas are incorporated in the sermon.

In August and September of 2021, the Worship Vision Team (worship planning) at the Church of the Village created its first worship series focused explicitly on teaching process theology to the congregation. Our guest preachers were Ignacio Castuera, Catherine Keller, and John Thatamanil (their sermons are included in this book). Immediately after that, we planned a five-week series on discipleship titled, "In the Way of Jesus: An Adventure of Imagination and Commitment." We had the audacity to invite renowned theologian, John B. Cobb Jr. We asked him to preach on three consecutive Sundays—and he readily agreed! As he said in one of the sermons, he had never preached on discipleship before, so this was an opportunity for him to grow (at 97 years old!). Two of those three sermons are included in this book.

At around that time, the kernel of what became this book began to germinate in me. In November 2021, I visited John Cobb for a week in southern California to get better acquainted with his work and the process community there. During that visit, I mentioned my idea for a small book of process-oriented sermons from Church of the Village, augmented by a selection from the small number of process-influenced clergy or congregations I knew were similarly engaging process theology. By then, I was telling colleagues I was an evangelist for process theology.

Being a full-time pastor in a significant ministry setting (and dealing with the challenges of the Covid-19 pandemic), the book project simmered on a back burner for more than a year. Then, I attended the 50th Anniversary Conference of the Center for Process Studies in February 2023. There, I described my vision for the book to Mary Elizabeth Moore, dean of the Boston University School of Theology (emeritus) and a long-time process proponent. She immediately replied, "Don't wait. Do it now. We need that book!"

So, in the spring of 2023, I asked the Church of the Village to grant me a 9-week paid leave of absence over the summer to get the book underway. Thanks to God's leading and my listening, early on, I met on Zoom with Thomas Jay Oord to get his recommendations for possible contributors to the book. I knew Tom because he had been a guest preacher with the Church of the Village, too. After I shared my vision of the book with him, he said, "I would like to co-edit this book with you." I leapt at the opportunity to work with Tom. He recruiting two other excellent editors, Vikki Randall and Nichole Torbitzky (who are also contributors to the book). I am so grateful for the skills, dedication, diligent work, and the generous collaborative spirit of our editorial team. I am convinced God inspired me to work on this book and then helped me co-create (with God and my co-editors) the conditions to be able to complete it.

This book is the first of its kind (and hopefully not the last). There are numerous books available on process-relational theology, open and relational theology, and open theism. Several valuable books have been written about interpreting and understanding biblical texts with an open, relational, or process lens. A few excellent books have been produced on preaching from a process-relational perspective.[1] A handful of important books are available on aspects of worship other than preaching.[2] However, what

---

1. See Norman Pittenger, *Proclaiming Christ Today* (1962) and *Preaching the Gospel* (1984); William A. Beardslee, John B. Cobb Jr., et al., *Biblical Preaching on the Death of Jesus* (1989); Clark M. Williamson and Ronald J. Allen, *A Credible and Timely Word: Process Theology and Preaching* (1991); Marjorie Suchocki, *The Whispered Word: A Theology of Preaching* (1999); Ronald J. Allen, *You Never Step into the Same River Twice: Preaching from a Perspective of Process Theology* (2022). See also, Casey T. Sigmon, "Engaging the Gadfly: A Process Homilecclesiology for a Digital Age." Ph.D. Dissertation: Vanderbilt University, 2017 and "Preaching in the Family of Process Theology," in *Preaching the Manifold Grace of God*, vol. 2, ed. Ronald J. Allen (2022).

2. See Norman Pittenger, *Life As Eucharist* (1973); Clark M. Williamson and Ronald J. Allen, *Adventures of the Spirit: A Guide to Worship from the Perspective of Process Theology* (1997); John B. Cobb Jr., Bruce Epperly, and Paul S. Nancarrow, *The Call of the Spirit: Process Spirituality in a Relational World* (2005, reissued 2022).

Preaching the Uncontrolling Love of God offers is largely novel. Our book is the first to provide a broad compilation of sermons, essays, and worship elements meant to show in practice and in specific contexts, how to present open, relational, and process theological perspectives to and for leaders and members of local churches.

The majority of contributors to the book are clergy who serve or have served in churches. The book also includes contributions from a few clergy who are now writers, scholars, bloggers, podcasters, or teachers. Ten contributors are current or retired professors of preaching, worship, theology, or religious studies who also preach regularly. Five are lay persons with strong theological backgrounds. Two authors write about their experience of incorporating open, relational, or process perspectives in their work as hospice care chaplains.

We have attracted 67 contributors and a total of 73 submissions. The clergy and lay authors belong to small, medium, and large congregations. Among the clergy contributors, some are relatively new to open, relational, process thinking, while others have been preaching and practicing these perspectives for decades. The largest percentage of contributors are from across the U.S. and Canada. In addition, we have clergy and theologians from India, South Africa, the Czech Republic, Switzerland, Denmark, and Great Britain. They belong to or emerged from a wide range of denominational and non-denominational backgrounds, including the Church of South India, the Methodist Church of Southern Africa, Brazilian Presbyterian Church, United Church of Christ, United Church of Canada, Unitarian Universalist Association of Canada, Anglican Church of Canada, Presbyterian Church in Canada, Church of England, various Baptist communities, non-denominational evangelicals, exvangelicals, Christian Church (Disciples of Christ), Church of the Nazarene, Vineyard movement, United Methodist Church, Episcopal Church, Evangelical Lutheran Church of America, and the Roman Catholic Church (U.S.).

Open, relational, and process theologians, clergy, scholars, advocates, and practitioners hold diverse and nuanced views on many theological questions. So, you will not find complete uniformity, consensus, or "orthodoxy" in this book. In fact, for most of us, the idea of strict orthodoxy or settled doctrine runs contrary to the view that the future is open and everything, always and everywhere is in process—*is becoming*. That includes God, who is relational, affected by creation, and changes in relation to changes in the created, evolving order.

Pastors are local theologians for their congregations. Their parishioners look to them for love, care, and affirmation. They also look to them for biblical interpretation and *theology that makes sense* and aligns with their lived experience, as well as what they read in the Bible. They hunger to grasp who God is and how God relates to them and to the world, even if they may not articulate it that clearly.

Christianity has been in a steep nosedive for decades in North America. This freefall was accelerated by the Covid-19 pandemic. People have left church for many reasons, but often rising to the top tier in polls and surveys are the exclusion of LGBTQ+ persons, the hypocritical behavior of many church folks, and a desire for intellectual integrity. Respondents are especially turned off by the anti-science attitude of so much of Christianity. Many refuse to believe in a God who they have been taught is all-powerful (omnipotent), yet who apparently refuses to intervene to end evil and unnecessary suffering. Often, this God is presented as coercive, controlling, all-knowing, and unchanging. Several sermons and essays in this book address these problematic theological concerns. I believe that open and relational theology and process-relational theology provide coherent, deeply spiritual, and biblically attested understandings of the character of God, how God relates to the world, and how the world actually functions.

I know from personal experience there is an audience hungry for these perspectives. In the Church of the Village where I serve, process theology has found a deep resonance. At a regional United Methodist clergy gathering in October 2023, I was happily surprised to get 20 clergy to sign up for a discussion/study group titled, "Learn to Preach and Practice Process-Relational Theology." While success is never assured, I am convinced that these perspectives have the depth and power to contribute to the renewal and revitalization of Christianity.

We, the members of the editorial team, hope this book will help you think deeply, learn, grow, laugh, question, and experience joy in the process. Life is an adventure. So is theology. And so is what we call "church." Enjoy the adventure.

Sermons from Open, Relational, and Process Perspectives

A Different Kind of Revelation

CHRIS S. BAKER

Humanity has a role to play in helping to make creation all it was intended to be.

Reading: Romans 8:18-21
Sermon to be preached in an upcoming series at
Columbus Community Church of the Nazarene, April 21, 2024

Have you ever played the parlor game "Six Degrees of Kevin Bacon"? One person names an actor. Then the players try to connect the named actor to Kevin Bacon in the fewest steps by naming actors with shared films. For instance, if the named actor was John Cleese, we would remember that John Cleese was in *Rat Race* with Cuba Gooding Jr., and Cuba Gooding Jr. was in *A Few Good Men* with Kevin Bacon. The theory is that every actor can be linked to Kevin Bacon within 6 steps, hence the name "Six Degrees of Kevin Bacon."

It is fun to think that Kevin Bacon's film repertoire is so vast that he can be linked to any actor. That may be the case, but it has been proposed that this phenomenon is not unique to Kevin Bacon. Rather, every living person can be linked to every other living person within six degrees of separation. Think about that! The web of interpersonal relationships we all have is so vast that we are connected within six links. We are all in this vast network of relationships. The staunchest of atheists and the strictest religious fundamentalists, the rich and the poor, people of all ethnicities, genders, and races are all linked together in six steps or less.

In our text today, Paul tells us that creation is suffering. It is easy to look around and see that creation-human and otherwise-is suffering. We think of wars and violence and the effect those have on creation. The consequences of climate change are all around us. We have yet to see all the effects of the bioengineering of our food. Fires rage and floods rise. If there is anything apparent when we turn on the news, it is that creation is suffering.

Paul tells us that creation is suffering, but it is not suffering because of its own choice. Rather, Paul tells us creation suffers because of a kind of "six degrees of separation" that we humans have with the world. See, not only are we connected to other humans in relatively few steps. We are connected to the non-human creation, too.

In the church, we often talk about how our actions have consequences for other humans. Because we are all connected in networks of relationships, our choices affect others. Often, our choices have effects we would not have predicted, both at the personal level and at the systematic level. We can take drug and alcohol abuse as an example. The ripple effects of drug and alcohol abuse go on further than the addicted person imagined possible. The inverse is true, too. Very often, the circumstances that resulted in an individual abusing drugs or alcohol are themselves results of the choices of others. In so many ways, our decisions ripple on and on, further than we might imagine.

Paul tells us that this is true in our relationship with the non-human creation, too. Creation has been "subjected to frustration, not by its own choice, but by the will of the one who has subjected it…" (Romans 8:20, NIV). Creation suffers because of the choices of humanity. Scripture tells us that from the very beginning, humanity was created to be godly stewards of creation. Humanity's vocation in Genesis 1 & 2 is to take care of creation. Adam and Eve—and with them all of humanity—are to be godly stewards of creation that work toward the prospering of all God has made.

Unfortunately, we humans have not lived up to our calling. God draws us and leads us to be faithful stewards so that all of creation might flourish. Too often, we have chosen not to cooperate with God. We see the effects of this failure of vocation in the Genesis story as well. The consequences of sin in Genesis 3 show a division not only between humans and themselves, and humans and God, but also between humans and creation. As Paul puts it, creation is "subjected to frustration…in bondage to decay…." Our failure to be good stewards has resulted in harming and damaging creation itself. We are all connected in a web of relationships, humans with each other and humans with creation, and the ways we live matter more than we could ever imagine.

In acknowledging the failing of humans to fulfill their vocation, Paul says something fascinating. He says, "creation waits in eager expectation for the children of God to be revealed…." Now, I grew up in the church. I was a teen in the '90s, so I recall multiple series of movies about the end times. Maybe you remember them too. They were the Christian version of horror movies meant to scare the hell out of you, quite literally.

If it could be said that we (conservative evangelical) Christians were waiting for anything to be revealed, it was the revelation of Jesus we were waiting on. We were waiting on Jesus to come back at the end of time and make everything right again.

We might expect Paul to say something like "creation waits in eager expectation for Jesus to be revealed..." But that is not what Paul says. Instead, Paul says creation is waiting for the revelation of the children of God. We humans have a role to play in helping creation to prosper. It is not simply that we are all waiting for the revelation of Jesus at the end of time so that he can make everything right. It is that we are all being invited by God now to be part of God's "making-the-world-right-project," to use N.T. Wright's phrase. God is calling us, drawing us, leading us, and luring us to steward creation well.

This ought to give us great hope. It is certainly true that because of the vast network of relationships we have, the negative consequences of our choices ripple further than we could imagine. But hear the Good News this morning: the same is true for the positive consequences of our choices. Those, too, ripple out and affect people in positive ways that we might never have dreamed of.

I mentioned that I grew up in the church. When I was young, my dad served as the youth leader in the church I grew up in. As you might imagine, my dad influenced a number of teens during that time. A few even went into the ministry themselves. One young man named Billy went on to one of our denominational schools and became a traveling preacher and evangelist. Years later, Billy came back to our church and lead a series of youth services. It was at one of these youth services that I decided to follow God's leading to go into ministry.

Now, do you suppose my dad had any idea when he was leading the youth group that Billy was in that any of that might happen? Of course not. At most, my dad might have seen gifts that Billy had that might serve him well as a pastor. But because of my dad's influence in Billy's life, and then because of Billy's influence in my life, I accepted the call into ministry.

Our negative choices have long-lasting ripple effects, but so do our good choices. Because of that, every positive act is significant, regardless of whether we think of it as a big or small act. Every act of love matters. Every tree planted matters. Every mouth fed matters. Every park cleaned, every hug given, every animal cared for, every single act of love has ripple effects far beyond anything we can imagine.

Yes, creation-human and otherwise-is hurting and suffering, but that is not the end of the story. At least, it does not have to be. God is drawing us to bring care and restoration to creation. Creation is waiting eagerly for the children of God to show up. Will we?

Chris S. Baker is a co-pastor at Columbus Community Church of the Nazarene in Columbus, WI, alongside his wife Teresa. He previously served as Associate Pastor involved in worship and discipleship in Upstate New York. Chris is currently working on a doctorate in Open and Relational Theology through Northwind Theological Seminary, exploring the intersection of Open and Relational Theology and the work of N.T. Wright.

Confession—A Homily in Missive Form

JOHN BALLENGER

All scripture is inspired by God and is useful for teaching....
2 Timothy 3:16a

I am so deeply sorry you have heard recent sermons in our fall Genesis worship series as a list of what is wrong with scriptural stories. I have not been communicating well. Pointing out and thinking about differences, contradictions, inconsistencies in a sacred story (or what I take to be differences, contradictions, and inconsistencies) in no way (to my mind) details what is wrong with the story (or more broadly speaking, the Bible). It rather notes that those who told the stories and wrote the stories and carefully, prayerfully, and intentionally put those stories together in order were obviously not primarily concerned about the consistency of detail.

Genesis 1 and Genesis 2 are two very different stories with different details, different order, indeed, a different God. That is not what is wrong with the Genesis creation accounts. That is what is right. That leaves room for God there. For the work of the Spirit still guiding us into truth. Room for the imagination to get past the details into the deep truth. Truth that is less about us propositionally affirming exactly what happened long ago, as it is about us experientially affirming (and celebrating) the truth we know today that the people of God have known and celebrated (and trusted) through the millennia.

We could then add all the other (also different) creation stories from throughout Scripture (Psalm 8; 19; 33; 89; 102; 104; Proverbs 8; Job 26; 28; 38; Jeremiah 10; Isaiah 11; 40; 45; John 1; Revelation 21). Differences, contradictions, and inconsistencies in details do not bother me in Scripture. I receive them enthusiastically as invitations to more thought and the possibility of intimations of deeper truth. And more.

With each additional version—each different version—I do not hear an insistent "God created like this" as the ringing refrain, but rather, "God is creating … as God is always creating … has always been creating." This is not just what God did; this is what God is doing now. And if God is not still doing this, then what's the point? Really, what's the value of *then*, if not to affirm *now*?

In the so-called story of the great flood, we noted a refrain of sorts: establishing an initial context, naming the same three elements (a systemic wickedness, a natural disaster understood as consequent judgment, and the identification of one good man) in a completely different order (compare Genesis 6:5-8 to Genesis 6:9-12). So, the story gives us repetition and difference within it.

Then, when the animals are invited into the ark, they are sometimes described as entering two by two (Genesis 6:19-20; 7:15), and sometimes divided into clean and unclean, with clean animals in pairs of seven (Genesis 7:2-3; 8-9). Now, animals invited into the ark two by two does not preclude seven pairs of two (they are specifically combined that way in Genesis 7:8-9), but specifically saying two by two to refer to all in some verses and specifically adding another distinction (clean vs. unclean) in other verses is a completely different way of imaging the animals—particularly notable as the distinction between clean and unclean animals had not yet been introduced into the story (cf. Leviticus 11; Deuteronomy 14). So again, the story gives us repetition and difference within it.

Maybe a background in poetry and literature conditioned me to focus on the differences in repetition. When anything is repeated, but with changes, that always indicates a deliberate invitation to pay attention and ponder. Again, not to undermine though. Far from such observations leading to rejection of the story, they make me wonder if it is in truth a story so true that it's been told in different times (before the Law was given and after), such that its relevance—what is most true about it—are not the details of one expression of it; one manifestation in time, but something more.

As is true (I profess) of much of Scripture, the story is repeated less as history than as theology, less as the particular details of one telling than as the consistent affirmation that God is always present—and always working in the chaos of all time with us for a way forward through the chaos with hope. And there it is again. The same refrain as noted in the creation stories. So. Not a flood story. A so-called flood story. Actually, completely uninterested in affirming the flood as God's punishment of wickedness. That's simply part of the given (the context) in which to affirm God's hopeful presence and will and work. This is then a story for the people of God facing any flood—all chaos.

And none of the details of the way that is conveyed seem as important to me as that truth: within the overwhelming realities of life, God is present with us, working with us for a better tomorrow. The story is the means of conveying that truth. The story is not about the truth of itself. It is the unfortunate legacy of too much of church history to have made truth a matter of the stories themselves rather than the truths the stories were told (and retold) to show.

Every time I read a Bible story, I am expecting not to read it the same way I have before. I anticipate being struck by a new perspective, a new possibility. For me, that is integral to my understanding of a living word and a Spirit ever guiding us into truth. A biblical story preached should never offer confirmation of the way we've always heard it but offer precisely the newness of what a living word brings to the ever new now.

So it is, you may remember (I do not presume you do!) a previous sermon on the so-called flood story (we really need a new name for it, don't we? The long arc bending out of chaos story?!). Back then, we focused on the question of what kind of God issues the kind of judgment described in the flood stories. (Totally not an issue this time when considering "judgment" part of the context in which to tell the story, not a part of the story itself). But that previous focus also raised good possibilities for reflection. We obviously do not question that a sometimes capricious God of omnipotent power and absolute control is depicted in the Bible. It is worth questioning why. We must question what that means to us today. And we note there is a God of love and presence affirmed in the Bible, too. And yes, I have trouble seeing how they go together. How can loving someone be reconciled with controlling them? And no, I am not willing to resign that to the mystery of the God utterly beyond me.

You have asked before if I limit God too much to my own understandings—the limitations of my own experience and thoughts. Yes. Of course. Who does not? Each of us within the recognition of the limitations (hopefully) of our own understandings, seeks some level of consistency to who we understand God to be. Some of us find that consistency in affirmations of transcendence or mystery. Some of us see only inconsistency and reject God. And some of us filter all images and stories of God through the lens of what we deem most important and so the measure of what is consistent (like love).

It should come as no surprise to you that I do not turn to stories for the answer or for Truth. Nor to some mystery of transcendence that absorbs inconsistency. I love the stories because of the different ways of imaging and speaking of God they evidence. Because it is then upon us (immersed in the Presence) to sift through all that the Bible offers, to assess, evaluate, discern, prioritize, and choose because the focus is not on right and wrong revealed in sacred text, but because God trusts us to choose to commit to right and wrong in our living.

Again, none of this makes the story (or the Bible or God) less real or less true or less important to me. Again, it is, in fact, the opposite. I am deeply sorry that what you have walked away with over the past several weeks is the sense that you cannot trust the Bible to be real. I obviously did not communicate what I wanted to—how the Bible is more real to me than any of the stories of the Bible, and God is more real because of that. That I do believe all scripture is useful for teaching (2 Timothy 3:16a), just that we are sometimes taught by what we reject.

I maintain the profession of a high and holy sense of sacred text—with attention to that which calls from beyond sacred text—though sacred text. I name that spirit of truth—breath of God. If you want to call it the wild wind of the imagination, God has long sailed those winds too! I hope some of this helps frame some of what I've been trying to do in worship and with Scripture. I'll be rethinking how I'm trying to do that.

In closing, you also wondered about visitors—about how someone visiting for the first time might hear what we're doing in worship. No doubt someone raised in a traditional evangelical faith, expecting what they've heard before, may not be comfortable. That is a risk. But a greater risk, I suggest, is posed to our future and our integrity moving into the future, by not leaning into honesty and openness. So, I hope a visitor with ears willing to hear and eyes willing to see and a mind willing to think would be attracted to a lack of defensiveness about questions. Indeed, to the embrace of questions. To the exploration of alternative understandings. To the synthesizing of sacred word with personal experience. To the love of a wider, deeper, richer, more open (or what I call a wider, deeper, richer, more open) theology and interpretation of Scripture that is not angry, not dismissive, but joyful, exhilarating, anticipating, and hopeful.

May it be so.

John Ballenger is a graduate of the University of Virginia (BA), the Southern Baptist Theological Seminary (M.Div.), and Brite Divinity School (D.Min.). John has served Woodbrook Baptist Church in Baltimore, Maryland for the past 20 years, having served churches in Georgia and Texas before that. He grew up a preacher's kid, a missionaries' kid (in central Europe), and has been described as a relentlessly creative lover of the Word—always reading, writing, thinking and rethinking. There's little he loves more than chasing an idea that might offer a different perspective.

"Palo dado ni Dios lo quita": My Mother the Process Theologian

IGNACIO CASTUERA

The faith we learn at home constitutes the core of our theological teachings. A loving home with loving relationships makes it possible to believe in a God whose primary attribute is love. The all-loving God is more real than the all-powerful images that enter our lives in later years.

Readings: Hosea 11:1-4 & Matthew 7:7-11 (*The Inclusive Bible*)
Preached at the Church of the Village (NYC), August 1, 2021

What a joy it is to return to the Church of the Village. And to be here live! Zoom has done marvels for us, and I want to be very grateful to whoever invented it. And I'm grateful to everyone involved with technical issues that allow us to spread the word. The Bible tells us to get to the highest point and proclaim from there the glory of God. And now the highest point is an electronic highest point, and I think the Church of the Village has found such a high point from which we can proclaim the word of God.

And we can share wonderful things such as photographs. When this was preached, I shared a photo which was taken right after my holy communion. My mother, on the extreme right, her sister, Rocha, I'm holding my candle, my grandmother, Conchita, and my grandfather, who was so tall. When they got married, my grandfather shared a joke that when he tried to grab her around the waist, he almost choked her. Family. We are family. We learn the best about the love of God in our families. It is so sad that there are families who do not share that, but I was blessed. I was blessed with a mother that, unbeknownst to her, was really the theologian in my life, the first theologian. It's true she sent me to the Salesian school and prepared me for holy communion and I learned that the church taught that God is almighty, all powerful, omnipotent, and all that. And then at home when she administered punishment—she had not read the Bible—but later she discovered that the Bible said spare the rod, spoil the child—she would say to us "see, I was right!" Sometimes in the middle of that physical punishment she would say "palo dado ni Dios lo quita"—a good beating not even God can take it away. So, I learned many years later about cognitive dissonance. God is almighty, but can't take away the beating my mother was administering. So where is this almighty God? That seed eventually developed into my understanding of God in a different way thanks to process theology.

I'm so glad and so blessed that she was the one that created the cognitive dissonance that opened me up to think about God in different ways. The biblical record is a constant struggle between the religion of the temple with rules and regulations and the religion of the prophets who in the name of God say the rules, regulations, and sacrifices are not what it is all about. I want the good deeds, the love of the people, I want you to love the people. Jesus did not just come up with the loving ideas of God as an *Abba*, a daddy, a *papito*. He had been fed by the bold teachings of the prophets. There we find the beginning of those tender elements. Not to the degree that Jesus taught them, but they were there. If you look in the Bible every now and then there is reference to God as someone who is like a parent. Some of those images are scary. God says I am like a she-bear defending her cubs. If you've ever done any hiking, they ask you to shout and make a lot of noise to keep the bears away. If it is a she-bear, forget it. Try to get away as soon as possible. So, that image of God, as a she-bear ready to defend her cubs, is a powerful image that has a little bit of tenderness (defending her cubs), but it really is a scary one.

The Bible passage that was read today, which comes from the prophet Hosea, is a little bit more tender. I was blessed being the oldest of four. I have a sister 9 years younger and a brother 13 years younger, and I had the opportunity to "teach them" to walk. Now, I didn't actually teach them, but I helped them as they start learning to walk. So that image of God saying it was God who taught Ephraim to walk is one that is filled with tenderness. Jesus is building on that. Our faith, our Christian faith, echoes that strong division in the Bible between the faith of the religion of rules, regulations, and rituals of the temple, and the faith taught by the prophets about a loving God, a caring God, a God who wants us to love each other and to spread that love. That is echoed in the history of our faith. Because it started with the teachings of Jesus. In that tenderness of a *papito*, an Abba, who could not possibly do bad things for the children. And that image of Jesus saying, "if you, filled with faults as you are, can give good gifts how much more your heavenly *papito*, your heavenly Abba." So that image is really one that impels the early church to become the force that it was in the Roman empire.

But Constantine saw that that force could be used for his purposes, and he took it over. And the Caesars of Rome were the ones who then hired the theologians of the church who then created the images of power that have been passed down to us. All of the attributes of Caesar were assigned to God and the vision of tenderness that Jesus and the prophets had given us almost disappeared. Whitehead wrote, "The brief Galilean vision of humility flickered throughout the ages, uncertainly." I'd like to think one of those flickerings was that statement my mother gave about God not really being omnipotent which opened the idea that there are other ways to talk about God.

Process thought really starts with a major challenge to the religious rituals, rules, and regulations of the temple. The religion of the God with the attributes of Caesar is challenged by the religion of love, of a caring loving God. It is not omnipotence that is important for us as followers of Jesus. Instead, it should be love. We should go out of this place and start every day by affirming this image of God and go out and say to everyone we meet: you are a child of God; building on that deep theological foundation that God is love. God is tender. God is a member of our family, not somebody far removed from us.

Our official rituals of the church, even the prayer that Jesus taught the disciples, betray the teachings of Jesus. We should not say "our Father who art in heaven," we should substitute, at least in our heads and our hearts, the most tender image we can possibly summon and use that as the opening of the Lord's prayer. *Papito*, Abba, my dearest friend—whatever and whoever has been for you the most loving image of the most loving God—that is what the beginning of that prayer should be. That is what Jesus meant when he used the Aramaic word, *Abba*.

A theology that starts there is going to take us to very different places from a theology that starts with images of power. We need the kind of power that flows out of believing that God loves me and loves everybody around me. Not just the bipeds that sometimes think they are the "primates" in creation and evolution, but everyone. The molecules and electrons, the ants, the beasts of the jungle, fish in the ocean, etc.—all of them God loves—each and every one. God doesn't only "love the little children, all the little children of the world" regardless of their color, God loves all of creation.

You can see why process theology is becoming more and more popular now that our whole household—nature—is under threat. We can see that threat as the consequence of failing to acknowledge that God loves all of creation. That love that I can feel deeply from God is a love that is extended to the whole of creation. So, it is not a leap to ask people of faith, believers in Jesus, followers of his teachings, that we now must be the defenders of the Earth. In one of his books, John Cobb says, Jesus' followers must become "earthists": defenders of the Earth. Earlier, in 1972, he wrote a book called, *Is It Too Late? A Theology of Ecology*, where he writes about defending nature.

If people had only listened back in the early '70s, we would not be in the difficulty we are in now. This is what we now must do as well. An omnipotent God is not going to come in from out of nowhere and "save creation" by his own power, as many conservative "Christians" claim. They say "no, we don't have to worry about it, God will do it all. God will come in." This false sense of security that comes out of a false image of an omnipotent God contributes to human actions and attacks upon the earth. We who believe that God is not omnipotent, but that God is loving and loves everyone, should be the ones who lead the way in the defense of the creation.

When Pope Francis wrote *Laudato Si*, those of us who are in the process camp thanked God that someone with the voice of authority that the Pope has can begin to move all people, not just the Catholic church, closer and closer to the vision of Jesus and farther and farther away from the religion of the empire.

In this very place, we are a reflection of the religion that Jesus wanted to see. One grounded in love that is spread out to others, other human beings, and to the whole of creation.

Ignacio Castuera was born in Mexico into a Roman Catholic family. He came to the United States for his college and seminary training. He is a retired ordained elder in the California-Pacific Annual Conference of the United Methodist Church, serving churches in Mexico, Hawaii, and Southern California during a 50-year career. He holds a Doctor of Religion from the Claremont School of Theology.

On Being Jesus's Disciple

JOHN B. COBB JR.

I urge you seriously to consider being a disciple of Jesus.

Reading: Acts 9:1-9
Sermon preached at the Church of the Village, September 12, 2021

I appreciate being asked to talk about discipleship. I have never written about it or spoken about it publicly before. So, I'm being given the opportunity to think. That's a challenge, but just the kind of challenge through which I hope I can continue to grow. In the last few years, I have sometimes said that if being a Christian is believing any particular set of things that Christians have believed in the past—the creeds of the time of the ancient Roman empire or the ideas of Anselm that have really influenced the church in the wrong direction—then I'm not Christian. I don't think that is what it means to be a Christian, but there are people who think it is.

But I want to state positively why I think I am a Christian. I am sure at this point in my life that I want to be a disciple of Jesus. So, you are giving me an opportunity to explain what I mean by that and why I am saying it with strength of feeling and commitment.

In order to do that, I have to set a little background. That's a process way of doing things. We tell a story—but trying to find a place to begin is difficult because each beginning is at the end of something else. Still, each story has to have a beginning and come to a point where it explains what one wants to communicate. Let me say that in order to understand or to emphasize process, one has to follow one of the two major traditions in the West. One of those comes from Israel. The sacred scriptures of Israel are mainly about process, often in the form of stories. You could say they're about history, but much of it is history simply in terms of individual lives—the Bible is a book of stories.

The other great tradition that has fed into the contemporary West is philosophical. That tradition is mainly seeking to explain everything, including all processes as growing out of regular and unchanging principles that govern the movement or change of substances. Plato, Aristotle, and Plotinus have influenced the thinking of the Western church away from the process thinking of the Bible. The rise of the natural sciences has intensified this influence. These have strengthened the substance thinking that has dominated Western philosophy. Stories are not the way of developing modern philosophy or science. What one wants to understand is how things always and everywhere are.

Whereas most people are sometimes very interested in what is happening uniquely in a few moments, and how it differs from whatever happened in any other moment, science wants to explain everything as the outgrowth of laws that are the same always and everywhere. Process thought teaches that much is the same always and everywhere, but there are also differences. No two events occur in exactly the same context, and because every event is affected by its context, no two events are exactly alike. For many purposes, the differences are unimportant, but in some instances, they are very important. In other words, we have the uniqueness of everything that is happening. We also have the enormous commonality of most events with some other events. Much of the explanation of all events is by universal principles and practices. But no event is completely decided by commonality of context and universal laws.

A few scientists and philosophers believe that as we examine the world in greater and greater detail, we discover that, after all, it is composed of events and processes rather than substances that obey universal laws with great exactness. Hence there is, at the margins of Western philosophy and the natural sciences, also a tradition of process thinking that can be related to the process thinking of the Bible.

Now, it is obvious that science has developed out of philosophy and because Western philosophy is primarily substance thinking, the task assigned to science has been to talk about what is always true. That doesn't mean that everything is always happening, but the basic pattern can be repeated. In science, it is very important that in the laboratory you can reproduce the same phenomena again and again. But when we remember the 9/11 catastrophe, many of us don't think of it as a repetition of things that happened in the past and could readily happen again. We view it as an absolutely unique event. Therefore, it is not dealt with by scientists in their standard studies. The historical explanation for which it calls is a quite different matter.

Scientists tend to think that, in principle, everything that happened on 9/11 can be explained scientifically, that is, without the appeal to purposes or aims. Historians think that an historical approach is needed. In that approach, purposes and concerns play an important role. Even scientists who do not regard such explanations as real explanations tend, for practical purposes, to appeal to final causes (Whitehead's "subjective aims") for many practical explanations. Some scientists envision the expansion of science to include Whitehead's "subjective aims," and this is not impossible. The resulting science would no longer require a separate discussion of history. One form of explanation, including both efficient and final causes, would be used for everything. That would be the ultimate goal of a process science. Process thinkers would still assume that thinkers confront some patterns of events that are highly repetitive for millions of years, and some events dominated by unrepeatable features.

This way of understanding science is not common among scientists. To explain why, we need to tell the history of science. If we know the history of science, we understand why it has focused as it has and ignored what did not fit. Historians can give us an historical explanation of why science in its present form seems so often to support deterministic and reductionistic thinking.

During the medieval period, Aristotle was the great philosopher/scientist and everything that was discovered about the world was interpreted in Aristotelian terms. This often led to the idea that one understands something when one understands what it is for. That is called an Aristotelian final cause. When you understand the role the heart plays in keeping animals, including human ones alive, you understand the heart. Final causes played a predominant role in much of the science of the Middle Ages. In the 17th century, people like Descartes—Descartes being a very influential figure—said no, final causes don't explain anything—what we want is to understand what makes things happen as they do. That is the efficient cause. And so, the final causes were ignored and rejected, and even denied. At first one could have said that was a methodology so that our energies would be devoted to explaining things in terms of what makes them happen not in terms of why they happened. But it got translated into saying there are no final causes, no purposes in nature. The natural world is completely lacking in purpose.

Now, in my view, that is not science. That is philosophy, and it is a very dubious philosophy. Purposes play a large role in my life. My guess is purposes play a large role in your life, too. But when we say that and try to explain ourselves in terms of our purposes, what we're saying is thought of as non-scientific—outside of the scientific world. In my view, this move on the part of science was a serious mistake.

There is no question that science is the best way of learning a great many things. But because we have a tendency to idolize science and to absolutize science and to say that if something is not scientific then it is not important to pay attention to, it is important for us to understand that if we are seeking the repetitive features of reality—what happens again and again and can be reproduced again and again in a laboratory, science is the best way, and almost the only way, by definition, of getting at the deeper truth.

Please do not take me as disparaging science. That is not at all what I mean. But damage is done if people start out worshiping science and taking it as the only source of reliable knowledge. History disappears. And the uncontrolled and unpredictable world that historians seek to understand and explain gets neglected. The reason it is important to think about this is that it is happening, now, in our universities. They are overwhelmingly focused upon science and the kind of thinking supported by substance philosophy. The social sciences are looking more like the deterministic natural sciences, since efficient causes are much preferred to final causes. This studying, and learning immense amounts about what is repetitive, tends to delay understanding when an event like 9/11 occurs. There are not many people whose university studies have prepared them to understand dramatically unique occurrences.

I think that those of us who still think historically have a very important contribution to make. Of course, it is possible to study science and then also add historical knowledge. But if you study things historically, you don't have to add scientific knowledge, you can include scientific knowledge. The historical approach is, or could become, the more inclusive one.

Now, of course, the historical approach is a process approach. Process thinking which focuses on events rather than fixed, stable entities, is able to include studies of fixed, stable entities. I think science has finally realized that if you analyze these stable fixed entities enough, you finally come out with events, that is, events are more fundamental.

Energy is more fundamental than mass. There are energy events that occur that have no mass. There is no mass that cannot be understood as equivalent to energy. So, process thought is more foundational than what most scientists retain. But my broader concern for today is to say that all of us, to some extent, think historically. I wish our education were not so prejudiced against that. I think we may have a chance of influencing education to renew an interest in the unique, the organic, that which does not fit into this repetitive mechanical world. We should not belittle the power and importance of what is mechanical and repetitive, but we should set it in a larger whole. If you have only this mechanical, repetitive world there is no meaning. If there is no purpose it is hard to talk about life being meaningful. But if you start with the historical, the event, the process, you can include all of the science and find that meaningful. We can study the history of science, and by studying the science we can see what it has accomplished and also its limitations.

Now all of this may not seem like it has anything to do with discipleship, but I want you to understand where I'm coming from. I'm coming from the view that history is of primary importance and right now we are living in what may be the end of history. Nothing could be more important than avoiding that. I wish that this could be said in the context of our leading educational institutions and be heard and understood. But, for example, it is very difficult for people who do not think historically to understand the importance of the fact that we are already living unsustainably.

So, today I'm going to go from this very broad indication of what is for me central. Even more important for us than the scientific world now so much better known, is the world of human relations, the world in which Jesus lived, taught, and acted. Within that context, we can say the historical world, we can ask what Jesus' role now is and why we should focus on this one particular person when we are speaking of discipleship.

This sermon is confessional. I have found great importance in what Jesus taught about how to live in that human/historical world. Whether it will strike others as so important, I do not know, I just can tell you how I discovered it and why it became so important to me. What I say may seem relevant to you—you may have had a similar experience. But it doesn't mean that everyone has to experience it that way. I think many people who have reflected about history seriously, and who have cared about the same things most of us care about, have come to similar but not identical conclusions as I.

From childhood, I have thought of myself in relationship through the wider history in which I was brought up. I grew up in Japan in a society in which most of the people were ethnically and culturally different. When I came to the U.S. for the first time, at the age of 6, to the state of Georgia—I heard the ways white people talked to white people about black people, and I was absolutely appalled. I list this as historical because I think this is a matter of history. The reasons people do this and the importance for history of the consequences of this kind of racism are now well known.

I was shocked by what adults commonly said, and I wrote in 1931, at the age of six, a little ditty that indicates that my feelings were very strong about this. I fancied myself a poet, but I have learned that I am not. All I meant by poetry was that certain words rhyme. I wanted to express my feelings about what we now call "racism." At that time the term "intolerance" was widely used, and I used it in my little ditty.

"Intolerance, thou art a curse than death itself, far, far worse."

For me, that was just the way it seemed then, and I think my life was set to seek meaning in trying to understand my life historically. This decision was reinforced when we again travelled from the Japan to the United States in the fall of 1939. This time we came via Europe. Great Britain declared war on Germany while we were crossing the Atlantic in the Queen Mary.

Although the American people did not want to get into another European War, President Roosevelt thought we should support our allies. He succeeded in provoking Japan to bomb our fleet in Hawaii, thus justifying an American declaration of war soon extended to Germany. My life was clearly shaped by global events. For me the biggest issue was whether to be a pacifist or participate in fighting Japan. Much as I appreciated the Japanese people, I considered Japan's imperialist ventures profoundly wrong and that ending them was an American responsibility.

At that time, I'm proud to say, the Methodist church was much more historically oriented than it is today. It was committed to what was called the "social gospel." The church nationally felt the responsibility to help young men in my position to understand the issues and to decide wisely. I went to a national meeting, and we had speakers who were pacifists and speakers who thought we ought to participate in the war. Despite my positive feelings toward the Japanese people, I decided I was not a pacifist and would take part in the war.

I am simply trying to say, the big decisions in my life were in a context of global history. I think global history plays an enormous role for all of us, but so many people don't pay much attention to it. In my case, it would have been difficult to ignore global history.

Given the fact that history has often been the context that has set goals for what I wanted to do, I am strongly convinced of its importance in shaping my decisions. I wanted to work for peace, and for years I thought the best place would be the government foreign service. I was gradually disillusioned about being able to work for peace as an employee of the government. I gave up the idea of serving the world through the government of the United States. But if one finds meaning in involving oneself in what is historically happening, one's knowledge of this will play a large role in one's decisions.

Then the question becomes, "How do you make those decisions?" I discovered that many Americans made them in ways that I did not think were good. It seemed that for many the selfish interest of the U.S., or segments of the population in the U.S., was more important than any type of global view. In the 1930s, Japan was the imperial power I was horrified by, but after WWII, the U.S. has taken over the primacy of that role in the world. American imperialism is something I strongly oppose, and I have to ask why. Some of my friends think that international action that is not for the U.S. is unpatriotic and one is being a traitor if one has a wider horizon than the national interest.

As a Christian, I find myself (along with all others) loved, and that my life can be lived out of that love. I believe that all of us are loved and that we can to some degree participate in that universal love. In Jesus we see what the fuller embodiment of that love brings about. In a Christian community, we find all loving all, or at least some tendencies in that direction. It is a unique way of reading a history that often seems cruel. But it is a self-validating way. Knowing ourselves loved and participating in that loving protects us from the worst of the distortions to which our understanding is always subject.

Two people I admire greatly for their contributions are Mahatma Gandhi and Martin Luther King Jr. I admire them because they embodied and fulfilled ideals that had come to seem to me the right ideas. But it is very interesting that, although one of them was a Hindu, it was from Jesus that both derived their central conviction that we all need to love our "enemies." I realize that the message that we should love our enemy is, in terms of my values, of ultimate importance. I want the world and humanity and civilization to survive, and I believe we will not unless we love our enemies.

It might be better if we use the word opponents, but I'm going to continue using the harsher word because that is the way we are acting today. Today, the U.S. has declared China to be its number one enemy. The fact that China threatens American global domination makes it America's number one enemy. That leads China and other nations, that know that the United States will not tolerate any threat to its control, to prepare to fight the United States if they must in order to have freedom to act in their own interest.

Viewing this situation after having learned from Gandhi and King that Jesus taught us to love our enemies, it became increasingly apparent to me that our only hope was for us all to love our enemies. That means that we would be disciples of Jesus. His followers have rather conspicuously ignored this message, but it would have saved Israel in Jesus' day. It could lead to peace in ours. Jesus identifies this as his message that was not part of the Judaism of his day. It rarely became the actual Christianity of the church in subsequent centuries. To expect the church to really push Jesus' wisdom on its members may indeed be unrealistic today.

But I do not see another way to move forward. I want to be a disciple of Jesus. This does not mean that I will ignore all his other teachings. Very few teachers have taught about love of friends as well as enemies with such passion and power. There is much else. Love of enemy needs to be taught in Christian churches like mine as entailing loving Trump. The failure to love our national enemies is accompanied by failure to love our political opponents. Jesus' message overall has profound wisdom. It seems to me to specify what is truly essential. I do not know who else I might follow.

The rather vague assumption in liberal American churches that we should love everyone, today, in liberal circles does not lead to great efforts to love Trump and his disciples. Both camps have many Christians in them but the way they talk about each other, the way they treat each other, is destructive. If we do not learn to love our enemies, history is going to end in utter disaster and catastrophe.

So, I urge you seriously to consider being a disciple of Jesus. The church is no longer a major factor in the American scene, but it still has a voice that could be influential.

As more and more people recognize how precarious is the future of humanity, more may also sense that they are called to spend their lives in discipleship of Jesus. Maybe others will follow the call to listen.

John B. Cobb Jr. is an American theologian, philosopher, and environmentalist. Cobb is often regarded as the preeminent scholar in the field of process philosophy and process theology, the school of thought associated with the philosophy of Alfred North Whitehead. He is the author of more than fifty books, and founder of many organizations, including the Center for Process Studies, the Cobb Institute, the Institute for Ecological Civilization, and the Living Earth Movement. At 98 years old, he is still actively writing, speaking, and organizing.

The Personal Experience of Discipleship

JOHN B. COBB JR.

Readings: Mark 1:16-20 & Amos 7:7-15
Sermon preached at the Church of the Village (NYC), September 26, 2021

I have considered myself a liberal protestant, but I realize that liberal Protestantism is dying and has been for some time. It has lost most of its vitality, and of course also its membership, already. We are closing liberal churches all over the country, and there doesn't seem to be any real notion of how we might change ourselves in such a way that lots of people would think what we were doing was important enough to take part in. I think it is important to figure out why we are dying and to think about how we might change. I think we are called to give serious attention to this question. At one time feeling a call to break out of orthodoxy and seek to be completely open and honest could generate strong feelings and a commitment that seemed truly important. Our liberal Protestant ancestors felt called to break through the limitations on their freedom. I want to think further about the importance of feeling "called."

The term liberal almost inherently means openness to whatever seems to be the best information, the best knowledge, the best thinking in the world around us. And I still want to be liberal in that sense. Openness is one of the things to which Jesus' disciples are called. But sadly, especially in the 20th century, after human beings became included in the natural world, the characteristics that had previously been attributed only to the rest of the world came to be attributed to human beings also. Increasingly, the supposed wisdom, the supposed insight of the supposed leaders of thought have become totally uncongenial to the Christian faith. Human beings understand nature as like the machines they make. When they view human beings as part of nature, they see us also as machine-like. In this modern view, humans have no more responsibility for what they do than do the machines that humans make.

If we adopt from the most respected thinking in our secular environment the idea that all that we do is completely predetermined, the Bible and the Christian tradition will be meaningless. If we open ourselves uncritically to what is unchristian, even antichristian, and try to adjust to that in our lives, there will be very little good news left. And as we liberal Christians work hard to open ourselves to the most respected thinking in our secular society, I'm afraid there has been very little authentic gospel in what we have been doing and saying in our liberal churches.

The ethos and the teaching of our universities, to which we have understandably looked as authorities with respect to matters of thought, has become explicitly non-theistic. But it is not only God that is omitted. From the beginning of the modern era, that is the 17th century, science made no use of final causes. "Final causes" just means purposes. Modern people thought that the natural world can be explained completely without any use of the notion of purpose, or aim, or goal. Then, when human beings were introduced into the world explained by science, we were told that our purposes don't amount to anything either. Values are not important. Everything is finally to be explained mechanistically. If so, maybe God created the machine a long time ago, but what people do now is determined by what they were determined to do then by their participation in the whole created order. That works out on its own. God does not make new decisions as the world changes. God has nothing to do with what happens in the global machine now. Values have no role. Purposes have nothing to do with it.

Now, obviously, it is not possible to preach a Christian sermon and completely agree with all of that. But so many of us have felt that even if we could not completely adopt scientific determinism, we must avoid giving offense to the modern thinkers who are considered the experts and the most advanced. For example, with respect to God, we very rarely hear, in liberal churches, that God has actually done something, that anything is to be truly explained by reference to God. To offer a theistic explanation of an historical event would violate the climate, the standards, the norms of our universities as they represent modern thought, supposedly, at its best.

But a God who does nothing, who explains nothing, is not very significant, and some liberals seek to keep the term, "God," alive by explaining that it is only symbolic. It doesn't have a literal meaning, and we won't actually say anything specific about what God does because that would not be acceptable. These liberal choices have led us not to say anything very distinctively Christian. One reason that we theists are being abandoned by younger generations in massive ways is that we have so little to say that is really good news, in a world that has little good news. In my view, we need to believe that we humans are not alone in seeking human survival, that there is always and everywhere an effort to increase value. That means that life and even human life have been brought into being by a power far greater than that of human beings, with which we can join and by which our efforts to increase the value in the world are supported.

All of that is to say, I think, there is an alternative for liberals to copying unbelievers. We don't have to continue in this obedience to a worldview that is hostile to everything Christians believe. We mustn't simply attack the atheistic/determinist world view. We are beneficiaries of the enormous expansion of information that its advocates have bequeathed to us and the enormous richness universities have added to our cultures.

I'm using the term "university" a little loosely. Universities vary. But, overall, they are the intellectual 'establishment.' There are many think tanks, research institutions, and other kinds of institutions besides universities that have bought into a common world view that we often call "modern." Its achievements have been enormous. Nevertheless, it does not explain much of Christian experience, such as our responsibility for what we do with our lives and our response to our calling. Viewed in relation to these dimensions of Christian experience, the world view is not adequate to the evidence, and this is becoming increasingly true.

That means that it might be possible for us to be very loyal and devoted to the evidence without accepting the interpretation of that evidence that is so contrary to our own beliefs. I will give an example of this: For a long time, as we learned more, it seemed that more things we thought, traditionally, needed to be explained by purposes and values could be explained, after all, simply by mechanical causes. So, there was a retreat, a legitimate, needed retreat, by Christians from some of the kinds of affirmations they had been making.

However, it is very interesting that in the last twenty years the evidence has gone in just the opposite direction. We have found there are many features of this world that happen to be exactly what is needed in order that life be possible. There is no explanation otherwise as to why they are just what they are. It seems to me to be natural to say there is some purpose in the universe. It seems that the universe, or something pervasive of the universe, wants life and has the ability to make adjustments in the nature of things that allow for life to come to be. Now we have not just one thing, where the chances of what happened that made life possible was one in twenty or even less. There is not just one stage at which the developments that made life possible were highly improbable. And the life we now have has progressed through many of these improbabilities. Perhaps there are a dozen such developments in the road to life. If there have been twelve steps in each of which improbable developments had to occur, the statistical likelihood of all this happening strongly indicates that another cause has been at work. More plausible is that purpose has played a role.

So, the evidence is that there is purpose in the universe, and, of course, that means there is God. But that is against the metaphysics, against the doctrine, against what has become interiorized as the very nature of science. So, some scientists are trying to persuade us all that the explanation is that there are millions of universes. No one had previously ever imagined that the universe is not the entirety. Of course, there might be earlier universes before the big bang. So, the possibility that there have been other universes is very real. but to go from

Some people regard modern reason as showing that if our life-filled universe had only one chance in a million of coming into being, then we may expect that there are hundreds of thousands of universities, perhaps millions. I'm trying to make one point—the worldview that liberals open themselves to when they open themselves to the leadership thinking of the modern world is not one that fits comfortably with the facts. It has to be stretched and is becoming increasingly fragile. We experience purpose; so, few of us really doubt its existence. Explaining some features of our universe as informed by purpose seems quite reasonable.

Now, there is one modern thinker, at least recent thinker, who was well versed in the science and mathematics of his day. Even though the strong evidence we now have of the unlikelihood of chance and necessity proving a plausible explanation of life, had not yet been found, he thought that there were plenty of reasons to recognize what were once called final causes as playing some role in all events. Alfred North Whitehead thought that all unit events constituted themselves around an "aim." He saw that the mechanistic world view, which still dominates, is not able to account for evolution.

There is something in the universe that works for life. We need organic categories of thought rather than mechanistic ones. And he offers us the philosophy we need. So, he enables us to understand that and how the universe is indeed uniquely and remarkably characterized by just what is necessary for life to appear in it. His view of an organic world fits the facts. It is composed of events each of which is purposive by virtue of God's participation in its self-constitution.

The continued exclusion of God as an explanatory factor in the universities is not based on evidence. It is a matter of clinging to ideas that once proved very fruitful. There is no reason for the church to share in this clinging. Indeed, this is by no means the only case where Christian tradition is better supported by evidence than the modern worldview. I want to spend what time I have left to talk about something that has been important to me in my understanding of Christian life but ignored by modern thought. That's what I'm referring to as the call.

Many years ago, I used the phrase the "call forward." We have to distinguish a call that is drawing us into the future in a distinctive way from the many, many elements in our experience, moment by moment, which are controlled by or reflective of the past. It is unique—it is often not very strong, but sometimes it is. The call of Amos, for example, must have been very strong for him to respond as he did. We can read about many other calls and responses in the Bible that are dramatic and intense. The term "call" is often used chiefly in relationship to these dramatic instances. But from Whitehead I learn that the way in which God is present in us moment by moment, can also be thought of as a call.

I like to use the term call forward. I thought I had originated it and was taking some pride in it. I thought everybody experienced the call forward but that it was especially in the theistic traditions, particularly Christianity, that the call forward is understood as God's call to us. When it is understood that way, and when we act on that understanding, it plays a role in our lives that it doesn't play in the lives of those who ignore it or do not have a way of understanding it.

I am also inclined to understand what I think everybody experiences, in terms of my own experience. I knew that this may be misleading or misdirecting, so I was rather pleased when I came across the expression in Zion's Night, the climactic book and work of Martin Heidegger, considered one of the greatest phenomenologists of the 20th century, who wrote, in German, of "der Ruf nach vor." That means just what "call forward" means in English. We were talking about the same experience. It meant that I was not erroneously reading an element of my personal experience into universal human experience. For me, it seems to be the most pervasive experience of the God of the Bible, the "Abba" of Jesus.

Heidegger could not explain it as I did because he was an explicit and emphatic atheist. He found that there was a call forward in human life, and he had to deal with the question, where does this call come from? I think he knew that the answer that had been around for a long time was that it came from God. Of course, an atheist cannot explain anything in that way. He came up with the view that we call ourselves forward. Heidegger decided that the call comes from ourselves.

I do not think that our feeling of being called is well described in that way. This explanation is forced on Heidegger by atheism, not comfortably supported phenomenologically. We can avoid affirming God by attributing to ourselves the role in experience that has led many to speak of the divine. But unless the reasons to deny God are strong, which I do not find to be the case, something Heidegger finds phenomenologically important is evidence of God's role in experience, not of what we do to ourselves. It is justified as the millions of universes are justified, only by an uncritical commitment to atheism.

There are other examples of this, but this is the one that I want to pursue. If we understand that there is a call forward and we understand there is reason to see God working in every event in the world aiming toward more intensive life, we can connect these two. We also can find out that God is working in us. God is making us, calling us to be more alive and that has specificity. If that is true, we are all experiencing God in a call that can imperfectly and without certainty be distinguished from all the other factors that enter into our experience moment by moment. This becomes the central, distinctive form of Christian spirituality. This is not an eccentric thing for a theologian to say, but when we ask, when do people pray with most sense of urgency, often it is when they need to make important decisions. And they do have a feeling that it makes a difference to God. God wants the right decision to come out of this. And Christians seek to align with God's will and purposes for them. That is an important form of spirituality.

Think of Jesus. There were two times that we were told he was engaged in the work of meditation and prayer very intensively. One of them was right after his baptism by John. He went into the desert and we have vivid accounts of how Satan tempted him. This implied that Jesus had some understanding of what he was called to do, but even understanding what God calls us to do does not guarantee that we will do it.

I don't think there's a particular reason to take the notion of Satan especially seriously. But if Satan means temptation, when he discovered that he has really remarkable spiritual powers, the question of how to use them was urgent and demanding. He was very eager to use them as God wanted him to use them. He spent some time alone before he came back into society and began his ministry of preaching and healing. Another time is in Gethsemane. When he felt called to go to Jerusalem, he knew that was very dangerous. John the Baptist was beheaded, and if he went to Jerusalem, it could easily mean his death. He knew that.

But when he learned that he had been betrayed by one of his known disciples, he prayed, intensively. He was asking God if it was all right to avoid this. Can I avoid this cup? Can I run away? I don't think it would have been impossible since he knew they were coming to crucify him. He could probably have slipped away, but he found that was not his calling. But it was an intense time of prayer.

Few of us want to live our lives in such intensity, but we also want to know what it is that God wants of us. Day by day, hour by hour, moment by moment we often do not even think of ourselves as making decisions. When we are making decisions or a lifetime nature, we are more likely to be aware of how they relate to God's call. At that time, "God" is not just a word about something mysterious that we can't say anything about. That God is the one by whom we are drawn to what is best moment by moment. Often, in a way, we already know what is best and it is simply a matter of urging into that direction. But often, we don't know what is best. God often lures us into acting in ways that are beyond our knowledge.

I said I felt called to produce a new sermon, not to produce the one I'd written out before... I think I was really called by God to do that. I think I felt that I had something more important to say to you in this, the last of my sermons, than sharing my ideas about topics on which of course I have views. They are important topics, but they are not at the very heart of what I understand to be the life of the disciple. I think disciples are those who seek moment by moment, day by day, year by year to find what God wants of them and to shape life around God's call.

Some of you may have been living with God in this way for a long time. For some, it is important to take time and really listen day by day. It can become a situation in which we feel God is making use of us beyond our understanding, beyond our rational decisions, and that to be guided and shaped in that way is a true blessing to us and sometimes through us to others. That is a fully developed life of discipleship.

We must distinguish between God's call and our "consciences." Too often conscience is a matter of some kind of internalized moral law or parental teaching. God may or may not have played a major role in fashioning it. But even if God has not been involved, consciences are important for all of us and often save society from problems even worse than it now experiences. But consciences can be badly shaped. I myself suffer as so many Christians have suffered in the area of sexuality because my conscience was shaped in a way that was not for my own good or for the good of the world. I am not alone in having internalized the view that sexuality is inherently unclean or demeaning. For some Christians "morality" is most centrally sexual restraint.

There is very little support for this kind of "conscience" in the Bible. Breaking out of this distortion is important so that our sexuality can serve God along with the rest of our lives. We must understand we are not talking about conscience when we seek to respond to God's call. We are really talking about something distinctive—we are talking about how God relates to us moment by moment and the possibility that we can hear and respond. And that this hearing and responding can become something that is no longer a struggle but is really the heart of our lives. It doesn't mean that we will not have all kinds of problems—we will still have anxiety, we will still suffer from diseases. We will realistically worry about the future of the church and realistically worry about the future of humanity on this planet. Responding well to the call forward doesn't resolve any of these problems. But when we experience ourselves as being in God's hands there is a kind of assurance, a kind of confidence, a kind of peace that passes understanding and gives us context in which we can suffer. We can even sin. We can refuse God's call at times, but we are still loved. We are still in God's hands. And we can still be opened, again and again, to being led and directed by God. I hope this may help you find the reality of God as a vivid part of your own life experience and one through which you can grow.

Amen.

John B. Cobb Jr. is an American theologian, philosopher, and environmentalist. Cobb is often regarded as the preeminent scholar in the field of process philosophy and process theology, the school of thought associated with the philosophy of Alfred North Whitehead. He is the author of more than fifty books, and founder of many organizations, including the Center for Process Studies, the Cobb Institute, the Institute for Ecological Civilization, and the Living Earth Movement. At 98 years old, he is still actively writing, speaking, and organizing.

An Evolving Sense of the Holy

FRANCES DEARMAN

Process theology reflects an understanding of ultimate reality whereby all that ever was is folding into the unfolding of the world.

Sermon preached at the Universalist Unitarian Church of Halifax, March 25, 2012

What is Process Theology?

"That's hard to explain."

Imagine a small brown cat walking towards wisdom, taking with her all she has learned, growing into knowledge with each new experience, and leaving each individual she meets also changed by that meeting. At the end of each day the cat is still herself, and yet also something new, re-shaped by each event she has experienced into something unforeseen and unforeseeable. In the simplest terms possible, that's Process Theology. Only you are the cat. And so is God. [from *Wabi Sabi*, by Mark Reibstein]

Process Theology emerged from a series of early twentieth-century events, academic in origin, and widely published. The individuals who propelled what we know as the School of Process Theology are named and known and lived very long lives. Generation succeeded generation. Initiator was succeeded by interpreter, who was in turn succeeded by wandering disciples, each with students of their own.

There is no church that preaches Process Theology specifically and exclusively; rather, the ideas of this school of thought have permeated into the seminaries where theology is taught, and into the public realm where theology is lived. Many of us may well hold some ideas that have the shape of Process Theology without ever having heard them named as such.

First, the initiator: Alfred North Whitehead (1861-1947): child of privilege, gifted academic, celebrated teacher. His family birthright was rooted in Anglicanism. His later preference leaned towards Roman Catholicism. He taught until the age of 76, first in England, then at Harvard. When he died at 86, his remains were cremated, and no service was held.

Whitehead was born into a world where absolutes were crumbling. Darwin was overturning our sense of who we are in the world. Scholarship was shattering our understanding of scripture and revelation. No less challenging for Whitehead—scientist and mathematician—Einstein was shattering the old certainties of Newton's physics.

Like Newton before him, Whitehead was led from physics into metaphysics—the theoretical philosophy of being and knowing.

Now, I am a "bear of very little brain." I hesitate to reduce a great mind like Whitehead to anything that I could understand. What I take away from what I have read is that Whitehead's foundational publication of 1929, entitled *Process and Reality*, defended God, but at the cost of radically altering the nature of God, a God no longer the God of Abraham—all seeing, all knowing, all powerful, active in time and beyond. In an age of science, of Darwin and Einstein, Whitehead gave us a god of limited power and knowledge, a god who evolves.

Whitehead was a great mind—and his prose could be impenetrable. And so emerged Whitehead's interpreter: Charles Hartshorne. Charles Hartshorne: child of privilege, gifted academic, celebrated teacher. His father was an Episcopal minister. Hartshorne emerged from a liberal Christian home, read Emerson's Essays as a youth and, in later life, joined the Unitarian Church.

After two years as a hospital orderly in France during the First World War, Hartshorne returned home to America, entered Harvard, and did three degrees in four years—BA, MA, and Ph.D. This was noteworthy, even for Harvard. Hartshorne's dissertation was a roughed-out cast of the philosophy and theology he would spend the rest of his life exploring.

Hartshorne had been Alfred North Whitehead's teaching assistant at Harvard. Later, Hartshorne went to the University of Chicago, taught philosophy there, and eventually branched sideways into theology. Generations of Unitarian ministers were taught by him.

I find myself much struck by the chain of generation in this School of Process Theology. Whitehead taught Hartshorne. Hartshorne taught many, over many decades—Hartshorne lived to be over a hundred and taught well into late old age. He published at 96, delivered his last lecture aged 98, and gave a good interview at age one hundred. He died at 103.

Charles Eddis, emeritus minister of the UU church in Montreal, studied with Hartshorne and his successors—a living link to the original thinkers. And his colleagues learn from Charles, and many others. Process theology is a concept with which most UU ministers are likely to be somewhat familiar.

Hartshorne, like Whitehead, defended theism; however, Hartshorne's God differed in some ways. For Hartshorne, God exists with the world in a dynamic, changing relationship. Also, God has two polarities, being both abstract and concrete. In the abstract, there are elements to God that do not change, like self-identity. Otherwise, God does change, growing in knowledge of the world as the world itself changes and develops.

Also, Hartshorne promoted the idea of pan-en-theism, that the world exists within the holy, much as an unborn child exists within the body of its mother. God is beyond the world, but still intimately connected with and encompassing the world—both in material events and in how we feel about them, for there is always an affective element in our awareness.

For Hartshorne, God was omnipresent, and therefore never absent from any event, even as events unfold. The question becomes, to what extent are we aware of this presence?

Perhaps Hartshorne's most accessible work, intentionally so, largely thanks to his wife and editor, Dorothy Hartshorne, is a small volume entitled *Omnipotence and Other Theological Mistakes*. I turn to my colleague, Katie Stein Sather, who has graciously shared with me her summary of Hartshorne's main points.

First Mistake: that god is absolutely perfect and unchangeable. Not so. God is a process, always in the process of change, according to Hartshorne. No one conception of god applies all the time.

Second Mistake: God is omnipotent, or all powerful. Not so. This idea leads to questions like, "Why would a loving God give me cancer? What am I supposed to learn from this?" Hartshorne would say that God is not in charge.

Third Mistake: Omniscience. Not so. If God is not perfect and not all powerful, then God cannot be all knowing.

Fourth Mistake: God's unsympathetic goodness—that is, that God does not suffer. Not so. If god is represented in each of us, then that sympathy—that shared feeling—is reflected in our care and concern for each other—so therefore God must share our pain.

Fifth Mistake: Immortality after death. Not so, says Hartshorne. There is no individual ongoing awareness after death, says Hartshorne, except for the memories we the living hold of those who have died.

Sixth Mistake: Revelation is Infallible. Not so. Process Theology rejoices that revelation is not sealed. Revelation continues.

Katie reminds us that Hartshorne rejected the notion of God as an "unmoved-mover"; his God moves and is moved, feels our joys and our pain, loves and is loved.

We have heard a brief summation of Process Theology, its main arguments, and its history. Later, I'll speak of how Process Theology might take shape in the pulpit and daily life. But first, let us consider the strongest arguments raised against this school of thought. These are two-fold: some theists find it too radical, some atheists find it not radical enough. Further, some are troubled that Hartshorne's God is imperfect. If God is imperfect, how is such a God worthy of our worship, some might ask?

Some are troubled by the nature of this pan-en-theistic God; Hartshorne's re-interpretation of the holy takes us well beyond Biblical revelation and also beyond the Trinity. This new God lacks divine foreknowledge and pre-destination concerning salvation. This new sense of the holy appears to deny or de-value the miracles attributed to Christ and the divine nature attributed to Christ. Hartshorne is seen to privilege an aesthetic admiration of the world in place of the holiness of God and the awe accorded to the holy one. Hartshorne makes little room for petitionary prayer or the survival of the individual into the afterlife.

Process Theology might also be found weak and wanting when confronting the problem of evil. In our post-holocaust world, an optimistic reluctance to wrestle with the sin and depravity of wilful human malice may seem an inadequate response to the work of religion.

So what do we do with this? How do we take it into the pulpit? How do we take it into our daily lives?

For me, the most significant element of this process school of theology is that, however we feel about god, we are given an image of the universe in which nothing is ever lost. All that ever was goes to shape all that ever will be. It is as if we were remembered in the mind of the holy, our hopes and loves and struggles carried there forever.

And so even when someone we love is adrift in dementia, they are held in the care we offer, in the gifts of care we remember. That mindfulness of care spills into the world and the future like a wave in the water from a pebble tossed into the sea.

And so even the still-born child, lost before the light of day, leaves a legacy of hope and care.

Whitehead was blessed with two sons and a daughter. One of his sons son died in action during the first World War. Hartshorne served as a medical orderly in France during that same conflict. Millions of young men melted into the trenches in that mess. My personal belief is that this is the great gift of Process Theology—that all those lives had value and were not entirely lost, because our connection with the lost is folded into our caring for the future. All that ever was is folded into all that ever will be. This belief might encourage us to walk lightly on the earth, to cease from attachment, as the Buddhists might say, to let go of our desire for fixedness and idolatries that deny the flow of time, knowing that our contribution is never lost.

Several of my colleagues were kind enough to share sermons that were consciously shaped around elements of process theology, each very different. I was intrigued by their choices, and I share the essence of them with you, to illustrate how process theology might play a role in our present lives.

One wrote of death and loss and transition, of the temporary and the transcendent in our lives. Preparing to depart from one pulpit to serve another, my colleague reminded the folks that all they had shared together would be folded into all their futures and would never be truly lost. Therefore, said my colleague, let us take our losses seriously, and honor them.

Another colleague picked up on the more abstract concepts, how the evolving theoretical plays out against a frozen ideal, how the dance of cosmos and chaos makes room for creativity and demands the exercise of our free will.

Another colleague framed their sermon to remind us that Charles Hartshorne was also an eminent birder, an ornithologist who argued that sometimes birds sing their song just for the glory of it. Process theology glorifies nature as the body of god. Process theology invites the imagination of those who find worth in nature, paganism, and feminism.

Another colleague, preaching the final sermon of their life, used process theology to explore final things, final in the sense of being shaped towards purpose, towards the future. Here we see the two poles that Hartshorne spoke of: first, the identity of the holy that is grounded in goodness; then the creative, evolving, unfolding potentiality, that we have free will and we choose to live in connection, aware of our responsibilities, and we commit ourselves to some finality, some purpose that relates us to the future and to the infinite.

I am most grateful to my colleagues for their generous sharing.

In conclusion, there is a school that teaches an understanding of the holy as creative and in motion, in which all experience, all affection, finds a home, folded into the ever-unfolding future. And so, nothing is ever lost.

The first of those who taught this school of thought wished to preserve their faith in God and Christ through this re-framing, and to cease burdening the holy with illogical powers and responsibilities.

However, we choose to name the universal integrity, the infinite reality that holds the universe together, god or not-god, the gift of process theologians to us is their belief that everything we do matters, that we are connected to all the universe and to the future. Our choices matter. Our lives have meaning in the world we help to shape each day. And that all that ever was is folding into the unfolding of the world.

May it be so.

Fran (Frances) Dearman is a retired Universalist Unitarian minister living in Victoria, BC.

Whose Light is it, Anyway?

TERI L. DITSLEAR

Admit it, sometimes scripture does not make sense, especially when we have learned the story, repeatedly using the one lens of tradition. Often the cherry-picked scriptures we can easily rebuff because of context. But what happens when a whole parable just seems to be so blatantly unfair, and God comes off mean and double-minded? This is where the story of the bridesmaids, the virtuous and the silly, never made sense in the first place. What if there was another way of understanding?

Sermon preached at Roots of Life Community, ELCA, November 5, 2023

It is important to remember that we are given permission to question our previously held beliefs. My time spent with Process and Open and Relational Theology, along with my studies of Panentheism, has led me to encourage people to be more curious and open about their tightly held narratives of stories in scripture and our ideas about who God is and is not, especially when those ideas are harmful. The Gospel is always Good News for everyone, all the time.

> Then the kingdom of heaven will be like this. Ten bridesmaids took their lamps and went to meet the bridegroom. Five of them were foolish, and five were wise. When the foolish took their lamps, they took no oil with them; but the wise took flasks of oil with their lamps. As the bridegroom was delayed, all of them became drowsy and slept. But at midnight there was a shout, "Look! Here is the bridegroom! Come out to meet him." Then all those bridesmaids got up and trimmed their lamps. The foolish said to the wise, "Give us some of your oil, for our lamps are going out." But the wise

> replied, "No! there will not be enough for you and for us; you had better go to the dealers and buy some for yourselves." And while they went to buy it, the bridegroom came, and those who were ready went with him into the wedding banquet; and the door was shut. Later the other bridesmaids came also, saying, "Lord, lord, open to us." But he replied, "Truly I tell you; I do not know you." Keep awake therefore, for you know neither the day nor the hour. (Matthew 25:1-13, NRSVUE)

"This is the Gospel of the Lord" and we respond, "Thanks be to God!"

It is this time in our church calendar, from All Saints Sunday until Advent, when we are reading about the end times from Matthew's Gospel. We get to hear a bunch of stories from cranky Jesus. It feels like the Good News of Jesus is hard to find. Beginning in Matthew 24, in the story about *keeping watch,* the last verse tells us if you are not aware when the master is to arrive, "the master will cut you into pieces and throw you into a place where there is weeping and gnashing of teeth." "This is the Gospel of the Lord!" we say, as if this is Good News? Today's version is a little milder but still, it is not good news for those of us who forgot to set our alarm clock—or had the dog throw up on the way out the door—or forgot to put the car in the garage and the windows are frozen and you have to scrape and defrost and then drive with just a little hole of vision. You know what I'm talking about? Things happen to waylay our best intentions.

Many of us have heard the story about the bridesmaids waiting for the groom and we were warned to be Boy Scout-ish, 'always prepared.' This moral of the story has always annoyed me because I often find myself unprepared, late, or willing to think that my friends will have my back in an emergency. This version of Jesus seems to tell us that no, we are responsible for ourselves only, otherwise we will not be given a seat at the table. Besides that, doesn't Jesus tell us often that we are to take care of our neighbor, give to the needy, look out for those who are misfortunate? Did Jesus just renege like a cheating card player? (See Matthew 5:42, 19:21, and 23:13.)

Why are the stingy bridesmaids held up to be virtuous? I mean, what about the words from Hebrews 13:16, NRSVUE "Do not neglect to do good and to share what you have for such sacrifices are pleasing to God. And "Now the whole group of those who believed were of one heart and soul, and no one claimed private ownership of any possessions, but everything they owned was held in common," from Acts 4:32-35. NRSVUE. Trust me, there is more, just Google "*sharing in the Bible*."

I must give a nod to preacher Nadia Bolz-Weber, who reminded us not so long ago that parables are not to be read as morals. They are not to be read as the ethical handbook of "The Virtuous Christian, or How to Behave to get to Heaven." We do not have to believe that we are going to be cast out if we forget to bring enough oil for our lamp, forget to make reservations, or put the car in the garage on a frosty night. She called it the parable trap, when we believe parables are the morality instruction book. Parables are simply truth tellers. Sometimes the truth is hard to find, but when you do find the truth, it sets you free.

One thing that has helped me in my spiritual growth is learning about the theology of Open and Relational Theology. One of my "aha!" moments includes being given permission to look at scripture from a non-traditional lens, rather than the way it has always been interpreted. Funny that the permission was given to me by myself. I was always put off by snarky, dark, cringy, bad mood Jesus, though I know he had his moments. My image was always children-loving, water- and food-giving, welcoming Jesus; the one who always embraced the misunderstood and the outcast.

Clearly, God created us with brains to think and hearts to discern truth. Open and Relational Theology helped me to understand that it is more than alright, it is called for to question our norms, culture, and even history. Being curious about why we believe the things we do is healthy and spiritually revitalizes our soul. Finding a group of people with whom we can safely converse about our questions is key to finding truth in a God-ordained world. Being open to who God is and who we are in God, while questioning the old ways of thinking, is best done in community and in loving relationship with each other.

Back to our parable. What if Revelation 22:5 was the verse that the unprepared bridesmaids should have held onto, instead of listening to the voices of the greedy bridesmaids? Revelation 22 states, flowing from the throne of God "there will be no more night; they need no light of lamp or sun, for the Lord God will be their light, and they will reign forever and ever (NRSVUE) Therefore, the unprepared and the prepared (whatever that means) bridesmaids will have all the light they need. The watchman was standing guard and all of the bridesmaids fell asleep. After all, the master's lamp could be seen in the darkness; the maidens did not need their lamps. The watchman was on the lookout. Maybe the unprepared bridesmaids were duped by the greedy bridesmaids, just like the snaked duped Eve into believing she would have a better life if only she would do what the Lord told her *not* to do.

It seems that all God, the master of the banquet, wants from us and the bridesmaids is a right relationship, to trust in the God of abundance, not a silly snake or greedy bridesmaids. "Your word is a lamp to my feet, and a light to my path," says Psalm 119:105 (NRSVUE). The unprepared bridesmaids, instead of relying on the light of the others around them or the light of Christ, ended up running around in circles, trying to fix the problem themselves. Maybe they were trying to keep up with the Kardashian girls who always had it together. Maybe they were worried that they were going to be shamed by their lack of resources. In reality, God loves to do things with nothing—it is God's favorite palette. Remember the fish, when there was not enough? How about in Maccabees, the teeny bit of oil that stayed lit for eight days instead of one? What about bringing light into darkness? How about bringing about life when things look barren? The bridesmaids either didn't trust God would show up without their lamps, or perhaps they did not think that they would be seen. Instead, they trusted the selfish bridesmaids.

We must admit we do this too, at least I do. Sometimes I believe what others say. I can jump to conclusions like it is an Olympic sport. How often do we get sucked into social media drama, unsubstantiated news reports, or even gossip around town? Maybe we have jumped into the fray and fueled the fire. How often have we been denied something we really want, and then later found out it was a scam? The big question is how often have we listened to a voice that was not God's? God's voice calls us "beloved," calls us "children," calls us "made in God's image," and any other voice is a damned lie. The snake, the selfish bridesmaids, and any other voice that does not call us into love is a voice that does not have our best interest in mind.

Teri Ditslear is an ordained minister of the Evangelical Lutheran Church of America (ELCA), graduated from Lutheran School of Theology Chicago, with an M.Div. and is working on her doctorate in Open and Relational Theology at Northwind Seminary. Teri is a pastor, mission developer of Roots of Life Community, ELCA, a Reconciling in Christ Church and part of the Wild Church Network. She is a certified Spiritual Director, a lover of Eco-theology, and believes that God is in all things.

The Earthquake of Easter

PATRICIA ADAMS FARMER

"The God of Easter rocks our world with radical, transforming, uncontrolling love."

Reading: Matthew 28:1-10
Sermon preached at Millersburg Christian Church (Disciples of Christ), Fulton, Missouri, April 16, 2017

"And suddenly, there was a great earthquake." And the earth quaked and the trees cracked and the rocks rolled. On that first Easter morning, transformation on a scale no one had ever seen began to shake, rattle, and roll its way into the world.

Resurrection. It is an earthquake, an upheaval, revealing a brand-new world of possibility, hope, and new life!

Having lived on the Pacific Rim for many years, I am well acquainted with earthquakes. They strike fear in me, let me tell you. My first California earthquake caused our three-story condo to sway back and forth, as if it were nothing more substantial than a tree branch swaying in the wind. Doors rattled, the floor rolled—and so did my stomach. I learned to keep a bottle of Pepto Bismol close by in earthquake country.

Then, years later, when living on the coast of Ecuador, a 7.8 earthquake destroyed our newly built beach home. Thankfully, we were not present for that one. But others were not so lucky.

So, I have always associated earthquakes with fear and destruction. But here in this passage in Matthew, we discover another kind of quaking—the kind that wakes us up, gets our attention, jolts us out of our everyday assumptions about the world. These are the earthquakes that break open tightly closed minds and hearts—the kind of quake that issues forth new life and fresh possibilities.

The Easter story in Matthew begins with this kind of earthquake: a quaking of pure wonder, awe, astonishment. This is what Mary Magdalene and the other Mary must have felt when they learned Jesus had risen. Astonishing, too, was the fact that the *women* disciples were the first to witness the resurrection!

These devoted and courageous women went to the tomb that Sunday morning with heavy hearts, expecting to anoint a dead body with spices. Instead, they experienced the shaking of the earth, the snow-white brilliance of an angel, and the amazement of an empty tomb. "They departed quickly from the tomb with fear and great joy."

"Fear and great joy"—the very definition of astonishment. We need to be astonished once in a while, don't we? In C.S. Lewis' *The Lion, the Witch and the Wardrobe*, there is a description of the resurrection of Aslan, the Christ-lion. Lewis speaks of Aslan's resurrection as "a Deeper Magic" embedded in the universe since before the dawn of time. As theologian Bruce Epperly puts it, "This deeper magic is not contrary to the laws of nature, but a deeper, more energetic reality that gives birth to our own personal resurrections and the power of life to overcome death."

Yes, the deeper magic of the universe rocks our world with the good news: Christ is alive, hope is alive—and love is stronger than death!

With this astonishing news, we are jolted out of our limited vision of ourselves and our world. In an instant, the two brave Marys in our text left the world of despair behind and entered a new world filled with hope and fresh possibility. This is the earthquake of Easter: it shakes us out of our everyday world with its heartbreaks, injustices, and might-makes-right philosophies; it cracks opens an astonishing world of divine possibility and spiritual treasure.

In the 1950s, there was a devastating earthquake in China. As a result of the quake, a huge boulder was dislodged from a mountain, exposing a great cache of wonderful artifacts and treasures from a thousand years ago. A new world became visible. This speaks to me on a personal level. After the devastating earthquake in Ecuador, a new world became visible to my husband and me. Despite our sadness and loss, we landed here, in a new place -- a place of grace and welcome, and yes, treasures in the form of new friends and fresh adventures we never imagined possible.

Our faith is built on resurrection possibilities, which offer hope when all seems lost. Just look at the women who witnessed the earthquake at the tomb. When the earth shook and the stone was rolled away that first Easter morning, they caught their first glimpse of a new world filled with spiritual treasures: a world where hope is alive, where suffering is transformed, and where power is turned on its head.

When the world values brute force and violence, we are astonished to see that, after all the destruction and suffering, it is love that survives—love that triumphs. Love is the greatest power in the universe because God is love. This earth-shaking power does not control or destroy because love cannot control and destroy. As theologian Thomas Oord reminds us, the God of resurrection is the "God of *uncontrolling* love." This radical, transforming, uncontrolling love becomes both our salvation and our hope.

We need to remember this when we experience the metaphorical earthquakes of the tragic variety, when our world is shaken or even turned upside down: a phone call in the middle of the night, a loved one dying, a job suddenly lost, or a relationship broken.

Sometimes our earthquakes come in the form of a spiritual crisis that cracks open a fresh vision of God. For me, it was discovering that God is not the Policeman in the Sky or the all-controlling bearded tyrant who determines everything that happens. Instead, I found the God of Easter, the God of uncontrolling love—the God who, in the words of philosopher Alfred North Whitehead, is our "great companion—the fellow-sufferer who understands."

Yes, the God of Easter resurrection is the God who suffers with us in this "veil of tears," and out of that shared suffering and deep presence fashions fresh possibilities for transformation and healing. This God of resurrection is never the author of tragedy and suffering, but rather the healer who lights the way for a fresh beginning. As co-creators with God, we can choose to follow this light out of our dark tombs and into the dazzling brilliance of new life.

But moving from death to resurrection, from darkness into light, from the world as it is, to the world as it *might* be, is not as easy as it sounds. We are so very addicted to thinking the worst, aren't we? Of course, sometimes fear is a good thing... that is, if we're being chased by a tiger. But when fear becomes the master of our lives and lodges itself like a boulder inside our psyche, our worldview, even our religious life, it keeps us prisoners inside tombs of spiritual darkness. Such entrenched fear leads to depression and despair or mutates into hate and us-vs-them worldviews. We find ourselves locked inside tombs of our own making. Deprived of fresh air, sunshine, movement, and connection, our souls begin to die a little more each day.

Jesus was very much aware of this human tendency toward fear. Twice in this passage in Matthew, we hear the words: "do not be afraid." Radical transformation can be a scary thing. Fear is more familiar, so we cling to what we know best. But in order to meet the risen Christ-- the God of Resurrection-- we must, like the two Marys, muster the courage to move past that heavy boulder of hard, stultifying fear, and accept the divine invitation to enter a world of fresh imaginings.

One of my heroes from history is the Dutch Jew, Etty Hillesum. Her diary is one of the most profound literary treasures of the Holocaust. Etty Hillesum was in her twenties when that Great Darkness began to swallow up Europe. As a secular Jew, a mystic, and an intellectual, she embraced inspiration from many sources, including, and especially, the Gospel of Matthew.

One of the most moving passages of Etty Hillesum's diary is a prayer she wrote on a dreary Sunday morning in 1942, when she knew her time of freedom was growing short. She wrote, "The jasmine behind my house has been completely ruined by the rains and storms of the last few days, its white blossoms are floating about in muddy black pools on the low garage roof. But somewhere inside me the jasmine continues to blossom undisturbed, just as profusely and delicately as ever it did. And it spreads its scent round the House in which you dwell, Oh God. You can see, I look after You, I bring you not only my tears and my forebodings on this stormy, grey Sunday morning, I even bring you scented Jasmine."

Etty Hillesum did not survive the war. But her courageous spirit could not be destroyed because the jasmines inside her refused to quit blooming. And everyone she touched felt her strength. When she left one internment camp to go to her death in Auschwitz, she threw out a postcard from the train that was later found by a farmer. It said, "We left the camp singing."

How can one not be moved, shaken, and astonished by such a courageous defiance of darkness?

The celebrated Christian writer Frederick Buechner said: "Here is the world. Beautiful and terrible things will happen. Don't be afraid." I think this is what Jesus was telling the two Marys that first Easter morning: Here is the world, my friends. Beautiful and terrible things will happen. Don't be afraid.

This is what Easter is about: a time to join together in singing against the darkness and injustice and tyrannies of this world -- and never letting fear have the last word. Come what may, in the Risen Christ, we have hope in this world, as well as in the next.

So, maybe it is time to embrace the resurrection possibilities within the earthquakes of life. Maybe it's time to let go of fear. Maybe it's time to renew our childlike capacity to be astonished. To open ourselves to the deeper magic in the universe. To be shaken and awakened by the Easter message that God is love -- and love, my friends, is stronger than death. Amen.

Patricia Adams Farmer (www.patriciaadamsfarmer.com) is an ordained minister in the Christian Church (Disciples of Christ) and the author of several nonfiction and fiction books including *Embracing a Beautiful God*, *Fat Soul: A Philosophy of S-I-Z-E*, *Beauty and Process Theology*, *The Metaphor Maker,* and *Fat Soul Fridays.* She is a regular contributor to *Spirituality & Practice* and *Open Horizons.*

On Rendering to Caesar and to God

RONALD L. FARMER

Most Christians are aware of the danger of "rendering to Caesar things that belong to God," but the danger of "rendering to God things that belong to Caesar," is often overlooked.

Reading: Matthew 22:15-22
Sermon preached at Oakland Christian Church (Disciples of Christ), Columbia, MO, October 22, 2023

"Politics makes strange bedfellows," they say, and how often the truth of this aphorism manifests itself! We see it in the political machinations of today, and we see it in today's scripture lesson from the Gospel according to Matthew 22:15-22. Among Jesus' verbal sparring opponents during Passion Week was an unlikely confederation of Pharisees and Herodians. They had quite different political and theological views, but they were able to set all that aside in order to present a united front in opposition to Jesus.

Despite the flattering (and ironically true!) words with which they began, the intention of these unlikely allies was to entrap Jesus by his own words. The question of paying the census tax—a tax levied on every adult within the Roman Empire—was far from academic in Jesus' day. The institution of this head tax in the year 6 C.E. sparked a resurgence of Jewish nationalism, whose flame the Zealots eventually fanned into the disastrous conflagration known as the First Jewish War against Rome (66-70).

Clearly, Jesus was trapped—or so his opponents thought. If he said that paying the tax did not violate the Torah (the position of the pro-Roman Herodians), then he would lose popular support. If he took the stance that the tax violated the Torah (the position of the Pharisees, at least in principle), then he risked being reported to the Roman authorities as a dangerous subversive, subject to arrest. Jesus perceived the hypocrisy of their flattering words and recognized their question for what it was: an attempt to put him to the test and discredit him with the crowds who flocked around him.

The tax could only be paid with a Roman *denarius*, so he asked his challengers for the coin. Now, in the opinion of most Jews of Jesus' day, such a coin was, in itself, idolatrous. In addition to the image of the emperor and Roman religious imagery, the coin bore the following inscription: "Tiberius Caesar, august son of the divine Augustus, high priest." When devout Jews were forced to handle such coins, they refrained from looking at them. Such idolatrous coins could not be placed in the temple treasury, hence the presence of moneychangers in the Temple's Court of the Gentiles, who changed Roman coins for other coins, such as the Tyrian shekel and half-shekel, which did not contain idolatrous images and inscriptions.

The fact that Jesus' opponents had no difficulty in providing a *denarius*, even in the Temple precincts where the verbal exchange took place, suggests that it came from one of the Herodians. In a move that doubtless shocked many of those in the crowd, Jesus forced his opponents to look squarely at the coin as he held it aloft and asked, "Whose head is this and whose title?" Of course, only one answer was possible: "The emperor's."

Jesus then uttered his famous dictum: "Give to the emperor the things that are the emperor's, and to God the things that are God's."

Historically, theologians have used this passage in two important ways. First, it has been used to support the notion that one can be both a good citizen and a good Christian. In the words of New Testament scholar Pheme Perkins, loyalty to God "does not require that God's people be defined by a theocracy embodied in a particular nation." Indeed, not long after Jesus' day, the Apostle Paul exhorted Christians to render taxes, respect, and honor to the governing authorities (Rom 13:1-7).[1]

No, the two loyalties need not clash.

But sometimes they do, and this is when the second theological use of the passage has come into play historically. One must distinguish between what belongs to the emperor and what belongs to God. As is typical with Jesus' teachings, this saying is in the form of a principle rather than a rule; application to a particular situation requires

1. Although Paul's theological and ethical teachings are anti-imperial, he nonetheless finds much of value in the Roman world. For a discussion of Paul's anti imperialism, see John Dominic Crossan and Jonathan L. Reed; *In Search of Paul: How Jesus' Apostle Opposed Rome's Empire with God's Kingdom* (San Francisco: Harper, 2004). For a process-relational analysis of Paul's anti-imperial thought, see John B. Cobb, Jr., and David J. Lull, *Romans*, in *Chalice Commentaries for Today* (St. Louis: Chalice Press, 2005). For a process-relational analysis of John's anti-imperial thought, see Ronald L. Farmer, *Revelation*, in *Chalice Commentaries for Today* (St. Louis: Chalice Press, 2005).

careful reflection. When governmental authorities demand something that, upon careful analysis, belongs to God, then a Christian must resist. Surprisingly—or maybe not so surprisingly—in the short interval between Paul's Letter to the Romans (ca. 57) and John's Revelation written from governmental-imposed exile on the island of Patmos (ca. 95), the nature of Roman governmental demands changed. Indeed, so dramatic was the change in what the government demanded, that rather than viewing the Roman government as "God's servant for your good" (Rom 13:4) as Paul had, John perceived that the emperor had become "the beast," a henchman of "the dragon" (Rev 13:1-10).

The creative tension between these two historical teachings derived from this passage has served Christians well for nearly two millennia. Living in a democracy, as we do today, it is all too easy to become lazy. We sometimes need to be reminded of our obligations as citizens. Promoting the common good requires not only our taxes, but also contributions of our time and energy. Likewise, there are times when we need to be reminded of the second historic teaching. Whenever laws or governmental policies demand more than is rightfully due, Christians must resist. Such resistance can take a variety of forms: from pressing for new legislation and voting one's conscience, to participating in peaceful protest movements and engaging in non-violent civil disobedience. Yes, the creative tension between these two teachings has served Christianity well.

But there is a third teaching implicit in Jesus' famous dictum—albeit one that has received scant attention in the history of Christianity. Not only is it possible to render to Caesar things that belong to God; it is also possible to render to God things that belong to Caesar. This error occurs whenever people conceive of God in terms of Caesar, in essence creating God in Caesar's image, only "bigger." This all-too-common theological error results in Christians picturing God as exercising coercive, controlling, unilateral power like Caesar, only raised to the *Nth* degree (mathematically speaking).

With characteristic eloquence, the philosopher Alfred North Whitehead expressed the seriousness of this all-too-common error: "The brief Galilean vision of humility flickered throughout the ages, uncertainly.... But the deeper idolatry, of the fashioning of God in the image of the Egyptian, Persian, and Roman imperial rulers, was retained. The Church gave unto God the attributes which belonged exclusively to Caesar."

Herein lies contemporary Christianity's fundamental flaw, the nearly ubiquitous error that alters, or at least taints, every other theological and ethical teaching and practice—including one's assessment of and vision for the social-political order. The most pressing need today is for Christians to recapture the original Galilean conception of the divine, for as I wrote in my commentary on the Revelation to John:

> A person's conception of divine power greatly influences his or her understanding of power on the human level. In fact, one's view of human power

> differs from one's understanding of divine power only in terms of quantity, not quality. Thus, if divine power is viewed as coercive, all-controlling, and unilateral, then the corresponding understanding of the highest/ideal form of human power will be coercive, controlling, and unilateral—like the power exercised by the beast, the Roman emperor. But if divine power is understood to be persuasive, all-influencing, and relational, then the corresponding understanding of the highest/ideal form of human power will be persuasive, influencing, and relational—like the power exercised by the Lamb.

As disciples of Jesus, let us seek to recapture Jesus' teaching, the Galilean vision, regarding the nature of divine power—power that is persuasive, not coercive; all-influencing, not all-controlling; and relational, not unilateral.

And that's today's good news.

Ronald L. Farmer served on the religious studies faculties of the University of Missouri, the University of Cincinnati, Chapman University, and Brandman University. An ordained minister in the Christian Church (Disciples of Christ), he has served churches in Ohio and Missouri. He has written three academic books (including *Beyond the Impasse: The Promise of a Process Hermeneutic*), two philosophical novels, and over five dozen journal articles and essays.

The *Psst!* of God

MARK FELDMEIR

The divine voice resounds throughout all space and time, overheard by the swirling stardust at the furthest corners of the universe and the stirring spirits of every living creature on earth—a voice that says, "Psst! You are meant for more. You're not done. You could become this..."

Reading: Exodus 14:10-29
Sermon reached at St. Andrew United Methodist Church,
Highlands Ranch, CO, September 17, 2023

Do you remember, as a child, when someone would ask, "What do you want to be when you grow up?" Maybe it was a parent or grandparent, a teacher, or a coach. "What do you want to be when you grow up?" The comedian Paula Poundstone once said that adults are always asking kids what they want to be when they grow up because they are looking for ideas.

What *did* you want to be when you grew up? I'm guessing you probably named a particular profession or vocation: nurse, teacher, veterinarian, truck driver, bomb tester, rock star, engineer, TikTok influencer, hedge fund manager.

Maybe these professions sounded adventurous, rewarding, or lucrative at the time. Maybe you even pursued one of them into adulthood and are actually dismantling bombs or managing billion-dollar hedge funds for a living today. But, for most of us, it probably never occurred to us back then that none of these professions have much to do with *being*. With some exceptions, they're mostly about *doing*, and we quickly learn to do them well without giving much thought to who or what we're becoming. So, chances are, we never actually got around to answering the deeper question—"What am I becoming?"

That's a question we should never stop asking until the moment we breathe our last breath.

What am I becoming?

Every being is implanted with an innate and enduring impulse to *become*. This impulse is inherent in all living things—not just humans. It is found in all of nature. Biologically speaking, it helps explain why we are humans and not eukaryotic cells or chambered nautiluses or duckbilled platypuses. Over nearly 14 billion years, this impulse said, over and over, *"Hey! Psst! Listen! Do you know that you're not done yet? Do you know that you could become this…?"* And, throughout time, from the simplest life forms like organelles and amoeba to the most complex life forms like homo sapiens and ecosystems, a brave and endless chorus resounded, sometimes faintly, in the face of enormous odds, saying yes, over and over, to the divine *psst* to become more. It's how we got here. Even now, in this moment, it's still happening. The divine *psst* still calls, waiting for our *yes*. We are still becoming. We are not finished yet.

This *impulse to become* is not merely biological. This is where Darwin fell short. We now know that beyond the known, visible world of cells and ions and molecules and atoms and electrons there's a mostly invisible and as-yet unknowable world of quanta and strings and fields and lots and lots of energy—all of which we know are participating in an elegant cosmic choreography we cannot accurately measure or even objectively observe. Even the universe, at this very moment, is still becoming, still expanding—at a rate of something like 42 miles per second. If it sometimes feels like the world is moving at a million miles an hour, you're not wrong. Not even the universe is finished becoming. Nothing is done yet.

It's like there's a divine voice resounding throughout *all* space and time, overheard by the swirling stardust at the furthest corners of the universe and the stirring spirits of every living creature on earth—a voice that says, "*You are meant for more. You're not done. You could become this…*" For millennia, people of faith have believed that this enduring voice is the divine voice spoken always and everywhere, from the very beginning of time—when God first looked upon the swirling, soupy, formless mess of empty space, and said, "Let there be light…" It wasn't a command so much as it was an invitation. God was saying, *"Hey, you—chaos. Psst… Listen: If you're ready, you could become this…"*

Who knows how long God had been saying *Psst*. But at a particular moment in time, the chaos finally said *yes*, choosing to become light and then life and then grass and trees and buzzing insects and creeping and crawling and walking creatures. That divine voice has been calling out ever since, over and again, to all creation, *"Hey, you. Psst. You are meant for more. When you're ready, you could become this..."* This longing to *become* is woven into the very fabric of the universe, reminding us that to remain what we are and who we are and where we are—unchanged and unmoved—is death. We are wired to become more—to go from there to here and then from here to there, from what we've been to what we could be, from a world of imposed limits to boundless possibilities, from bondage to the past to a future of greater freedom and adventure and novelty.

This is why we love stories about people or groups of people who cry out for freedom in the face of physical or spiritual forces that enslave them—Rosa Parks, Bob Marley, Nelson Mandela, ordinary Ukrainians fighting for freedom, twelve-steppers and people in recovery from all kinds of abuse—they are all, in some way, bravely answering the call to become more. Some of the most memorable stories and movies are about the human struggle for freedom to become more—*The Odyssey, The Grapes of Wrath, Shawshank Redemption, Gladiator, Four Years a Slave.*

One of my favorites is *Barbie.* At the heart of the *Barbie* movie is a story of our human longing to become more. It is a parable that even Jesus might have told. It poses the question we all must answer: will I choose to live in Barbie Land, a world that is manufactured and predictable and not real, and where nothing—including me and my life and my future—can ever change? Or will I dare to journey to the Real World where, despite the risks and the pain and the challenges, I can become more?

This longing to become is why the Exodus story is so universally resonant and relatable and enduringly archetypal. In the story, Egypt is the place of slavery, the Promised Land is the place of freedom and novelty to which God is calling the people, and their journey from Egypt to the Promised Land is the timeless paradigm for the human struggle to become more—and the obstacles that seem to be always in the way. The word exodus means "the way out," or "the road of escape." And who among us hasn't longed for liberation from something that constrains or threatens our wellbeing, our potential, our future? Who hasn't felt trapped or paralyzed by forces or circumstances that control us? Who hasn't ever felt some hopeful impulse to take a step toward becoming more, only to doubt ourselves or the source of that impulse or the possibility of ever arriving?

The Exodus story speaks of two kinds of struggle: the outward struggle for freedom that people endure in the face of real oppression in this world, which, for marginalized people, makes the Exodus story *their* story of liberation. But it also speaks of the inward, spiritual struggle for freedom we all experience as humans, and the divine call to embark on a journey of liberation that leads to the possibilities of becoming.

According to the story, the Hebrews are slaves in Egypt. Moses convinces them to flee their captors. He covertly leads them out of Egypt, but their captors fiercely pursue them.

Considering the odds, we assume this is going to end badly. But the Hebrews get a head start. Things initially are looking good. Their over-under on survivability seems favorable. They are making great headway and it's all looking wonderful until, suddenly, they discover their exodus—their "road out"—has led them straight to the dead-end shoreline of the impassable, impossible, unimaginable Red Sea. And now, Pharoah's army is swiftly closing in on them, and they're trapped between the Red Sea and Pharoah's marching death squad, and it occurs to them that they're probably going to die.

But that's when the divine voice speaks—that same voice heard everywhere, since the very beginning of time. The voice says, *"Hey, if you're ready, you can do this, you could become this…"* The voice uses different words here—but it is the same message. "Do not be afraid, stand firm, and see the deliverance that the Lord will accomplish for you today… The Lord will fight for you, and you have only to keep still." (Ex. 14:13-14, NRSVUE). What the voice was saying was, *"You're not done yet because God is not done yet."* Don't we all long to hear that voice in the face of whatever Red Sea we're facing?

But this is where the story gets so weird that many find it unbelievable. The details about what happens next are difficult to reconcile from a purely rational point of view. According to the story, what happens next seems entirely implausible. First, that impossible, impassable Red Sea actually splits in two, leaving an opening of dry land running through the middle of it. And we moderns might say, *Hmmm…*Then, all those panic-stricken Hebrews agree that there is really nothing at all unwise about a mass migration through a parted sea, nothing sketchy about all those fish frozen in the walls of water, with eyes wide open, just staring at them. And we moderns might say, *Hmmm…* And then, just as the Hebrews make it out safely on the other side, the walls of water crash down on Pharoah's army and the Egyptian soldiers are drowned—thousands of lifeless, bloated bodies washing up on the shorelines while the praise songs of the righteous rise up over the whole scene. And we moderns might say, *Hmmm.*

History is always written by the victors, and while these details make for a great story, don't let this great story get in the way of its deeper truth. You don't have to believe that any of those details are factually true to hear its deeper truth. You don't have to believe that it always takes some supernatural act like the parting of the sea to get you through your troubles. You don't have to believe that the physical laws of the universe must somehow be suspended so you can inexplicably walk through a real-life crisis unscathed. You don't have to believe that your own worst enemies must ultimately die or suffer in order for you to finally be set free. This story doesn't ask us to believe the unbelievable or the impossible in order for something good to happen. It doesn't ask us to do anything at all, actually. Did you notice this? There are no commands on that shoreline to do anything—except this: to not be afraid, to stand firm, and to be still.

I love this divine advice: do not be afraid, do not run away, do not react impulsively.

These are the instructions given to the Hebrews at the shoreline of the Red Sea. And what is the Red Sea? For them, it was real. But for us, it's a symbol. In ancient times, the sea was a symbol of chaos, the untamed parts of nature—the dangers, threats, and forces of death. It was to be avoided at all costs because lurking beneath its surface were all the things we can't see and all the demonic forces we manufacture in our minds—leviathan, sea monsters, unknown beasts with sharp teeth. The sea is a symbol for whatever obstacle, fear, or force of resistance stands in the way of our freedom to become whomever God is calling us to be next.

For us, on any given day, it might be real injustice, oppression or systems or institutions that repress or harm or hold others back. It might be depression, anxiety, addiction, or some inner personal struggle. It might be the loss of a job or relationship, some past event from which we've never healed, or some present event that's turned our world upside down and rendered us helpless and deeply vulnerable. The sea changes from day to day, but the message of the divine voice is timeless: you can do this, you can become this, so do not be afraid, do not run away, do not react impulsively. The story says that, on the journey of liberation, the real Pharaohs of this world are always banking on the possibility that we *will* be afraid and *will* run away and *will* act impulsively. Pharaoh only holds onto power when we give in, give up, cash out, sell out, concede and recede into a lesser version of ourselves. Fear, retreat, and impulsivity constitute the oxygen that keeps Pharoah alive.

Months ago, the church campus where I pastor was vandalized because of my congregation's inclusive welcome of LGBTQ persons. The Pharoah of hate assumed we'd be fearful and run away and react by becoming a lesser version of ourselves. It didn't know that people of faith are no longer citizens of Egypt. Pharoah no longer has power over us. Our way is through the sea and we'll never become whom God calls us to be until we stand at the water's edge, take courage, stand our ground, and be still while we work and wait for the barriers—the waters of exclusion—to finally part.

You can get the people out of Egypt, but it's hard to get the Egypt out of the people—unless they choose to live unafraid, to not run, to not react impulsively. But the story also says that, on the journey of liberation, God is always out in front of us—going to battle for us in ways we don't see or understand. Each of us experience and describe that "divine combat" differently. But the story says that God is always for us and before us, and that in every Exodus we are never closer to God than when we are standing at the water's edge.

At this moment, countless people stand at the shoreline of some seemingly impossible and impassible sea in their lives—many of whom cannot see a way out. It leads them to a place of hopelessness and resignation. Every day in the US, 132 die by suicide—more than 5 every hour. If you are standing on that shoreline, or fear that someone you know is, the Exodus story is a story for you, too. God's *Psst* is spoken everywhere, to everyone, reminding all of us that there really is a way through the sea. God is with for us and before us. That can be so hard to hear when we're in the grip of despair and cannot see a way through. In the US, more people than ever are giving up. But what I've learned from survivors of attempted suicide is that this timeless wisdom of not reacting impulsively when you're at the water's edge can make all the difference.

In 2020, Kevin Hines jumped off the Golden Gate Bridge. He'd been suffering from Bi-Polar Disorder, crying out for help—but no one answered. He took a bus to the bridge and jumped. He somehow survived, and he says what so many survivors of attempted suicide confirm: "The millisecond my hands left the rail, it was instant regret." Hines says he instantly lamented his impulsive decision. He fell 220 feet through the air at 90 miles an hour, knowing he didn't want to die, that he'd made a mistake. The impact was severe, but he miraculously survived—thanks to a lone sea lion that came to his aid, keeping him afloat until he was rescued. Today, Hines is a suicide-prevention advocate whose message is that if the one in despair can keep from acting impulsively, he can be saved. And so it is for all of us, at whatever shoreline we find ourselves, when we listen for the voice of the God who is for us and goes before us, saying, *"Hey! Psst! Listen! Do you know that you're not done yet? Do you know that you could become this…?"*

Mark Feldmeir is Lead Pastor of St. Andrew United Methodist Church in Highlands Ranch, Colorado. He holds an M.Div. from Claremont School of Theology, where he has taught homiletics courses, and has written four books, including his latest *Life After God: Finding Faith When You Can't Believe Anymore (Westminster John Knox Press: 2023).*

Deep Withness

JONATHAN J. FOSTER

Science and faith harmonize along the idea that the entire universe—micro into macro, immaterial into material, and humanity into divinity—is flowing back and forth in complex waves of relationship. This "deep withness" is reality. It has profound implications for both your life and the life of the entire world.

Sermon preached at Mission Church, Lenexa, Kansas, 2019

Once, when our youngest was about three, he got into trouble. I know it's hard to believe that the little guy would break a rule, and honestly, his transgressions were few and far between, but something happened, and as a result, he was sent to "time out."

Later, after time out was over, and after I had forgotten about the incident, I loaded him into the car to head down the road and run an errand, he quietly said, "But Dad, you still wuv me, right?"

It's been almost 20 years, and my heart still aches thinking about his question.

I pulled over, jumped out of the car, opened his door, and gave him a big hug. With my body draped over him and the car seat, I said, "Hey, bud, there's nothing you could ever do to make me stop loving you."

I remember giving him a big kiss on the cheek. He just smiled and stared up through the moon roof, as if he knew it all along, as if he was cool, as if there had never been any doubt.

You and I are emerging out of a variety of different backstories, and though I doubt anyone walked in here asking the three-year-old's question—"But, God, you still wuv me, right?"—the reality is, your backstory could be full of difficult, challenging, and even hurtful experiences. It'd be understandable to wonder about God's love for you.

To begin to address that issue, I want you to know upfront that I'm committed to the idea that God is love. I don't know anything for certain, but by faith, I suspect this is true. It's a remarkable claim, really, and means more than just God doing nice things.

Put it this way: That God is love is a deeper statement than God is lov*ing*. Lov*ing* suggests something God may do (or the shadow side of this idea, something God may not do), but love suggests what simply is. And what simply is (as if any of this is simple) is that love is with us. Where else would love be?

If God is love and love is with us, this would mean that God is not a separate being, an entirely different entity that chooses from time to time to move into our world to do something lov*ing*, because, well, God is already *here*. Love is here. It's something I call a deep withness.

I suspect deep withness is the reality.

Interestingly, while science has no interest in making claims about God's presence, the idea of withness is present within what it reveals, as well. It turns out that our best science, both in biological, physiological, and even psychological ways, tells us that everything is connected to everything else—plants and oxygen, soil and climate, gravity and physics, desire and imitation, viruses both virtual and biological, etc.

And, of course, the sacred text hums with this reality. The psalmist in Psalm 139 says, "Where could I go to flee your presence?" Jesus assures us in Matthew 28:20, "I am with you always, even unto the end of the world." Paul reminds us in Acts 17:28 that "in him, we live and move and have our being."

In light of this, one could say that both science and faith harmonize along the idea that nothing is entirely separate; that the entire universe, from the micro to the macro, immaterial into material, and humanity into divinity, is flowing back and forth in complex waves of relationship. It's all one song (i.e., uni-verse).

Separateness is an ontological impossibility.

Therefore, broadly speaking, one could also say that Americanized Christianity, with its interventionist-God coming from somewhere else to order everything in the beginning, only to come back at the end and destroy everything (of course, after extracting a select group of people) is a perspective that is fundamentally opposed to reality.

"The greatest ally of God," as Richard Rohr says, "is reality."

Reality might be telling us of God's deep withness; God's presence to all things, in all ways, across the full spectrum of matter throughout the universe, and across the full spectrum of humanity in all its splendid, interesting, and interconnected shapes and forms.

God with …

- *The physical: throughout our variations of height, skin pigmentation, eye color, or hand dominance. (Who would dare say that the left-handed are out? Hold on, the church did that once.)*
- *The emotional: in our waves of depression or confidence, hope or pain, guilt or assurance. (Who would say that those who are depressed are out? Oh, yeah, the church did that once, too.)*
- *The mental: across our range and spectrum of intellect, intelligence, reasoning, and imagination. (Who would dare say the disabled are out? Sigh, been there, done that.)*
- *The sexual: across a range of phenotypes, chromosomes, desires, and proclivities. (Who would dare say these human beings are out? Oh, wait …)*

Reality doesn't really care about what the church or culture says (or what the church-culture says)… reality just keeps moving on. Deep withness is here.

I love this thought. It helps me and I hope, it helps you.

And there's more, particularly for those of us interested in the way Jesus lived, for he showed us that to enjoy God's deep withness to its fullest, we might consider extending it to others.

I want to approach that sentence again to clarify what I'm not saying; I'm not saying that if you don't extend withness to others that God is no longer with you. No, God no longer being with you is not possible. The judgment has already been made, and it's a judgment of love. In the same way, there is nothing my children could ever do to make me stop loving them, so it is with God. There's nothing you could do to make him stop loving you.

So, I'm not saying this is a transactional thing, that you must give love away in order for God to love you. I'm trying to say something less conditional but still very real; less definitive, but still very true…that is: according to the life of Jesus, those who live most resonant with God's deep witness are those who are interested in being open *to* and *with* others. The one accentuates the other.

In other words…

- *You're not earning God's favor by being hospitable; rather, being hospitable opens you up even more to God's favor, which is already freely flowing.*

- *You're not manipulating the machinery of grace by laying your life down for others; rather, by laying your life down for others, you are giving up all control of manipulating anything and fully trusting in grace.*
- *You're not proving your good worth to God by going out of your way to help someone; rather, going out of your way to help someone proves God's good worth.*

Each of these statements, I think, is worthy of careful reflection, but in the time that we have left, I want to highlight the last idea, the idea that God's worth is somehow attached to our thoughts and actions.

This is both a beautiful and troubling idea.

Let's suppose, as we've already begun to do, that God is not an outside omnipotent deity watching us from a distance, but that thing inside of us energizing us to love. And that as we love, God is revealed to the world. We already take for granted that God has no localized physical body, so one can see fairly easily (as if any of this is easy) that moving, working, and helping is a way to actualize God in the world.

Etty Hillesum, I call her Saint Etty for her indefatigable work with family and friends in the face of the Nazi concentration camp powers, wrote of the importance of our actions and our ability to "enable God to be God." I find St. Etty's idea to harmonize with one of my favorite philosophers, Jack Caputo, who says that while God insists, it's up to us whether God exists. And I find Jack's idea to harmonize with one of my favorite people, Jesus, who, in stories like the one we call The Good Samaritan Story, emphasizes the idea of God needing humans, even those who were formerly thought of as being out "of the fold," to actualize his love into the world.

Each of these people might be saying that God is in the process of becoming and is doing so by way of our thoughts, prayers, and actions. The deep withness is constantly and forever being birthed into the world, what the theologians from long ago called incarnation. But incarnation isn't just what happened in the stable on that first Christmas; incarnation takes place all the time, moment by moment—God loving the world by becoming the world, us loving God by becoming God.

Was Jesus God? Yes.

Are you God? Yes

Haha, do I mean these two statements in the exact same way?

Do I mean to strip Jesus of the unique way he embodied God? No, not really.

But do I mean to strip you of the unique way you embody God? No, not really.

Each of us (along with all creatures and matter in the cosmos) is caught up in the invitation to partner with God. Open and relational theologian Andrew Davis calls this incarnational back and forth between divine and human, "ethical theosis." It's simultaneously the awareness of deep withness, the gestation of its possibility, and the birthing itself into the world moment by moment.

So, with all the uncertain-certain faith I have, I want to say that God's affection for you runs deep and that you will never be forsaken. Additionally, I think that as you lean into this reality, it'll catalyze incarnation in you, which just might open others up to the reality that God is with them, too. In this way, deep withness is the hope of the world.

As we close, I invite you to pause, close your eyes, take a deep breath, and realize the deep witness inside of you.

All around.

And in the presence of that love, consider one way in which you might lean even more into its depth.

Jonathan J. Foster is the husband of one and the father of three. He's an author, podcaster, pastor, has degrees in open and relational theology and mimetic theory, and leads lovehaiti.org. Mostly? He likes to hike. Learn more at jonathanfosteronline.com.

When God Is a Baby

RICARDO GOUVEA

In Jesus, we find the revelation of a God that is different from what most people imagine, a God who is shown to be fragile, who is open to adventure and has taken the risk to become a human baby out of utmost love for us.

This will be a sign to you:
You will find a baby wrapped in cloths
And lying in a manger.
Luke 2:12

When God is a child there's joy in our song.
The last shall be first and the weak shall be strong,
And none shall be afraid.
Excerpt from the hymn Hope is a Star

Preached Sunday, December 3, at West Flamboro Presbyterian Church, Dundas, Ontario, Canada

Christmas is a great opportunity to rethink our ideas about God, the one whom Jesus called "Father" and who theologians say was revealed to us in Jesus. If our minds are jovial and flexible enough, we can discover new things and have new insights. This is what is required in a quest such as this, in which we are exploring the Good News with the help of the new perspective offered to us by what has been called process, relational, or open theology.

At Christmas, we use the word "epiphany" in reference to the birth of Jesus. Epiphany is a word commonly used to signify a sudden manifestation or perception of the essential nature or meaning of something. And this is what happened when Jesus was born, a manifestation and a perception of the essential nature and meaning of God. Epiphany means, literally, "a manifestation from above," and is used in anthropological studies for the apparition of anything considered to be sacred to a people in their myths such as, for instance, when a god appears. In that case, we call it a "theophany," a manifestation of the divine. This is where we should start our reflection, realizing that Jesus Christ was a theophany for the apostles and for those who followed them. In Christ we have a manifestation of God. Yet, this sense of Jesus as a theophany has been obfuscated by our doctrines and rituals, unfortunately, and needs to be recovered.

When we start from the notion that Jesus was a theophany, we realize that all of Jesus should matter to Christians, and not just the crucifixion of Jesus. I am appalled to perceive in some Christians songs and sermons that the monotonic message that Jesus dies on the cross to save me has invaded Christmas as well, and that even Christmas songs have to mention the cross and the resurrection, and poems and sermons explaining that was the meaning of Christmas.

I am not saying the cross does not matter, nor the resurrection. What I am saying is that those Easter themes are not the meaning of Christmas, and that we may miss the meaning of Christmas if we bring these Easter themes into it and obscure the true Christmas themes such as the advent and the epiphany or, as I have suggested above, the theophany of God in the person of Jesus. If we presuppose that this is a theophany, a very orthodox and ancient notion, then all of Jesus matters, for Jesus revealed God to us from the very first moment.

At that very first moment, Jesus was a baby lying in a manger. Yet, what child is this? Who is this babe, the son of Mary? John the Evangelist tells us at the very beginning of his Gospel that Jesus is "the Word made flesh" (1:14) and (1:1) that "the Word was God." This is what we call "the Incarnation," that is, God became a human being; indeed a human baby, which is a paradox; for what is divine is, by definition, not human; and what is human is certainly not divine. And this paradox is one of the most sacred statements of ancient Christian doctrine.

Let's call it "a mystery." The infinite became finite, and the eternal became temporal, and infinite possibility became subject to the basest human necessities, as Søren Kierkegaard (1913-1855) said in *Philosophical Fragments* (1844). The inferences we can take from this are astonishing. It means, first of all, a re-consecration of matter itself, effacing the distinction between the material and the spiritual. Matter becomes sanctified. It also means the sanctification of time and history, for now, time and history became the abode of God. Beyond that, it also implies the sanctification of the human condition. In theological language, is means the annulment of the curse, of the lapse, of the fall of Adam, in Christ the Second Adam. It is a redeeming birth.

That the Eternal Word became a baby also points to something even more shocking that goes against the grain of our accustomed theological conceptions; it denotes the sanctification of tenderness and fragility. All tenderness and all fragility became sacred, for God was revealed to us as fragile and tender. If God became a baby, this has theological consequences that should be faced and considered. The Incarnation and the theophany of God in Christ speak to us, therefore, of God's own frailty, fragility, and they speak also, wonder of wonders, of God's interest in taking risks; for the tenderness of babyhood is very risky, and God took that risk, out of love.

God took this risk out of God's ultimate and absolute love for us because God is indeed "amipotent," that is, he is capable of utmost love, as we can learn from the books of Thomas Jay Oord (1965-), particularly, *The Death of Omnipotence and Birth of Amipotence* (2003). I am talking about Agape love, that is, compassion, mercy, solidarity, forgiveness, respect, service, and care. This is what the Father of Jesus is utterly capable of. The measure of God's love is love without measure. Yet, God's love, God's utmost "amipotence," seems to contradict our regular, traditional ideas about God's omnipotence. Indeed, in Paul's letter to the Philippians we read about God's *kenosis*, that is, God's self-emptying without which the Incarnation is unthinkable. Without God's self-emptying (Phil 2:5-11), there is no redemption, and there is no reconciliation; it is "always winter, but never Christmas," like C. S. Lewis (1898-1963) said so poetically in *The Lion, the Witch, and the Wardrobe* (1950).

So, when God is a child, God's "amipotence" becomes evident, and forces us to reconsider our old conceptions regarding God's omnipotence. Otherwise the narrative becomes a meaningless masquerade, which is exactly what it has become in fundamentalist theology, where the babyhood of God and all its fragility and risk are just pretense. It isn't true that God is frail and that God took a risk. Of course not, says the fundamentalist, because God is sovereign and omnipotent, and there was no risk whatsoever and God has not become frail or fragile or tender, because such adjectives are inapplicable to God. Yet, the fundamentalist is wrong, led astray by a rationalistic theology. He does not see the paradox; he does not see the theophany; he only sees what his "religion of the right doctrine" allows him to see, as Rubem Alves (1933-2014) explains in his book *Protestantism and Repression* (1979; English translation, 1985). The "religion of the right doctrine" teaches that we are saved by having beliefs. This is how the slogan of Martin Luther (1483-1546) is understood; "salvation by faith" becomes salvation by having the right beliefs or embracing the right doctrine, instead of the slogan's true meaning, which is salvation by trust in Jesus Christ, trust in God's grace (Agape love) revealed to us in Christ.

The Incarnation of the Word is the greatest of mysteries, and the greatest of mysteries is ultimately about love; about Agape, divine love. The divine baby is a call to us to live in love; it is a call to adopt the Agape Principle as the fundamental rule of life, of practice and of faith. It is a call to make Agape into our *regula fidei*, our rule of faith, as St. Augustine of Hippo (354-430) suggested.

When we see with the eyes of faith that God is a baby, we see God's love and we finally understand the depth of divine love. Then we can hear the call to embrace love as a life principle. This God calls us to love as well, with divine love. We are not naturally inclined to divine love, but we are enabled in Christ to love as God loves. If we bring Christ into our hearts and accept the risk of becoming Christlike, this mystical union enables us to love others in their otherness, and all of God's creation with love without measure.

When we see with the eyes of faith that God is a baby, we see God's love in its utmost depth, and we are taken by it into heaven, and we are absorbed by God's love, and we love God back with the deepest love possible, and this perfect love drives out all fear (1John 4:18), including all fear of God and of judgment and of punishment, for God is love (1John 4:8). Then, driven by the power of love, we can become disciples of Jesus Christ, followers of Jesus in his love, and we can become ourselves, in Christ, a manifestation of God's love, as Christ is manifested in us.

This is what mature faith looks like; not a relation with God of eternal childish dependence, always asking for things, and for protection and deliverance; but rather a friendship (John 15:15) and a partnership in love for the release of the transforming power of the Holy Spirit upon people and society and the world at large.

When we embrace mature faith, we do not ask anymore what God can do for us; we rather think of what we can do for God, out of love. And that is all that matters, for God is a child, and as such God calls for our help, for our tender love and care.

Such a thought brings holy peace, heavenly peace, like that of the silent night we sing about, in which God became a baby; for when God is a child, the last shall be first and the weak shall be strong, and none shall be afraid. Yes, peace is that tricky; but in the theophany which is Christ we can find true peace. We find Immanuel, God with us. And if God is with us, who can be against us? (Romans 8:31)

We should put aside the toxic image of God that was inculcated in many of us. We must dismiss the image of God as a harsh, stern judge, always watching us with judgmental eyes ready to cruelly castigate us sinners that we are, or even worse, ready to castigate Jesus instead of us, so that honor is kept and forgiveness might be granted. For God has revealed God's own being, nature, and character to us in Christ as a poor little baby who needs and wants to be tenderly embraced, who needs and wants to be loved, and who wants to become our friend and play with us. God is not a menace. In

Christ, we see God crying and asking for our attention and our care, the lovely divine baby who wants to be loved. Baby Jesus, who is not only God-with-Us but also God who has become just like us.

Religion is a two-edged sword. It can make one a saint or a demon. Religion can be based on love, but also on fear. The Christian faith has many times been presented to people in the last two thousand years as a religion based on fear. It is tragic that this became so common; for a religion based on fear is useless. Yet, the Christian faith can also be presented as built upon love, upon compassion. And this seems to me to be the true nature of the Gospel, the Good News. Then we see a different picture altogether; a salvation offered by God within history and within the human condition, and not as an alternative to history and the human condition, as it is presented many times by the ultraconservative. They see the Gospel as merely a ticket to heaven, to a life beyond this world, beyond history, and beyond humanity. If God became human, he embraced humanity forever; and God became part of human history and embraced it.

God loves humans so much that God decided to become one of us, Jesus Christ. God doesn't want to condemn us; God wants to be with us, to become our companion, to entertain us, and to be entertained by us forever. As Leonardo Boff says in his book *O Sol da Esperança* (2007), every child wants to be an adult, and every adult wants to become rich and important like a king, and every rich, important person wants to be a god; but God wanted to be a child. This shows us how lovely God truly is.

Marie-Louise von Franz (1915-1998), the Swiss thinker, wrote two great books about the archetype of the *puer aeternus*, the eternal child that lives within us, that we must never stop being (*Puer Aeternus;* English translation, 1997). The child within sends us to the past in delightful memories in moments of healthy nostalgia. The inner child keeps us always able and ready to play and to be like children, simple and adorable, like Jesus taught us to be. Yet, the *puer aeternus* in us also leads us toward the contemplation of the future with the promise of renewal, teaching us the need for curiosity and for flexibility, as is typical with children, always open to new possibilities. Jesus told us we need to keep childhood alive in us so that the Reign of God may be real for us, and in us. We must be in mystical union with the baby Jesus.

A baby wrapped in swaddling clothes, poorly dressed, the child of a poor family, born in a cattle stall and lying in a manger with animals around. Jesus was not born is a palace, like the magi thought at first. He was not born in the temple either, surrounded by priests. He was born in a stable. And that is a sign to us, the angel said, This will be a sign to you: you will find a baby wrapped in cloths and lying in a manger. (Luke 2:12) Let those who have eyes to see, and are not blind, let them see it.

Joseph and Mary were travelling due to a census that aimed at charging all with heavy, intolerable tributes to be sent to the emperor who wanted to be worshipped as if he were a god. This is the context of Jesus' birth that we celebrate at Christmas. It is okay to be part of the sophisticated and noisy celebration as long as we do not forget the circumstances of Jesus' birth, and that even today we are still surrounded by social injustice, and that there can never be peace on earth without justice. Even today, there are many poor children in the world that have no food to eat, no warmth, and no Christmas.

Jesus was born in a stable, according to Scripture, because no one had space to spare or any compassion for his pregnant mother, a traveler from distant Galilee. The women and children of our world are still suffering due to the lack of compassion and sensitivity of many. This is why Christmas is about caring, and sharing, about welcoming, accepting, embracing, humanizing those who have been dehumanized. It is thus that we arrive at the full meaning of Christmas and of the Gospel; for this is how Christ is born not only in Bethlehem two thousand years ago but also in us today, the hope of glory. As Paul the Apostle proclaims, "the mystery that has been kept hidden for ages and generations, but is now disclosed to the saints. To them God has chosen to make known among the Gentiles the glorious riches of this mystery, which is Christ in you, the hope of glory." (Col 1:26-27)

Ricardo Gouvea was born and raised in Brazil. Now he is a Canadian citizen and lives with his wife, Lilia, in Paris, Ontario. He is a professor of theology and religious studies, currently teaching sessional courses at different schools, and is the pastor of West Flamboro Presbyterian Church in Dundas, Ontario. He earned his Ph.D. from Westminster Theological Seminary, and has eight published books in Portuguese, plus many chapters and articles both in Portuguese and in English.

Everything Happens for a Reason?[1]

ADAM HAMILTON

Rather than a micromanager or absentee landlord,
God influences and gives freedom.

I'm not a fan of the phrase, "Everything happens for a reason." It is, at best, a half-truth. To explain what I mean, I'd like to offer three critiques of this idea.

First, if everything happens for a reason and that reason is God's "plan," then whatever happens must be the will of God. Therefore, I cannot be held responsible for my actions; I was only doing what I was supposed to do. If I cheat on my wife, everything happens for a reason. If I text while I drive and I killed someone, it must have been the victims "time." I did these terrible things, of course, but it was God who put me up to them to accomplish some greater purpose. I was only doing what God demanded.

Second, saying "Everything happens for a reason" implies that God intended for everything to happen. Ultimately, God willed and caused each. Every rape, every murder, every act of child abuse, every war, every terrible storm or earthquake that claims the lives of people, every child that dies of starvation, happened because God planned and willed it.

Third, if everything happens for a reason as part of God's plan, the results are fatalism and indifference. Fatalism says we are powerless to change what happens in life. Whatever will be will be. For instance, there's no reason to wear a seatbelt; if you are meant to die in a car accident, you will. Why work out and take care of your body?

---

1. Adaptation from *Half Truths* by Adam Hamilton © 2016 Abingdon Press. Used by permission. All rights reserved.

When it's your time, it's your time. Diagnosed with cancer? Don't see an oncologist and consider treatment; you are resisting God's will. Don't like the President? You need to get behind them; they must have been God's choice.

Calvin's Determinism

Is this really how things work?

Theologians speak of God's purposes and way of working in the world as the doctrine of providence. The term typically refers to God's governance of the cosmos, including our world and everything in it.

Christians who believe in God's providence also typically believe in divine sovereignty. But there are very different ways of understanding God's providence and sovereignty among Christians. One alternative draws from John Calvin, a brilliant lawyer, theologian, and pastor who lived from 1509 to 1564. Calvin wrote the *Institutes of the Christian Religion* when he was just 27. He was writing in response to Catholicism of his day.

Calvin is best known for his particular understanding of the sovereignty of God. He believed that everything happens by God's will and command. He writes in the *Institutes*, "No wind ever rises or rages without [God's] special command." Many today call this "theological determinism."

Calvin believed that people have children or remain barren, not for some physiological reason, but because of the hand and will of God. He believed God governs the very thoughts of your heart. Although you might think you've had an original idea, God really placed the idea in your heart. And thus everything that happens, for good or bad, is "fixed by God's decree." One corollary to this, which Calvin is known for, is believing that we have no choice whether we'll accept God's saving grace or not. He believed God predetermined some to be elect and saved and some to be damned for eternity in hell. In fact, God predetermined this before any person was born.

There are many things I appreciate in Calvin, but this element of his teaching is not among them. I understand that in a world where there is much uncertainty, doubt, and questioning, one temptation is to assert God is in such complete control that his hand ordered every detail of life. This is only comfortable, of course, if you are among the elect God chose for heaven. And it's comfortable as long as you don't think too long and hard about the monstrous things that happen that must be, according to this view, God's will.

Calvin could claim some scriptural support for his position. Some biblical authors saw the world in these terms. Yet I believe the overarching witness of scripture is that God's governance is not as a micromanager who controls everything minute detail in our lives. In this other biblically supported view, God gives people freedom and empowers them to make their own decisions, even if they will sometimes make the wrong decision.

Consider the creation story of Adam and Eve. God says, "Be fruitful and multiply, and fill the earth and subdue it; and HAVE DOMINION over the fish of the sea and over the birds of the air and over every living thing that moves upon the earth." God creates the cosmos, sets the laws in motion by which the universe operates, and then he gives dominion over the earth to the man and woman. Does this mean that God is not still ultimately in charge? Of course not! But God has given us the freedom and responsibility to rule over this planet on his behalf.

Throughout scripture, God lays out the right path and warns of pursuing the wrong path. We see this in Deuteronomy where Moses has just recited the Ten Commandments and the rest of the Law. Notice what Moses says next as he implores the Israelites: "I call heaven and earth to witness against you today that I have set before you life and death, blessings and curses. Choose life so that you and your descendants may live, loving the Lord your God, obeying him, and holding fast to him; for that means life to you and length of days." If people were simply going to do whatever God put on their heart to do, what would be the point of this powerful challenge? The Israelites have real choice. They can obey God, hold fast, and love and find life. Or they can turn away and find death. Why call them to choose if, as Calvin's thought implies, they cannot choose?

We regularly make choices. Some are moral, some are amoral. I enjoy riding my motorcycle, but I recognize that every time I ride my motorcycle it could lead to my death. Will I blame God for my injury if something happens when riding my motorcycle? Of course not. Will I have been hurt or killed because it was God's will? I don't believe so. Is God still sovereign if I have the freedom to get on my cycle, and even if I die on it? Yes.

You have choice too. So does the person who doesn't think they have a drinking problem and goes drinking and driving. So does the CEO without a moral compass who makes decisions that enrich his pocketbook, but which will eventually lead to the company's bankruptcy and thousands of people paying the price. So does the person who hurts children. God doesn't will these things. But they're possible because God gave us dominion, even though he has ultimate sovereignty.

Deism

Let's look at a second view of providence. At the opposite end of the theological spectrum from Calvin's determinism is a theological philosophy popular in the 18th century. It's the belief system of some of America's founders, and it's usually called "deism."

This view of providence held that God created all things, set the laws of nature in motion, gave humanity dominion over the earth, then stepped away. According to deism, God takes a completely hands-off approach to the affairs on earth. God cares, but does not intercede.

Deism makes no room for God to be at work in our world. If it's true, God did not liberate the Israelite slaves from Egypt. God did not speak through the prophets or send Jesus to show us the way. God does not guide us by his Spirit or in any other way influence the events here on earth.

Yet, according to much of what we read in scripture, God *is* influencing the affairs of this world God sent Jesus to save and deliver us. God forms, shapes, guides, and, on rare occasions and for reasons we may not fully understand, even intervenes in the affairs of this world in miraculous ways.

In sum, Calvin's determinism and Deism's hands-off deity offer very different pictures of God's providence and sovereignty. In the first, God is a micromanager; in the second, God is an absentee landlord. The truth is somewhere between the two.

A Better View of Providence

The reason most things happen is not because God willed them. Our decisions and the laws that govern nature are the primary reasons "things happen." As I was preaching on this theme, a member of my congregation sent me a meme that says, "Everything happens for a reason...but sometimes that reason is that you're stupid and make bad decisions!"

A little harsh perhaps, but this captures far more truth than to say that the result of our bad decision was really God's will. God *does* superintend. God *has* a broad will and plan for humanity. God *does* guide us by the Spirit, and through the scriptures, in church, as we pray, and through other Christians. God empowers, strengthens, and walks with us. But God *does not force us*.

LaVon, my wife, once bought me a fitness watch for Christmas. It encouraged me to walk 10,000 steps a day, and the watch actually counted my steps. When I was inactive too long, it vibrated on my wrist to tell me to get moving. But the fitness band could not make me walk, exercise, or take better care of myself. I have to do that. But it could nudge me, reminding me that I'm supposed to do these things.

In some sense, that is one picture of how God governs and superintends. God wrote the laws of nature, gives us the gift of life, has given us the Spirit, the scriptures, the church, our conscience, other people. God walks with us. He has shown us what is good and what he requires of us. But God also gives us freedom to walk in his path or away from it. This is part of what makes us human.

I want to mention one other thing God does. It's captured in an oft quoted passage from Paul's letter to the Romans: "We know that God works all things together for good for the ones who love God, for those who are called according to his purpose."

That passage *doesn't say* God makes everything happen for a reason. It doesn't say whatever happens was God's will and a part of God's plan. It says that whatever happens, God can and will somehow force good from it for those who love him. He will bend evil to accomplish good. The good times and bad, the times of great joy and terrible pain, do not happen because God wills them. *But God will use them.* They ultimately become a part of our journey in God's eternal kingdom.

At Church of the Resurrection, we have a small chapel named for a retired pastor named Ray Firestone. Ray had lost his wife in a train accident while he was parenting three small children. He once shared with me a clipping, published anonymously, that'd found helpful in capturing the relationship of God and suffering:

> Suffering is not God's desire for us, but it occurs in the process of life. Suffering is not given to teach us something, but through it we may learn. Suffering is not given to punish us, but sometimes it is the consequence of our sin or poor judgment. Suffering does not occur because our faith is weak, but through it our faith may be strengthened. God does not depend on human suffering to achieve his purposes, but sometimes through suffering his purposes are achieved. Suffering can either destroy us, or it can add meaning to our life.

Does everything happen for a reason? Not if by that you mean that everything that happens is the will of God and is part of God's plan.

Our church was barely five years old when a 3-year-old was struck and killed by a car. I've been blessed to be their pastor for almost 30 years. Years after Austin's death, his mother wrote me reflecting on her faith and how it had changed in the year's since his death:

> After Austin died, some people told me it was his "time." But I was having a hard time believing in a God who would plan to take my child at age three. I came to learn that tragedies weren't part of God's plan, but that God gave us free will, and sometimes bad thing happen. Understanding this helped me to turn to God instead of away from Him…Since Austin's death, I believe that my faith has grown and continues to grow. His death changed the way I view God and my faith. I no longer have a naïve, child-like faith where God protects you from all harm and makes everything ok. It's a deeper faith that has been tested through tragedy. I know God doesn't promise me a pain-free

> life, but he promises to always be there to love me, comfort me, and guide me. My faith gives me something that people without faith don't have—HOPE, hope for the future and the knowledge that I will see Austin again in heaven.

Between the picture of the micromanaging God, who causes everything to happen, and the absentee landlord God not involved in our lives or world, is a God who grants human beings freedom. This God allows us to take risks. Tragedy is not caused by God, but used by God. And we have the assurance that, in the end, "death has been swallowed up in victory."

Adam Hamilton is the founding pastor of the United Methodist Church of the Resurrection, Leawood, Kansas. He is the author of many books and small group studies. This is an excerpt from a sermon he preached. Later, an expanded version was published in Adam's book, *Half Truths: God Helps Those Who Help Themselves and Other Things the Bible Doesn't Say* (Abingdon Press, 2016). Abingdon granted permission for its use.

The Underbelly of Novelty

BETH HAYWARD

Sometimes life lands you in unchartered territory and the novelty threatens to undo you.

Sermon preached May 2, 2021 at Canadian Memorial United Church, Vancouver BC.

The year I turned fifty, I left a job I loved and a city where I was deeply rooted. I moved across the country with my family and settled in to see what was next. Some people thought I was brave, courageous, adventuresome. Others were impressed with how deeply faithful I was to uproot without any vocational plan. Some people assumed I must have a secret plan. (I did not). What reasonable person leaves a perfectly settled life without a plan?

The wholesale uprooting of my life was carried out on a bit of a whim. I was starting to feel stuck and something in my gut seemed to say: "throw the chips in the air, see what comes, the Holy Spirit will show up if you make the first move." A month before my fiftieth birthday, I found myself sitting in my new home without a job or a plan, wondering when the Holy Spirit was going to show up and reveal my next best step. It's possible that what appeared to others as deep trust that "all will be well" was a thinly veiled desire for change, any kind of change, and at any cost. I just wanted something new. I was aching for novelty.

Novelty is a tenant of open and relational theologies. The aspect of it that I was after can best be explained as the idea that every single moment is dripping with fresh possibilities for creative transformation. It's kind of like a hyper focused way of living in the moment. I think the contemplatives understand novelty best, with their capacity to stay in this moment without judgment. I, however, am not a contemplative!

I've always been drawn to new experiences. I spend more time looking for the next new thing than I do celebrating past achievements or grieving failures. I didn't think my new life would be easy, but I thought the novel would land before me with some clarity. It didn't. There was no clarity. It was more like living in chaos. Everything was new, but nothing stood out as the worthiest course of action.

In my efforts to figure out what to do with my life, I did what all good pastors might do (signal eye roll emoji), I read about novelty. I might have prayed about it, but instead, I read. I learned we run toward novelty, not so much in the pursuit of purpose but because: dopamine.

Psychologist Winifred Gallagher says that dopamine intensifies our arousal and arises as an intense form of "go for it!" It's such a powerful evolutionary force that we need to be careful to question whether novelty is working for us or whether we're under the spell of all things new. In this information age, one could pursue novelty as a sort of perpetual numbing fix. On the eve of my half century mark, I knew one thing for sure, dopamine was not going to pay my bills and take care of my countless grown-up responsibilities. I was feeling lost and second guessing my decision to throw away all semblances of security. The new was letting me down.

This is the brick wall I hit after turning my life upside down. I was counting on the dopamine to carry me when, in fact, it was supposed to catapult me in a new direction. I learned quickly that novelty was not going to sustain me. It was more like the yeast in the dough, like a bee in a bonnet. We're not meant to cling to novelty, but to take the gift it gives us and bring it into ourselves so that the next moment, the next decision, is the better for it. This may have been where I set myself up for disillusionment. I took the drastic steps of upending my life, seeking the novel... and assumed God would take my lead and keep the novel coming. This is where 0pen and relational theologies always trip me up. I like that God is in relationship with us, luring us to the next new thing, until it gets hard. Then I just want "Father God in the sky" to float down and fix it!

I may have chosen the novel, but sometimes we're thrown into it. Think of those life altering events like births and deaths and lost jobs and broken relationships. Sometimes we find ourselves in a new reality that leaves us completely disoriented or aching for the past. John Cobb says that chaos makes its contribution to novelty, which is a good thing because my search of it left me in a whirlpool of chaos. Novelty is not just what is new and beautiful. Everything is new, so novelty is all that is new—the good, the bad and the ugly.

After finishing reading the psychology, philosophy, and theology of novelty, I finally turned to the stories of my faith tradition. I wasn't convinced that the Bible would have anything to offer at this crossroads, but I was desperate. My all-time favorite biblical story is The Road to Emmaus (Luke 24:13-35). Talk about a tale of novelty—on Easter day two companions head out of Jerusalem because the future they were counting on has crumbled in an instant. Everything is new in the most devastating sense.

These shell-shocked followers of Jesus leave town because their new reality is unbearable, because their dreams are shattered, and their faith shaken. They've heard about the resurrection, but it makes utterly no sense to them. As far as they're concerned, this new circumstance is destined to lead them right back to where they started, without a hope or a plan.

I'm always struck, in this story, by the breaking of the bread moment. When the stranger breaks the bread at the table in Emmaus, they go from lost to found, from wandering aimlessly to an unstoppable sense of drive. When the stranger breaks the bread, it's as if a window is cracked open and the rush of fresh air overtakes them, and they get to their feet.

Before their eyes are opened, they miss several other opportunities to lean toward the gift of the new. They dismiss the resurrection—the novel. They don't have a clue when the scriptures are being broken open to them—novel. The good news seems to be that when we miss God's invitation to say yes to the novel, the invitation will be extended a thousand times again.

We live in a time when the novel is our new reality. It used to be that we could rely on things to be the way they always were. It used to be that past experience was a good predictor of the future. This isn't true in a world seized by the effects of climate change and devolving trust in institutional ability to address real life struggles. It's not a case of "everything old is new again," it's more like everything old is utterly unreliable and the new is truly new.

It's funny sometimes where Spirit can lead you. In the past, Emmaus helped me understand lost hopes and resurrections, but when I look at it today, I keep seeing the table, the simple table with the broken bread. That seemingly insignificant moment is when they see the Holy in their midst. It's at that point when they receive the sustenance to carry on and completely alter their course. That's the moment they turn back to the very place where their dreams were destroyed, only to find a fresh calling.

The first thing I did after purchasing a new house, in a new city, was order a custom-made live edge spalted maple table. I visited the carpenter's workshop, ran my hands along the rough timber, locally sourced and left to rot before he gathered it up for a resurrection of sorts. Spalted maple is half rotten wood. I thought its imperfections were beautiful.

The table, like the move itself, was a bit of an impulsive purchase. I don't regret either. The table represents some sort of hope and commitment to community. When it was finally delivered, it was an imposing structure in a modest home. It stood there strong, perfectly imperfect, and empty nearly all the time.

The table is a concrete embodiment of the novel. I move past it countless times a day, touching its promise and lure. It whispers to me the hope of community; a place to share in all the beautiful and ordinary things of life. It nudges, a tangible reminder to build circles of love and friendship, to extend hospitality. The table is where I practice listening for the voice of the Holy Other calling toward the next best step.

We hosted 19 people around that table on our first Thanksgiving. As we slowly consumed the last morsels of pumpkin pie, a particularly wise 21-year-old looked me in the eye and asked: "when you're preaching, do you aim to ground people or move people?" His insight floored me. My response was inadequate, but his question lingered; it was fresh, it was novel. His question informs my weekly preaching in the small, not-dead-yet congregation that called me to be their minister. They are aching for a resurrection of sorts, and they seem to think someone who is practicing attending to novelty might be just the companion they need.

When life offers us things that anyone in their right mind would be fearful of we, like the two companions, have that first instinct to retreat. Even a road to nowhere is better than standing still in an awful novel reality. Eventually, the companions find their way back to Jerusalem, and the place they go with determination is to the upper room where the others are gathered. The Bible doesn't tell us if there was a table in that upper room, but I like to think there was. It might have been the same upper room from Thursday's meal. In returning to those with whom they share broken hearts, they find the first thing required to walk this novel path is a good meal with old friends.

Novelty reorients, moment by moment, to a new future; not with well thought out plans but with a whisper and a promise. A five-year plan, a mission statement with goals and metrics, is not new. Novelty is more like an intuition, like the draw of something exciting, alluring, but without any proof that it has the substance to deliver. Novelty lures us toward the future, but always an unknown future. I kind of like that. It makes me feel like uprooting my life in search of something new that might have been divinely inspired, not merely an articulation of my mid-life crisis.

Beth Hayward is an ordained minister in the United Church of Canada. She has over twenty years of experience serving congregations. Beth writes and speaks about the practice of ministry from an open and relational perspective. She hosts a podcast called Souls in Soles, https://soulsinsoles.podbean.com/. You can connect with her through her website at http://bethhayward.org

Generosity on Tap

FRED HERRON

Insights from pantheism illuminate a vision for panentheism.

Reading: Proverbs 11:25
Sermon preached at Living Water Christian Church, November 12, 2023

The indigenous wisdom of pantheism can be beautifully integrated with a Judeo-Christian vision of nature. As I understand Open & Relational theology, God is always in partnership with creation, not controlling and dominating creation, but partnering, permeating, influencing, and co-creating at every moment in loving solidarity with all creation. This vision of panentheism is beautifully illuminated through the practices of generosity in a gift economy.

I was about eight years old when my dad enrolled me in a YMCA program called Indian Guides in Prairie Village, Kansas. It was my first introduction to North American indigenous culture. The program was eventually critiqued, and the name was changed to Adventure Guides. But for me, as an eight-year-old, I didn't understand all the different perspectives which were contained in that critique. As a kid, I ended up loving indigenous culture. I started reading books about indigenous culture and started studying the history of all that happened with indigenous peoples: the broken treaties, the stealing of the land, and the indoctrination of European perspectives on land rights. I didn't know any of that when I started Indian Guides, but I developed a love for indigenous peoples because of the program.

And it was a love that continued throughout my whole life. I appreciate the indigenous vision of seeing all of nature as living beings. It's a healthy vision. There are passages in the Hebrew and Christian scriptures which reference mountains singing and trees clapping their hands (Isaiah 55:12). If you read Psalm 19, notice that the first Bible for all living beings is nature itself. Psalm 19 observes how all creation speaks—the voice of nature speaks—and it sees all of nature as living beings from which we can learn. I have always loved nature, and I love the indigenous vision of nature.

I recently read a new favorite book on indigenous culture. As many of you know, I love bicycles, and I love books. If you hang out around me long enough, I'll encourage you to ride a bike, and I'll recommend a book or two. The book is by Robin Wall Kimmerer entitled *Braiding Sweetgrass*. She published this book with a small press back in 2013, but it's one of those books that every artist dreams of. It basically became popular by word of mouth. Over the last 10 years, it has sold 1.6 million copies. Robin studied as a botanist, but her family background was of mixed descent with a strong indigenous heritage from the Algonquin tribes, particularly the Potawatomi tribe from the Great Lakes region. The subtitle of her book is *Indigenous Wisdom, Scientific Knowledge, and the Teachings of Plants*.

As we explore the topic of generosity, I think Robin Wall Kemmerer's book, which integrates indigenous wisdom with scientific knowledge, has some beautiful insights which need to be integrated with our Judeo-Christian tradition.

The first insight comes from the indigenous origin story of humanity. Robin opens her book with the origin story of how humans landed on this planet according to her Potawatomi tradition. It's the story of "Skywoman Falling." Skywoman existed in the sky before she fell to earth. Skywoman steps through a hole in the sky, falls through the sky, and plunges towards dark waters. As she's falling, geese see her and flock to her aid and catch her to soften her fall. As she falls, she hits the dark waters and begins to plunge into the depths of the dark water. Other animals see this and move to her rescue. A muskrat swims down, pulls her up, and gives his life for Skywoman. As the muskrat takes his last breath, he's got some mud in his hand.

A turtle offers her support for Skywoman and says: "Put the mud on my back." Skywoman is rescued by the animals and the turtle. As Skywoman expresses her gratitude, she begins to spread the mud on the turtle's back and dance in gratitude on top of the mud, which then begins to expand. The whole earth expands out of this mud on the turtle's back. According to Potawatomi tradition, North Americans live on Turtle Island. That's the name of our homeland, Turtle Island, according to indigenous peoples.

What's beautiful about this story is that humanity is in harmony with nature, not at odds with nature. That's a big point—an origin story where humanity is in harmony with nature, not at odds with nature.

One of the ancient Near East origin stories from the Hebrew Bible starts in Genesis 1 &2. What you see is humanity made in the image of God, men and women, both fully made in the image of God. And they're placed in a beautiful garden sanctuary.

The whole garden is like a garden temple. In Genesis 2:15 humanity is given responsibility to "tend and watch" the garden and all of creation. Humanity's task is to tend, to guard, to watch, to care, to steward, to nurture, and to live in harmony with all creation. It's a vision of harmony with nature. It's a beautiful vision.

Unfortunately, what happens for many Christians, in various Christian traditions, is that they start the Christian origin story in Genesis 3. Genesis 3 is a story of shame, cursedness, and banishment from the Garden of Eden. For some people in Christianity, the "Original Sin" of Genesis 3 becomes the origin story. I think if you start with Genesis 3, you end up distorting the origin story. Shame is certainly a condition which humans experience. I have experienced deep, dark shame, but shame is not our true identity. We need to be healed from shame. Genesis 1 & 2 describes our true nature and true calling—one of Original Blessing and Goodness. Genesis 1-2 calls us to live in harmony with nature—in sustainability, mutuality, and reciprocity with nature. Shame banishes us from the garden, and we live in enmity with ourselves, each other, and the planet. We need to learn from indigenous wisdom and restore a vision of Original Blessing from Genesis 1 and 2.

The second insight Robin gives us regards how indigenous culture values a gift economy versus a commodity economy. Kimmerer reminds us of how Europeans arrived on Turtle Island with a different view of the world. Europeans didn't see nature as living beings with which to live in harmony and reciprocity. Rather, they viewed nature as a commodity—a commodity which could be conquered, owned, bought, and sold. Commodities can cease to be gifts. Gifts create harmonious relationships with the gift, the giver, the receiver, and the co-creator.

Think about it, we human beings can't live on our own when we're first born. The fact that you exist means that you have received gifts of nurture and support just to be living and breathing right now. You've received thousands of gifts which have been bestowed on your life in order for you to exist. Gifts of food, water, clothing, shelter, and love, all of which derive from nature, family, friends, and acquaintances.

We have to draw upon nature for living water and bread of life, and we thrive in loving community with people and nature. But if we view everything as a commodity, we begin to lose the relationship with nature and with each other. So, for example, how many of you have ever received a gift from somebody that was just a commodity, that was purchased at a store, maybe a big box store? They gave it to you as a gift, but it really didn't mean a whole lot. Anybody have some items laying around their house or in your closets or in your garage that were just simply a commodity? And the origin of that particular gift is almost meaningless, right?

On the other hand, how many of you have received a gift given with love which produces a loving relationship with the giver? Every Christmas my mother would decorate a Christmas tree, and on that Christmas tree she would hang the ugliest Christmas ornament that you could imagine—front and center. It was a Christmas angel I made for her when I was in the first grade. It was made out of something like flour and water. It was like a Play-Doh angel. Remember the Pillsbury Doughboy? It was a female version of that, a chubby little angel with wings, short legs, and a big chubby belly. I shaped it with my hands and painted golden hair and blue wings. I think it's one of the ugliest angels I've ever seen. Over the course of time, its wings fell off, and then its legs fell off.

After a few decades, it was just a head and a body, but it still made its way onto the Christmas tree. And my mom cherishes that gift. You understand why it's not a commodity, right? There's a relationship with me, the gift, and my mom. But honestly, if we could learn to live like that with all of creation, with all of nature; if we could begin to restore the relationship with gift, giver, creator, and receiver, with what we eat, with how we live, and with how we love; then we would be living in the loving, self-giving, ever creating heart of God.

There's a beautiful vision that Robin Wall Kimmerer is trying to reclaim by writing *Braiding Sweetgrass*. She's trying to restore this vision of generosity, of receiving and giving gifts, and of seeing all of life as a gift. We have a relationship with all living beings and nature and people who give into our lives. And then we give back with love and beauty and grace and generativity.

Proverbs 11:24-25 reads: "Give freely and become more wealthy; be stingy and lose everything. The generous will prosper; those who refresh others will themselves be refreshed" (NLT). I don't prefer the word "wealthy" because we all of a sudden think of bank accounts, but what we're talking about is a vision of generosity and reciprocity. If you want to reap what you sow, don't just sow one seed and check on it every day and pull it out of the ground just to see if it's working. That's sowing with stinginess. Sow everything generously. And then don't worry about how it comes back, but trust that it will come back. This is reciprocity, a karma of sorts—sowing and reaping. It's a gift-type economy where we give and sow freely, generously out of a heart of love and gratitude because we've received so much. We keep those gifts in motion, and there's a flow and a relationship between the gift, the giver, and the receiver.

Indigenous peoples cherished a gift economy where everything's in motion. You give and you receive; and you receive, and you give. But all of a sudden, European settlers didn't see it that way. Indigenous peoples were stigmatized as "Indian Givers" because they wanted something back. But no, that wasn't the vision. It wasn't like giving a single seed and then expecting something back in return, but it was a vision of gifts in motion. One of scattering seed all over, and then it comes back. And there's a reciprocity of love with nature, with living beings, and with humans. That's the flow of generosity—the heart of God—a gift economy.

Think about Gollum in *Lord of the Rings*. When he got the ring, what did he say? "Precious" and "Mine." "It's mine." So that's the stingy version. But the generous will prosper, and those who refresh others will themselves be refreshed. Think about the difference between homegrown, homemade versus store-bought commodities where there's no relationship. Our calling is to move into a gift economy.

Robin Wall Kimmerer also brings out the difference between gift economy and private property. As you know, indigenous people didn't believe that someone could own the land. The land belongs to the land. Mother nature owns the land. The Great Spirit infuses the land. People don't own the land. We simply live in reciprocity with the land and with nature. We receive gifts from it, and we give back to it. We live in sustainable ways with nature, with living beings, and with one another. But Europeans were more like Gollum when it came to the land: "It's mine."

I hope you've figured out by now that you don't take anything with you when you transition in death. You leave it all behind. Remember the statement: "There's no U-Haul's following a hearse." I've done hundreds of funerals, and everybody leaves everything. Who owns it? Who owns your stuff? Who owns your house? Who owns your car? Who owns your things? Robin Wall Kimmerer shows that in a gift economy, nobody really owns it. It's all a gift in motion.

We can't own it. We can share; we can receive; and we can give. We can live in harmony. But if we try to own it and possess it, then we are moving off course. According to Psalm 24:1, who owns the earth? Psalm 24:1 says: "The earth is the Lord's and everything in it, the world and all its people belong to him for he laid the earth's foundation on the seas and built it on the ocean depths" (NLT). So God owns it. It's not ours. It's on loan. Everything that we have is on loan. And Robin Wall Kimmerer beautifully illustrates through her tradition how we desperately need to return to a vision of a gift economy—for our own well-being and the well-being of all living beings and the planet itself.

Everything is in motion, and we strive to keep it in motion. God is always self-giving and co-creating with all of creation. And we live in that reciprocity with all living beings. And we recognize that it's not ours. It's a gift that we've received, and it's a gift to be shared. There's a responsibility that comes with the gifts that we receive, and there's a responsibility to share the gifts that we receive. There's an interesting verse that most people have never read or noticed in the Torah. The first five books of the Old Testament (The Hebrew Bible) are called the Torah. One of the Torah passages, Leviticus 25:23 says: "The land must never be sold on a permanent basis, for the land belongs to me [God]. You are only foreigners and tenant farmers working for me" (NLT).

So ancient Israel did not own the land. It was on loan. I think that's really what the Torah's pointing towards. The Torah is more in sync with the indigenous wisdom of a gift economy. There's a celebration every fifty years called Jubilee in the Torah. People who have lost land and fallen into debt are forgiven. Debts are forgiven and land is redistributed. Jubilee resets everything. The land, which is owned by God, is redistributed to stewards, not owners. We can steward resources with a new vision of gift economy.

With this vision of a gift economy, Robin Wall Kimmerer calls us to live in harmony and gratitude with nature, other living beings, one another, and the plant itself, and she encourages us to practice ceremonies which deepen our sense of gratitude and connection. According to Kimmerer, we can create our own ceremonies or rituals for gratitude, thanksgiving, and awareness. Kimmerer learned rituals from her father—despite his own distance from the Potawatomi tradition due to the practice of cultural genocide—who attempted to instill in her the ways of indigenous wisdom.

Kimmerer recalls how they would go on family camping and canoe trips in the Great Lakes area, and every morning they would make coffee. When her father made coffee every morning, he would boil it and pour off the coffee grounds that rose to the top, similar to the ancient coffee ceremonies in Ethiopia. He would pour the coffee grounds into the land, and they would become one with the humus. He would give thanks to Tahawus, which was the indigenous name for Mount Marcy meaning "cloud splitter," and the Great Spirit.

Kimmerer often asked her dad how far back in history the coffee ceremony originated. She wanted to know the richness of that history because as a trained scientific botanist she had lost some of the magic of the indigenous teachings of plants and nature. She was thinking that there was some special, magical tradition that extended back in ancient indigenous practices.

However, Kimmerer records her father's response and her own reflections:

> "I've been thinking about the coffee and how we started giving it to the ground. You know, it was boiled coffee. There's no filter and if it boils too hard the grounds foam up and get stuck in the spout. So the first cup you pour would get that plug of grounds and be spoiled. I think we first did it to clear the spout." It was as if he'd told me that the water didn't change into wine—the whole web of gratitude, the whole story of remembrance, was nothing more than the *dumping* of the grounds?
>
> "But, you know," he said, "there weren't always grounds to clear. It started out that way, but it became something else. A thought. It was a kind of respect, a kind of thanks. On a beautiful summer morning, I suppose you could call it joy."

> That, I think, is the power of ceremony: it marries the mundane to the sacred. The water turns to wine, the coffee to a prayer. The material and the spiritual mingle like grounds mingled with humus, transformed like steam rising from a mug into the morning mist.
>
> What else can you offer the earth, which has everything? What else can you give but something of yourself? A homemade ceremony, a ceremony that makes a home.

The first Bible is nature itself. Psalms 19 declares: "The heavens proclaim the glory of God. The skies display his craftsmanship. Day after day they continue to speak; night after night they make him known" (Ps 19:1-2; NLT). It's a beautiful way to immerse ourselves in the loving, self-giving heart of God who co-creates a gift economy with all of creation.

Fred Herron is a Prodigal Pastor who loves cycling, rock climbing, hiking, and storytelling. He earned degrees from Baylor University (BA), Southwestern Baptist Theological Seminary (M.Div.), and Fuller Theological Seminary (D.Min.). He founded and pastored Vineyard Church in Kansas City, MO which grew to several thousand people (1990-2019), and he worked on a Ph.D. in the Hebrew Bible while pastoring a megachurch because he loves learning. He went through a spiritual and emotional meltdown which led to him founding Spirituality Adventures in 2021 and connecting with people in recovery, deconstruction, and religious trauma through blogs, podcasts, meditation events, and groups. He is also the new Lead Pastor of Living Water Christian Church (DOC) in Kansas City, MO (2023).

Creator, Christ, and Comforter

GREG HOOVER

The sacred blur of the Trinity comes into focus through the lens of uncontrolling love.

The following is a Trinity Sunday sermon. It explores the Trinity from an open and relational perspective. In the Western liturgical calendar, Trinity Sunday is celebrated every year on the first Sunday after Pentecost. The sermon was preached at St. John's Episcopal Church, Harrison, Arkansas, June 4, 2023.

The day I was ordained to the priesthood, I asked a retired priest what he had learned from his many years of active ministry. He thought for a moment and then he said, "I learned to always take my vacation on Trinity Sunday, so I don't have to preach on the Trinity!"

Well, today is Trinity Sunday and I'm not on vacation. That's because I love this day and all it has to teach us.

Over my years as a priest, I've known many people who have struggled with the idea of the Trinity. At its best, this spiritual struggle can function as a kind of Zen Koan—a seemingly unanswerable question that a disciple wrestles with until their ego is overwhelmed and they have a flash of insight.

But rather than wrestle with the Trinity like Jacob wrestled with the angel, many just seem to drift away from the faith community. Others seek out another spiritual path, one without a trinity with which to wrestle. But this proves to be difficult, too, because we find this idea of the divine as a trinity or sacred triad throughout the world's great wisdom traditions.

For instance, in Judaism, the mystical teachings of the Kabbalah speak of God manifesting in creation as three spheres—Kether, Chokmah, and Binah (which means crown, wisdom, and understanding). These names do not represent three separate gods, but rather make up a sacred triad, which is one in essence and purpose.

The Hindus speak of Vishnu, Brahma, and Shiva, but these three are unified in Brahman, the one universal underlying divine substance of all reality. Likewise, our Buddhist sisters and brothers teach a sacred triad of Buddha, Dharma, and Sangha.

Even Quantum physics speaks of the Cosmological Singularity—which physicist Frank Tipler suggests is the scientific name for God—which contains three singularities but in one infinite point. Tipler writes, "The Three are One," and he even says, "The cosmological singularity is the Judeo-Christian God."

We could go on, but the point here is that there seems to be something within the human soul or collective unconscious that resonates with the idea of the sacred as a trinity. Different names and different symbols are used, but the underlying intuition seems to be a perennial spiritual concept throughout the world's wisdom traditions.

But now for something less heady.

When I think about the Trinity and the different words or names that we traditionally use to describe it, I often think about an episode of *Veggie Tales* about the life of St. Patrick.

In one scene, St. Patrick is trying to teach the concept of the Trinity to the pagans of ancient Ireland. And so, St. Patrick holds up a shamrock, and says, "God is like a shamrock." And the people all bow down and worship the shamrock, and they say, "Oh great shamrock!" So, St. Patrick says, "No, no, the shamrock is just a *metaphor* for God." And then the people all bow down again and worship, and say, "Oh Great Metaphor!"

This cartoon makes a good point.

Trinity Sunday is the day in the Church year when preachers all over the world will try to explain the Holy Trinity in the space of a few minutes. Well-meaning but sometimes misleading metaphors will be given as preachers make heroic attempts to explain the divine as, in the words attributed to St. Patrick, "the three in one and one in three."

In Christianity, we use symbols, analogies, and metaphors to describe the indescribable. But some of us make the mistake of taking the metaphors literally, and we miss the deeper message. And then we bow down and proudly proclaim, "Oh, great metaphor!"

Please don't misunderstand me. There is nothing wrong with using metaphors and analogies. They can be very helpful, and I use them myself all the time. However, one of the great intellectual tragedies of the modern world is that many of us have lost the ability to think symbolically.

This impacts our ability to understand the Trinity as we continue to use the traditional symbolic terms of Father, Son, and Holy Spirit. Because of this, to many people, the Holy Trinity has become something of a sacred blur. So, to help clarify our spiritual vision, this morning I want to share with you a lens to see the Trinity more clearly.

The lens that helps bring this sacred blur into focus is the uncontrolling love of God. Through this lens, we see that the Holy Trinity is not just an old man, a young man, and a bird. Nor do we experience the divine as a lonely king on a throne, controlling subjects from his lofty perch with unidirectional coercive power.

Furthermore, through the lens of God's uncontrolling love, we will begin to see the unity of God expressed as active, responsive, and creative, and not just use the word "trinity" to mean a kind of tritheism in disguise—the belief in three separate gods with three subjects of consciousness. It will also help us see that the Trinity, to quote Keith Ward, "... is not three people sitting in a bowl of soup."

Through this new lens, we see the Trinity as the dynamic and relational presence of uncontrolling love, moving and flowing through all creation, including through all of us. It is within this dynamic presence of uncontrolling love that we live and move and have our being. In this understanding, the Trinity is less like a triangle and more like a circle, eternally flowing in time in a continual process of growing and becoming.

In this model, the power of the Trinity is seen as the power of love, and the power of love is the greatest power in the universe. But love is a different kind of power than most human conceptions of power. The power of the Trinity is not seen as controlling or unidirectional, but rather as loving, inspiring, and relational, inviting us on the grand adventure of exploring together an open and undetermined future.

It calls us to see God's power as a shared power, a living relationship of mutual interdependence, grounded in love. This sacred call invites our active participation, cooperation, and partnership with the Trinity to heal our bodies, our souls, and our world. In the words of Thomas Jay Oord, "When we cooperate with the possibilities of love—no matter how big or small—we partner with the God of the universe."

In this framework, it might be helpful to think of our Trinitarian language differently. For a moment, let's reimagine our traditional terms of the Father, the Son, and the Holy Spirit. Instead, let's speak of the Trinity—the active, living presence of uncontrolling love—in fresh terms of *Creator*, *Christ*, and *Comforter*.

This fresh language helps us see the Trinity in a new way. The Creator is pure uncontrolling love, the Christ is the human face of that love, and the Comforter is the universal spirit of uncontrolling love who interconnects everyone and everything. In contrast to being "the unmoved mover," this dynamic Trinity is the most-moved mover. This Trinity works cooperatively by influential love.

Out of love, God as Creator continually forms, inspires, and empowers others. As the human face of that divine love, Christ leads us by walking alongside us, modeling the uncontrolling love of God as present within all our relationships. Christ is our fellow sufferer who loves us and who understands. And the universal presence of the Comforter continues to actively nurture us with this divine love, both from within and without.

As a spiritual practice, we can remind ourselves of this by making the Sign of the Cross slowly and mindfully, and saying, "*In the Name of the Creator, and of the Christ, and of the Comforter.*"

Not only does this dynamic Trinity, this living presence of uncontrolling love, flow through everyone and everything. In a deeper sense, this dynamic divine presence of love is also the very ground of our being, our own true nature, and our deepest and interconnected Self. This relational presence of cooperative, uncontrolling love that is the Trinity is primary. *In the beginning was the relationship.*

In the Trinity, God, us, and all of creation relate to one another, and everyone is free to give and receive the love of God. We are many and one at the same time in a divine community of love, grounded in the Holy Trinity.

Through Christ, we are invited to participate in the life and love of the supremely relational Holy Trinity; in the words of Jesus, to be grafted into the vine. We are called into an active, dynamic, and living community of uncontrolling love that is the presence of the Holy Trinity among us and with us.

This relational love shared between the Creator, the Christ, and the Comforter becomes the guiding principle of our lives. In the words of the New Testament, "*Watch what God does, and then you do it, like children who learn proper behavior from their parents. Mostly, what God does is love you. Keep company with [God] and learn a life of love. Observe how Christ loved us. His love was not cautious, but extravagant. He didn't love in order to get something from us but to give everything of himself to us. Love like that.*" (Ephesians 5:1-2 MSG)

When I Celebrate Holy Communion, I always pause at the moment when I put a drop of water into the chalice of wine. To me, this seemingly insignificant moment contains a deep and meaningful truth related to our discussion.

As wine aficionados will tell us, a single glass of wine has a trinity of three levels or layers of aromas and flavors that continually change over the course of its life. To me, the chalice of communion wine represents divinity—this Holy Trinity of whom we have been speaking, this dynamic, open, and relational presence of uncontrolling love—and the drop of water represents our humanity, in all of our brokenness and imperfections.

The drop of water flows into the wine and the wine embraces all the individual molecules of the drop of water. Although the water remains water and the wine remains wine, we can no longer separate the wine and the water. In a sense, the water is both one with the wine and yet maintains its own separate identity. They are not two, they are not one. The fancy theological term for this is *non-dual*.

This is eternal life—realizing our oneness with the life and love of the active, creative, and dynamic Trinity of Creator, Christ, and Comforter, yet maintaining our individual existence at the same time.

There is nothing more exciting than this.

This is the great adventure.

We are invited to participate in the divine life and timeless love of the Holy Trinity, and be grafted into the vine.

This new vision of love and unity allows many of us to affirm the Trinity once again. We can find meaning as we sing or say the beautiful words attributed to St. Patrick:

> I bind unto myself today,
> The strong name of the Trinity:
> By invocation of the same,
> The Three in One and One in Three

In the Name of the Creator, and of the Christ, and of the Comforter, *AMEN*.

The Rev. Gregory Hoover, an award-winning writer, has worked as a professional actor, behavior therapist, and Episcopal priest. Father Greg loves his children, international travel, and the great outdoors. He is the author of *The Pain Killer* (Black Rose Writing, 2022), a true-crime novel that explores a famous series of unsolved murders from the perspective of Open and Relational Theology, and *The Witching of the King* (Black Rose Writing, 2021), a historical mystery novel that features William Shakespeare as an amateur detective and incorporates open and relational ideas.

God Who Never Lets Her Children Go

CHRIS JORGENSEN

The biological phenomenon of "fetal microchimerism" offers us a glimpse of a God whose love will not let us go.

Reflection for special worship service called "Advent Interrupted: A service for all grieving infertility, miscarriage, stillbirth, and infant loss." Hosted most recently online by the Urban Abbey United Methodist Church in Omaha, Nebraska, December 8, 2021

Advent is a Christian season that has been historically relentless in its insistence on celebrating pregnancy and birth as categorically joy-filled and hopeful. Preachers have talked about the world being pregnant with possibility. Images of Mary, swollen-tummied, hand on her diaphragm, looking downward in expectation, have emblazoned countless church bulletins. A traditional theology of "God is in control" would make one think that every difficult pregnancy should turn out like Mary's. Even with hardships, the child would be born. Hope would spring anew into the world. It would be so because life and birth are God's will.

This theology leaves no room for the reality that miscarriage, stillbirth, and infertility are experienced by so many expectant parents. It leaves unanswered the question of "Where is God when the life and birth of a child is not the outcome of one's deepest hopes?" This question, like the question of suffering in general, is not easily resolved with logic and rationality. It is perhaps better answered with art and ritual and an opportunity to encounter God, even in the midst of one's grief.

For that reason, since 2015, the Urban Abbey (a United Methodist coffeeshop-church) in Omaha, Nebraska, has offered those grieving miscarriage, stillbirth, or infertility a worship service called "Advent Interrupted." This service was created by my dearest clergy sister, Rev. Debra McKnight, following her own experience of miscarriage. The service includes liturgical elements such as music and scripture and reflections by those who have experienced this particular kind of loss. When she first created the service, Debra asked me to include a poem and some reflections I wrote for her following her miscarriage. I share it here as an example of a liturgical invitation to reconceive God's presence and activity as relational, loving, omnipresent, and powerful even when God cannot unilaterally fulfill our deepest yearnings:

Microchimera is the title of a poem that I wrote for my dear friend Debra McKnight when she was the pastor already at Urban Abbey, and I was finishing my seminary degree thousands of miles away at Drew University. She had experienced a miscarriage, and like so many other things in life, there was nothing I could do to fix it. But I could do what we can always do, which, of course, is listen and grieve alongside, and pray for our hurting loved ones.

As I grieved alongside Debra, the first words of this poem arose in my mind. "What we lose is flesh and hope…" and I began to think of what we keep when we experience miscarriage or the loss of any child, for that matter. And I remembered, from a random article I once read…microchimera. Microchimera are cells that cross the placenta from the fetus into a mother's body. Scientists know about them because they found cells with Y chromosomes in women, and wondered, "What is that Y chromosome cell doing in this woman's body?" Turns out, it came from a son she once carried. So scientists studied these things, and learned that you can find cells from a fetus not just in a mother's bloodstream, but in her organs…her brain, in her kidneys… because these clever little cells, wherever they land, they transform. They develop into the kind of cell that is needed there.

This is not rare. Scientists believe that every person who has ever been pregnant has these microchimera, these cells that make this statement true: "our children are literally a part of us." Amazingly, every child we have ever carried, even the ones we have lost, are literally…literally lodged inside us, helping to ensure that our hearts, though they may be broken, continue to beat.

And so, I wrote this poem for my friend Debra, and I invite you to pray it with me.

Microchimera

What we lose is flesh and hope,
A tiny body in which an expanse
Of imaginings and love
Had taken up residence.

What we lose is a longed-for daughter,
A yearned-for son,
A sibling to a toddler,
Who will not understand this.
Except in her mother's sighs,
Her father's lingering hug.

What we keep is love and void,
A phantom emptiness,
Neither spoken nor named.
What we keep is quite reasonable sorrow
And futile dreams of a life run its course.
What we keep are microchimera:
Cells drifted across the placenta and lodged
In a mother's body, brain, and heart.
Audacious physical relationality.

What God keeps is all of this:
Flesh and hope and love,
A daughter, a son, a playmate,
Void and emptiness and dreams and memory,
Cells alive and cells extinguished,
Matter and spirit,
Interweaving and transforming.

In God, all is gathered
And nothing is forsaken.

Thanks be to God.
Amen.

Chris Jorgensen is the Lead Pastor of St. Andrew's United Methodist Church in Omaha, Nebraska and its global digital campus All Saints Online. She earned her M.Div. from Drew Theological School. She delights in seeing the power of God's love transform lives through the theologically expansive and LGBTQ-inclusive faith community she serves.

God's Seedy Power

CATHERINE KELLER

Whose power is more like a seed than like a sovereign?

Readings: Genesis 1:1-2, Matthew 13:1-10 (adapted from NRSV)
Sermon preached at the UM Church of the Village (NYC), August 15, 2021

Yes, I am Catherine, she/her. It is a joy to be back—even virtually—on the very good earth (speaking of those seeds) of the Church of the Village.

I am honored to take part in this series of introductions to what is called process theology. I can't imagine better introducers than the first preachers in this series, my good friends Rev. Ignacio Castuera and Prof. John Thatamanil.

I want to pick up where John left off, with the world of process and relation; and with the great alternative reading of God's power, that process theology has been teaching for more than half a century. Alternative to what? To the standard assumption that what we worship is an omnipotent, all-controlling God; that nothing happens apart from the will of God; that if God is in control, "he" (very much a He-God) must be willing the evils of the world, the violence, the injustice: because otherwise he would intervene to prevent them. So, he wants to teach us a lesson or to punish us.

In other words, God must be somehow willing the current horrors of the world—this COVID-19 plague, the coming collapse of Kabul, the fires, the floods.... But sorry, I already preached here a year ago on the Apocalypse. So today the first reading was of the very opening of the bible. The beginning. Not the End.

For in process theology, creation is always beginning again. Every moment. With every one of us. Every creature in the universe. We live in a universe of perpetual becoming. In fact, the word genesis in Greek means becoming. The creation is a work in process. And what is that process about? Theologically speaking, it is about God's relationship to all becoming creatures. And that is a relation not of coercion but of calling: the Genesis "let there be." That letting-be is not omnipotent control but the invitation to become.

The invitation is what, in process theology, is called the "divine lure." The lure is God's offering of possibility, moment by moment, to every creature—from a primordial photon of light to all the levels of creaturely life. And yes, to each of us humans. Moment by moment: an invitation, not a determination. Not an omnipotent power of creation from nothing—which isn't a biblical idea: the Bible features a creation from the deep, not from nothing. "You moved on the waters, you spoke to the deep." The ocean of Genesis 1.2—the waters of primal chaos, of potentiality. (I've written a book on that!)

As it happens, that creation from chaos called me in a personal way. I grew up in a family of great chaos, psychic damage and alcoholic violence, constant moves, but—PTL—not without love. So, the kind of order one can shape out of chaos rather than out of a neat void spoke to me. I am grateful that I discovered process theology relatively early. And soon I landed with the world's leading process theologian, John Cobb, in California over 40 years ago, where I would study process theology with him. Wondrous that you will hear him yourselves, and for 3 Sundays!

In the creation narrative, God is not giving orders to be obeyed but luring forth our universe. And the creatures themselves are invited to collaborate: the waters, the land, and again the waters bring forth the biological life of our planet. And when humans are finally created, we are invited to consciously cooperate in this relational creativity—in the image of God. With each emergence, God expresses delight—ooh, that's good! And altogether—wow, very good. That is an ancient prescientific story. But it has resonance with very science-based process theology.

Process theology is about creative relating—or relational creativity. And it is focused not just on our relationships to each other up close, but at the same time to a vast world of others. It tunes us to our life right now, moment by moment—and on our choices at each moment—whoever we are, whatever past choices and influences have shaped us. It takes these in as part of the present moment—and calls us first to tune to the ultimate relationship—the relation to the ultimate itself, which we here still call God.

We always have some freedom—to respond more, or less, to the divine lure. What is the content of that lure? It is in process theology always a possibility: a possibility for this very moment, a possibility for something more beautiful; more ethical; more loving; something more tuned to the needs of my neighbor; something conducive to social justice, to planetary stewardship and sustainability.

Something better—for you individually. Yet in this vision, our individuality is inseparable from all the fellow creatures of our world. As at this gathered moment, we are influential upon each other. And always there's the element of freedom—for instance, to ignore these words, to repress them, or to take them in and allow your own insights to test them. It is a freedom saturated by its context—by the oddity of this Zoom medium, by the beauty of the liturgy and music still echoing. Freedom in process theology can go many ways: can be the irresponsible response—as in "why should I get vaccinated or wear a mask?—It's my free choice." Or freedom can express itself in some degree of responsiveness, responsibility, to the lure to enhance the health and life of our world and ourselves as part of that world.

But the divine lure is not the same as other relations—it precedes them moment by moment—letting be, letting become. The divine lure seeds each moment with fresh possibility. Possibility, not certainty. So, there we are in the great parable of Matthew 13. As soon as I received the invitation to be part of this series on process theology, the parable of the sower called out to me. There may be no better illustration anywhere for the divine lure. For the lure is precisely the seed of possibility.

Matthew's parable makes clear that God's will has nothing to do with some coercive power, some all-controlling ruler. The seeds are tossed, a great multiplicity of them. They are so delicate, so obviously the opposite of a word of command. Yet Jesus is talking about the "kingdom of heaven." And so here and elsewhere in the gospels when kingdom language is used—the Greek *basileia*—we must not miss the irony. Jesus is teaching a kingdom not of this world of rulers, of coercive powers and oppressive structures. But the very opposite: a basileia grown of these generously thrown seeds, each landing gently, almost imperceptibly, forcing nothing. This alternative kingdom is a subversive mockery of authoritarian power. That is why some of us sometimes pronounce kingdom as kindom.

These delicate seeds land—wherever you are. Whatever you are. You might be going about your own business, going your own way. So, you may resemble that path some seeds fall on—they don't have a chance. You don't notice them, and the birds enjoy them. Or you might, at the moment, be a bit hardened—like the rocky ground—and the seeds do sprout, you give new possibilities a chance—but they can't get rooted, your hard, stony places block growth, your virtuous responses remain shallow. And so new possibilities get scorched and wither. Or your life is too full of thorns, of tangled complexities, unresolved grief that tears into the moment, or hurts that jab and turn to aggressions—thorny issues that choke off new growth. And there is also all that good soil: you take in the seeds and you yield a rich harvest. But notice that the sower is not micromanaging this agricultural activity: this is no condescending up close daddy-god, this tosser of seeds.

As I prepared for this sermon, I was taking in the new and devastating UN report on climate: "Code Red for humanity"—still barely enough time for us to make the big difference needed to prevent environmental cataclysm. And I recognize that sometimes I just ignore it and, like the impermeable path of the parable, go about my business; or I do little shallow things like self-righteously turn off the lights behind my husband; or I get tangled by all the thorny complications of dealing with other pressing issues, personal and political—and amidst the thorns, I do next to nothing. And then maybe sometimes I take in the possibility of making a difference, and some grain does grow.

My point is about process theology's lure. God is offering possibilities even now. And certainly here, in this church! But it is up to us to realize them, to take them in deeply enough to bring them to fruition. God will not step in and fix climate change or any other crisis, not even my intimate ones—this God does not work like that, the universe is not created that way: God tosses to us the seeds of possibility. And we actualize them not at all, or a little bit, or fruitfully. And this sowing is always going on, moment by moment. There is always a new beginning—and we can singly and collectively ignore it or make superficial changes—or actually grow that basileia together.

But do I really want to call these possibilities seedy—with its suggestion of "gone to seed," of shabby, indeed like a seedy reputation, sordid, dirty. A seedy, dirty basileia? Well, of course, that is exactly how the classy folk saw the homeless Jesus and his riffraffy movement. That lowly Galilean bore no resemblance to Caesar. So, the full range of seediness might keep us honest. And that dirt—isn't that metaphorically and materially the earth, the ground, of our shared life?

Process theology has God seeding the world—not just once at the Big Bang, or in occasional interventions, but moment by moment—amidst whatever shabby scenes. And global warming is starting to make those smoky, burnt, droughty or flooded scenes proliferate. But God did not will this summer to be the hottest on record. God is not deliberately permitting climate change and the human injustices it will amplify. Humans are doing it, and some of us—probably not worshippers at the Church of the Village—much more than others. But God will not step in and fix it. Nor is this God's plan for the end of the world.

The process God doesn't send disasters to punish or teach us. But certainly, those seeds of possibility do call us to learn lessons from any disasters we face. God does not do the repair work for us, but does make it possible. We may take in the seeds or not, or just kindasorta. The seed does not determine what kind of soil we are; what kind of soil we are determines if we heed the seed. And there are always real social, relational, or psychological reasons for our stoniness or our thorniness—or our receptivity. But then how we respond in this moment, responsibly or otherwise, influences all our relationships and can change our social world. This is a vision of an earthy relationality in perpetual process.

But the process God is not only the purveyor of the lure—the sower of the seeds. The one who seeds possibilities. This God is also the one who receives whatever we become—moment by moment. That is another aspect of the kingdom of heaven—it takes in all that takes place, it hosts the world; it integrates it within God. In other words, God feels all that happens. Feeling it all in its living process—in its joys and in its sorrows. As in the body of Christ in Corinthians, we are members of one another, which is to say, interconnected but extremely different members of a divine body. As John Thatamanil made clear last week: the process God is not the medieval Unmoved Mover. Making everything happen, and unmoved, unaffected, by any of it. Process theology says this: God is not the Unmoved Mover but the Most Moved Mover.

Unlike classical omnipotence, God's power is the power of a relational love to seed possibilities and then take in (harvest) their actualizations. That means—to receive all that can be received, all that does not simply contradict the love of God, the God that is Love. But this cosmic love does take into itself the traumas and the suffering. So, as you heard last week, Whitehead called God "the Fellow Sufferer who understands."

In this way God is also in process, is also becoming—not static and not changeless. Doesn't that detract from divine perfection? Not at all. God is perfect—in the sense of whole, wholly good, loving—but not in the sense of changeless, static, eternally the same. The Creator's continuity from aeon to aeon is expressed in the cosmic process of uncontrolling creativity.

And so, we do not pray to this God to fix our problems for us. But to inspire us, to lead us, to teach us how the chaos and the seediness of our lives can be creative. Our rock-hardness can be broken up, our thorns less prickly. And if this is true for our own funky lives, with our moods and issues, it is all the more true for our collective life, with its global delusions, destructions, code red, its lost chances. But also its last chances.

So, we pray to you who "let be" the light of our galaxy, who called forth over billions of years our astonishing Earth, who delights and suffers with all of us creatures—we pray that we may together grow the seedy possibilities of your will. On Earth as it is in heaven. Amen.

Catherine Keller is Professor of Constructive Theology at the Theological School of Drew University, where she has trained ministers and theologians for over three decades. She writes quite a bit. *On the Mystery: Discerning Divinity in Process* offers an accessible introduction to process theology. Her most recent book is *Facing Apocalypse: Climate, Democracy and Other Last Chances* (2021). She is a member of the Church of Saint Paul and Saint Andrew (United Methodist).

Is God a Superhero?

HYUNHUI KIM

What kind of power lies behind the ability to speak in different languages on the day of Pentecost?

Reading: Acts 2:1-13
Sermon preached at West Grove UMC, Neptune, NJ, June 9, 2019.

"Jesus is my Superhero!" This energetic song from the Hillsong kids in 2004 has been loved by many children in Sunday schools ever since. The lyrics children enjoy most goes like this:

> Jesus, you're my superhero. You're my star, my best friend.
> Yeah, yeah, yeah, yeah, yeah, yeah, better than Spiderman
> Yeah, yeah, yeah, yeah, yeah, yeah, better than Superman
> Yeah, yeah, yeah, yeah, yeah, yeah, better than Batman
> Yeah, yeah, yeah, yeah, yeah, yeah, better than anyone
>
> Yeah, yeah, yeah, yeah, yeah, yeah, better than Yugioh
> Yeah, yeah, yeah, yeah, yeah, yeah, better than Barbie
> Yeah, yeah, yeah, yeah, yeah, yeah, better than Action Man
> Yeah, yeah, yeah, yeah, yeah, yeah, better than anyone
> Jesus, you're my superhero.

When singing this song, the children shout out the name of each hero, along with a distinctive movement aimed at representing that individual. In the visual images for this song, Jesus appears in hero costumes. Can you imagine the vigor and energy that the children generate as they mimic the characters of these superheroes? A sense of excitement and enthusiasm always fills the space the moment the song's intro is played.

What comes to your mind when you think about a "Superhero"? Perhaps you think of the useful and cool superpower that each heroic figure possesses: superhuman strength, speed, and senses; the ability to wall-crawl, bat sling, become invisible or fly. However, the sort of power represented by the capacities of each hero is the kind of power that dominates and controls others or circumstances. To be powerful seems to mean projecting one's will over others.

Life isn't fair, and contradictions and injustice prevail in our society. We all experience these things at times—some more, some less. These kinds of experiences of unfairness and injustice are likely to make superheroes and their stories fascinating for us, and also highly influential. Such a fascination is not a childish obsession. It is more than that. Tales of superheroes in movies or books seem to trigger our strong longing for the absolute power that can defeat, control, and fix the evil, vice, and injustice we experience in this world.

We often project a similar understanding of what it means to be powerful onto God's character. In our prayers, hymns, or praise songs, God's power is often described as absolute, unlimited, or sovereign. But is divine power exclusively depicted in that way in Scripture? Is there any other way to understand divine power?

I find another interesting insight into power in the movie, "The Lord of the Rings." Unlike the sort of heroic tales that rely on the absolute power possessed exclusively by the heroic figure, the story of "The Lord of the Rings" seems to tell us that hope for peace and justice cannot flourish in the absolute power possessed by a single figure. Rather, the book implies that peace and justice only begin with the end of absolute power.

The notion that absolute power is an illusion as implied in "The Lord of the Rings" is affirmed in the biblical text, Acts 2:1-13. This passage is often referred to on Pentecost Sunday, for it celebrates the receiving of the Holy Spirit in a special way. The passage describes how suddenly there is a noise from heaven that sounds like a strong wind blowing, and separate flames of fire hover over the heads of each of the people who have come to Jerusalem from all over the world to celebrate a Jewish feast (Acts 2:2-4). In this moment, the people receive the power of the Holy Spirit to speak different languages.

The day of Pentecost, when all present are full of the Holy Spirit, is interestingly the day when fullness of power means being multilingual. The power bestowed by the Holy Spirit is the power to speak different languages! What kind of power is it? In what ways does this power suggest divine power? What does it mean that the Holy

Spirit brings this special kind of power to the people accompanied by symbols of wind and fire?

The power to speak different languages! It sounds fascinating, especially for those who are struggling to learn a new language, for those who want to travel to different countries and to experience new cultures. Language isn't just about words. It has power and its power is greater than we can image, since it is not just a tool of communication but it is also a means of impacting our cultural, ethnic, national, and personal identities.

The power of language has long been recognized. There is a story of the power of language in a chapter in Genesis that goes in a completely opposite direction from that which is affected by the Holy Spirit in Acts 2. It is the story of the tower of Babel.

This story reveals humankind's desire for power represented in the act of building a tower that reaches into the sky. The goal of building this tower with its top in the heavens is eternal fame (Gen. 11:4). In the story, the power the people long for is the kind of power we expect in the stories of superheroes, even though the purpose of that power may be different. The thoroughly hardened bricks they make for this tower-building project illustrate well the nature of the kind of power they seek (Gen. 11:4).

We then see God countering the human desire for a strong and hardened brick-like power. God understands that the goal of centralizing power is facilitated by use of the same language, so God causes the people to speak different languages, which confuses and thus scatters them (Gen. 11:8-9). It seems that God here is proclaiming the end of the power to control, rule, and dominate. God only discloses the meaning of speaking in different languages much later, in the story of the day of Pentecost recorded in Acts 2.

While the power of control is represented in the image of the hardened bricks in the story of the tower of Babel, the metaphors that represent the day of Pentecost, when power is given by the Holy Spirit, are fire and wind. Fire and wind are not hard like bricks, and neither can they be stored. Instead, they are flowing and flexible. And the power envisioned in these flowing and flexible images is something that persuades, lures, and encourages us to celebrate differences.

Here, we find an interesting comparison. The power longed for and sought by human beings has to do with controlling, dominating, conquering, and ruling, but the power given with the coming of the Holy Spirt is the power to speak different languages, the power that fosters diversity and multiplicity.

This power does not manifest in one reflection, one knowledge, and one narrative. The power of the Holy Spirit is the kind of power that de-centers a single reflection, a single knowledge, and a single narrative, and instead inspires the multiple stories and testimonies that we experience in our own unique and different lives. The power that the Holy Spirit brings to us is the power that lures us to be open to diverse experiences, identities, and thoughts. This divine power encourages us to embrace flexibility and fluidity.

The speaking of different languages causes confusion for the power that seeks control, as we see in the story of the tower of Babel in the book of Genesis 11. When we understand the nature of the power reflected in the image of the hardened bricks, we see that the differences among us are obstacles to the sort of unification that people of Babel seek.

However, in the divine power manifested on the day of Pentecost, differences promote opportunities for new learnings, new experiences, new ways of thinking, and new creativities. Unity no longer means sameness. This divine power invites us to understand unity differently, and a clue to this new understanding is found in the scene of the people gathering on the day of Pentecost. For although all speak different languages, everyone nevertheless understands the message in their own tongues! If divine power works in this way, differences are not something to be erased in the interest of unity. Instead, unity is only truly experienced when we seek a harmony of differences in interrelated and interdependent relationships with God and each other.

Unity in harmony is what we experience when completing a jigsaw puzzle. Think of the thousands of pieces of different shapes, sizes, and colors in a jigsaw puzzle box. When all these different pieces are put together, they reveal a unified image.

The divine power revealed on the day of Pentecost empowers differences—different languages, different personalities, different gifts, and different abilities. Different cultures, different skin colors, different eye shapes, different hair textures, and different genders. These variations do not simply manifest mere differences. Instead, like the pieces of a jigsaw puzzle, each difference is a related difference.

Divine power is the power that lures us to explore God's mysterious beauty in the entangled relations of the differences inherent in God's creation. Divine power is the power that persuades us to be open to new possibilities to work together with these related differences to reveal God's goodness, justice, love, and peace. Such divine power, poured out on the day of Pentecost, has been flowing throughout history and to the present, empowering different stories and testimonies of God's love and grace.

The day of Pentecost is regarded as the birth of the church. If the first followers of Jesus Christ received such power on the day of the birth of the church, is that power something that we need to attend to and strive for in our practice as a church?

So, friends, when the wind touches your face and blows your hair, please be reminded that the divine power is encouraging you to nurture your own uniqueness. When the wind makes the branches dance, be reminded that the divine power is nudging you to awaken your awe at the beauty of the divine creation, and to do one small action and take one small step to support justice for the earth. When you see the weaving candle flame on your dinner table or on the altar in the church, be reminded that the divine power is luring you to shine your own light where it is needed. When you feel the warmth of little fires, be reminded that the divine power is empowering you to share your warmth with someone who needs it the most.

Are we still waiting for the absolute power that a heroic figure might bring to control, defeat, and fix what we consider unfair and unjust? Let us stop longing for such illusive power to change the world and make it better. Instead, let us open ourselves to the divine power that is continuously luring us everywhere, from all directions, and at this very moment, to call forth the goodness and justice that we want to see in our lives, our communities, and our world.

HyunHui Kim is an ordained elder at the United Methodist Church. She earned her M.Div. and Ph.D. in Theological and Philosophical Studies from Drew Theological School. Her cross-cultural experiences have been formative in her ministry and studies. As a constructive theologian, she is passionate about ensuring faith is vitally connected to the contemporary world and its pressing concerns.

"Lean Not on Your Own Understanding": Trusting Together

ALEXIS LILLIE

When life feels unbalanced or inequitable, we need one another to help each other see what is possible, remember where we've been, and hold what feels too heavy.

Reading: Proverbs 3:1a, 5-6 (*The Inclusive Bible*)
Sermon preached at the Church of the Village (NYC), October 22, 2023

"My child, do not forget my teaching.... Trust in the lord with all your heart and do not rely on your own insight. In all your ways, acknowledge [God] and [God] will make straight your path." (Proverbs 3:1a, 5-6 NRSV)

I have grown a lot in this particular area of my life, but my default state is to have difficulty discerning paths forward when there are multiple options. I tend to second-guess myself, to play everything out to the bitter end in my mind and catastrophize how my choices could go wrong. I can easily paralyze myself by overthinking and over-analyzing all the options. I have trouble trusting—trusting my own inner divine wisdom, trusting that the Spirit is weaving goodness into my life, trusting that I am surrounded by people who care about me and who are going to help ensure, as much as possible, that I am going to be ok.

Part of how I have grown in trust is to allow myself to exist more and more in community. I have learned to practice vulnerability so that I'm able to more readily rely on the wisdom and discernment that comes when others know you deeply. For me, I have outgrown some of my internal lack of trust by first developing others-trust.

The story I always share to illustrate this is the journey that led me to become a military chaplain, which I did for almost ten years in the Air Force Reserve. I was in seminary and considering what my options would be for ministry. The idea of chaplaincy had intrigued me and crossed my mind, but I didn't think much of it. I was raised in the military, so I have always had a heart for working with service members. But I never really considered working in the military myself, since I devoted nearly the first 20 years of my life to it as a family member! However, over the course of several months, two separate people—independent of each other—mentioned to me the possibility of becoming a chaplain in the Reserves as something I might be called to.

On my own, I had a curiosity about the possibility of chaplaincy, but I didn't quite trust it. It might not have been brought to fruition were it not for the insight expressed by others whom I trusted and that I was in close relationship with. This support gave me the additional trust I needed to step into the opportunity.

In this way, trust is developed with others and not in a vacuum. Even when we are making decisions for ourselves and drawing on our inner wisdom, we are doing so affected by, and through, all the various relational touchpoints we have. We are learning to trust something greater than ourselves.

If we reflect on our passage today, we might be drawn to the obvious, and correct, interpretation of the passage: that this "something other than ourselves" is the divine, God. But back up a few verses to the first part of the chapter. These proverbs are being told by someone. The teacher is giving instruction to the reader, or in the case of the original community, the hearer. Ancient communities passed things down verbally through sharing and storytelling. This type of instruction happened in community by necessity. The speaker is inviting the listeners to learn from them, and from one another.

So yes, the reader is told to trust God, but what if part of developing *any* type of trust in the first place actually happens in community? What if God's trustworthiness is made manifest by others?

I want to note, this is different than *only* trusting "something other than ourselves." It's not that inner wisdom, or even "our own understanding," does not exist or is not to be trusted. Rather, we are developing these trust muscles in relationship with others.

Why would developing trust in God become a communal endeavor? It makes sense for a few reasons that I will mention here and then expand upon.

- The community sees what we can't
- The community remembers what we forget
- The community holds what becomes heavy

In these ways, we build multi-directional trust: with ourselves, and with things that are greater than us: the divine and our community.

First, we nurture this trust by seeing communally what may not be seen if left to the individual. When we are with others, we are part of a whole, and we see ourselves in relation to others. We provide wisdom and discernment to and with one another. We support one another. As we are seen in community, we grow in ways we simply cannot when we are on our own. God speaks to us through those in our community as we develop others-trust, which can then grow into divine trust.

This often happens to me within the community of Church of the Village. I am a "doer!" I love checklists and systems and getting things done. I need to be in relationship with people who remind me it is ok to get out of the weeds and imagine, envision, create, and re-create. I can trust these different ways of doing things, even find God in them, because my community is in it with me!

Think also of my Chaplain story. I was intrigued by the idea, but it may have stopped there if it weren't for multiple others speaking this as possibility into my life, inviting me to trust what came next.

Second, the community helps us remember what we might otherwise forget. This is something I practice on my own sometimes by reading through my journals. When I look back a few months or a year, here are some things in there I have *definitely* forgotten. (To be fair, some things should stay forgotten!) But for the most part, it is life-giving to read through the things I have gone through and remind myself, especially in trying times, that I have gotten through difficult things in the past and I can trust the same will be true in the future.

There are ways to do this for ourselves, individually (like reading through journals), *and* it is really powerful to have someone speak this truth over you. To remind you of what you have walked through, because they were walking with you. To reflect back to you how you got through what you were facing, that everything is temporary, and you (in community, and in relationship to the divine) can overcome.

Plus, it is a two-way street because when you are in consistent relationship with others, you are *being* accompanied, and you are also accompanying. So *you* are witnessing others' journeys of endurance as well, and in turn, providing those reminders, these trust opportunities, for them when they go through difficult times.

Finally, the community can help hold what becomes heavy. Like I mentioned, there are some things we get through that we'd rather forget, and while we're in the middle of them, they might be too heavy to bear alone. In this way, suffering also happens in community. We learn to trust that our suffering can be experienced in solidarity, and perhaps even diffused a bit when it is held by others.

There's no denying these have been heavy weeks. I cannot imagine the depth of communal suffering taking place specifically in Gaza, and throughout Holy Land. It has rippled out around the world to be felt by everyone in some capacity, and certainly caused suffering in our own community. In this, I have seen how we bear one another's burdens as much as possible. Our trust in one another--and in "something greater"--grows when we experience others helping to carry our burdens.

At the end of our passage for today we're told if we do these things—if we develop trust, if we don't rely only on ourselves, but engage with God by engaging with community—we will be on a God-infused path. I don't know about you, but some of these paths that I am on, and that I am seeing around me, they don't feel too God-infused. Not the least of which is the "path" that seems to be unfolding in the Holy Land. And I get angry about that. I get angry when I'm trying to trust, trying to do the "right" things, and life still feels some ways in shambles. Whether on a global stage, or personally. When day-to-day life gets challenging. When finances are hard. When a relationship ends. When you are trying but you feel like you still can't make the change you want. This stirs up some righteous indignation, which makes sense.

Also know, Proverbs are their own type of literature. They exist all over, not just in the Bible, and they are not promises. They are wisdom sayings, but they are not guarantees. It's not that if you input "this," you're guaranteed the output will be "that."

I invite us to consider not that this then makes God *less* trustworthy, but rather that it makes life in community *more* necessary. When reality is doing its thing, when life feels unbalanced and we want that input/output model, we need to help one another see what is possible; remember where we've been; and hold what feels too heavy.

This builds the trust that we are seeking as, together, we learn to rely on the divine Spirit that is powerfully present in and through our deep reliance on each other.

Alexis Lillie serves as the Minister for Leadership and Congregational Development at the Church of the Village in New York City where she is passionate about viewing the subversive life of Jesus as a blueprint for the systems-inverting work of justice today. She graduated from Union Theological Seminary in 2014 with a Master of Divinity degree and is ordained with the Christian Church (Disciples of Christ).

The Ground of Everything

TIMOTHY C. MURPHY

We should affirm God as the creative ground of everything,
the condition upon which anything can exist.

Reading: Acts 17:22-28a (NRSV)
Sermon preached at Plymouth Congregational Church of Fort Wayne,
UCC, May 12, 2019 (Mother's Day)

Our scripture for this morning is the story of Paul speaking in Athens. There are many god figurines in their religious marketplace, so to speak. They have a statue marked as being to an unknown god, and it is here where he finds his opening. What I really like is how about Paul describes God:

God made the world and everything in it.

God is never far from us, even if we strain and grope to find her.

Yet God does not reside in any shrine or figure we create to try to capture her.

The very life and breath that we have comes from God.

Finally, and most importantly perhaps, God is the one "in whom we live and move and have our being."

This is a nice summary. It displays an understanding of creation's dependency on God. Grander than our images, beyond us, and yet fully present with us. The source of our very life and breath; that's about as essential as you can get in my imagination. Cut yourself off from that and you won't last but a minute. Paul mentions boundaries that are assigned; there are boundaries and conditions in which we can live and thrive. But when you go outside those habitable zones, we're in trouble. Scientists talk about a goldilocks zone when searching for planets with potential life on them. Too hot or too cold, and life can't thrive. Too close or too far from a star, too much or too little atmosphere, it's a delicate balance.

Even on our planet, we need to stay within a few miles of sea level. When astronauts remain in space for long periods of time, their muscles begin to atrophy, and their bones weaken. Without gravity, our bodies simply begin to fall apart. In my lifetime, if we ever have human missions to Mars, keeping our bodies healthy for the long journey may be one of the most difficult challenges.

We depend on so much for living and thriving. Everything that exists depends in some way on something else. As the theologian Rosemary Radford Ruether writes, "An animal depends on a whole ecological community of life processes of plants, insects, other animals, water, air, and soil that underlie its existence." And the same is even truer for human beings. Ruether goes on to say that our job is to be "the caretaker and cultivator of the welfare of the whole ecological community upon which our own existence depends." *(87-88, Sexism and God-Talk)* Ultimately, that whole existence depends on God. This passage in Acts points to this reality, in whom we live and move and have our being.

It had special relevance this week as I was reading the United Nations' report published this past Monday. You may have seen it in the news, highlighting the strain being placed on our planet's life systems. Written by 150 scientists in over 50 countries, over 3 years, and surveying 15,000 academic articles, they have made a truly massive report. It spans several thousand pages. I just read the 39-page summary.

The headlines, as being reported, are on the surface admittedly grim. There are an estimated 8 million plant and animal species on our planet, and extinction threatens fully 1 million of them over the next decades. As one of the authors of the report said, "The essential, interconnected web of life on Earth is getting smaller and increasingly frayed… This loss is a direct result of human activity and constitutes a direct threat to human well-being in all regions of the world."

The authors do not pull any punches, and they name five of the biggest drivers of this dynamic. They are, in order of the impact they have had up to this point: 1) land and water use, which is expanding the areas of cities, farms, clearing our wilderness areas for development and extracting resources, 2) direct exploitation of organisms, which includes things like overhunting and fishing to the point of collapse of a species population, 3) climate change, which is leaving species unable to adapt fast enough and reducing their areas of habitat; and this is one that they expect to increase in influence over time if left unchecked, 4) pollution that would include toxins in land, water, and soil, and 5) invasive alien species, which is accelerating and comes from our increasingly globally connected world and travel.

Though it's not been discussed in any US news coverage I've seen, the report talks a great deal about how humanity's relentless pursuit of economic growth is also a major part of the problem. What we measure, and what we don't measure, fundamentally warps our understanding of development. As they write in one of their summary points, quote, "Economic incentives generally have favored expanding economic activity, and often environmental harm, over conservation or restoration. Incorporating the consideration of the multiple values of ecosystem functions and of nature's contribution to people into economic incentives has, in the economy, been shown to permit better ecological, economic, and social outcomes." That just means you need to include the health of the environment when calculating development holistically.

They give lots of advice on what can be done and has been done so far at smaller scales to solve this problem: we can end subsidies and incentives to destructive practices, we can introduce incentives that value nature's contribution to people, and enforce existing regulations, among many, many other actions. What is needed as they see it, is quote: "the evolution of global financial and economic systems to build a global sustainable economy, steering away from the current limited paradigm of economic growth" and limited measurements like gross domestic product for more long-term views of economics and quality of life.

In what I consider to be the understatement of the entire report, they admit that this will be hard, as quote "Vested interests may oppose the removal of subsidies or the introduction of other policies." You don't say so. If they needed a theologian to summarize, it would simply say: Expect oppression and social sin.

Now a critic might say, are we supposed to not use anything? Return to pre-modern nomadic life? Well, no. Since the formation of human societies, people have taken a portion of what the earth produces for their own sustenance. There's no way around that. As the philosopher Alfred North Whitehead once said, "Life is robbery."

Why doesn't that end all life? Well, there is a regenerative capacity of the planet—every year the earth produces life and creatures, and resources. But for the vast majority of human history, we did not take more, we did not use more than the regenerative capacity of the planet to heal itself. That is no longer true. As a matter of fact, today we use 50% more resources than our planet can regenerate annually.

Said another way, human society uses 1.5 planet earths worth of renewable resources. It will be even more as poor countries catch up to our rates. We'd need 4 planet earths if the world lived like we did in the US. No closed system can sustain infinite growth in the use of resources. That includes our planet. There is a point of equilibrium where if you go beyond, you are simply eating the future.

Let's compare it to a financial example. Let's use retirement savings. Say you've been fortunate, you've worked your whole life and built up a nest egg to help cover your golden years. And let's keep the numbers simple: say you can cash out 20 thousand dollars a year to help cover your living expenses, and if you do so, the principal of your retirement will never diminish. You're just using the interest. But say maybe you want to take an extra trip or somehow require more money. So instead of 20 thousand that year you take out 30 thousand. That's 50% more than what is sustainable.

If that happens one year, that's not great, but it's also not a crisis. If you go back to sustainable levels, you should be ok. But what happens if you take out 50% more than you can afford from your retirement every year? You're going to be eating into the principal more and more each year, because each year you eat into the principal, you eat into the capacity for it to regenerate. If you keep doing this, your retirement account will generate less revenue. And if you don't stop, it will eventually be exhausted down to zero. Yes?

Now, if you're just concerned about the length of your life, that's not necessarily a bad plan. Most people draw down their savings over the course of retirement. But what if you didn't need that account to last just one generation? What if it needed to last longer, not two generations, or ten generations, but 100 generations? Using anything more than the regenerative capacity of the account would be self-destructive. The same is true for our planet. Basically, we are consuming our future capacity to have life on our planet.

The report suggests that, while it will be very difficult, transformational change is possible. Nature can be conserved, restored and used sustainably. And one of the things that they say will help are different visions of what a good life entails that do not include ever-increasing material consumption, but lowering total consumption and waste, along with other actions. I could say a lot more about alternative ways to calculate economic welfare such as inclusive wealth accounting, natural capital accounting, or even de-growth models. It could mean things like the reforestation of North America as a form of holistic economic development.

The change we need includes, among other things, changing our paradigms, goals and values. That is one of the strengths of our religious imagery and traditions, especially in some of the less well-known voices. One of those is what's called ecofeminist theology. That may be a new term for some of us. Ecofeminist theology thinks about God and our world in light of the concerns of surprise, surprise, ecofeminists.

You're probably familiar with feminism, which is at its most basic the quest for equal rights for women vis-à-vis men. So, ecofeminism is based the notion that women's rights and the protection of the earth are connected efforts.

Ecofeminism started in the late 1980s and early 90s—where it combined the insights of feminism and ecology, exploring how male domination of women and the domination of nature are interconnected in terms of their values and institutions. In the dominant systems that got us to where we are today, male has been placed over female as more important, just as human was placed over nature. Women were devalued and assumed to be closer to nature and natural processes, which was understood to need to be controlled by male power and rationality. Ecofeminists argue that to fix social inequalities between sexes and classes, we have to fix both human and nature hierarchies as well. We can't separate them out.

It just so happens that the UN report more or less agrees 30 years later, saying explicitly that land or resource insecurity and declines in nature have greater impacts on women and girls, who are most often negatively affected. Ecofeminist theology takes these insights and explores how they impact our understanding of God and how we are to live with one another on this earth.

Several ecofeminist theologians have offered alternative images of God that I believe can help. One such person is Sallie McFague, an Episcopalian and retired professor of theology, who seems to take a cue from Paul's speech in Acts when she writes, "God is not primarily the orderer and controller of the universe but its source and empowerment, the breath that enlivens and energizes it." (*Body of God*, 145) She goes on to say "God [is] the source of our being, the source of all being, not as the one who intervenes from the outside to initiate creation, patch it up, or direct it, but as the one who supplies us with the breath for all the incredible rich, teeming fecundity and variety of life." (*Body of God*, 146)

McFague proposes thinking about the universe as God's body, where God is the spirit of the universe that gives it life. In this way, God's creative action is not something that happens once in a while from the outside. Rather, it is continuous and universal inside work that sustains and empowers life moment-by-moment, without which all life would end. To destroy biodiversity thus becomes an attack on the very creative, life-giving acts of God. To the extent God acts through creation, such attacks diminish God's ability to work with the world if there's less world to work with.

But, like Paul would say, this does not stop God. We see God *through* creation, mediated through matter, through life, but we do not see the face of God *in* creation. Rather, creation helps us see the back of God, much like Moses saw God's back at Sinai, but not the face.

By affirming God as the creative ground of everything, the condition upon which anything can exist, as the song we earlier sang said, God is the womb of life and the source of being. In this way, we can affirm God as mother. This can be a powerful image. Again, following McFague, in God's relation to the world's creative process, God is like a "Mother who encloses reality in her womb." (*Body of God*, 152) Just look at your bulletin cover with Mary Southard's "Sheltering Mother." Creation, all that is, within and surrounded by God.

On this Mother's Day, we can celebrate the divine mother, who, without her constant presence, nothing would be able to persist and endure. For that, we can give thanks. As much time has been spent in Christianity thinking of God as Father—all the songs, prayers, sermons, etc.—God as Mother should now be able to get her due. We could use this image every week for 50 years and barely crack the patriarchal assumptions that are deep within our tradition.

Still, like any image, we should not make this one into an idol either. God as Mother is liberating for some. It can remind us of the love many of us have received from our mothers. It can redefine what it means to be a mother, especially if we had a poor relationship with them. But it can also be a metaphor that gets in the way, just like "Father God." Though admittedly, it is less prone to abuse if by simply being less common an image.

But ultimately, whatever imperfect images we use to describe the Divine, God as the ground of everything reminds us of the intimate link between the creative process of our world and our own vulnerable but beautiful quest of flourishing. If we want to live in a land of milk and honey, not just now, but for the next seven generations and beyond, where biodiversity may flourish as God intends, we must find a way to live in balance with the rest of creation. Part of that may be new, ecofeminist images of God, who is the ground of everything.

Some of you may know that for the last week of April, I was in Halifax, Nova Scotia for a week of continuing education. On our last night, my travel cohort went to see a showing of the musical, "The Color Purple," based on the book by Alice Walker and later movie.

The show beautifully captures the values of a god who is the ground of everything, the one moving in nature, and encouraging its flourishing, the matrix of becoming, that womb of creative power, who can take us from situations of hopelessness, of disempowerment, of despair, leading us to lives where we can see who we are, all that connects us, and who we can be.

As the lyrics of the final song attest:

God is inside me and everyone else
That was or ever will be
I came into this world with God
And when I finally looked inside,
I found it
Just as close as my breath is to me
And then…

Like a plate of corn
Like a honeybee

Like a waterfall,
All a part of me

Like the color purple
Where does it come from?
Now my eyes are open
Look what God has done

Plymouth Church, look at what God has done, is doing each day, and will do, in and through us, and all creation, the whole world, if we but say yes to that creative power that resides, and moves in us. Thanks be to God, our Mother, our ground, our source, our Spirit, our Life, of everything that was or will be, now and forevermore. Amen.

Timothy C. Murphy currently serves as Senior Pastor of Plymouth Congregational Church of Fort Wayne, IN, a position he has held since 2018. He previously served as the Executive Director of Progressive Christians Uniting in Los Angeles and as a visiting professor at Claremont School of Theology. His justice and service passions include dismantling racism, combating economic inequality, and addressing climate change, among several other areas. He is the author of three books, the most recently being an illustrated children's book entitled *Jesus Learns to Glow*.

"Abide in Me": A Process Perspective

SANDRA G. NIXON

It's no accident that process theologians love the gospel of John.
It's mystical, cosmic, non-linear, and relational.

Reading: John 14:15-21
A sermon preached at Trinity-Grace United Church, Vancouver, Canada,
May 14, 2023

"If ye love me, keep my commandments. And I will pray to the father, and he will give you another comforter." These are the opening stanzas of a choral anthem by Thomas Tallis, one I sang often when I was part of a church choir years ago. It's based on the well-known scripture passage from the Gospel of John.

In the lead-up to Pentecost, we'll be hearing an increasing focus on community and unity. We will hear Jesus addressing his disciples, preparing them for a time when he will no longer be with them as a physical presence. And as part of that, Jesus will promise that the Father will send another Advocate, "the Comforter," who will be with them, not just as individual followers, but with the community as a whole. That Comforter, that Advocate, is the Holy Spirit.

We hear this in the passage from John today, which is a continuation from the earlier part of the same chapter, where Jesus tells the disciples: "I am the Way, the Truth and the Life."

It's all part of Jesus' final speech in the Gospel of John—which he delivers to his followers just before his arrest, trial, torture, and execution.

It follows the "classic form" of a farewell speech: Jesus addresses the survivors' needs and fears; then he gives instructions for their future behavior; and finally, offers glimpses of the otherwise-unseen-but-present other world, and of future events.

It is also very typically John—which means: very much *non-linear*.

You see, John—especially in his reporting of Jesus—is not terribly concerned with recording "history," per se. He's not trying to document exactly what Jesus actually said; or where he went; or who he met. John wants us to *see* Jesus for who he really is. That is why John's reporting of Jesus comes across so convoluted and confusing: he repeats and circles around; switches tenses and reverses statements—all to confound our linear "seeing," so that we might *really see*.

And that means adopting a sideways glance—and a non-linear approach—to interpreting this passage.

So let's look a little closer to see what we can "really see"...

"If you love me, you will keep my commandments" (John 14:15 NRSV).

Really, there was one commandment Jesus gave his disciples, at the last supper: "Love one another as I have loved you." (Although I suppose you could add in "feed my sheep" for good measure.)

Note—as Rev. David Ewart (www.holytextures.com) notes, this shouldn't be read with a finger-wagging, stern warning tone of voice. For John, this is more a statement of plain common sense logic. What is the commandment? "Love one another as I have loved you." (John 15:12, NRSV) Therefore: If you love me, you will keep my commandment.

Jesus could have also said it this way: "Those who keep my commandments are those who love me."

In the next verse, since Jesus is about to leave them, he now promises that he will ask God, and God will send them a helper, the Spirit of truth. The "world" cannot "see" this spirit, because it has not "seen" Jesus. Yet this Spirit will abide in the disciples as Jesus abides in them. And this spirit, this advocate, is the Spirit of truth.

Again, this is not a conditional promise, as in: "If you love me, and then keep my commandments—*then* I will send the Spirit. It's simply another statement, "*And* I am sending you the spirit."

A brief sidebar: The underlying Greek word which is translated into English as "truth" here is the word *alethea*. In Greek, an initial letter "a" is like our English "un." "Lethe" is the river in Greek mythology that the dead drank from in Hades in order to forget their past.

And so "a-lethea"—translated as truth—essentially means "un-forgetting"—so in a way it means waking up to; remembering; overcoming oblivion; being alive and vital; and not being deceived by false ideas or desires or scams. In other words, truth is *seeing* what is as it actually is.

We often focus on the spirit in those re-assuring terms of a comforter and advocate, and forget that a special role of the spirit is to also help us see the truth—and then, presumably, to act on it, or in alignment with it.

But there is also a reassuring, unifying message here from Jesus—framed in the language of *abiding*.

When we hear the word *abide* used today, it's in a couple of contexts: either in the sense of accepting ("I will abide by the group's decision.") or more of tolerating ("If there's one thing I can't abide, it's ketchup on Kraft dinner.").

But when it's used in scripture, it has a slightly different meaning. It's a more active kind of verb meaning "to remain" or "to stay."

"Abiding" is one of the themes running through John's gospel: Jesus abides in the Father, the Father abides in Jesus, Jesus speaks about abiding in his followers, and his followers in him, and the Spirit abides in them as well (and so on).

This abiding theme gets repeated a lot, and not just in this passage. It's a key "non-linear" piece in John, which means it's key in pointing us to a truth. And as archaic perhaps as the "abiding" language feels, it also feels like there's something there.

"The Spirit of truth, whom the world cannot receive…abides with you, and will be in you … I (too) am in my Father, and you in me, and I in you. Those who love me will be loved by my Father, and I will love them and reveal myself to them" (John 14:17, 20-21, NRSV).

Have you heard of the transitive property—one of those things we all learned in middle school math class?

For John, Jesus, God, the Spirit, and his followers are all inter-changeable terms within this concept of abiding—and within the parameter of love. For example, if Jesus is abiding in you, and I love you as Jesus loves me, then I am loving Jesus (who is abiding in you).

So…to recap: "abiding" results in this mystical, non-linear union of God, Jesus, Spirit—and us.

And then we read:

"Those who love me will be loved by my Father"—which essentially means: "Those (in whom I abide) who love me will be loved by my Father (who loves me and therefore also loves those in whom I abide)."

And again, just like with "abide," the word translated as "love" also has several meanings. In the context of this passage, the word used in the Greek is "agape" which has the meaning of God's unconditional, unbreakable, *covenantal relationship* of love, kindness, and mercy.

This is the kind of love Jesus is talking about—an active and faithful *relationship* more than any kind of *feeling*.

"I will not leave you orphaned."

One of the phrases from this passage which really stands out for me is when Jesus says, "I will not leave you orphaned."

And for me, this—and the use of the love language, really gets to the heart of Jesus' message and how John wants us to "see" Jesus.

At its most basic, the message, the *reality* we are meant to see, is that we are not orphans; we are not fundamentally alone in this world. And it's more than there being some external spirit out there helping and guiding us.

What I believe this passage affirms is that in some fundamental, mysterious, energetic, and spiritual way, we are not "on our own." Rather, we dwell in Christ—we abide in Christ, and Christ dwells in us—through an unconditional and unbreakable relationship.

One of the key ideas in process theology and process-relational thought in general is the concept of "inter-becoming."

The main idea is this:

Everything in the universe is in the process of becoming. And that process is relational.

All things—*all things*—grow and evolve together. This we are learning is a fundamental characteristic of reality, of how things are related—from the cosmic to the quantum.

It's no accident that process theologians love the gospel of John. It is mystical, cosmic, non-linear and relational—just a few of Process-Relational Thought's favorite things (as the song goes).

And it seems to point towards a reality that modern physics is just beginning to confirm.

And what, you might ask, does this understanding of reality look like—or how does it express itself—as theology? As a faith statement?

Well—let's try this:

> "All I'm saying is simply this, that all life is interrelated, that somehow we're caught in an inescapable network of mutuality tied in a single garment of destiny. Whatever affects one directly affects all indirectly. For some strange reason, I can never be what I ought to be until you are what you ought to be. You can never be what you ought to be until I am what I ought to be. This is the interrelated structure of reality." —Dr. Martin Luther King Jr.

It was just this way of seeing reality (his attunement to real truth) that gave MLK the hope he had and maintained that the "Beloved Community" he famously envisioned was in fact possible. This embodied his vision of a community in which everyone is cared for, loved, and belongs, and poverty, hunger, and hate are eliminated.

At its core, MLK's vision was one of community structured around belonging and connection—two things that are sorely lacking in the western world—with devastating impacts.

And why it's so crucial that as people of faith, we remain lovingly faithful to the message of Jesus and the truth as John has so elegantly revealed for us. The truth that we truly are connected. To each other, to all living things—as are our individual journeys.

Just as the branches of a vine are connected to the trunk and nurtured by the roots, which in turn communicate with and help—and receive help—from other trees in the ecosystem—all of which is further supported by a vast mycelial network—we, as branches of the Christ vine, as part of God's vastly interconnected, inter-becoming world—we too are part of the "God ecosystem"—based in loving relationship and a mystical abiding in one another that really can, in and through the spirit, do more in and through us than we can ask or imagine.

Thanks be to God.

Sandra G. Nixon is an ordained minister in the United Church of Canada. She earned her M.Div. at the Vancouver School of Theology and has been in active congregational ministry for over twenty years. She currently serves as Coordinating Minister with Trinity-Grace United Church (www.tgucvan.com) in Vancouver, Canada. Sandra lives with her family in Richmond, BC and enjoys west coast gardening, cooking, kayaking, and yoga.

God Is Not in Control—Thank Goodness!

THOMAS JAY OORD

If God is in control, life makes no sense.

Reading: Ephesians 5:1-2
Sermon preached at the Church of the Village, November 14, 2021

I'd like to explore a question I suspect just about everyone has asked: "If there is a God, and it this God loves every one of us perfectly and omnipotent, why doesn't this God stop the genuine evil, the pointless pain, the unnecessary suffering that you, and I, and so many around the world endure?"

Some of us ask this question because we've suffered personally. Others ask because we know someone who suffered in some horrific way. This question isn't a side issue that we think about every once in a while. If the polls are correct, it's the number one reason people say they can't believe in God. And I suspect this question of suffering is the number one question people who believe in God ask.

In what follows, I'm going to be bold: I propose a solution to the problem of evil.

If we consult the Bible for an answer to this question, we'll find various responses. Many passages talk about God's power, God's love, and evil. Unfortunately, some biblical texts paint God as unloving. Some even say God causes evil. But many others portray God as opposed to evil. And they say God wants us to oppose evil.

I've titled this sermon, "God is not in control—Thank Goodness!" Of course, many people say just the opposite. They say, "thank goodness, God is in control." But does it make much sense to think a loving God causes or allows evil? If God is in control, God must be able to prevent evil. And yet evil occurs. I will argue we should be thankful God is *not* in control.

The passage I've chosen to spark our discussion of God and evil is this: "Be imitators of God, as beloved children, and live in love, as Christ loved us…" (Eph. 5:1,2a). The Apostle Paul makes the bold claim that his readers can be like God.

How is it possible for creatures to be like the Creator? Well, I don't believe Paul is saying we can be omnipresent, like God is omnipresent. I don't think he believes we can be omniscient. There are many ways we cannot imitate God. According to the passage, Paul thinks we can imitate God when we "live in love." We can imitate the God of the universe when we love.

Our ability to imitate God by living a life of love is possible because God loves us. "We love because He first loved us," according to First John. Our best example of what love looks like is Jesus Christ. Putting it altogether, the passage seems to say we can imitate God by living lives of love. And Jesus is our best example of what that looks like.

Let's return to questions of evil. Would a loving person—divine or creaturely—cause evil? Would this loving person allow the evil that person could stop? Is God someone who either purposely makes bad things happen or stands back and allows them?

I live in Idaho, and there's a good size stream that runs behind my house. In the hot summer months, my three daughters sometimes play in the stream to cool down. Imagine that one afternoon I'm in my backyard doing yardwork. Let's say my daughters have gotten into an argument and my oldest daughter takes the head of my youngest and puts it under the water. She's trying to drown her sister. Suppose I'm close enough to wade out into the stream, intervene, and prevent my daughter's death. But instead of helping, suppose I stay in the yard. I might even say, "I'm not causing this death, but I'll allow it. I'll permit my oldest daughter to drown my youngest."

If I did not prevent the evil I could have stopped, I would not be a loving father. No one in my subdivision would vote me "Father of the Year." My wife would be angry beyond description.

Many people think God can single-handedly prevent evil in the world. They believe God allows the evil God could prevent. God chooses not to thwart free will, they say, or chooses not to interrupt the laws of nature. Does that make sense? I don't think so.

People have wrestled with questions of God and evil for millennia. You've probably heard some of their answers. "It's all a part of God's plan," some people say. Others say, "Everything happens for a reason." Others say, "Heaven's choir needed another angel." Or people claim God is trying to teach us a lesson. None of these answers makes sense to me or to most people I know.

One of the better answers to evil points to creaturely freedom. They say God gives us free will, and we sometimes abuse that freedom. Most people who appeal to freewill also believe God could override our freedom or fail to give it. But if that's true, we rightly wonder why God doesn't remove freedom from those who do horrific evil, as the story of my daughters illustrates. After all, if I could override my older daughter's freedom and prevent the killing of my youngest daughter, that's the loving thing for me to do. Saying God *chooses* not to take away free will doesn't provide a full answer.

Those who have considered the "answers" I've mentioned find them wanting. In response, they metaphorically reach into their back pockets, and they pull out a big mystery card. Then, "KACHUNK," they slap that mystery card into the conversation. They say, "Who are we to understand God?" Or, "God's ways are not our ways." Or, "God is infinite, and we are finite."

Of course, there's always a measure of mystery in theology. I don't think I have God figured out fully, and I am highly suspicious of those who act like they do. But playing the mystery card when questions are vexing can be an escape from rethinking our most basic views of God. It can prevent us from searching for and find an actual *solution* to the problem of evil.

I don't play the mystery card. I'm going to propose an actual solution to why a loving and powerful God fails to prevent genuine evil. God didn't drop this answer directly into my head in a controlling fashion. I'm uncertain the answer I propose is correct. I find it highly attractive and convincing. And I know many people who agree.

I've given my answer in various books, especially *God Can't: How to Believe in God and Love after Tragedy, Abuse, and Other Evils*. It's an answer with five dimensions. And I want to address each briefly, because together they provide an actual solution to the problem of evil.

The first dimension to this five-fold answer is by far the most controversial. It says God simply *can't* prevent evil single-handedly. I'm not saying God *won't*, as if God could stop evil but chooses not to. I'm saying God *can't* stop evil single-handedly, because God can't control anyone or anything.

Those like me who read the Bible might say to themselves, "God can't? That surely can't be scriptural. Where is this coming from?" It surprises many to discover there's biblical support for the idea God can't do some things. The writer of Hebrews says God can't tell a lie. The Letter of James says God can't be tempted. The psalmist says God can't grow tired. Hosea says God can't abandon us. My favorite passage is Paul's letter to Timothy: "when we are faithless, God remains faithful, because God cannot deny himself."

What if "God cannot deny himself" means that God can't be other than God? And what if God always loves? What if it's God's immutable nature to love, and this love is always self-giving and others-empowering? And what if God's love is always uncontrolling?

If divine love is uncontrolling and God always loves, God can't prevent evil through control. Because God loves you, me, every creature, and all creation top to bottom, God can't control you, me, any creature, or all creation top to bottom. That's the first big idea we need to solve our questions about God and evil: God can't single-handedly prevent evil.

The second idea says God cares. God is not aloof, sitting on mars eating popcorn, looking down on us. God isn't watching us from a distance muttering, "Suffering from a pandemic? Sucks to be you!" No.

The second idea says God empathizes as one present with absolutely everyone and all creation. God experiences joys and the sorrows, suffering and excellencies. When you suffer, you have God as a fellow sufferer who understands your suffering.

The third idea we need to embrace addresses healing. Some who endure pain and difficulty say, "I'm not really looking for an answer to why God didn't stop what happened. I just want to get over this. I want to be healed."

God is in the healing business. But God can't heal single-handedly. If God could, God has favorites, right?! If God picks some to heal all at once and all alone, God must not like some of us very much. After all, we're not healed. God is trying to heal everyone and everything in every moment, but there are real obstacles to healing.

For healing to occur, we need to cooperate with God, or the conditions of the creation need to be conducive. Creaturely forces, factors, and actors sometimes oppose God's work to heal. And because God can't control anyone or anything, God can't single-handedly overcome those factors. Because sometimes obstacles prevent healing now, I believe some healing must wait until the afterlife. I believe in life after death and I look forward to existence without the pain-ridden body I now have.

Now to the fourth dimension of this solution to the problem of evil. It says God squeezes whatever good can be squeezed from the bad God didn't want in the first place. I often hear people testify to when they've gone through a difficult time and then they've seen something positive come from it. In response, they'll say, "The bad must have been God's plan. God knew I needed to grow."

Jimmy told me his first marriage was horrible, but his second was great. He thought it must have been God's will for him to go through an ugly divorce so that he could find the right person on the second try.

We don't have to think like Jimmy does. We can believe God works with whatever circumstances we encounter. God works with us and others to squeeze something good from the bad God didn't want. When something good occurs, we don't have to believe God foreordained or even foreknew it. It's not part of God's "plan."

The final dimension to my solution to evil says we all have roles to play in overcoming evil with good. You and I play a role in love winning. God actually *needs* us.

When some hear me say "God needs us," their heads metaphorically blow off. They've been told that God is totally self-sufficient, not in a "need" relationship. God can up and do whatever God wants to do.

If you have a view of God who does *not* need us, you won't have a solution to why evil occurs. Those who deny God has needs are typically the ones who play the mystery card. However, if God calls upon creation to join the work of overcoming evil with good, then part of you and me is essential to the work of love. What we do matters. The way we live, eat, hang out with people, work with partners, families, enemies, bosses, coworkers, politicians, and the earth...matters. It matters to God, and it matters to the unfolding of history. Everything we do impacts God's work of love.

That's my five-fold solution to why a loving and powerful God fails to prevent evil. I think it fits the general witness of scripture, although I know some passages that don't support it. I think it's eminently reasonable and fits our experience. And it fits with what it means to follow the Apostle Paul's instruction to "imitate God, as dearly loved children, and live a life of love, like Christ loved us."

If love tries to overcome evil instead of causing or allow it, you and I can join the uncontrolling God of love in overcoming evil with good.

Amen.

Thomas Jay Oord, Ph.D., is a theologian, philosopher, and scholar of multi-disciplinary studies. Oord directs the Center for Open and Relational Theology and the Open and Relational Theology doctoral program at Northwind Theological Seminary. He is an award-winning author and has written or edited over thirty books. A gifted speaker, Oord lectures at universities, conferences, churches, and institutions. Website: thomasjayoord.com

Wholly Other God—I Am... (Dot, Dot, Dot)

AMANDA OSTER

The Divine is not a person to know, but an invitation to explore.

Readings: Exodus 3:14, Genesis 12:1, Psalm 34:8, 2 Corinthians 5:7, Hebrews 11:1
Sermon preached at various rural churches in North Dakota, of different denominations, over a span of a couple years

Amanda delivered this sermon on various occasions in different churches where she was invited as a guest preacher. Even though none of the settings would be considered progressive or leaning toward Process or Open and Relational Theology, they all welcomed and embraced the message. Because it is "process-lite," it introduces Open and Relational theological concepts alongside traditional themes, perhaps making new and challenging ideas a bit more palatable. This approach might be used as a bridge in moving people toward a more Open and Relational/Process perspective.

In the book *Ten Questions Christians Are Asking*, David Jeremiah includes a story about Albert Einstein who was a brilliant scientist but also known to be erratic, forgetful, and scatterbrained. As the story goes, he was on a train not knowing where his tickets were. The ticket attendant stood there waiting for him to produce the tickets as he patted his pockets, checked his hat, rifled through is bag, briefcase, and even overturned his socks. Finally, the young man replied, "It's okay, Dr. Einstien, I know who you are and I'm sure you bought a ticket. If you end up finding it, let me know. Otherwise, no worries." The young man continued down the aisle, taking tickets from other passengers, and when he turned around, he saw Einstein on his hands and knees searching under and around his seat for the missing tickets. The attendant hollered toward the back, "Really Dr. Einstein, it's okay. I'm sure you bought a ticket." To which Einstein hollered back, "I'm sure I did, too. I just can't remember where I'm going."

Have any of you had a week like that? If so, I hope that our time together will give you some peace of mind and help you navigate your journey a little better. Maybe you'll even be a little closer to finding what you're looking for, kind of like Einstein's lost tickets. Let us pray.

In literature and theology, the Divine is often referred to as "The Wholly Other"—wholly as opposed to holy—meaning *entirely and completely*. In humanity's effort in to make sense of and explain this Wholly Other, we anthropomorphize, which is a technical term that means we attribute human characteristics to non-human things. Such phrases as *the hand of God reaching down to touch us*, *the eyes of God watching us*, *the Lord exulting over his people with singing*, and even the gendering of the Divine with *he* or *his* and the use of names like God, Lord, King, etc. are all indicators of anthropomorphization. Even Jesus anthropomorphized when he referred to the Divine as Father God and gave the Ultimate Mystery a singular locative identity when saying "He" was "in heaven." Michael Gungor was correct when he wrote in his song *White Man:* "God is not a man. God is not a white man. God is not a man sitting on a cloud." In fact, as much as it may rattle some who hold to traditionalist ideologies, we could just as well refer to God as she, for God is not human at all.

God, if I may refer to the Divine by that title, is infinite. Even if we should say something like "in God's entirety,"—which is an attempt to capture or express a grandiosity like the Grand Canyon—such phrases infer a measurability, even if God's "bigness" is vaster than the oceans. In our sincerity, we might wish to extend our arms wide in order to gather ourselves to God and wrap the Divine in a hug, but we know it's not possible, no matter how we might try. For God is not made of carbon and oxygen and calcium and hydrogen. God is not measurable, physically literal, or even bound to a location. God is wholly other.

Nevertheless, throughout time, humanity has set about creating activities, developing habits, and carrying out sacred rituals meant to somehow experience this God that isn't human but affects us humans in transcendent ways. Experiences of God might be accompanied by a change in heart rate, cascading tears seemingly unbidden, unexplained calm amid personal chaos, or a swelling of emotions that makes a person think and feel their chest might possibly burst completely open. Try as we might, and surely we will try, we cannot fully describe and express what happens to us when we "encounter God."

So often we get hung up on the verbiage, the rituals, and the pronouns that define our experiences that we conflate those things with God itself. Our preferences as human beings, our desires to know and solve the puzzles and problems that plague us lead us to concretizing the ineffable. We gravitate toward bible studies that ask us to fill in the blanks, and in so doing we feel a sense of accomplishment. But, what if experiencing the Divine is less about fill-in-the-blanks and more about ellipses (those three little dots in a phrase that indicate a pause, a hesitation, a trailing off thought, or a silence)? How might that change how we walk about this great earth?

Imagine asking your friend a question, and instead of a full reply, they respond with, "Well, I heard…", leaving you hanging with those three little dots. What do you do? If you're like me, you raise your eyebrows, open your eyes a little wider in wonder, maybe even give a little side glance. You gently lean in and wait for your friend to continue, your entire posture saying, "tell me more." In essence, what you're doing is responding to an invitation. You're stepping into your friend's thoughts and motives and doubts, trying to shake out what's in there. "You heard, WHAT?! Tell me. I want to know what *you* know."

Approaching the Divine as a series of ellipses rather than a defined being is, in my experience and in my opinion, the better way, even if I am still sometimes prone to seeking a definition of the Mystery we call God and write it in the blank.

For all of us who have found ourselves in a strange relationship with Christianity's holy text, the Bible, maybe there's a reason for all the holes in Scripture, all those things the Bible doesn't make absolutely clear or doesn't talk about at all. It's in those places where we are invited to lean in and wonder and wrestle; where we are given space to *come taste* and *come see* as the Psalmist wrote in Psalm 34:8. Perhaps it is in this tasting and discovering that we find that being with God is not about figuring it out, but about being together.

In Exodus 3:14, the Bible recorded Moses having a conversation with the Divine. In this account, God called Moses to leave his wilderness living and go back to Egypt to compel the Israelite people to leave and establish themselves as a distinct people elsewhere. Moses asked the Divine, "But who are you?" To which God replied with this well-known comment, "I am that I am." I used to read this as a definitive, concretized statement as if there were an asterisk attached with the comment, "and that's final!" But then I learned that the writers of this story constructed the naming in such a way as to, perhaps, let readers know the Divine is unfinished, yet to be determined, fluid, in process, mysterious, and has infinite potentiality. In the Hebrew language, it could be translated, "I will be what I will be." In other words, "I Am…" (dot, dot, dot). What does God mean? The Divine's pronouncement of itself, rather than a definition, is an invitation of discovery and exploration and perhaps not just for Moses, but for God, too. Moses' acceptance of the I Am, then, is an acceptance of adventure and possibility; a journey into the great unknown *with* the Great Unknown.

We can see that this invitational theme of exploration and the ongoing discovery of mystery was true for Abraham also in Genesis 12:1 when Abraham felt compelled to leave the land he knew to travel to a yet specified destination. God impressed upon Abraham to leave and go, and the place he was to settle would be determined at a later date. The great creative force of the universe didn't give Abraham the entire picture of itself, of Abraham's life ahead, or even the next dot on the map. Instead, Abraham simply felt the nudge to leave and go and would later receive what he would need when the time was right. It is possible God knew where that eventual place would be, or perhaps God and Abraham would discover that place together, co-creating a magnificent life as they traveled in partnership with one another. I happen to think it was the latter and not the former.

Again, we see this vagueness when Jesus called his first disciples in Matthew 4:19. When Jesus said, "Follow me," he gave them one descriptor: "and I will make you fishers of men." That's it.

How many of us, myself included, are prone to hesitate, become anxious, and stay rooted in place at an invitation until more of the blanks get filled in? Or, until we have a better picture of what we think God looks like and the "adventure" comes with a well-planned itinerary? But what if that's not how the Divine is to be approached, and that's not how it works? What if life, like God, wasn't meant to be managed and figured out but, instead, experienced?

I have a friend who has suffered from miscarriages, and it's been a process of sorrow and longing and difficulty for her. We've talked a great deal about suffering and how often, as Christians, we don't suffer well. We try to take comfort from well-intended phrases such as, "God doesn't waste anything in your life, including suffering," but we simply want the suffering to end—waste or not. We want answers. We assign blame. We look to all our faults and guilt ourselves for our failures. We thrash and writhe and yell. These are human reactions to pain, and we sometimes try to look for a source outside ourselves to just fix it all and take it away.

Yet, I wonder if maybe Love doesn't come to us and say: "Yes, this is hard, but no adventure of life is meant only to be easy. I can't make the hard go away, but I am with you. I will walk this out with you."

Imagine you've been trekking through the jungle all day, and you still haven't gotten through all the lush, dense vegetation as day turns to night. The dark becomes so deep you can't see past your face and the air so heavy it seems hard to breathe. Your water bottle is nearly empty. You have stinging blisters on your feet, and you feel you can't go on, but there is a fire that still needs building and a hammock that needs hanging, if you are to have any relief at all. What's more, there are deadly creatures of all kinds in the jungle, and not a piece of dry wood can be found. No matter how much you pray for a divine intervention, a miracle, you'll have to dig deep and do these things yourself, for God is not a man that can roll up his sleeves, so to speak, and do them for you.

We *could* believe that the Divine's lack of intervention is proof that God is withholding good in an effort to test faith, but I'm not convinced this is how the Divine interacts with the created universe. What if it's more like an invitation to lean in… (dot, dot, dot)? What if this Relational Mystery promises presence and experience, and says, "I promise, I will be with you on the adventure that is your life and it will be something! No, your journey won't be like anyone else's, it's not supposed to be. But, if you talk to other adventurers, you might find some common themes; you may even learn a thing or two. If you feel like screaming in the dark, go ahead. If crying brings release, do it. If all that makes you feel better, great, but it won't make the morning come faster. It won't transport you to a different location; you'll still be in the jungle. In the morning, however, you can pack up and go back the way you came, but there's a lot more that lies ahead, in Me and in you. Whatever you decide, I will be with you."

Many of you are probably familiar with the poem "Footprints In the Sand" that describes two sets of footprints on the beach that become one, and when the voice of the poem asks God where the second set of prints went, God says, "That's where I carried you." Don't we just love that idea? But how often do we find that life isn't like that at all? If we were to be honest, what our footprints look like is that at some point the two, nice orderly sets break apart, and instead of becoming one, we see one set of footprints become a muddled mess with the sand all turned up, zigzagging hither and yon, crossing over and doubling back. We see a set that have become "disordered." Maybe that's when life got overwhelming and you were plunged into darkness. Maybe that's when you struck out on a creative endeavor that others "warned" you about. Maybe that's when you decided to dance with the Divine instead of walking a straight line. There's something beautiful about the two becoming one, but there's also something exciting and thrilling about tearing up the sand and plunging into the darkness, the mystery, the unknown.

The question that lies before us is this: what will each of us do with our one wild life? Will we see it for the adventure it is? Will we partner with the Divine in scary, messy, beautiful discovery? Or, will we sterilize our lives and God, too, and miss out? Will we try to tame the wildness that is God, or will we accept the invitation of the Great I Am (…) to journey in new ways through life that are more real and more alive than we ever thought possible? Will we embrace both the mystery and confidence of faith that the Bible speaks of in 2 Corinthians 5:7 and Hebrews 11:1 and walk by faith even when we can't see our way in the dark? Will we keep going when all seems lost and we can't find the tickets that will get us there?

I began with Albert Einstein, and now I want to close with Albert Einstein. The thing with this great man is that he had a group of close friends that knew well of his brilliance but also his absentmindedness—they kept pretty good tabs on him and regularly helped him out. If the story is true, his friends wouldn't have let him get too far off the beaten path before intervening. And, if *that* were the case, I wonder how long Einstein spent looking on the floor and rummaging through his stuff before sitting back, looking out the windows, and enjoying the ride, knowing that he was in good hands. And because he had a "welcoming committee" back home, it would be a grand story to tell!

Whatever we decide, whatever path we take, may we all be able to take comfort in what is around us and say in similar words of the Psalmist: I have truly tasted of God, and It is good; oh, so good! And I have seen something Wholly Other, and it is good; oh, so good! I want more… (dot, dot, dot).

Amanda Oster earned her MA in Missional Leadership from Trinity Graduate School and has served various ministry roles throughout her adult life. Amanda is a lay theologian, the founder and director of Lyra Ministries, and the host of the very infrequent *(un)Done podcast* that focuses on issues of faith outside of church. She lives with her family in rural North Dakota.

The Sanctuary of Openness

REBECCA ANN PARKER

Those who have rejected standard concepts of God as inadequate for their spiritual and moral life enter a space of openness in which new understandings of God can arise.

Explanatory Note: In *Process and Reality*, Alfred North Whitehead rejects several classic concepts of God, including God as Unmoved Mover, as Omnipotent, and as Moral Ruler. Process philosopher Charles Hartshorne follows suit in *Omnipotence and other Theological Mistakes.* Openness to new understandings about God is a hallmark of process theology.

A few summers ago, on a pretty evening, I sat on the porch with my father and gazed across the still water of Wollochet Bay as the setting sun drenched the cedar trees in golden light. A fleet of honking Canada Geese glided in from their day's outing and landed with a graceful splash, returning to the cove of rushes they came to every night. Overhead, the osprey soared out from her tree-top nest, where her younglings peeped incessantly for food. She glimpsed a fish jumping for dragonflies, swiftly dove into the water and rose with a flash of silver in her beak.

We sipped our after-supper coffee in silence and then my dad, an 88-year-old retired United Methodist minister, waved his hand across the scene like a magician unveiling a magic trick and shook his head in wonder. "Just look at this marvel of life before our eyes! Look at how everything is interacting, how everything works in circular motion to create the whole." He paused thoughtfully, then, with an impish smile, added, "Who knows whether the source of all this is one God or many gods?"

I enjoyed my father's delight in the life of the lagoon, but I was amazed that, after nearly 70 years as a Christian minister in which he faithfully represented the one, true God, he happily speculated that there may not be one God at all! Then I realized that my father's buoyancy of spirit, his openness to entertaining a thought about divinity that went beyond what he had held as a core belief, was born from his lifetime of loving God.

To love God, truly and deeply, is to hold one's certitude about God without grasping, knowing as Alfred North Whitehead said, "the merest hint of dogmatic certainty as to finality of statement is an exhibition of folly." For the love of God, we must let go again and again of what we think we know about God, repeatedly opening our mind and heart to new intuitions regarding an ultimate reality that has not finished revealing itself to us.

Whether you feel there is one God, or many, or no gods at all, devotion to the sacred source, which some call God, requires you to think critically and carefully, and in disruptive ways, about who and what is meant by God. To orient your life to radical openness about God can carry you to surprising places, and can hone your heart, mind, and actions as a citizen of the circle of life.

A first step towards loving God is to say "No!" to that which is not God. This is the starting place for many thoughtful people of conscience. Atheism is better than uncritical devotion to unworkable or harmful conceptions of God. Many sensitive people at one point or another have said "No!" to that which is not God.

The Despotic Judge condemning sinners to hell: this is not God.

The Warrior King deploying crusaders to massacre infidels: this is not God.

The Fickle Fixer who might make everything ok for us if we just ask in the right way and make the right bargain: this is not God.

The Old White Patriarch in the Clouds, ordaining men to rule over women, and anointing whites as the superior race: this is not God.

The Provider of Material Abundance who showers earthly prosperity upon those who hate gay people, reject socialism, and defend the right to bear arms: this is not God.

The Ruler of Creation who plans to destroy this Earth in a cataclysm of ecological disaster and global warfare and rapture the true believers into a new creation: this is not God.

Protest of unworthy concepts of God is at the heart of serious faith. When we embrace the scriptural tradition that says God is Love, then Love becomes our measure for the adequacy of any religious claim. Love requires that we reject any view of God that contradicts what we know Love to be and to do. We say no in the name of Love.

In addition to the explicit theological claims about God that contradict Love, there are implicit secular claims that must be questioned as well. In his recent anthology, *"God Is Dead" and I Don't Feel So Good Myself,* John Stanley writes, "We must analyze the reigning 'gods of our time,' those ideologies that demand our ultimate allegiance." He names these as "nationalism (the pursuit of national interest and national security at any cost), technologism (the pursuit of scientific discovery and technological advancement at any cost), and economism (the pursuit of profit and economic expansion at any cost)" and goes on to comment:

> We would do well to pause and reflect upon the kind of world these gods have bestowed on us, or I should say, the kind of world we have created in our submission to them—a world characterized by escalating violence and the rise of the military industrial machine, human alienation from nature and vast environmental degradation, the threat of nuclear destruction and biological weaponry, the commodification of reality where people become reduced to things in a market where everything has a price, and a rapidly widening gap between the world's rich and the world's poor—and ask ourselves whether the gods of our age are as benevolent as we have taken them to be, and if they are truly worthy of our service.

Being a serious person of faith involves saying no to myriad claims about God and demands for our ultimate allegiance that have amplified suffering and injustice in the world rather than alleviate it.

Saying "no!" is not an easy path. Quite the opposite: it launches you into a process that may require you to let go of comfortable assumptions, question authority, reject the dominant culture and counter the dictates of loving only your own kind or your own country. You will have to ask not only "who is God?" but also "who am I?" and "what is Love?"

This spiritual path is known as the *via negativa*—the path of negation—in which, bit by bit, one dismantles nearly every claim about God. Negation empties your conceptual mind and takes you to a void, an unfilled space that I call "the Sanctuary of Openness," a place carved open by what has been taken away.

In this space of radical openness, a different spiritual and ethical awareness can begin to arise in our lives. For beyond saying "no!" there is a hidden "yes!" to something deeper that impels our no. As the philosopher Camus has observed, "Beyond the no of every true rebel there lies a yes." That "yes" hidden within our "no" anchors our spiritual and ethical ground; it marks our deepest intuition of rightness and reality, but we may not even have a name for it.

In the Sanctuary of Openness, we offer hospitality to one another's unfolding spiritual discernment. Some find stability resting with the silence—we ground ourselves in holy emptiness, in a-theism, accepting radical responsibility for our choices and actions without attributing our loyalty to anything beyond our own deepest self. We are content only to give our allegiance to that which we judge to be worthy of our devotion, and we are at peace with the unknown.

Others of us find in the Sanctuary of Openness an emergent intuition of holy presence, arising and calling to us. John Caputo, an a-theologian, writes:

> I do not believe in the existence of God, but in God's insistence. I do not say God 'exists,' but that God calls. God calls upon us, like an unwelcome interruption, a quiet but insistent solicitation...God emerges here and there... not in the bound volumes of theology but in loose papers...restless hope, where ...non-knowing is not a lack but the open-ended venture in the human adventure.

Asian-American feminist theologian Rita Nakashima Brock, in *Proverbs of Ashes*, arrived at a new sense of God after a long journey:

> And this is how I can speak of God: a presence gradually unfolded by life in its richness and tragedies, its devastating losses and its abundance; a power calling us into a fullness of living; a passion for life, for good and ill; an unquenchable fire at the core of life, glimpsed in light and shadow.

In the Sanctuary of Openness, something beckons us beyond the idolatries we have rejected. The mind and heart can slowly become attuned to that which addresses us, which asks everything of us and offers everything to us while remaining unseen, un-nameable, and un-known. We sense that which abides with utter reliability and yet is elusive, that which is all pervasive and yet opaque, that which is at once one and many. We feel the presence of that which does not answer us when we call, and yet calls to us. It speaks to us from leaf and branch, and stream, from osprey splash and setting sun, from stars above and dreams within, from the faces of children, in the sounds of lovemaking and birth-giving, and in the last breath of the dying.

In the Sanctuary of Openness, the hidden artist inside of us appears. Human beings who have cleared away unworthy notions of God and stepped beyond the rule of the world's principalities and powers begin to speak new and different names

Spirit of Life, Fount of All Blessings,

Dream-keeper, Spinner and Weaver of our Lives,

Most Intimate Friend,

Mother of Us All,

Breath, Wind, Fire.

Alice Walker's character Shug says, "My first step from the old white man was trees." Alfred North Whitehead called God, "The Poet of the World," "The Fellow Sufferer Who Understands."

In the Sanctuary of Openness, we can speak in an alternative voice, and we can hear alternative voices arising from unexpected places and from subdominant traditions—black lives, queer lives, women of all colors, communities that have had to take their spiritual wisdom underground to survive. We press beyond established images and claim the presence of the sacred arising from our lived experiences of life's beauty, of our need for solace in pain, our search for strength to hold out against folly, our longing to remember lives well lived and lives taken too soon, and our desire to find some way to say, "thank you."

In the Sanctuary of Openness, we listen to the world as it speaks to us, like my father and I listened on the porch that summer evening. In quiet moments, God's presence cracks open from its hiding places, shattering orthodoxies into pieces, and leaves us standing here in a polydoxy of wonder.

My father died that next winter. As he lay dying, I asked him, with some hesitancy, if he would like me to pray for him. He nodded. I ended the prayer with the scripture: "Whether we live or die, we belong to God." "Amen!" he said in a full voice, raising his hands with all the strength he still had.

My father was a sailor as well as a preacher. As the little boat of his life crossed the bar into the open sea, the great depths of the unknown mystery remained uncontainable by any human definitions. And yet, he was buoyed by love and by one certitude. He knew his life was embraced and carried by that greater life.

That was my father's faith. I learned to trust it from him. You, too, may feel this way. Or your faith may be different.

Your questions matter—
Your openness matters—
The yes hidden with your no matters.

This is how we offer profound reverence to God: by staying anchored in love and buoyant upon the waters of mystery.

Rebecca Ann Parker is Professor of Theology Emeritus and President Emeritus of Starr King School for the Ministry and Co-Founder of The Braxton Institute for Sustainability, Resiliency, and Joy. She is author of *Blessing the World*; co-author of *Proverbs of Ashes* and *Saving Paradise* (with Rita Nakashima Brock), and co-author of *A House for Hope* (with John Buehrens).

Holy Transformation

GARY PATERSON

A Process meditation on Revelation 21:5b
"Behold! I am making all things new."

The following sermon was one that I shared several years ago, as Moderator of the United Church of Canada, when we gathered in Cornerbrook, Newfoundland, for our triannual General Council. As a denomination, we were (and still are) facing many challenges (familiar to most Mainline denominations), and this was a point in time where we had come together to talk about our future. During the past three years, I had criss-crossed the country, preaching or leading workshops, with many different congregations. I would frequently begin with the bad news—"In the next several years many, many of our congregations will close…including, perhaps, this one." Then I would say, "But there is good news, for we are a people who believe in resurrection. Perhaps we are unsure what that means in our present situation, but we still trust that God can breathe new life into dry bones. The Holy One can bring about a new creation, even though, right now, we don't know what that will look like, and we are scared of the death that is implied."

The theme of our General Council was based on half a verse from the 2nd to last chapter of the Bible… "Behold! I am making all things new!" (Rev. 21.5b). My sermon, as part of our opening worship, cracked open these seven words, phrase by phrase, hopefully enabling people to see new possibilities.

It was a sermon that I continued to rework and have presented in one form or another to several congregations, particularly when they were feeling challenged by the aging of their membership and shrinking finances and numbers.

I have come to realize that this sermon embodies my own "credo"—my trust that the God who is Love is revealed in me, in other people, in all my relations, in the entire creation. This God is not "a" person, but is not less than personal. This God, who can only be described through metaphor (often expanded into "story"), is involved in the unfolding of the universe (including the church), bringing about transformation… which is perhaps another word for resurrection. Although I do not explicitly mention the words "process theology" in the sermon, it is omnipresent, and undergirds the whole of what I am saying. This includes the understanding of who God is, how God has power, how we are called to behold and relate to this Mystery, and how we can be sustained by the promise of transformation—the "new." As the British-Swiss philosopher Alain de Botton has said, "The difference between hope and despair is a different way of telling stories from the same set of facts."

So, sisters and brothers, we gather from across Canada, here in Cornerbrook, Newfoundland, to participate in the United Church's 42nd General Council. We begin our Council, as always, in worship and in prayer, filled with hope and faithfulness, along with many questions and wonderings. So take a deep breath; hold it; now, let it out slowly; and then another…in…out. Let us come from where we have been and let us be where we are.

The theme of our Council is half a verse of Scripture from the second to last chapter of the Bible—Revelation 20:5b: "Behold, I am making all things new." So simple, so straightforward, this proclamation, this promise; seven words, all composed of one or two syllables; nothing fancy—and yet profound, scary, hopeful, challenging, exciting, worrisome…and…really, could it be true?

So, here's what I propose for this sermon, maybe reflecting that long ago I was an English teacher and remain a lover of words. I am inviting us to spend time with each word or phrase, lifting it up, examining it, as if it were a rare gem, shining, bright, rich in depth, calling out to us, demanding our full attention. Seven words—one sermon—fifteen minutes (hopefully).

And then, at the end, since any worthwhile sermon calls for engagement and dialogue, I'm going to ask you to turn to a neighbour and share which word speaks most evocatively to you at this moment in your faith journey. And why? What might your "chosen word" say about you, about the church, and this General Council, about what God is calling us to be and do?

Here we go: and the first word is "Behold." It helps to imagine the word written in caps, followed by an exclamation mark or two: BEHOLD!!—meaning, pay attention, look and listen; taste, touch and smell; feel and be mindful. In the King James Version, the word "behold" shows up 1298 times in the Bible—to Jacob, on the run: "Behold, I am with you and will keep you…."; with Moses: "…and behold, the bush burned with fire and was not consumed….”; to the prophet Jeremiah, “Behold, I have put my words in thy mouth.”; to the shepherds of Bethlehem, “Behold…I bring you tidings of great joy….”; to Thomas and the other disciples, “Behold my hands and feet….”

The basic premise of this word is that God is active in the world, is part of what is happening in the universe, is present in every moment—the omnipresent God. And our task is to see and hear the Holy Presence, to be open, ready, receptive, discerning. God is not so much a proposition, but an experience. We believe in God because we behold; although because we believe, we behold differently and more deeply.

Behold!—a summer's night when the sky is alive with stars; or when you are awakened by the dawn chorus of a thousand birds singing to greet the sun; or when a child runs up, so excited to show you a shiny beetle she has caught. Behold, and see the image of God in every neighbour, especially those who are different from you; especially those who are in need, who are hurting, whose suffering you might rather not see. “Behold!” says God; don't turn away.

Sometimes our poets help us see—Elizabeth Barrett Browning, for instance:

Earth's crammed with heaven,
And every bush afire with God.
Only those who see take off their shoes,
The rest sit around and pluck blackberries.
(from Aurora Leigh)

Or let me share some words that I scribbled down when walking by the ocean in Vancouver:

“Speak, Lord, for your servant is listening,”—
though I'm a little hard of hearing these days.
But with the wind in my face,
and my heart a monastery of open stillness,
I wait—
for there is a crack in everything,
that's how the light
gets out.
Watching for holy signs, I slowly walk the seawall:
waves ripple endlessly over sand and rock
gulls arc across the sky
and English Bay a-glimmer with golden light.

Answering God's invitation to "behold" leads us to awe, which sometimes can feel overwhelming, even frightening, because of the vastness of this Mystery, but ultimately, such awe moves us towards a new sense of wonder, and from there, it's an easy step to praise and gratitude.

"Behold! I am making all things new."

Now, the second word, "I"—but who is this "I" that is speaking? Certainly not the visionary writer, John of Patmos; not the multitudes of martyrs and elders; not the angels. No, it is the Holy One, (with John serving as a mouthpiece), God speaking directly and personally to the reader, the listener—to you and to me, to us, to the church, the community.

We say "God," knowing that this is shorthand, as we try and name and comprehend the Mystery in which we live and move and have our being; the Spirit, the Energy, the Breath that permeates all creation, so far beyond us...and yet, inside our bodies, our blood and bones. Over and over we turn to metaphors, and find ourselves drawn to the personal, hence the pronoun "I"—this Mystery is not an "it." But we need to be aware that when we are using metaphors such as Father, Mother, Lover, Friend; we must not take them literally, for God is not a person, no matter how big and vast; and further, to reify any one image is to lose the wisdom of multiplicity. God is not "a being" but perhaps better, the ground of being, or even being itself...but strangely and wonderfully, never less than personal, relational.

This is the God who speaks to Moses out of the burning bush, "I AM WHO I AM." Or the God who speaks through the poetry of the prophet Isaiah:

He who created you, O Jacob, [insert your own name]
He who formed you, O Israel: [again, insert your own name]
Do not fear, for **I** *have redeemed you;*
I *have called you by* name, *you are mine.*
When you pass through the waters, **I** *will be with you,*
And through the rivers, they shall not overwhelm you;
When you walk through fire you shall not be burned,
And the flame shall not consume you.
For **I** *am the LORD your God,*
The Holy One of Israel, *your Savior....*
You are precious in my sight,
and honored, and **I love** you.
*(*Isaiah *43:1-4)*

God is a "whatever" that is a "whoever," relational, connected to us and with us. And, trusting in this truth, perhaps one of the best descriptors for this most amazing "I" is to say that "God is Love."

Which leads me to say that this mysterious God, this "I" who is Love, is revealed in the life of Jesus. Of course, there is a multiplicity of revelations…from nature itself, the first incarnation; and through women and men of other faith traditions. Yet we who seek to follow in the Way of Christ might dare to say that Jesus is God's "best selfie." We can imagine Jesus as a lens through whom we see God, that sharpens our vision; with Jesus also functioning as a lens through which God beams light and love to and upon us.

The writer of John's gospel proclaims that, "Whoever has seen me [Jesus] has seen the Father" (Jn.14:9). And at various times, Jesus declares, "I am…the Way, the Light of the World, the Bread of Life, the Good Shepherd, the Vine. This last image is particularly evocative, because we all become the branches attached to, energized by, abiding in the mystery of God revealed in Jesus.

Hear the words of another poet, Rainer Maria Rilke, from "The Book of Hours"—

I am, you anxious one.
Don't you sense me, ready to break into being
at your slightest touch?
My murmurings surround you, like shadowy wings.
Can't you see me standing before you,
cloaked in stillness?
Hasn't my longing ripened in you from the beginning,
as fruit ripens on the branch?
I am the dream you are dreaming.
When you want to awaken, I am that wanting.
I grow strong in the beauty you behold!
And with the silence of the stars
I enfold your cities [your bodies, your churches]
[all] made by time.

We are called to love this "I," this God, with all our heart, soul, strength, and mind (Luke 10:27). We are called to remember that here and now, wherever we find ourselves…in church, in family, in neighbourhood, in the wilderness, God is present, and wanting to be in relationship; is seeking us out, waiting and hoping for our response, wanting us to fall in love, and to recognize and accept that we are already beloved.

And we respond, seeking to nurture this relationship, with prayer and spiritual practices, with openness and vulnerability, with silence and time, with heartache and joy, with confession and trust.

"Behold! I am making all things new."

Two words, so far... "behold" and "I"—does either call out to you? No? Yes? Maybe? Wait, don't answer the question yet—instead, let's keep going and look at the next phrase, "am making." Again, it must be the English teacher in me, the grammar nerd, but I love the tense of this action verb. It's called the continuous present," or even better, "the progressive present," which is to suggest that the "making" is always happening, is ongoing, is in constant process, always becoming. Such an understanding of ongoing creation fits well with our new scientific cosmology, as we discover the 13.8-billion-year journey our universe has been on and look to the mystery of this incredible creation unfolding over trillions of years to come.

God is engaged in time and history. "Creation" is not something that happened long ago, with God now watching with minimal interest. This "I" is still in the "making business," still getting involved; as we say in our United Church creed: "We believe in God who has created and is creating...." This progressive, continuous present tense contradicts any deistic vision, where God winds up the clock of the universe and then steps back, letting the world do its own thing. And, also, it challenges our functional atheism, where we give lip service to God's involvement, but truly act as if it's all up to us.

But that does bring us to the question of "how" God works. So, not distant and uninvolved; not an interventionist God, who occasionally stirs things up with a divine "big stick;" but also not the God who is omnipotent, totally running the show, over-riding any real choices made by humans, operating with a divine blueprint where everything is predestined. Not that kind of God at all.

An alternative understanding is to trust that God is involved in our lives, in the world; God operates in partnership with creation, active and powerful, but not all-powerful. One theologian claims that God's power is best understood as "uncontrolling love" (Tom Oord).

Over and over, in every moment, we are called upon to make choices. Most of them are automatic, almost unconscious, so shaped are we by our context, our past, our...well, you name it. But what if, even as the past rolls into the present moment and constrains our choices, what if in precisely that nexus of past, present and future, God is to be found, experienced, with energy, offering support, love, new possibilities, novelty? What if God is luring us towards a new vision, inviting us to choose the option among all possibilities that is most loving, most compassionate, most just, most life-giving, not just for ourselves, but for others, for the world. The future has power, like a magnet, pulling on us, drawing us forward into something new.

We are called to discern where God is active, in what direction the Holy is pulling us; we must read the signs. And then, we respond. We hit the dance floor, with God as our partner, leading the way in this grand adventure, moving forward, step by step, towards new possibilities of beauty, complexity, joy, and justice.

Or not. For we are free to ignore God, to act in ways that limit life, for ourselves, for others, for the earth. There are consequences from those decisions, sometimes disastrous ones—not as some holy, divine punishment, but because that's the way the world works. However, instead of judgment from God, this Uncontrolling Love continues to be present in us and with us; is present in the next moment, and the next moment, always presenting and energizing the choices that will, in this new context, maximize life.

So "[I] am making"…and God calls us to discern and respond; God offers visions and dreams; God shares energy and love so that we feel empowered to choose that which is life-giving. And this back and forth never stops. So think about your life; your family; your community; your neighbour; your church…and know that God is the mix of it all.

"Behold! I am making all things new!"

So, next phrase—"all things." Now, that's a pretty big order, "all things," or as the New Jerusalem Bible translates, "the whole of creation." Let me introduce a twenty-dollar theological word—"panentheism"—a fancy way of saying that God is in everything, and everything is in God. That's not the sum total of God, who is more, beyond time and space, beyond our imagining. But it is mindboggling just to ponder the notion that all things contain God-energy, all are sustained by God, all are in process, changing, being made and remade, over and over and over. From quarks to plankton to insects to humans to planets, to stars, galaxies, and black holes.

Let's start close to home…with ourselves, recognizing that each one of us is included in "all things"—you and me; we are each of us a tiny part of the whole of creation; the energy of God is within us, and all around us, and we are in a constant process of being made new. We often lose sight of this deep truth, caught up in our own personal struggles of self-worth, unable to be open to grace, dealing with trauma, both received and given. Can we ever simply accept that we are accepted? (Tillich). Can we embrace the forgiveness that is on offer, always present? Can we recognize our innate beauty and value, knowing that we are a precious part of creation, and the world would not be the same if we were not alive and present, empowered by God's energy and love?

Now stretch the phrase beyond yourself, recognizing "All things" embraces all human beings, including all those with whom you have difficulties, don't get along with, discriminate against. Although the DNA of any two people on earth is 99.6% identical,

unending wine at a wedding feast;
the last supper: break bread—eat, pour wine—drink;
the next supper: same upper room, with wind and fire for everyone.
The table's long; then longer still ...
(Gary Paterson)

We realize that a different life is possible, through the grace of God; that a different world is possible, if we say "yes," if we are open to this holy dream of justice, beauty, complexity, peace, joy, and compassion. We are called into a radical openness and we respond with a trust that enables us to let go of what is, filled with hope, that with the God who is Love, within us and all around us, we will keep on keeping on.

So...seven words—"Behold! I am making all things new. Now it's your turn. What word speaks to you, what ideas are evoked, what questions arise, what metaphors are illuminating? Choose your word or phrase; turn to your neighbour, and let's see what we will behold. Let's discover how even this conversation, with the grace of God, might contribute to making all things new.

Gary Paterson was ordained in 1977 as a minister in the United Church of Canada, now retired, having served congregations in Vancouver, from "skid row" to the downtown "Cathedralesque" church. In 2012, Gary (who is married to the first openly gay person to be ordained in the United Church (1992) was elected to be the Moderator of the National Church, the first openly gay person to be elected as the head of any major denomination in the world.

Living with a God Who Can't

RONALD S. PELT

The purpose of this essay is to share, as a layperson, my introduction to process-relational theology. For me, this way of imaging God opens new vistas and possibilities of understanding what having a relationship with God really means. I hope it will whet your appetite and encourage you to learn more.

My faith journey has been just that, a journey. Born and raised in the south, I was raised as a Southern Baptist. My parents were sincere, hardworking people who wanted me and my two older siblings to be good people. They wanted us to know that there are rules and boundaries in living with others, consequences to breaking those rules, and hope for improvement, including being forgiven and forgiving others, if at all possible. There was, in the church we attended, the expected amount of fear, fire and brimstone, but I don't think either of my parents fully bought into that kind of God.

The stories and interpretations of them I was taught in Sunday School about the wages of sin often scared me, but the stories about the life of Jesus and the things he said and did attracted and comforted me, with the exception of what some of the people in his life were capable of doing to each other and to him. Because a part of me always rejected or wanted to question some of what I was taught (because I wanted God to be lovable and fair) I always held back on being a full-throated devotee of what I was taught being a Christian meant by those teaching me.

I have all my life been a searcher, for Truth and an authentic way of living in this world. The one constant that I have found is the powerful reality of Love. My experience of being loved by my parents, siblings, friends and my late wife has given me a solid grounding in *that* reality.

I was introduced to process theology when I heard my current minister quote one of his seminary teachers, Dr. Frank Tupper, regarding the question of why God would or would not intervene in healing or curing a suffering child faced with a critical health issue. "God always does everything God can do," was Dr. Tupper's answer. At the time I don't think I understood the true meaning of that statement. My minister went on the explain that Dr. Tupper was speaking of a God who *could not* suspend the laws of physics or nature without taking away our basic freedom of being a human rather than a puppet. Further, this was not a Santa Claus or genie-in-a-bottle God. When I began reading and discussing Whitehead and Teilhard as well as the more contemporary philosophers and clergy who are teaching and preaching process thought and theology, I have found it to be one more refinement of the God I have always been yearning to know more deeply. The first time I really thought about a God who was not immutable, all powerful, fully aware of the future, my future, I realized that I no longer believed in that God anyway. But I couldn't put this awareness to words in a way that made sense to me, let alone try to explain it to someone else. While attending a recent conference on process philosophy, I realized that elusive God still caught me, still *lured* me to quote a process term.

So, what I am currently left with is the desire to dig deeper, learn more from others in this field of thought, and wrestle with the following questions:

1) What is it like to worship and seek relationship with the God who, by definition, cannot change or suspend the laws of nature?

2) What lures me towards this God? Why would I not choose to follow an omniscient, all powerful and controlling God with all the answers and solutions? What would this require me to give up? What would I gain?

3) What impact would process theology have on my day-to-day life as a person, a man, a Christian?

Here is what I have discovered so far from this new way of thinking and encountering God:

1) My old definition of worship has changed. I do not see worship as putting on a show of praise or adoration as a way to somehow manipulate God into thinking that "HE" has my loyalty. Process theology opens me to being in relationship with a mutual becoming with an all-loving God, rather than an all-powerful one.

2) The attraction to me of this God is not that God has all the answers, but that God goes through the questions with me. This does require me to give up the comfort of a God who will magically save me from the fear and pain of loss, but that is replaced with the intimacy of a God who loves me enough to grant me freedom from being a puppet or pet and believing in me as much as I do God.

3) The God I am becoming more in touch with is one who also gives me the responsibility of making minute by minute and day by day choices and decisions that aren't always easy, but ones that give me the opportunity to discover my own life; the same freedom that I have always wanted my children to have in living their own paths. This God also knows I will fall short and does not condemn me for being imperfect.

In case you're wondering, I am finding I do not have to let go of my sense of awe and wonder in following this God. In fact, I think I am learning to better live with mystery. A couple of years ago, I took training in contemplative prayer and I meet with a group on a regular basis. This is teaching me to calm my mind and pay attention to the becoming God who is often set before me like a burning bush. I am reminded of one translation of Moses' conversation before that burning bush. He asked God who he should tell Israel had sent him. The answer was, "I am becoming. Tell them that I am becoming has sent you to liberate them from their bondage."

This God is truly liberating me from fear and challenging me to love more fully. It is not an easy discipleship, but it is an inspiring and hopeful one.

Ron Pelt is a 75-year-old widower, artist, and a retired professional counselor. He is a member of a progressive Baptist church in Charlotte, North Carolina. His faith journey has taken him from a Southern Baptist beginning to the Presbyterian Church USA, and finally to a progressive Baptist church. In the gaps he has explored Buddhism, Taoism and the writings of Ram Dass, Alan Watts, John Spong, Paul Tillich, Lawrence and Harold Kushner, Jon Dominic Crossan, Marcus Borg and, more recently, Fr. Richard Rohr, Thomas Merton, Thomas Keating and Ilia Delio. Most recently he has been reading the process philosophy/theology of Alfred North Whitehead and Teilhard de Chardin. He lives in Matthews, North Carolina.

Should I Scrap the Trinity?

DANIEL J. PETERSON

Sermon that could have been: a no-holds-barred reflection on the nature of the Trinity in conversation with quantum physics.

For some time, theologians have conjoined discussion of the Trinity with that of process, open, or relational theism.

Process thought owes its inception to the philosopher Alfred North Whitehead who drew upon quantum physics to develop a new, dynamic understanding of the universe.

A helpful way of defining *quantum physics* comes from Clayton Crockett, a philosopher of religion. "Quantum physics studies matter at the subatomic level," he writes, "where it behaves in ways that defy our common sense." Rather than seeing reality through a microscope as a collection of tiny bits of matter, quantum physics focuses our attention on the stream of becoming that gives rise to the "relative stabilities" of the cosmos we identify as objects. Activity or "process" lie at the heart of everything.

Process theologians have since developed Whitehead's discussion of God as it occurs within his most popular work, *Process and Reality*. Rather than inhabiting an altogether different order of being, they claim, God constitutes and exemplifies worldly processes as they appear at the most basic level of *this* reality, *our* reality.

But how does it preach? Can quantum physics in conjunction with process theology illuminate Christian doctrine in a way that resonates with people sitting in the pews?

The sermon that follows (edited for publication) reflects my attempt to bring together a rudimentary understanding of quantum physics with classical Trinitarian theology. I preached it on Holy Trinity Sunday at Queen Anne Lutheran Church in Seattle where I am the pastor. Its message culminates in what I consider to be the greatest contribution of process, open, or relational theism: the observation that suffering and evil *do not* come from God.

The Message

Today is Holy Trinity Sunday, the only festival day Christians following the lectionary devote to a teaching of the church rather than an event in the life of Christ or the tradition that followed in his name.

As someone who likes to think about faith, Holy Trinity Sunday is the one Sunday of the year where I get to open my toy box and share with you what's inside. Instead of preaching on prophets or parables, I get to peak my head through the clouds and gaze with you at heavenly abstractions. I get to do theology. I get to talk about God.

For today's message, therefore, I plan to interpret what it means to say that God is three-in-one and one-in-three by comparing the Trinity with quantum physics. Both speak the language of paradox. Quantum physics tells us that at the most basic, microscopic level of reality, physical "objects" like quarks or electrons exist as waves *and* particles simultaneously. Scientists refer to this as the "wave-particle duality."

When we speak of the Trinity, we likewise point to a duality within God. On the one hand, God possesses what the theologian Daniel Migliore refers to as "three centers of personal distinction" (Father, Son, and Holy Spirit). At the same time, each of these "persons" reside in a matrix of love. This makes the Trinity a paradox too, a "relationship-person duality." We even have a name for this relationship. We call it love.

Love requires a plurality of "persons" to exist even as these "persons" are bound to each other in the oneness of their relationship. This "dance," to quote the title of a popular hymn, makes God three-in-one and one-in-three.

One of my favorite descriptions of the Trinity comes from Michael Himes, a Catholic priest and former professor at Boston College. He writes, "I think I can say, without too great an exaggeration, that the entire doctrine of the Trinity is an enormous [explanation of] that phrase in the First Letter of John [4:8] that God is [self-giving] love. From that metaphor spins out the whole of Trinitarian theology."

An Important Accent

Now let's add some nuance to our discussion. Recall my reference to the "wave-particle duality" of quantum physics: an electron exhibits properties of both. It can appear like a wave of energy. At the same time, it resembles a particle or "thing." By placing "wave" in front of "particle," which I did earlier, the accent falls on the primacy of relationship.

Are you confused? If so, a definition might help. The word "electron" is simply a combination of the words electric and ion. Notice which comes first. Linguistically, the answer is clear: the wave, the pattern, the buzzing and whirling of electricity, ever so slightly precedes the "thing," the particle, the ion.

The same is true of the Trinity. If we start with three "persons," we turn God into a bizarre constellation of three separate beings. This leads us to raise nonsensical questions like how three separate beings can somehow be the same being, after which we shrug our shoulders and chalk it up to mystery.

1 John 4:8 offers us a different point of departure. It says not that God is three persons who happen to be in love, but that God *is* love. This renders the relationship that exists between the "persons" of the Trinity primary.

When speaking of the Trinity, in short, we should start with the communion of love, the dance, the buzzing and whirling of electricity that exists between the persons rather than as the persons themselves.

Are you still confused? Consider Yahweh, the "name" for God we find in the Hebrew Bible. As Rabbi Rami Shapiro explains, "*YHVH* isn't a noun, but a verb... *YHVH* is an activity, be-*ing* itself rather than a being or even a supreme being.

The twentieth-century theologian Karl Barth expresses the same idea. For him, the being of God is an *event*. Because God is an event, speaking of God is "like trying to follow *a bird in flight* with your eye. The living God is always on the move" (Peter Bolt).

So, why does this matter?

It matters for two reasons. First, speaking of the Trinity in dynamic rather than static terms lifts the burden of having to believe—against reason—in the identity of three and one. (I think here of the theologian Paul Tillich who defines the task of apologetic theology as the removal of "artificial stumbling blocks.") Prioritizing *activity over stasis*, moreover, allows us to resist the temptation to pin God down, to reduce God to an entity or being whose existence is determined by the greater whole of reality rather than being the eternal *rehearsal of love* that gives rise to physical reality as its deepest source and groundless ground.

What a message for Holy Trinity Sunday: an unfettered, no-holds-barred reflection on the nature of the Triune God in conversation with quantum physics, one that shows how religion and science can work in tandem, how they are two swords that should never cross (Martin Marty).

But then I think of our second lesson for today, Romans 5:1-5. Here Paul ostensibly implies that "everything happens for a reason," that suffering somehow reflects God's will. This, in my mind, creates an even *bigger* problem for faith than the intellectual conundrum of believing in a TriuneGod. I wonder : should I scrap my attempt at describing the Trinity, or can it illuminate the problem of suffering from a theological perspective?

My Problem with Paul

Suffering has a purpose for Paul. It compels him to rely on God's power rather than his own, enabling him to do "all things through [he] who strengthens me " (Phil. 2:13, NRSV). God allows the thorn Satan had delivered to Paul's flesh (2 Cor. 12:7, NRSV) to linger *for a reason* which Paul unpacks in Romans 5:1-5: suffering produces endurance which builds character which leads to hope. It teaches us lessons.

I have no doubt we can learn from our suffering. As a boy I learned from my constant struggle with life-threatening asthma never to give up, to fight, and that quality of my character has served me well as an adult. My problem with Paul is that not *all forms* of suffering improve our character or make us better people. Suffering can bring us to our knees. It can destroy us.

I wish, therefore, that Paul had qualified his view of suffering by saying that it *can* produce within us greater endurance or better character. Unfortunately, Paul did not have the luxury of carefully nuancing everything he wrote. His letters appeared amid persecution, the kind under Nero that would eventually lead to his death.

There is something Paul wrote that we can change, however, not because we disagree with the apostle but due to a common mistranslation of a subsequent passage in Romans as evident in the majority of English Bibles.

Amid All Things

In Romans 8:28, Paul offers what seems to be the definitive explanation of suffering: "we know that all things work together for good for those who love God, who are called according to his purpose" (NRSV). Whatever trials we endure supposedly come from God. The Almighty supposedly works in a hidden way. We may not understand why suffer occurs, but we should trust that God has a plan, that everything happens for a reason, that "all things work together for good."

The oldest copy we have of Romans, on the other hand, says something different. Instead of indicating that God makes "all things work together for God," it says, "in all things God works for the good" (NRSV). Paul, in other words, "means not that all circumstances in this life are good for us...but that amid *all* these *things* God's purpose prevails" (*New Oxford Annotated Bible*, Rom. 28, n. 28-30; italics original).

God is *not* the one who causes us to suffer for some kind of inscrutable or mysterious reason. Instead, God as the power of love works through our trials the way God worked through the cross and resurrection of Christ, bringing renewal out of death, glory out of pain, and healing out of misery whenever possible. These things (life, renewal, and healing) come from God. Amid all things God works for the good.

The Good News

Dear friends in Christ, it turns out our reflection on the Trinity was not in vain. Instead, it gave us a vantage point from which to deny the claim that God uses pain for pedagogical purposes (i.e., to teach us lessons about faith).

Over the years I have seen more than a few of you suffer. I have been with you as you have laid to rest spouses, siblings, parents, and children. In circumstances like these, I have no words except to say except that God is love, which Paul confirms in the *oldest* copy we have of Romans 8:28.

Since God *is* love, the dance, the buzzing and whirling of electricity that exists as the relationship between the Father, Son, and Holy Spirit, then we cannot attribute suffering to God as part of "His" plan. That would be a contradiction.

The good news, the gospel, rejects the claim that God causes us to suffer "for our own good." God is not our enemy or an abusive parent. Instead, God remains with us "amid all circumstances" as pure, radiating love. God as love never abandons us, even if God cannot bandage all our wounds.

Today, let us commemorate the One-in-Three and Three-in-One by remembering God's nature: love, the secret power made manifest in and through the resurrection that cannot be conquered in life, even when life or suffering feels like it has conquered us.

Glory be to the Father, and of the Son, and the Holy Spirit.

Amen.

Daniel J. Peterson earned his Ph.D. in systematic and philosophical theology from the Graduate Theological Union in Berkeley. Formerly an instructor in theology at Pacific Lutheran University and then Seattle University, he is now the pastor of Queen Anne Lutheran Church in Seattle. In addition to various articles, he is the author of *Tillich: A Brief Overview of the Life and Writings of Paul Tillich* (Lutheran University Press) as well as the co-editor of *Resurrecting the Death of God* (SUNY Press).

"God Grows and Matures with Us"

KIM PURL

God's open and relational nature with Moses reveals a mutual growth and maturity from tyrants to servants.

Reading: Exodus 39:32 & 43, 40:34-38
Sermon series preached at Immanuel United Church of Christ,
Wright City, Missouri, November 12 and 19, 2023

We made it! We are at the last sermon in our Exodus series.

We have journeyed with the Children of Israel from slavery in Egypt to the unlikely birth of Moses. He is a spared Hebrew baby boy living in the tension of Pharaoh's palace. Moses flees to Midian after killing an Egyptian. Living like *hakuna matata* he marries and starts a family leaving his past behind. Then there is the burning bush, back to Egypt, ten plagues, Passover, parting of the sea, Mount Sinai, the Ten Commandments, and then the Golden Calf. It all broke. God. Moses. The tablets. The people.

If you were to ask me what was new for me on this journey through Exodus, I realized the rocky state of mutual relationship with God's people as a give-and-take for both God and the people. Yes, God, along with the people had to adapt, change, and realign. That's a big idea when most of my life I have heard that God never changes, only people.

Since sin has barred the way back to Eden, it makes sense that moving forward God partners with broken humanity to discover the potential of abiding together amidst the mess. Peter Enns in his book, *Exodus for Normal People,* states that Exodus is quite possibly God's best try at recreating the Garden of Eden, a place where God and all that is created are in harmony. Although Exodus is a roller coaster ride of great highs and lows, and in weariness God tries to ditch the Israelites; the covenant with Abraham is spared by a thread. What a rocky relationship!

The tightest relationship in Exodus is God's partnering with Moses. Their relational dialogue in problem-solving was intriguing. God changed. Moses changed. AND I changed in what I understood of my relationship with God. What if God grows with me in our partnered relationship? What if God has also grown in grace and love?

I had these relational questions in Exodus 32-33. God and Moses discuss their disgust and smoking hot anger over the Israelite's worship of the Golden Calf. God tells Moses of a plan to wrathfully consume the people and start over again with Moses, much like the story with Noah. Moses reminds God to keep the covenant that was promised because God will lose a strong reputation to the defeated Egyptians. God accepts the suggestion and holds back as if God has human qualities. After all, we are made in God's image.

The relationship takes a troubling turn and becomes violent, abhorrently abusive, and confusing. When Moses sees the Golden Calf, he gets irrational and calls the people to him who are on the Lord's side. He says that the Lord wants the people to go through the camp butchering disobedient relatives like an ancient holy war. This is not something that God has said. It appears Moses carries out a slaughter that he asked God not to follow through with. The slaughter of three thousand becomes a barbaric ordination for the Lord's service and a blessing. When Moses returned to the Lord, he requested God's forgiveness of the people's sins. God does not forgive. God encouraged Moses to go ahead and take the people to the Promised Land and God will stay behind. In a double gut punch, God strikes the people with a plague for their sins to add to the overly aggressive corporeal punishment. Although Moses and God are on speaking terms, their relationship with the Israelites is overly abusive and broken.

Out of the blue in Exodus 33:12 and following, Moses comes to his senses and has a heart-to-heart talk with God about their excessive abuse. After wielding a powerful hand with the people, Moses calls on God to forgive, restore relationship, and go with these imperfect people into the promised land. If not, the only option without God is to not go anywhere at all. God's presence is what makes God's people who they are: a people whose God is with them.

A divine God listens to the human request of Moses. God agrees with Moses and recommits to go with the people. This is profound. Our relationship with God is a partnership where human interaction matters to God. The human side of the partnership isn't always on the receiving end of the relationship but actively in dialogue and experiencing life together with life-changing outcomes.

From this convincing moment, Moses becomes bold in his relationship with God, not bothered by limited humanness. Confidently, Moses asks God to prove their relationship is unshakable, "Show me your glory." This showing of glory reminds us of the close relationship God shared with Adam and Eve in the Garden of Eden.

If we think through our human desires, we crave to have close proximity and relationships with great leaders. We want their autograph and a photo to prove we were close to them. God lives with us relationally, showing us glimpses of God's glory, glimpses of heaven on earth, in case we would ever doubt.

Without fanfare, God forgives and starts over again. New tablets are made. The tabernacle is built to completion in all its details. Today's passage reveals the completion of the tabernacle. God's glory fills the tabernacle. All is well in the world again. God lives among God's people. Yet, it is a far cry from the Garden of Eden. This is the desert wilderness. Nothing lives apart from God. In this desert place, God alone provides water, manna, and clothes that don't wear out. This is God's glory.

But this restored relationship didn't last forever. In time, the people sinned again. God's judgment fell on them again. Exile. Separation from God. And a long, cold silence.

These cold dead silences seem to be dead ends. Could these merely be portals that offer creative space to begin again? Endings create opportunities to put a stop to unhealthy patterns, learning from what didn't work. Moving forward together with God, we learn from our past and allow new possibilities to form and take shape.

Then at the right time. A messenger from God shared good news with Joseph and Mary.

God once again adjusted to what we needed. God was coming to us in the form of a human body, leaving a pillar of cloud and fire in the past.

Jesus, God's glory among us! Open and relational to each of us uniquely, living fully among us, continuing to journey with us in our foibles, taking the form of a servant to us, as we abide together. In solid relational commitment, Jesus submitted to our human misunderstandings of him. He was crucified, dead, buried, but on the third day was resurrected. Creating another major shift in the depth of the openness of our relationship, Jesus ascended to heaven and poured out an open-ended, relational Holy Spirit to fill us full to overflowing into our world. A Spirit abiding as God's glory. We carry this holy glory in our portable temple into the wilderness of our world. Practical. Portable. Loving God, loving others, loving ourselves.

Looking back on our Exodus journey holds more depth than looking back on what we have learned about God and Moses. It is beautiful to consider how God relates openly with us today. Whether the journey with God is painfully on the rocks or a glorious walk in the garden, our relationship with God is always moving and growing for the best of us and God together. I can trust a God who adjusts and grows with me and beyond me.

That is the glory of God revealed to me. Amen.

Kim Purl is a pastor at Immanuel United Church of Christ, Wright City, Missouri. She earned her D.Min. from Eden Theological Seminary in diversity and faith studies. Kim blogs for her church at immanuelucc.online and on her site at missouripastor.org.

To Be Emptied

VIKKI RANDALL

The assumptions we have about Jesus and the "omnis" shape our understanding of divinity and our life of faith.

Adapted from a sermon preached at First Presbyterian Church, Altadena CA April 30, 2023.

When he was five years old, our son Josh really loved bugs. So when we learned that there was an exhibit of giant bug sculptures at our local arboretum it seemed seemed natural to take him.

We arrived and were given a map to find the bugs hidden throughout, a fun scavenger hunt for enormous bugs carved out of beautifully polished wood.

We quickly found our first bug, a giant bumblebee, where it was displayed with a circle of rope around it and a sign that said, "Don't Touch." As we admired the artwork, a man in a baseball cap came up, ducked under the rope, and began touching and poking the sculpture.

We moved on to our second bug—a gorgeous dragonfly with a six-foot wingspan, perched by a lake. It had the same rope circle, the same sign that read, "Don't Touch." As we were admiring it, the same man joined us, again ignoring the sign to poke the piece.

This scene played out again and again as the same man with the baseball cap kept showing up to push and prod the sculptures. We were too timid to confront him directly, but we would remind our son, "Josh, the sign says, 'Don't touch'." Josh would reply loudly, "I'm not touching—*he's* touching!" But it made no difference.

Finally, we arrived at the last sculpture—a grasshopper at the top of a small waterfall. And again, the same man came up, ducked under the rope, and began poking. In fact, he pulled on the grasshopper's wing so hard that it came right off!

This took things to a new level. Now that he had actually damaged the artwork, it seemed imperative that someone throw this guy out. But there were no security guards to alert, so our only choice was to return to the volunteers at the entrance.

But at this point we had crisscrossed the 127 acres, ending up on the far end of the arboretum. Our kids were tired, so we stopped to rest. We noticed a bulletin board with photos showing the creation of the artwork. We enjoyed seeing the evolution of the sculptures as they grew out of solid blocks of wood.

Then we came to the final photo, of the artist in his studio.

It was the man in the baseball cap.

The man's identity had been hidden from me by my expectations and assumptions.

Emptying

Just as knowing the artist's identity changed the way I interpreted his actions, so also the expectations and assumptions we have about Jesus filter the way we read and understand the New Testament. Today we'll look at some of those assumptions we have about Jesus to gain a clearer picture of who Jesus is, particularly the meaning of the incarnation—that Jesus is God in human form—God with us.

Our text today is Philippians 2:5-11. I'm going to read now from the New International Version (NIV)—we'll compare that with other translations in a moment. In these verses, Paul is quoting an ancient hymn that brings us to the very center of our faith: the person and nature of Jesus Christ.

> Your attitude should be the same as that of Christ Jesus:
>
> Who, being in very nature God, did not consider equality with God something to be grasped, but made himself nothing, taking the very nature of a servant, being made in human likeness.
>
> And being found in appearance as a man, he humbled himself and became obedient to death—even death on a cross!
>
> Therefore God exalted him to the highest place and gave him the name that is above every name, that at the name of Jesus every knee should bow, in heaven and on earth and under the earth, and every tongue confess that Jesus Christ is Lord, to the glory of God the Father.
>
> — Philippians 2:5-11 (NIV 1984 ed.)

What is being celebrated and honored in Phil. 2 is Jesus' incarnation—the notion that in Jesus, God takes on human flesh. The hymn parallels an event, recorded in John 13, when Jesus and his disciples gathered in an upper room. Jesus unexpectedly takes on the role of a servant to wash their feet.

Paul describes this act of incarnation as Jesus "emptying himself," using the Greek word *kenosis*. This is the same word found in John 13 when Jesus pours out water on the disciples' feet. But here it is Jesus himself who is poured out. What's happening is something that goes to the core of who Jesus is. It changes not only the way we understand Jesus, but even more so the way we understand the very nature of God.

Why does Jesus do this?

The first question we might want to ask about this emptying is: Why does Jesus do this? Returning to our text—this time in the NRSV translation.

> Let the same mind be in you that was in Christ Jesus, who, though he was in the form of God, did not regard equality with God as something to be exploited, but emptied himself, taking the form of a slave, being born in human likeness.
> — Philippians 2:5-7 (NRSV)

The two translations are very similar, with one key difference. There are several ways to translate the conjunction in verse 6, all viable in the Greek. One way is how the NRSV has translated it: "<u>though</u> he was in the form of God... Jesus emptied himself." This is the way most of us tend to think of the incarnation—as something Jesus did "though," or "even though," he was God. We tend to think of the incarnation as a momentary pause in Jesus' divinity—something later resumed in the second half of the hymn when Jesus is exalted and given the name above all names.

But notice again how the NIV translates it—"*being* God... Jesus emptied himself." This is an equally valid translation. Gerald Hawthorne goes even further in the Word commentary, translating it "*precisely because* he was God... Jesus emptied himself."

What Hawthorne and the NIV are highlighting is the belief that the incarnation is not a momentary exception to Jesus' divinity. Rather, they suggest the incarnation is the *precise fulfillment*—the ultimate expression—of what it means to be God.

Jesus doesn't empty himself <u>*despite*</u> being God. Jesus empties himself *precisely because* he is God.

In John 14:9, Jesus says that if you see him, you've seen God. Jesus is the clearest picture we have of God. If Hawthorne and the NIV are correct, then Phil. 2 changes the way we understand Jesus and his incarnation. It changes our whole understanding of divinity—of what it means to be God.

What is Jesus emptying himself of?

Next, we ask: What exactly is Jesus emptying himself of? Some commentators see Jesus emptying himself of divine glory, the indignity of becoming human.

But I think there's a better answer. Building on themes found in Eastern Christianity, some theologians associate this emptying with setting aside the "omnis"—omniscience, omnipresence, and omnipotence—or God as all-knowing, all-present, and all-powerful.

That might seem odd to us at first. We have been trained to think of the "omnis" as the very definition of divinity. However, that notion comes from Greco-Roman philosophy more than biblical revelation.

And in fact, the notion that the "emptying" of Phil. 2 is about Jesus setting aside the "omnis" makes sense. It is consistent with what we see in the Gospels, where Jesus usually appears to be bound by space and time, not knowing some aspect of the future. Even the miracles of Jesus are usually portrayed as Jesus drawing not on his own power, but on the Holy Spirit.

But traditionally, Christians believe that Jesus is fully God and fully human. While the picture of Jesus as bound by space and time, with limited power and imperfect knowledge sounds fully human, does it endanger the fully God part of the equation?

One way to look at the question is to differentiate between *relative* attributes and *essential* attributes.

Our family loves to play telephone Pictionary. We've come up with some shorthand ways to represent each family member. If we draw someone with a beard that's our son, Josh. Someone with a manbun is my son-in-law Matt. My husband Rory is always represented with a pocket tee.

Those are all distinctive qualities—things that set them apart. Yet—are they defining qualities? Would Matt still be Matt without his manbun? Would Rory still be Rory without his pocket tee?

Of course, they would. So, we see all sorts of attributes that may at first seem defining—someone with a beard or pocket tee—that are, in fact, not defining. They can divest themselves of these attributes without losing their essence. Their essential nature—their "Roryness"— is something much deeper and more essential.

I believe that at the incarnation Christ divested himself of the relative attributes of omniscience, omnipresence, and omnipotence, but retained the things essential to divinity.

So, what are these "essential attributes"?

It's challenging to describe God, so most statements about God are metaphorical. The Bible describes God as a rock, a parent, a midwife, and a mother hen. But one of the few non-metaphorical declarative sentences about God is 1 John 4:8: God is love.

It doesn't say "God is loving," or "has love" or "does love"—but *God is love*. Emil Brunner says that "God is love" is the most daring statement ever made in the human language. Love is God's defining characteristic.

Coupled with the earlier thoughts about *why* Jesus empties himself, we can see that Phil. 2 makes a radical, audacious statement, not just about Jesus and the incarnation, but about the nature of divinity itself. In Phil. 2, Jesus shows us that the essence—the defining, core attribute of God—is not the relative assets of omnipotence or omniscience. Being God is not about being the biggest dog on the block, ruling over all by virtue of strength and might. Rather, Jesus shows us that the defining, essential characteristic of God is radical, sacrificial, incarnational love.

This is why Jesus is exalted and honored in vv. 9-11, why "every knee should bow." Not as a reversal of the emptying that came before, but as a celebration of it. Every knee bows because, in Jesus, we can look beyond our faulty assumptions and see God as God truly is. That changes everything.

What does this mean for us?

So, what does this mean for us today? What changes for us as we go forward?

After Jesus washed the disciples' feet, John 13:14 tells us he told them to do likewise. Both John 13 and Phil. 2 are urging us to follow Christ's example of sacrificial, self-giving love.

Theologian Greg Boyd has said, "the most powerful predictor of the quality of your life is your picture of God. Allow your picture of God to be shaped by Jesus."

If our picture of God is shaped by power and control, then that's what will take shape in our lives. As we go out into the world, we will see our job as taking charge, being in control.

But the picture of Jesus found in Phil. 2 is one not defined by control, but rather by service and sacrificial love. Boyd describes this as "power under" rather than "power over." As we live out our life in Christ, may we be shaped by this picture of Jesus, defined not by control, but by incarnational, self-giving love.

> Come, Lord Jesus come. Come into our hearts today. Help us see you ever before us—in the face of every person we meet, created in your image. Help us draw near to you and set aside our desire for control or power over and

embrace instead your calling to power under. Help us live that out in a beautiful and broken world. Amen.

Vikki Randall lives in Monrovia CA, and has 28 years of pastoral experience, serving large and small churches, mostly in PCUSA. She received a D.Min. in spiritual formation from Azusa Pacific Seminary and has served there as adjunct faculty in undergrad theology since 2003. She is passionate about transformation and experiencing God's presence.

"Life's Unfair—and It's All God's Fault!"

TIM REDDISH

"Life's unfair—and it's all God's fault!" is a common enough assertion, but did you know this sentiment is to be found in the Bible?

Reading: Ruth 1:6-21; 4:13-17 (*NRSV*)
Sermon preached at St. Andrew's Presbyterian Church, Amherstburg, Ontario, May 9, 2021

The astute reader will realize that this sermon is not explicitly from a process theology perspective. This is deliberate on my part as I do not typically try to shoehorn my open and relational theism into my sermons since that could be critiqued as eisegesis. Nevertheless, this particular sermon is consistent with a process perspective, as the divine action or influence in this story is very much one of being hidden or behind-the-scenes and largely instigated by Ruth. Furthermore, at the end of the story the narrator leaves the reader convinced that God has been at work.

"Life's unfair—and it's all God's fault!" Have you heard your mother say that? And let's face it, mom's (and wives) do have a lot to put up with. For example, whoever tidies the home—and it's still usually moms even today—will find it all messy again within 24 hours, and that's rightly frustrating. Often children *won't* listen, husbands *don't* listen, and life can sometimes seem so unjust. "I don't deserve this," says a mom, "This isn't what I expected; parenting is so hard, juggling a home and a career is so difficult, I give, give, give—life's just cruel." And if you're a single mom, it's understandably even worse. Nevertheless, you don't have to be a woman to say, "life's unfair—and it's all God's fault," men say it too. And sometimes we say that and *mean* it! We have to blame *someone*, and who better than God?

You might be surprised to know that this angry sentiment is in the Bible and comes from the lips of Naomi, as we heard in our reading from Ruth (see Ruth 1:20-21). And she seems to have had a point. Naomi had married Elimelech, whose name means "My God is King," and from a traditional Jewish perspective, God had blessed them with two sons. We are also told that the family were Ephrathites from Bethlehem, and this introduces some bitter irony to the story. "Bethlehem" means "House of Bread," yet the story begins with a famine (see Ruth 1:1). But there is worse news: the family had moved to Moab for a time and, while there, Naomi's husband had died. Now, her two sons married Moabite women, Ruth and Orpah, and they lived in Moab for a decade when, we are told, the two sons also died. No wonder Naomi was drowning in her sorrows; we can truly empathize with her. In those patriarchal times, that meant Naomi had zero security and was effectively homeless. There were apparently no children, no young heirs with any rights, so the label "Ephrathite" meaning "fertile" or "fruitful" was also just a cruel joke! "Life's unfair—and it's all God's fault," says Naomi, and we can perhaps begin to appreciate why she feels abandoned by God. But there is more. Naomi's two daughters-in-law were Moabites, and this clan were widely viewed by Jews with deep disgust because they were descendants of Lot through his eldest daughter (see Gen 19:30-38). We have to therefore see a racial element here. Just as the Samaritans were despised by Jews in Jesus' day—and that clearly adds power to the parable of the good Samaritan (see Luke 10:25-37)—in a similar way Ruth and Orpah being Moabites is relevant in this story. Incidentally, the unsure dating of the book of Ruth is a factor here too. I assume an early post-exilic date, during the time of Ezra and Nehemiah when there was a bias against foreigners and inter-marriage (see Ezra 9:1-4; Nehemiah 13:23-27; Deuteronomy 23:3.)

That is the background to the book of Ruth, which despite its obvious initial tragedy, is a beautiful, uplifting, pastoral story with multiple themes in the context of *relationships*. It is a parable concerning a woman whose life has fallen apart, a woman who eventually finds a new family, and a man who finds a wife. It is also a story about love, loyalty, and kindness far beyond any cultural expectations and beyond anything that the recipient expects or deserves to receive. The book of Ruth is also a story concerning racism, prejudice, and being the outsider, and about how to survive as a woman in a man's world. It's not the Jewish equivalent of a cheap romance story. It's all about God's involvement in the lives of ordinary people. The story portrays God's provision behind-the-scenes through human action, as well as through chance (see Ruth 2:3, which says, "as it happened" (NRSV), and 4:1. In fact, the story's narrator only mentions God's action explicitly in Ruth 1:6 and 4:13, the rest is implied through the words and actions of others.) Above all, the story illustrates what it means for God to be a *redeemer* and a *restorer*. Let's explore it briefly.

Naomi hears that Israel's God has provided food for his people (Ruth 1:6), so she decides it is time to leave Moab for Judah, and Ruth and Orpah come along as traveling companions. At some point along the way, perhaps nearing Bethlehem, Naomi says to her two daughters-in-law, "Go back each of you to your mother's house" (Ruth 1:8, NRSV). Naomi wants the best for Ruth and Orpah; she blesses them in the name of Israel's God for their kindness and loyalty, but the time has come to recognize that the legal bond they had together through marriage (rather than a blood tie) is long over. Ruth and Orpah are young enough to remarry Moabite men, and so Naomi urges them to consider their future as best being served back in Moab. The response is tears and grief. They said to her, "No, we will return with you to your people" (Ruth 1:10, NRSV). Naomi then spells it out again in the context of the customs of the day (i.e., Levirate marriage, see Deut 25:5-10), saying she has no men up her sleeve that she can magically conjure up as husbands for them. That realism is also mixed with grief and a sense of hopelessness, in that Naomi concludes, "No, my daughters, it has been far more bitter for me than for you, because the hand of the LORD has turned against me" (Ruth 1:13, NRSV). Consequently, it doesn't make any logical sense for you align yourself with me, says Naomi. And the response is more tears and grief. We are told Orpah obeys her mother-in-law, kisses her, and returns; she has done absolutely nothing wrong in that. Ruth, however, defies commonsense and clings to Naomi (see Ruth 1:14).

We then hear one of the most remarkable speeches on love, loyalty, and commitment in the whole of the Bible: Ruth tells Naomi, "Stop urging me to abandon you! For wherever you go, I will go. Wherever you live, I will live. Your people will become my people, and your God will become my God. Wherever you die, I will die—and there I will be buried. May the LORD punish me severely if I do not keep my promise! Only death will be able to separate me from you!" (Ruth 1:16-17, NET). Ruth is absolutely determined to stay with Naomi. The deaths they have both experienced have created a bond stronger than life. Regardless of what sorry future they could expect together, Ruth will abide with Naomi. Ruth recognizes that she may be rejected as an immigrant, or worse—as a Moabite; even so, Naomi's Jewish people will be her people come what may. But more than that, Ruth will align herself with Israel's God. And she vows that she will eventually be buried alongside Naomi. Ruth is willing to die to her past so that she and Naomi may live anew. What a declaration!

If Ruth's speech wasn't dramatic enough, when they finally arrive at Bethlehem, the narrator then gives a further speech of Naomi's. It's been ten harsh years and the women of the town barely recognize her. Naomi, whose name means "pleasant" or "sweet," says, "Don't call me "Naomi" anymore, call me "Mara"—which means "bitter"—for God has dealt bitterly with me. I went away full, but the LORD has brought me back empty" (see Ruth 1:20-21). "Woe is me," complains Naomi. Evidently, the loss of her husband and two sons was all God's fault in Naomi's mind.

When you hear this story, with whom do you most identify? Ruth or Naomi?

Here is another question: "Who does the *narrator* want you to align with? I encourage you to read this short book again and decide for yourself. I suggest, however, that the original Jewish readers were faced with a dilemma. Ruth's admirable loyalty and kindness might have encouraged them to think that they ought to behave like that. But could they get beyond the fact that she was a shunned Moabite? This is, in fact, a story of redemption and restoration. But who needs redeeming here? Is it really Ruth? Perhaps Naomi is the character that most closely mirrors the attitudes and experiences of the people of God—including the church. As is already evident, it's Jewish Naomi who really needs redemption in the story. Faithful Ruth is, unknowingly, God's surprising agent in accomplishing Naomi's reversal from bitterness to joy. Yet how can that be? Ruth is not Jewish! This story, then, is about *reform* as well as *redemption*. But for that message to be heard, the people of God in every generation must identify themselves with the one who needs to be redeemed, to have their lives turned around. This only works if we can be persuaded that the behind-the-scenes efforts made by an ever-faithful God on Naomi's behalf will be made by God on our behalf as well—and, in this case, through an unexpected avenue: Moabite Ruth. Yes, we ought to be like Ruth, but do we recognize that we are, in fact, more like Naomi, with a sense of entitlement and blaming God when things don't go as we expect? Who do we want to blame for our griefs and life's hurts? For cancer and COVID? Are we with Naomi and blaming God?

The story of Ruth and Naomi moves on. There is an apparent chance encounter with a wealthy landowner called Boaz, who turns out to be a kind, Godly man, and a distant relative of Naomi (see Ruth 2:1, 3). Boaz, on hearing the story of Ruth's loyalty to Naomi (Ruth 2:11-12), allows Ruth to glean grains of barley with his servants in his fields. On hearing this news, and as Naomi's grief begins to heal, she invokes the LORD's blessing on Boaz for his kindness and generosity (Ruth 2:20). It would appear as if Naomi is even beginning to think of God as a potential source of blessing. One thing leads to another, both romantically and—in the end—legally, and Boaz marries Ruth, and they have a son (Ruth 4:13). The story starts in tragedy and bitterness, and ends in a grandson, an heir, and joy (Ruth 4:14-17). The women of Bethlehem proclaim to Naomi that the child will restore her life and be the source of security and nourishment in her old age (see Ruth 4:15). They also attribute this blessing to God and to Ruth's kindness, love, and loyalty that is worth more than *seven* sons.

There is a further crucial point: The child of this marriage of a Jew to a Moabite is the grandfather of Israel's great King David. Ruth was therefore instrumental in blessing *all* Israel, and blessing the *whole world* because she is also mentioned in the genealogy of Jesus (see Matt 1:5-6). One of the underlying questions is can a non-Israelite, even a despised Moabite, become part of God's people. Clearly, the answer is "Yes." God can—and does—achieve his redemptive purposes through all kinds of people, and in the least likely of ways. One of the messages of the book of Ruth is that God chooses to redeem those, such as Naomi, who seem to have done little to deserve redemption. That is a feature of divine *grace*. In fact, the book of Ruth is primarily concerned with the faithfulness of God rather than the faithfulness of the people of God.

Let me conclude with a comment and a question. I, like you, have often heard the saying, "Everything happens for a reason." On one level, this seems fatalistic. Sometimes it is used to imply God knows the reason—though we cannot, but not to worry, "Everything will turn out alright in the end." I believe such phrases, though well-meaning, offer little comfort. While Naomi may now have a grandson, she remains a widow. Clearly, redemption doesn't *restore* everything. Nevertheless, I believe God is the "Life-Maker" *not* the "Life-Taker." I also believe that: "Nothing is wasted in God's economy." Tragedy and loss, though not from God, can—with God's behind-the-scenes influence and with the loving kindness of others—result in something good and beautiful that benefits others in unforeseeable ways. As you look back on your life, my hope is that you can also recognize signs of God's faithfulness as tragedy, disappointment, and even bitterness have been transformed into new opportunities and joy. If that is the case, give thanks to God and be a blessing to others.

And my question is this: Who are the "Moabites" that we disdain today who might actually be a surprise blessing and a means of our own redemption?

Tim Reddish has a Ph.D. in Physics from Manchester, UK, and an M.Div. from Knox College, Toronto. In late 2022, he retired from St. Andrew's Presbyterian Church, Amherstburg, having been their minister for nearly 5 years. His previous career was as a physics professor at the Universities of Windsor (Ontario) and Newcastle upon Tyne (UK), researching in experimental Atomic, Molecular and Optical Physics for 25 years. He spent his formative years in Nigeria, where his parents were missionaries, and has a diverse church background—Assemblies of God, Baptist, Anglican, and Presbyterian. Tim and his family moved to Canada in 2002. His first wife, Anne, died of cancer in 2011. His son, Philip, and his family now live in Edmonton and Tim is a grandfather of three. Tim remarried eleven years ago and enjoys being a stepdad to four young adults. He and his wife, Mary, live in Old Riverside, Windsor. He loves reading theology, watching British detective stories and period dramas, F1 racing, and photography. He is also the author of four books and co-editor of another (all available from Amazon), including *Does God Always Get What God Wants?* (Cascade, 2018).

On Not Giving Up

MANUEL SCHMID

Our life is not a construction kit according to a fixed blueprint. It is a creative chaos in which God demonstrates the Divine love for us.

Reading: 1 Cor. 13:4-7
Sermon preached at the International Christian Fellowship, Basel, Switzerland, May 2, 2021

The Vision of Love

Remember the last wedding you attended. Yes, it was certainly very romantic and heartwarming. But actually, isn't it totally crazy at the same time?

Everyone knows what ugly catastrophes can result from marital relationships. It is a known fact that when you uncompromisingly pledge your love to someone, you also give them the power to drive a spike through your heart and cause wounds that will never fully heal. Everyone knows stories, mostly from their immediate environment or relatives, in which a love story turned into an unparalleled drama, a mudslinging, a feast of destruction.

Trust in each other is slowly lost or cruelly abused until former soulmates become two strangers or even enemies. The wife learns that she has been cheated on by her partner. All the repulsive stories come to light, and she lies awake at night struggling with the abysmal pain of rejection. Or the husband is left for another, and he's still wearing the wedding ring five years later because he can't bring himself to acknowledge the end of his love. On Christmas he locks himself in and gets drunk because he can't stand the loneliness haunted by all the memories....

Not to mention the fate of the children.

No, it seems to be a clear-cut case: one would have to warn strongly against marriage!

In fact, the bride's parents should hold up large banners in front of the church saying, "Don't do it!", "Think again!" The groom's siblings would have to jump up during the ceremony and shout without restraint, "Say no!" to prevent disaster. Or best of all, kidnap the priest in advance. In any case, all those present at a wedding would have to bite their lips or avert their eyes in horror as soon as the bride enters the center aisle.

There is probably no other situation in which you can be more deeply hurt, more severely disappointed, more permanently discouraged than in a marriage that comes to a bad end.

And still the daredevils have not died out!

Every year, couples get married anew—every early summer, the door of our refrigerator fills up again with wedding announcements and invitations. Even people who have already been through a divorce, who have experienced the breakup of a marriage with all its hurts and bitterness, often walk down the center aisle of the church a second time and get involved in a partnership yet another time.

How is that possible? Why on earth do people risk such an unpredictable endeavour?

There is probably only one reasonable answer—and this is also the reason why seasoned men furtively wipe away their tears of emotion at weddings and women get goose bumps in hottest midsummer: because the vision I have of a successful marriage, the vision of community between two people who love and are there for each other and write a common history together—because this vision grips me more than the fear of the dangers I could run into with it. Because I am convinced: I am willing to pay the highest price for the prospect of a living love relationship with this person.

Love is worth the risk.

A Very Fat Book

This is what makes God willing to stick to the Creator's story with us, to take the risk of love—this is what makes God vulnerable and pay even the ultimate price to win us for the Savior's love: the vision of sharing a home with you and me and with people from all countries and cultures. To live with us in community.

And God pursues this goal with an amazing perseverance.

Sometimes theology students or even visitors to our church services have complained to me about the appalling volume of the Bible. Secretly, of course, behind closed doors—as a good Christian or prospective pastor, you don't want to embarrass yourself—but let's be honest:

Who still reads such a thick book nowadays?

Because that's what it is, the Bible—not slim, not full-figured, it's—you can't sugarcoat it anymore!—really thick! Do we really have to struggle through all these pages? Couldn't God have given us a shorter book—one that reads more quickly and leads more quickly to the glorious end?

Yes, of course the Almighty could have done that—actually everything speaks for the fact that the Creator intended exactly that when God called this creation into being! Considering only God's plan, the Bible would probably have simply become a folded brochure with the story of creation and the last two chapters being from the revelation.

But God is not the only one involved in this story—it is ***not God who makes this story fifteen hundred pages thick—t is us!*** We humans, with our tendency to refuse to trust God and to do our own thing, we humans, with our stubborn self-will and incorrigibility—*we are the ones* dragging out this story like Peter Jackson dragged out the film version of "The Hobbit"!

The size of the Bible, in other words, does not prove that God cannot be brief—this thick book proves that Almighty God does not give up fighting for God's people, for all humankind, for us!

This long story shows unmistakably that God is willing to pay any price to win us for fellowship with the Heavenly Father! "God will not let us go,"—that is the headline for this chunk of a book!

Over literally hundreds of chapters, it describes what God has done to win the love of humankind and to preserve the relationship with humanity. Through countless setbacks and disappointments, the Almighty holds fast to Israel, is not deterred by their waywardness, and is willing to start over again and again. This is a highly complex, long-lasting relationship story full of dead ends, detours, and unexpected turns—not a straight course toward the goal, but rather an expedition on rough terrain—a path that demands everything of God.

Vulnerable, but not Weak

But let us not neglect to talk about Jesus Christ himself.

Nowhere does God come closer to us and willingly become more vulnerable than here, in this infant in Bethlehem, in this man from Nazareth.

Jesus proves how serious God is about our Savior's vision for us.

In Jesus, we encounter this God in person, who has been writing the Creator's love story with us since time immemorial—but at first, it looks as if the rebellion of God's creatures, our self-will and brokenness, will get the upper hand.

Jesus ends up on the cross.

This God who willingly becomes vulnerable through the Savior's love for us, this God who designed us to be the Creator's counterpart and seeks our communion, is literally driven out of Jerusalem in Jesus Christ—chased out of his dwelling place—and executed as an outcast. Is this the frustrating end of the greatest love story of all time?

We should not be deceived.

Certainly, this God, revealed to us in Jesus Christ, unsurpassably demonstrates the vulnerability of the Creator's love. But Jesus also proves God's perseverance, God's holy intransigence in how the Lord deals with us human beings. This God never loses sight of the Almighty's goal, and even through death, Lord God finds ways to reach us.

Yes, Christ is vulnerable—but not powerless.

He lets himself be disappointed—but he does not lose heart.

He lets himself be rejected—but he doesn't give up.

He is executed—but he does not stay dead.

In Jesus Christ, we encounter a God who, precisely ***through*** vulnerable love, defeats the powers of death and blasts open the tomb—not only literally in his resurrection, but also in the lives of countless people: Jesus overcomes that which draws humanity away from the presence of God. Our Savior's uncompromising love takes on our mistrust and selfishness, which sets humanity on a course of destruction from the very beginning and drags God's whole creation down—and the Savior wins our heart again.

Christ is not deterred by Peter's fear and cowardice, in which he denies his friend and makes off—no: Jesus later searches for Peter and gives him a new opportunity to testify to his love for him and to continue writing the story with him. He does not give up on Peter; he does not write him off after his failure, but makes of him the leader of a revolutionary Jesus movement.

This Jesus is not discouraged by the hostility of the religious leaders who had longed for his death and plotted against him—no: he later meets one of the most zealous persecutors of emerging Christianity and wins in him one of his most passionate followers. Of all people, the former Pharisee and Christian-hater, Paul thus becomes the greatest missionary of the Jesus movement.

Neither does Jesus allow himself to be intimidated by the malice and cruelty of the Romans—no: still on the cross he speaks forgiveness to those who have maltreated and tortured him; he dies with love in his heart and on his tongue. This moved a Roman centurion, who observed and was responsible for the execution of Jesus, so much that he became convinced: "This was indeed the Son of God!" Countless other Roman citizens subsequently become believing Christians—and the message of Jesus is carried on Roman streets throughout the world.

Don't be fooled: ***this God, who revealed the Savior as Jesus Christ, achieves with persistent love what manipulation and control will never accomplish—God wins the love of people and continues to write the Creator's story with them.***

This Jesus does not let us go. He writes his story with us and reaches the goal with our lives, even through setbacks and resistance. Including our foolishness and stubbornness. God does not give up on us!

LEGO

Our son is an absolute LEGO fan. He had already started building Duplo towers when he could barely crawl—and the fascination with these little colorful building blocks has never left him. For many years, there was no greater joy to be had than spending time with him building LEGOs. Even when the sun came out for the first time after weeks of rain—our son didn't want to go out to the playground—he wanted to stay inside with his building block projects.

Sometimes you can learn something about God and life just by playing with children.

One day, a light dawned on me when I was sitting in front of a mountain of LEGO bricks with our son a few years ago to build something together with him. That's a special moment. Infinite possibilities lie before us: what can't be made of all those building blocks!

I suggested: "Let's build an unbeatably fast, sporty car!" Our son was immediately on board. We set to work, and he eagerly assembled the elements, picked out the wheels and other special parts. But the longer we built the thing, the less it looked like a car. At some point, my son got frustrated: this is not a car, this thing would never be able to drive. And I, too, had to finally admit: *As a car,* this had now really become unusable. Of course, I can't *say* that, and as I held our construct in my hands, an idea came to me: yes, it won't be a car—but what we have before us here is the *precursor of a magnificent submarine*! Our son was spontaneously inspired by this alternative plan, and so we left out the wheels and continued building, trying to achieve a semblance of a submarine. Unfortunately, this attempt did not meet with success either—and soon our son complained again: 'but this is not a submarine at all!' The mood threatened to tip again, he felt he had screwed everything up and will never be able to become a great engineer. Then the scales fell from my eyes: this was not a car, nor a submarine—this was the *hull of a huge spaceship!* Come on, son, don't be discouraged, we are constructing a spaceship! As if in ecstasy, we continued to work, digging with renewed vigor into the LEGO pieces and assembling a spaceship that would have made even Captain Kirk green with envy. And at the sight of which I suddenly understand more fully God's way with us.

Many Christians imagine God's story with us as a LEGO kit according to instructions: like a cardboard box with a picture of the final result on the front and 1537 parts inside. In addition, a construction plan—a fixed plan for our life—and God is now working through this with us page by page. Everything is counted. Every particle has its predetermined place here. A huge project with thousands of elements—and these must absolutely land in the right place, so that it results in what God has in mind for us.

But the stories God writes in the Bible with the Creator's people and individuals give a different impression—they are actually much more reminiscent of the interactivity and flexibility of free LEGO building between a Father and Son.

And that's good news.

Perhaps you look back on capital mistakes that you have made, on things that you have brutally screwed up—people whose trust you have gambled away, financial mistakes that have cost you dearly, professional decisions that you bitterly regret, moments of personal failure you can hardly forgive—and you get the impression that you have assembled some parts of your life completely wrong. You know: if life is put together according to a predetermined construction kit, then it will at best become "modern art" for you, but nothing that really comes to fruition.

Don't be deceived: God pursues divine purposes with you through all mistakes and dead ends—always at least one idea ahead of you!

And even if you remember deep hurts and traumatic experiences in your biography—maybe indeed the breakup of your marriage with all its pain and disappointment, maybe even the experience of psychological or physical abuse, maybe the mourning for a loved one you lost—and it feels as if you have been robbed of important "components" in your life; it feels as if the "kit of your life" is incomplete and no one can give you back the missing pieces, remember:

God Almighty remains in your life!

And if the Creator doesn't make it drive, it will swim, and if the Great Inventor doesn't make it swim, it will fly—in any case, the One who started this story with you doesn't get sidetracked, doesn't get intimidated, doesn't get rattled:

God will weave your shared story to a good end, together with you!

Many thanks to Mark Moser for his help with the translation of the text!

Dr. Manuel Schmid is a philosopher and systematic theologian. He worked as a pastor of a Swiss youth church for 17 years and has been running the pioneering digital project "RefLab" (www.reflab.ch), which publishes podcasts and videos for the past five years. "RefLab" is part of the Reformed Church of the Swiss Canton of Zurich.

"Future Needs a Big Kiss"

LUKAS TARGOSZ

In an unpredictable world full of suffering and pain, we need to find a relational God who responds to our decisions with heavenly embrace—and then surprise him with faith and love.

Readings: John 15:15, 1 Corinthians 3:9
Sermon preached at Element, Hradec Kralove, Czech Republic, on October 21, 2018

"Future needs a big kiss," sings U2 in their hit song, "Get On Your Boots." I have been reminded of that phrase repeatedly in the last couple of years: when my wife struggled twice with life-threatening cancer, and between these two cases we had two years of the COVID pandemic with ongoing lockdowns and restrictions. Years of constant change. Years of ambiguity. Years of uncertainty. Years of struggles and yet, hope. In a moment of despair, I was silently singing, "Future needs a big kiss." It really does! A kiss of hope. A kiss of wonder. A kiss of embrace. Are we ready to embrace uncertainty and open future? Our life depends on it. I really believe so.

I recently saw a joke on Facebook about a woman looking for the perfect man: a man who doesn't hang around pubs, cleans up, folds his laundry, goes to bed early, eats what is presented to him, and so on. At the end it asked, "Where can you find such a man?" And after that, it quipped, "In prison." It looked so good at the beginning: a predictable and reliable man… just not exactly free. We want freedom in our lives and decisions. At the same time, we realize that freedom should be accompanied by responsibility. But freedom always comes with the risk of irresponsibility. This is true of other people, but it is also true of us, isn't it? All of us stand at a signpost from time to time, wondering which direction to take. We know our choices are important. For we all know or suspect that choices become habits, habits form character, character forms our personality. In a sense, we really do become the outcome of our choices. The longer we follow a chosen path, the more that chosen path becomes part of who we are. And in doing so, the number of possible paths we can choose from also shrinks. But there was a signpost at the beginning that offered direction. We need to learn how to make the right choices in a world of many options.

Here's the thing: *everyone who talks about the future has a particular concept or worldview about the future*. In our culture, we put a lot of emphasis on predictability. We rarely realize this more than when we find ourselves in a culture of unpredictability. Look at travel, for example. When I am driving down the main road in Hradec Kralove, I drive calmly at the speed limit and do not really slow down before every intersection, because I expect other drivers to follow the rules. (Of course, sometimes they don't, and then we have an accident.) However, when I was in Asia recently, I noticed a different road order. Traffic flows slower but smoother because everyone is constantly moving, sometimes in quite unpredictable directions. Everyone there is anticipating the unpredictable. Or look at the perception of time. In our culture, we say that the church meeting will start at 10:00 a.m., and so we start at exactly 10:00 a.m. When I was in Africa recently, I was picked up for church at 9:30 a.m. and when we got there 15 minutes later, it appeared that worship had already begun and we were late. I asked when the meeting started. I learned that it had started 45 minutes earlier. Church went on for six hours—a completely different perception of time and rules than I am used to.

Why am I talking about this? *Because a culture of predictability leads us to positive things like planning and order, but it also leads us to fear what we cannot control, like the future*. I think we all see what that kind of fear can do to us. We don't know how to work with uncertainty. We have this idea that not knowing where to go is always a bad sign. This also translates into Christian theology. Most Western theology is built on the idea of a God who is in control, who never changes, who gets everything he wants. We speak of an unchanging and constant God. We assume that God is outside of time and therefore either has planned everything according to his will or at least knows in advance what decisions we will make. Because of this, we use various slogans that sound so good, such as 'everything happens for a reason,' 'nothing is new under the sun,' or 'God is in control.' We could address each of these phrases. If everything happens for a reason, then even evil is part of God's plans, but Jesus' friend John wrote that there is no darkness in God. If there is nothing new under the sun, then a lot of the Old Testament prophets and John the Seer, who wrote *Revelation*, would be wrong when they say God is doing new things. If God is in control, then Jesus underestimates

God's control when he exhorts us to pray for God's will to be done in the world as God intends it in heaven.

What if indeed the future is not completely given and planned? What if the image of an unchanging and static God who controls everything, even prepared everything, and knows our every decision in advance, is not really the Biblical image of God? What if we find a different image there? Two verses have had a significant impact on me personally. Everything changed when I realized that God wants to be my friend. Not just Lord and Savior, but friend with a relationship. Jesus told his disciples. "I no longer call you servants, because a servant does not know his master's business. Instead, I have called you friends, for everything that I learned from my Father I have made known to you" (John 15:15, NIV). This is remarkable. And all the writers in the Bible affirm this concept of a friendly God. Abraham, Moses, and other characters could tell the story. Besides, my friend wants to do something with me. Paul wrote (1 Corinthians 3:9, HCSB), "For we are God's coworkers." Consider, God has chosen me to be his co-worker. I can change the world with him. I can create the future with him. That is amazing! Because of these two concepts, I began a journey of seeking a better understanding of God's nature. After all, friendship does not tolerate a programmed, cold, and robotic relationship. Cooperation implies that I am participating in something. It's not just an act. It's real. But if God has planned everything and knows everything, then this is all just a sham.

I began to wonder if our idea of a constant God who never changes, who is not influenced by us, and who accomplishes everything he wants, is influenced by something else. We owe the idea of perfection as predictability to the Greek philosophers, especially the idea of an unmoved mover. This immovable mover was the model of perfect constancy. God alone sets things in motion, but nothing moves God. When some theologians wished to identify this idea with the God of the Christians, it necessarily implied a God who would not be affected by anyone or anything. He is fully sovereign. He does everything for his glory. He even uses evil to accomplish his purposes. And since he has either set everything in motion himself or knows how things will move, then our job as Christians is to find what God wants and do it. Our job is to move in God's will because what God wants, he will accomplish. Prayer is not meant to move God; it is meant to move us. God cannot be surprised.

There is, of course, a real problem with this concept. This picture of God does not match the picture of the God of the Bible. Quite a different—and very relational—picture of God emerges there; one of a God that can be surprised and hurt. How do we explain so many stories in the Bible where God changes his mind or does something new? How do we explain the power of prayer to move God's heart? How do we explain that when the sick King Hezekiah learned he was going to die and prayed in tears that he lived another 15 years? After all, God sent the prophet Isaiah to tell Hezekiah that God heard his prayers and saw his tears—and responded to them. How do we explain God's bargaining with Abraham over Sodom, with Moses over Israel, and with Jonah over Nineveh? We could go on. The image of the God of the Bible that Jesus presented to us is that of a parent who wants us to feel his closeness, to talk to him, to ask him for things. God wants to tell us back things we do not know (revelation) and to work with us (mission). *It is indeed a dynamic, not a static relationship.* What kind of picture of God do we find in the Bible? *We find a relational God who allows himself to be moved by his creation, who changes opinions and intentions, and who responds to our decisions.* We find a God who takes our prayers seriously and who responds to his creation. How much will this change our approach to the future and our search for the right direction? I dare say quite fundamentally.

The early Christians knew they were in a spiritual war, and that sometimes God would not get what he wanted. That's why they learned to pray that God's will would be done the way he wanted it. It wasn't automatic. They knew that their decisions really mattered. They knew that their faith, love, and their journey had an eternal impact on everyone they met. This attitude toward the future changed when some early Christian theologians applied the pagan philosophy of immutable perfection to the Christian God, obscuring who, as the Trinity, had relationship in a core of his being. After all, John writes that God is first and foremost love—that is the core of relationship. God is not primarily unchanging and static consistency, holiness, or even omnipotence. These are philosophical concepts that we may need to think abstractly, but the image of *God in the Bible is powerfully relational, responsive, and surprising*. Such a God has an open future. Such a God is not above time, but is with us during the time he himself created. What does this mean? Does it mean a rejection of omniscience? By 'omniscience', we usually imagine that nothing happens without God's approval and explicit permission. *Some open thinkers declare that God knows every variant of the future and can work with whichever variant a person chooses.* He can work with us even when we miss what God would want for us (we call this God's will). He adjusts. He may not know in advance exactly every decision we will make, but he can assume well, since he knows us best. But then, we can still surprise him by choosing a better (or worse) direction than we would normally do. Does this mean that God plans nothing? No. He plans. But, he does not coerce. For example, God does not really plan the specific person for you to marry. He gives you enough clues to know what kind of person would work for you, and he leaves it up to you to decide within those clues who you want-and then, together, you build a marriage that honors God and pleases your parents.

God has created room for us and our choices. In this, he is like good parents. He took a huge risk in doing so. His primary motivation was love. If everything was predestined—we should always know what God wants and act accordingly. But, if the future is open—we should live as it pleases God, who wants the best for us, trusting that he will walk with us in life. See? The stress shifts from "finding God's specific will" to "walking in his ways motivated by love." Because of this, we can surprise God. Sometimes badly by foolish decisions, but also positively by our faith, love, willingness, hope. Such a search for the right direction in a world of many possibilities would be a real joy for us. Because future needs a big kiss.

Lukas Targosz is the senior leader of Element, a church focused on reaching atheists and agnostics in his native Czech Republic. He earned a Masters of Arts at Alphacrucis College in Sydney, Australia and at Sydney College of Divinity. He is the author of a few publications, most recently *Christianity in Five Words* and a lecturer on leadership, having taught in over two dozen countries on six continents. He loves U2 and ice hockey.

Surf the Seas of Change with Love

LIBBY TEDDER HUGUS

God compassionately saves us from the overwhelm of internal and external pressures, inviting us to take courage when life is beyond our control.

Reading: Matthew 14:22-33
Sermon preached at Shepherd of the Hills Presbyterian Church, Casper, Wyoming, November 12, 2024

Aims of this sermon:

- To Know… God is not in control but aims to rescue us from chaos. How we respond, cooperate, and participate with God's love is up to us.
- To Feel… the invitation of Jesus to take heart, take courage when we're over-whelmed and over-crowded.
- To Do… reorient our confession to the religion of love and the law of kindness brought to light by the gospel so that we will be imitators of God and lovers of all.

Introduction and Confession Time

I have a confession to make: I really crave alone time and I have a healthy fear of open water, and when I get overcrowded either literally by the world around me or internally by my fears and anxieties and need for control, I get exasperated.

So, I can relate to both Jesus and Peter in this passage.

The gospels repeatedly show us that Jesus is taking the time to rejuvenate his wholeness in body, mind, and spirit by going away to pray.

Jesus models to us that he is his best resource.

Being plugged into the source of God's presence and love is the only way to replenish his ability to love, lead, serve, enact miracles, and prophetically call an entire nation to a more radical shalom.

In Matthew's gospel, this is the first time the writer explicitly refers to Jesus going away, alone, to pray. *So, it's a "listen up" sort of literary device:*

Hey, listen up reader: Jesus is taking a significant action here, pay attention to what that action is and why Jesus is taking that action.

This is Jesus' second attempt to get away to a quiet place—the first one was cut short by the crowds for whom he had compassion, when he met them in their need in order to heal their sick.

Crowded

Jesus' life was indeed crowded: with curious onlookers, hungry followers, needy disciples, judgmental and sometimes hostile religious officials, and greedy, power-thirsty governmental rulers; not to mention the internalized pressure of his personal calling and vocation.... The external landscape was crowded with pressure. The internal landscape was crowded with big feels, big awareness, big longings....

Jesus was anointed by the Spirit of the Lord to bring good news to the poor, proclaim release to the captives, recovery of sight to the blind and to set free those who are oppressed, to proclaim the year of the Lord's favor.

That's no small calling and anointing.... That's crowded, in it is own way.

Skeptical

What are we to do with gospel narratives like these?

Ghost-like appearances, walking on water, near-drownings, theophanies (God appearances) and confessions.... It would make for viral social media content today and binge-worthy television streaming.

I can see the Instagram Reel or streaming television preview now:

"Point of View [POV]: You wanna walk on water like your ultimate guru and almost drowned!"

According to the gospel writer, Matthew, the context leading into this particular occurrence in Jesus' life and times reveals some crowded and dramatic occurrences.

- John the Baptist's beheading: the man who was present at Jesus' own baptism and commissioning into ministry was murdered. Imagine the grief, the bewilderment, the awkward question of 'when is my turn coming?'
- And then, a massive miraculous feeding of thousands of hungry followers. They showed up physically and spiritually hungry, under-nourished, in need.

Immediately after these pressure-cooker events comes the scene we're learning from today:

Jesus walks-on-water-appearance and Peter's terrified-yet-brave-confessional.

And to follow all of those crowded occurrences, Matthew writes about how Jesus went on to heal many in the Gennesaret region.

Jesus' life was crowded with persecution, needs, presence-making encounters and healings.

Theophany

A theophany is an encounter with God when God appears in observable form....

Jesus was a lifelong theophany, and when Jesus appeared to the disciples, walking on the Sea of Galilee, it was for them a theophany: an encounter with God.

Jesus' presence is radical: radically divisive, radically political, radically threatening, radically healing, radically aware of people's physical needs, radically challenging to people's spiritual fears and failings.

Jesus' presence is not neutral—it confronts injustice, lack of wholeness, short-sighted-faith, boot-shaking-fear, ill-health and religious pretense.

Me Too

My life is crowded too. Like Jesus, it's crowded with people's needs and asks and wants and preferences and pressure to perform, prove and be perfect.

It's crowded with awareness of how unjust and broken the world around me is, the looping-on-repeat parts of human history that refuse, as yet, to surrender to the interdependent reality of God's kin-dom[1] come to earth.

---

1. Kin-dom here is a coined term replacing kingdom and representating the sibling-hood of all God's people rather than a metaphor of hierarchy and oppression.

Like Peter, it's crowded with my inner fear and disbelief; with my isolation from the person of Jesus as he is, vs. who I think he should be.

Jesus often appears to me as nothing more than a fleeting ghost like whiff in life's fierce storms.

Squinting, I ask, is that him? Is that who I think it is?

Like Peter, I fleece my relationship to God with if-then negotiations about who God says God is and how Jesus appears to me:

"If it's you, God, then command me to and I will get out of this boat!"

Crossroads

It's here that modern day disciples can intersect with this ancient gospel narrative: *at the crossroads of crowded and faithful.*

Jesus boldly challenges Peter to a faithful response to the radical presence of love when Peter is overcrowded with the most fear, in the deepest crisis, and shaking with a lack of trust. God challenges Jesus to a faithful response to the racial presence of shalom when the crowds around him are testing this reality: beheaded prophets and oppressive rulers; hungry and sick; afraid and faithless humans. God is eliciting a faithful response.

At the crossroads of crowded and faithful, we're invited to follow Jesus: to surf the seas of change with love as our center of gravity; we're invited into the reality of God's love inhabiting our earth.

It's an invitation to become aware of our location in life's crowded storms; it is a plea that God will save us and an assurance that even here, we will find the presence of Love when we're farthest from land than we've ever been.

This is the gospel at the eye of the crowded storm: a God of love who will find us smack in the middle of the chaos.

Sometimes we initiate the chaos we find ourselves in; sometimes the chaos is circumstantial to being humans on an overcrowded planet with other overwhelmed humans.

We cannot control the wind and the waves, but we can choose to surf: we can choose to find our center of gravity in love's presence, we can choose to receive the love of God extended to us in the stormy seas of overwhelm.

Will we know love when it shows up in our over-crowded life storms?

Will we recognize our rescue when it comes to our aid?

"Jesus Saves" is shorthand in popular culture as a slogan for being rescued from that which condemns or tempts us.

In this gospel narrative, we're yet again confronted with how Jesus saves us and from what Jesus saves us.

"Take heart, it is I; do not be afraid," says Jesus.

And here is where the good news shines forth: immediately after Peter asked to be saved, Jesus reached out his hand and caught him.

When we are at our most crowded, our most afraid—when we cry out in desperation to be saved from drowning in the chaos, *immediately* Jesus is present and says take heart (take courage); do not be afraid.

God's love is never absent from us in the chaos.

God is not the causer of chaos; and God will always answer us when we cry for help.

We're saved from our overwhelm and saved by the one who meets us in the middle of the storm.

Not outside of it, not in spite of it, not to escape it, but in it.

Reoriented Confession

'When they got back in the boat, the wind ceased and those in the boat worshiped him, saying, Truly you are the Son of God.'

The Wesleyan tradition's founding preacher and theologian was John Wesley. His way of forming disciples became known as Methodism. At one point in his own crowded journey, he was interacting with a "skeptic" of the Christian faith and responded with the following:

"What religion do I preach? The religion of love; the law of kindness brought to light by the Gospel. What is it good for? To make all who receive it enjoy God and themselves: to make them like God; lovers of all; content in their lives; and crying out at their death, in calm assurance 'O grave, where is thy victory! Thanks be unto God, who giveth me the victory, through my Lord Jesus Christ'." (John Wesley, *An Earnest Appeal to Men of Reason and Religion.* 1743)

When we are at our most afraid, most shaken and crowded, Jesus reveals the religion of love, the best news of all:

presence in the overcrowded places,
salvation when we may just drown in overwhelm,
an *invitation* to take heart, take courage, and
confess our allegiance to the revelation of Love in our midst.
Immediately, Love is present, available to us.

My confession shifts because of this gospel passage. I can relate to both Jesus and Peter in this passage. At the crossroads of crowded and faithful, I can see how Love met both Jesus and Paul in the middle of their overwhelming life storms.

Like Peter and the other disciples in the wind-battered boat, when Jesus enters the storms of my life, I can only see him for exactly who he is: the Beloved of God sent to rescue me from my chaos, my howling doubts and fears and overwhelm; and the chaos around me, the injustice and frantic frenzy of greedy, needy humans.

It causes me to worship, to appreciate, to ascribe value to the One before me who reveals the incredibly good news: Love is with me IMMEDIATELY when I ask for it.

Love reaches for me when I lose sight of my centering Savior, challenging me—even at the crossroads of crowded and faithful, to never doubt the power of love and courage in my chaos.

We cannot control the wind and the waves, but we can choose to surf. We can choose to find our center of gravity in love's presence.

I confess to the religion of love and the law of kindness brought to light by the person of Jesus. Jesus is the clearest representation of God's ever-present Love.

We can cling to that in any crowd, any storm, any lonely place where we find ourselves praying for more heart, more courage.

At the crossroads of crowded and faithful, we're invited to follow Jesus: to surf the seas of change with love as our center of gravity; we're invited into the reality of God's love inhabiting our earth.

"Take heart, it is I; do not be afraid," says Jesus.

Amen and may it be so.

A Prayer of Reorientation (from the Buddhist tradition):

May I be at peace,
May my heart remain open.
May I awaken to the light of my own true nature.
May I be healed.
May I be a source of healing for all beings.
May you be at peace,
May your heart remain open.
May you awaken to the light of your own true nature.
May you be healed,
May you be a source of healing for all beings.

Post Sermon Dialogue:

- Can you relate to Jesus and/or Peter in this passage? If so, how exactly?
- What do you need from God when you're most overwhelmed and crowded?

- How can you re-orient your confession of who God is when you recognize God in your chaotic life storms?
- From what does God rescue you and to what aim does God rescue you?
- How can you surf the seas of change with love as our center of gravity in your spiritual practice this week?

Libby Tedder Hugus is a Reverend, Coach, Author and Speaker. She was the organizing Pastor of The Table, a radically inclusive spiritual community in Casper, WY. She is the lead mental fitness coach at Resonate Coaching. Libby loves mountain air and international submersion travel. She believes generous hospitality can and will heal the world. You can find her online at www.resonatenow.live.

“What Do I Love When I Love My God?”

Theology as Critique and Prayerful Imagination

JOHN J. THATAMANIL

Good theology reforms the concepts we deploy in speaking about God, and good theology also refreshes the poetry in our prayers and liturgy. Process theology does both!

Reading: *John 17:20-24* (NRSV)
Sermon preached at the Church of the Village (NYC), August 8, 2021

Like it or not, there’s no avoiding theology. Every Christian has ways of imagining and understanding God. Most often they are passed down to us through families, church communities, and the culture at large. We acquire our working theologies largely by osmosis. Taking ownership of and responsibility for what we believe about God, the world, and ourselves—that’s what it means to do theology. Sadly, Christian communities have received the message that theology is best left to the professionals. “People, don’t try this at home!” We have come to believe that only people with Ph.D.s in theology are theologians. That professionalized understanding has done incalculable harm to the church and the world.

So, let’s get to it: what is theology, and why does every Christian have an obligation to do theology? Theology is the work of asking St. Augustine’s great question, “What do I love when I love my God?” What do I love when I love my God? Here’s St. Augustine:

> But what do I love when I love my God? Not the sweet melody of harmony and song; not the fragrance of flowers, perfumes, and spices; not manna or

> honey; not limbs such as the body delights to embrace. It is not these that I love when I love my God. And yet, when I love Him, it is true that I love a light of a certain kind, a voice, a perfume, a food, an embrace; but they are of the kind that I love in my inner self, when my soul is bathed in light that is not bound by space; when it listens to sound that never dies away; when it breathes fragrance that is not borne away on the wind; when it tastes food that is never consumed by the eating; when it clings to an embrace from which it is not severed by fulfillment of desire. This is what I love when I love my God."

Woo, that is some steamy theology, no?—stunning in beauty and poetry! St. Augustine is profoundly sensual in talking about God even he says that loving God is not like loving material things. What can we learn from Augustine's way of imagining theology?

First things first. We often think that theology is a matter of the head and not the heart. It has something to do with how we critically analyze God-concepts. But that is not where Augy begins. Oh, sure, he gets pretty heady too. He can mix it up with the best of them. But his core question is meant not for the mind alone. Instead, he puts forward a question of the heart. He asks, "What do I *love* when I love my God?" For St. Augustine, theology is a matter of critical desiring not critical thinking alone.

What you desire, that is the object of your worship. That is your God. So, we had better be sure that what we desire is worthy and true. Theology, then, is the business of critically investigating our desires so that we can be sure that it is really God whom we are worshiping and desiring.

We do theology not just when we write theology books. The most basic form of God-talk is talking *to* God—what we say to God in our prayers and liturgies. Prayer is theology's first language. And that first language deeply shapes our hearts. When we speak to God in prayerful yearning and longing, who then do we imagine God to be? Who or what are we longing for? Can you see why that is so crucial a question? Theology's first and foremost task is a matter of tuning our hearts so that our praise, our prayers, and our longings are worthy rather than misdirected. The 4th century theologian, Evagrius, put it this way, "The theologian is one who prays truly; the one who prays truly is the theologian." Theology asks, "Am I praying truly?" When I say that I long for God, what am I really desiring? Is the object of my devotion not God but an idol? If it is an idol, I better smash it!

Another observation: Augustine's language *about* God is not far removed from the language he uses in speaking *to* God. That is why it is so sensual, erotic, and poetic. Think of the difference between the language you use when writing a love letter and the language you might use to describe your beloved to a stranger. Love letter language is the language of poetry. Description language, *about-language*, is often the language of concept. *To-language* sounds like Romeo singing praises to Juliet in Act 2, Scene 2:

> But soft! What light through yonder window breaks?
> It is the east, and Juliet is the sun.
> Arise, fair sun, and kill the envious moon,
> Who is already sick and pale with grief,
> That thou, her maid, art far more fair than she.

The first language of theology is symbolic, mythic, and poetic. Juliet is not the Sun, but to Romeo she fairer than the envious moon. God is not Father or Lord, but we use these words to speak the longings of our hearts as they respond to God's parental and directing care. The first language of theology is the poetic language of intimacy.

But even poetic language can fall short and become idolatrous. A poetic symbol can be mistaken for a concept. Say "Father God" too often, and you might forget that you are speaking in poetry. You might come to believe God is, in some sense, literally and conceptually male. Say "Lord" too often, and you might come to think that God is like an earthly Lord who exercises controlling and sovereign power. The end result: we worship not God but maleness and controlling power—destructive idols that have the power to consume us and disfigure our common lives. That is why we must keep asking the basic question of theology, "What do I love when I love my God?"

But smashing idols is only part of theology's job. Repeat any poetic term too often and it can grow stale and lifeless. So, theology also stands in creative need of new poetry. Good theology *reforms* the concepts we deploy in speaking about God, and good theology also *refreshes* the poetry in our prayers and liturgy. Process theology does both!

Process theologians believe that both our poetry for God and our concepts about God are likely to go awry for a host of reasons. Let's focus on just one: many of our core symbols for God come from an age in which the only form of political power was ruling power. Any wonder then that many of our symbols of God are pre-democratic? Kings do not share power. They wield it unilaterally. Democratic life—at its best—is about shared power. Kings tell us what to do; we cannot return the favor. They can influence us; but they remain above the fray, and we cannot influence them. Is this starting to sound familiar? Because kingship plays so much a role in our imagination, we have come to believe that God creates the world; the world in no sense creates God. The world needs God like a kingdom needs the king, but God does not need the world. The world is really related to God; but God is not really related to the world. These core theological claims rest at the heart of many classical theologies. Do you see how these ideas are rooted in a vision of unilateral, controlling power, power from on high?

What does it mean that so many of our core symbols for God are pre-democratic? How might this penchant for royal symbols be misshaping our hearts? Might we need serious symbolic rehab to wean us from our addiction to the symbolism of sovereign power? Process theologians are absolutely convinced that we desperately need to rethink our ideas about power! Despite what we say about love, Christian symbolism leaves us vulnerable to the love of power rather than the power of love.

Our bad ideas about power are rooted in a far deeper problem. The root of our trouble rests, well, in how we think about everything or every *thing*. Let me be a bit cryptic: process theologians affirm that there are no things anywhere in the world. Sound crazy? Sure. But give it a moment. Process theologians hold that the world is composed of events not substances. We know even the most solid seeming things in the world, rocks, mountains, and tables, are actually composed of subatomic particles. And those particles are not particles—they are not bits of tiny stuff. Particles are themselves nothing but complex patterns of energy. From Einstein on, we know that matter and energy are not two different things. Matter just is energy in a stable configuration. If a pattern endures, it gives the appearance of being a thing. But scratch the surface, and you can see that every "thing" is actually a community of processes nesting inside processes inside processes and so forth. Hence the term process theology.

Why does it matter to theology whether the world is made up of events not things? Why should people of faith care? You might say, "This sounds like physics or philosophy to me, not theology." I'll simplify and say that it comes down to one word: relation. If we think that the world is made up of independent things, substances, then it is natural to fall into a billiard ball worldview. Each of us (God included) and everything in the world is like an isolated billiard ball sitting independently on a pool table. The 9 Ball sits next to the 8 Ball, but each is what it is quite apart from the other. The 8 Ball has no effect on 9 Ball. Now, I might use the cue ball to knock the 8 into the 9, but all three balls are only in "relationship," if you can call it that, at the moment of impact. They are what they are in splendid isolation. In a billiard ball universe, relationships are external and optional. Things are what they are apart from relationship. In a universe of things, the power of a thing depends on its capacity to affect without being affected. Imagine a billiard ball that is so dense that when another ball strikes it, it does not move. Or imagine an enormous billiard ball just mowing over and crushing all the others. That's what power looks like in a world of things.

But what does power look like in a world of events and processes? Oh now, that is quite something different. Events feel and respond to other events. A process is richer, more interesting, and more complex to the degree that it can *include* other processes into its own identity. One repeated note may be beautiful but not very interesting. But a symphony that includes a variety of instruments each offering its own distinctiveness into a larger whole—now that is intriguing, subtle, and complex. The conductor who can hear, feel, and respond to each note and each instrument and bring them together is the richer conductor. In a relational world, power is response-ability, the power to respond.

Things sit next to each other. You can only affect them from outside. And you can affect them only by pushing them. The power to push hardest and the power to be impervious to pushing—that's what power looks like in a "thing world." Processes/events are energy flows. They can enter *into* each other. They are never to be found in just one location, and they are what they are only in relationship to each other. The power to feel, the power to include, the power to respond—that's what power looks like in a process universe.

The more complexity a symphony can include without descending into chaos, the richer it is. If the world is more like a symphony in which we all play our distinctive part, but then contribute to a larger whole—if that's what the world is, rather than like a pool table, then we must reimagine power. Each musician doesn't just play her own note or instrument oblivious of others. Musicians offer their part in responsiveness to and in relationship with each other to compose something larger than each can do in isolation.

In a symphonic universe, or better yet, in an improvisational jazz universe, the power to listen, to feel, and to be affected—*that* is true power. In a universe of events, the ultimate power is the power of relationship. The power to let oneself be affected, to be responsive, and then to offer your own creative contribution is more important than the power to push. In a process universe, each event is what it is only because of its capacity to feel, take in, and then respond to every other preceding event. In a process universe, relationships are not optional; to be is to be in relationship. In a process-relational universe, I mask up because you are in me, and I in you.

In a responsive and relational universe, the power to pull is more important than the power to push. If every event in the universe is a relational response to the rest of the universe, then, the power of persuasion is more important than the power of coercion. We are creatures embedded in networks of relationship; coercion can only rupture that network. In any case, there is no standing above it barking orders from on high.

Now perhaps you can see why all this matters for how we think about and imagine God. To live with an antiquated and obsolete view of the world is sure to result in an antiquated and obsolete view of God.

In a world of things, God is the unmoved mover. God is utterly unaffected. In a world of things, God is omnipotent. God can do anything He wants. God does not share power.

In a world of process and relation, God is the *most moved* power. God has the great power to be deeply affected and enriched by what transpires in the world. The world can contribute to God's life because God has the power to feel all events and then creatively respond. In a relational world, the power to feel and the power for creative response is greater than the power to push and to control. Now that is the kind of responsive power that God possesses.

In a world of things, God can only exercise power by controlling them. In a world of events and relations, God exercises the power of appeal by persuading and luring us toward greater beauty, goodness, and truth. God's power is like the power of a candy bar over a child. The candy bar does not *push* the child. The candy bar pulls and lures the child. But only the child, exercising her own power of choice, can decide whether to eat the candy bar or not. Likewise, God lures us by the power of love and leads us into our own growth into life abundant. But only we can say yes or no. We are free and responsive creatures living in a relational world with and before a relational God.

In introducing these process ideas, I have largely been speaking conceptually—using "about" language. But let me conclude by returning to "to-language"—the language of intimacy.

> Holy One, who came to us as the Lowly Galilean and not as Caesar, who lures us by your beauty into lives of rich relationship and mutual love, we know that you are One who lives in relationship and is relationality itself. We know that you are in us and we are in you, even as you, the Word, abides in that Primordial and Spacious Silence from which all things unfold. We know that you are no unfeeling rock, but instead one who tenderly feels our joys and our sorrows. "Earth-Maker, Pain-Bearer, and Life-Giver,"[1] you are the Fellow Sufferer who understands. We pray that you lead us into richer and more beautiful ways of speaking to you and about you. Deepen our desire for you and our desire to serve the world you so richly love. Amen!

John J. Thatamanil is Professor of Theology and World Religions at Union Theological Seminary in the City of New York. He is the author of *Circling the Elephant: A Comparative Theology of Religious Diversity* (2020) and *The Immanent Divine: God, Creation, and the Human Predicament; An East-West Conversation*. His areas of research include theologies of religious diversity, comparative theology, and philosophical theology. He is an Anglican but much else besides. Specifically, he studies Advaita Vedanta and Tibetan Buddhist traditions both academically and spiritually. He is a

1. This evocative threefold naming of Trinity is taken from the New Zealand Prayer Book.

Past President of the North American Paul Tillich Society and the first Chair of the American Academy of Religion's Theological Education Committee. Most recently, John has been ordained as a Priest in the Anglican Diocese of Islands and Inlets where he serves as Volunteer Associate Priest and Diocesan Theologian. He is also an Associate Priest in St. Mark's Church-in-the Bowery in New York.

Is God in Control?

BARKLEY THOMPSON

How do we make sense of the idea that God "has a plan?"
What if God is not all-powerful?

Reading: Romans 8:26-39
Sermon preached at Saint Mark's Episcopal Church,
Little Rock, Arkansas, July 30, 2023

For many years, beginning in college or maybe even high school, I kept a folded slip of paper in my wallet. Written on it in blue pen was a single bible verse. The crease in the slip had been folded and unfolded so many times that the paper was almost torn in two. The ink had run and faded. My handwriting was so scrawled that I must have written down the verse in a moment of haste, or perhaps near panic. The verse was Romans 8:28, which is included in our epistle reading today and which many of you probably know from your own memory, or bumper stickers, or gauzy social media memes: "We know that all things work together for good for those who love God, who are called according to God's purpose." (NRSV)

What an enormous comfort. I don't remember what I was going through when I hurriedly jotted Romans 8:28, but I do know that for a long time in my younger life I read it often, and relied upon it, and was exceedingly glad St. Paul had originally written those words. "We know that all things work together for good for those who love God, who are called according to God's purpose."

It did not take long in life, however, for the verse to raise as many questions as it provided soothing answers. And as time went on, others I encountered in life would quote this verse back to me in situations for which it didn't seem to ring true. Romans

8:28 was deployed as another way of saying—a scriptural proof-text—that God is in control, directing all events, large and small. Rather than instilling deep peace, it began to make me deeply uneasy, as if invoking Romans 8:28 was an attempt to keep the thin façade of a shoddy religious worldview from cracking. Sometimes Romans 8:28 was invoked with regard to relatively small or trivial things, but not always. The straw that broke the camel's back for me—and I share this as gently as I can, knowing that there is no greater grief in this world—was the first time I, as a priest, had to bury a child. With good intentions and a loving heart, a parishioner said of the child's death, "We know that all things work together for good for those who love God, who are called according to God's purpose." And she followed it up with the modern corollaries, "Everything happens for a reason" and "God needed a new little angel." To my ears, these words, deployed in this way—both the scripture and the add-ons—seemed less a comfort than a taunt. The implication was that God *took* the child, that God *caused* this thing to happen, and that, somehow, the death of a child was good as part of God's orchestrated plan.

Hear me say: I didn't believe it then, and I don't believe it now. Whatever St. Paul means by Romans 8:28, it isn't that. God does not will the death of children. God does not lead people to run red lights and engineer automobile accidents. God does not manipulate the world in such ways.

But St. Paul speaks truth, so how are we to understand his claim in Romans 8:28? In what way *does* God weave all things together for good for those who love God and who are called according to God's purpose?

It is helpful here to draw on the thread of Christian thought known as "process theology." Process theologians don't see our experience in the world as a scripted performance, with us merely playing out parts God has already written from beginning to end. Such a world would be like a marionette on a string, and in it God would, indeed, be the author of each event that occurs, including the most senseless and horrific. Instead of such a world, process theologians imagine the cosmos as still unfolding, still emerging, still in process (thus the name of their school of thought), and in which even God, along with us, can be surprised, overjoyed, and grieved by what transpires in each moment.

This renders God more intimate and relatable, because God is experiencing each novel moment in the world as we are, with wonder, and whimsy, and shock, and maybe even confusion. But how can this be? It is possible because process theology also takes very seriously—perhaps more seriously than any other theological school of thought—the creation's free will, or said differently, our own role as *co-creators with God. We* speak, act, birth things into being alongside God, and it is often our human action, both individually and collectively, both immediately as when we run the red light or distally as when, for instance, our pollution of the earth increases societal incidence of cancer, that ushers in pain and leads to grief. God grants *us* the latitude by our own free will to create things good and ill in this world, and our creativity can thrill or shock, overjoy or grieve, *even God*. This is another way of conceding that, in and through our God-given freedom, God is *not* entirely in control.

Given all of this, how would a process theologian interpret Romans 8:28? How would she say that God weaves all things together for good?

In process theology, God holds within Godself as potential—not yet created—the best of all possibilities, for each individual and for the creation as a whole. And in each emerging moment of existence, God always sets before the creation the best possibility. I think we can grasp that. You and I both know in moments large and small in our lives the experience of having before us the next step, not yet taken, that feels best and right, that will contribute something meaningful to the world or will help you flourish. Those best-possibilities-set-before-us are how and where God acts, and that internal feeling—that tug forward, when we know which next step is right—is what the process theologians call God's "lure," calling us toward the good and the best for us. That surely seems like God weaving together all things for good, doesn't it?

But you and I also know that more often than not, we shut our ears, eyes, and hearts to God's lure. We ignore the best possibility God sets before us, and we choose otherwise. God does not do that *to* us, and God does not impede our free will. God sets before us the best of all possibilities, and then we choose to take that, or some other, step into the future.

Every moment of our lives, big or small, mundane or momentous, is a forked path, a decision point between one thing or the other. In the moment, we choose God's good, or we choose otherwise. And when we choose other than God's good, sometimes that good—whatever it was in that moment—is cut off forever. Life doesn't include mulligans. We do things that cannot be undone. Our decisions have real and often irrevocable consequences.

Process theology concedes this reality entirely. In our freedom, we co-create alongside God, but unlike God, often what we create is *not* good. But here is where process theology grasps Paul's great truth in Romans 8:28: In each moment, as soon as we decide, as soon as we act, as soon as we do something that takes us a step down the wrong path, a step away from God's *previous* good for us, God readjusts and sets anew in front of us, in light of our past decisions, the very best of all possibilities! And then we choose again. And then, taking into account the consequences of *that* choice, God sets before us the best of all possibilities.

Think about it this way: it is as if God is a cosmic GPS. When I'm driving, Google Maps provides me the best route for my journey, but I may choose to turn left when the GPS tells me that a right turn is the best way to go. My bad choice may put me behind an accident, or in road construction, or onto a flooded street. Thankfully, the moment I choose, Google Maps recalibrates, and given the consequences of my choice, Google Maps offers me the *new* best possible route for my journey. It does not ignore the choice I've made, and it must respond in light of my previous choice, but with a newly recalibrated route, it offers me the new best way forward. And eventually, no matter how many wrong turns I stubbornly make, Google Maps will see me safely to my destination. It will weave the best route through my journey.

In our lives, God does the same. God has granted us a world of wonder and freedom, and for that we are thankful. But the flip side of that gift is that in our freedom we can choose poorly, and do damage, and the world can do damage to us. That damage is real, and it can be, for God as well as for us, impossible to undo. But that does not mean we are bereft, hopeless, or alone. No matter what bad choices we make, or no matter what the world does to us, causing us disappointment and pain, God is always there, in the next emerging moment of our lives, calling us toward the best of all possibilities for us. Always. In every moment. In that way, God lures us forward, never giving up on us. God truly weaves together our worst and our best moments until hope against hope, God looks upon our lives and says, "It is good."

The Reverend Barkley Thompson is the rector of Saint Mark's Episcopal Church in Little Rock, Arkansas. Barkley previously served parishes in Collierville, Tennessee and Roanoke, Virginia. Immediately before coming to Little Rock, he served as dean of Christ Church Cathedral in Houston, Texas. Barkley is the author of *Elements of Grace* (2013), *In the Midst of the City: The Gospel and God's Politics* (2018), and *How Can We Know the Way?: Reflections on Belief, Salvation, and Eternal Life* (2023).

Go Back to Galilee

NICHOLE TORBITZKY

The empty tomb is not an ending, but an invitation to begin again.

Reading: Mark 16:1-8
Sermon preached at Sibley Chapel, Lindenwood University, April 9, 2023

When I was a child, I did not like Mark's version of the resurrection story. It seemed wrong. Why wasn't Jesus there? Where was he? What better thing did he have to do than be there in person to show the women that he's beaten death and set us free from our bondage to sin? And still, as an adult, just like the women at the tomb, I'm a little unsettled by this ending.

Let me back up and tell you about Mark's version of this story. Each Gospel has its own slightly different version, yet Mary Magdalene is at the tomb in all four versions, and in each version some form of an angel is there. In two versions, Jesus makes a brief appearance, and in one of them, Mark, Jesus doesn't show up again. In Mark's story, Jesus is taken down from the cross Friday shortly before the Sabbath begins and work must stop. Jesus lays in the tomb all day Saturday. Then Sunday, when the Sabbath is over, the women come to the tomb with spices to prepare the body properly for burial. Joseph of Arimathea had taken the body down, wrapped it in cloth, put it in a prepared tomb rather than a natural cave, and rolled a large disc shaped stone in front of the entrance. On their walk to the tomb, the ladies are worried about how they are going to roll that big stone out of the way. Turns out, that's not a problem, because when they get there, the stone is already moved and the body is gone. Instead, there is a "young man" that we assume is an angel, who tells them that Jesus is not here, he's been raised from the dead, and that they need to go tell Peter to meet Jesus in Galilee. The gospel ends with the women fleeing in fear, "and they said nothing to anyone, for they were afraid."

I remember flipping through an old Bible in a used bookstore and I happened to land on this passage. The previous owner had written here at the end of Mark, "Somebody told." My guess is that the writer is intending to say that Mary said nothing to anyone on her way home but did indeed tell the Good News to Peter when they got back to the disciples. It is fitting that the bedrock upon which the "Foundation of the Church" stands is the preaching of women.

If some of you were reading along in your Bibles, you might see headings called the "Shorter Ending" and the "Longer Ending" at the close of Mark's gospel. Scholars agree both endings were later additions—the longer ending being a much later addition. I honor their attempts because Mark's ending leaves us with the sneaking suspicion that Jesus' resurrection might be a little unsettling. We human beings don't like unsettling things. We want to exclaim, "Christ is Risen" and then get on with the pagan rituals of eggs and bunnies because they are so much nicer than empty tombs, missing saviors, and frightened, grieving women. Yet, Mark leaves us unsettled. Mark isn't all that interested in "proving" that Jesus was resurrected. Instead, Mark is interested in putting us, the reader, in the middle of an existential crisis, a faith crisis. Mark prompts us to ask, "Why is Jesus not here?" "Why don't I get the tearful reunion hug that makes everything feel better?"

I think it is because Mark may have known that the situation of the people that read his gospel is very similar to the situation of the people experiencing these events. So many of us spend so much of our time "fleeing" from stuff. So many of us spend our time refusing to transcend the things that bind us to patterns of living that are destructive of the good God wants for us. Let me tell you a story. Maybe you've heard of Father Greg Boyle, a Jesuit Priest who, beginning in the 1990s, started a ministry in the heart of Gangland LA to help young men and women get out of the gang life. He tells the story of a young man helped by the program who now helps others through it. His name is Hosea. He had been a heroin addict and gang member. As Hosea tells his story, he says, "I guess you could say my mom and me, we didn't get along so good. I guess I was 6 when she looked at me and she said, 'Why don't you just kill yourself, you're such a burden to me'." Well, the whole audience did what you just did, they gasped. He said, "It sounds way worser in Spanish." And everybody did what you just did. And he said, "You know, I guess I was 9 when my mom drove me down to the deepest part of Baja, California and she walked me up to an orphanage and she said, I found this kid'." Then he said, "I was there 90 days until my Grandma could get out of her where she had dumped me, and she came to rescue me." And then he tells the audience, "You know my mom beat me every single day. In fact, I had to wear three t-shirts to school every day." And then he kinda loses the battle with his own tears a little and he says, "I wore three t-shirts well into my adult years because I was ashamed of my wounds. I didn't want anybody to see them. But now my wounds are my friends, I welcome my wounds. I run my fingers over my wounds." And then he looks at this crowd and he says, "How can I help the wounded if I don't welcome my own wounds?" If one didn't know Hosea's story, most of us would be inclined to judge this kid who went to prison, is covered in tattoos, a gang member, homeless, and a heroin addict. But he was never seeking anything when he ended up in those places, he was always fleeing this story I just told you.

It seems like human beings usually have something that we're fleeing from. For most of us, the thing that causes us fear isn't as dramatic as Hosea's story, or even the story of the women at the tomb. Most of us were not abused by our parents or helpless witnesses to the injustice of persecution and execution of an innocent man. But maybe some of us have been. Maybe some of us have something else just as strong that causes us to run. What do we run to? For Hosea, it was drugs and gangs, until he found a home and hope with Jesus. For the women at the tomb, it was the same. They ran in terror, but history tells us they found home and hope with the resurrected Christ.

As a child, I judged the foolishness of God; I indignantly wondered why Jesus wouldn't be there. Maybe this is why—not just that Jerusalem is physically unsafe for followers of Jesus, but maybe that people are going to run. We're simply wired to run from our brokenness. We run away from it and into whatever will relieve the suffering, but truth be told, there's only one safe place. With God. Who isn't stuck in our fear and brokenness.

That doesn't mean we're abandoned or betrayed or left to fend for ourselves. Jesus tells us, through the women at the tomb, "I am waiting for you." This invitation isn't only for the disciples. It's for us too. The writers of these stories wrote not just to record them for future generations; they wrote to persuade people. They wrote because they knew that there will be people who have never met a disciple who will need to hear the story of Jesus…us, and billions of people like us.

Mark writes this story and tells us exactly why the foolishness of God isn't so foolish after all. A crucified and risen God is the God we've been looking for the whole time but couldn't find in Zeus. In Christ, God is made known, not as the sender of lightning bolts of wrath (like Zeus), who uses violence to get his way. In Christ, God—that which is truly divine in this world—is made known to us in an empty tomb. We learn that God—what is truly divine, is divine *not* because of his power to coerce. God is divine because God has the power to forgive when forgiveness seems impossible. God is divine because God has the power to love when loving seems not just hopeless, but useless. God is divine because God has the power to take up our cycles of violence and oppression and injustice and anger and fear with grace that has the courage to say, "I am enough to take this horror and never pass it on, not flee from it, not give retribution; but take it, and keep it, and fix it in myself, and offer in response the totally unexpected grace of forgiveness, peace, and love." It is so much more difficult to respond to evil with love. And yet, because it's God we're talking about here, that's what we get. And that is how we know it's God.

God knows people run from our brokenness, and God gives us a place to run to.

"He's not here. He's going ahead of you to Galilee." For us readers of this gospel—for those of us who cannot literally travel to the Galilee to find the risen Christ—this reference to Galilee is Mark's shining moment as a writer. Jesus is risen, and we, those of us who cannot go, are directed to Galilee. But in Mark's gospel where is Galilee? If you only have this book in front of you, and no chance of going to Galilee yourself…where is Galilee? Easy—flip back to the front of the book. You're there, back in Galilee. Now that we've been to the empty tomb, now that we understand what being the Messiah was all about for Jesus, we need to go back and read the gospel again. We need to hear Jesus' parables afresh, see the miracles anew. We need to re-consider Jesus' every word and act in the light of the empty tomb and God's inexhaustible love for us. Because only then will we, by the Spirit, see and understand the nature of God's kin-dom. And the nature of that kin-dom is grace, grace, grace.

We humans call this foolish. It's crazy, first of all, to send Jesus knowing that humanity was bound to make the wrong choice. Counterintuitive, at least, to meet human rebellion and sin without an equally violent response. But, crazier still, to continue to extend loving forgiveness in the resurrection. This all-too-human response fails to see that God's foolishness is wiser by far than human wisdom. God works in the world by refusing to accept our failure as the truth about us. God answers our failure not with wrath, but with another chance to get it right. In the resurrection, we receive God's judgment: forgiveness. God will work with us, like God worked with Hosea, to bring out the best possible in us. We are freed from our bondage to those things that keep us from doing the good that God envisions for us and the world. God certainly cannot force us out of cycles of violence and sin, because God does not coerce. But God refuses to fall victim to the evil that insists that our failure is all we can be. *God knows better. God knows us better.* God responds to each failure with an offer of redemption that acknowledges the truth of our troublesome pasts and yet refuses to leave us there. God responds to each of our triumphs with rejoicing and an offer to build on that victory.

How do we do that? Now that we've seen Jesus die on the cross, and know the tomb is empty, we understand that the only place to run to is back to Galilee. Not in hopes of the instantaneous miracle that Jesus will "poof" and fix all our hurts like a magician, but because the stories tell us how, in Christ, we can stop running. Our wounds aren't magically erased from our pasts, but the power they hold over us can be erased from our futures. Amen.

Nichole Torbitzky is an Associate Professor of Religion and University Chaplain at Lindenwood University. She earned her M.Div. from Pittsburgh Theological Seminary and her Ph.D. from Claremont Graduate University. She serves as the editor for the Process and Faith lectionary series (https://processandfaith.org/lectionaries/#gsc.tab=0) and is working on a book about Process thought and atonement theory.

God of Grief, God of Love

TRACY L. TUCKER

A funeral homily might afford the perfect opportunity to apply Open and Relational thinking in a real life or death experience.

Grief shows up in countless ways and often at unexpected times. Most of us have experienced grief or loss well before the first time we have lost someone to death. Perhaps someone you loved and maybe even depended upon has moved away. Perhaps the unhappy event of a divided or split family has touched your life. It might be that the loss of a career or vocation has become a reality for you, either directly or indirectly, and now your sense of security is at risk. The point is that grief and loss are, or will be, part of each of our lives. Consequently, it makes no sense for anyone to broadly label grief as an emotional or psychological weakness or deficit. Grief happens, and ignoring its impact leads to a very unhealthy soul.

Perhaps you recall in John's gospel how the sisters of Jesus's friend Lazarus sent word to Jesus, alerting him to Lazarus's serious illness. Martha urged Jesus to come quickly so he might prevent Lazarus's untimely death. Jesus, however, was on a mission and did not feel compelled to be in a rush. By the time Jesus arrived, Lazarus was in the tomb.

Notice in this story that Mary was impatient and wanted Jesus to acknowledge her grief.

> Now Jesus had not yet come to the village but was still at the place where Martha had met him. The Jews who were with her in the house consoling her saw Mary get up quickly and go out. They followed her because they thought that she was going to the tomb to weep there. When Mary came where Jesus

> was and saw him, she knelt at his feet and said to him, "Lord, if you had been here, my brother would not have died." When Jesus saw her weeping and the Jews who came with her also weeping, he was greatly disturbed in spirit and deeply moved (John 11:30-33, NRSV).

Jesus's response is to invite Mary and the other mourners to escort him to Lazarus's tomb. The empathetic person that he was, Jesus was affected by the grief of those around him and by the time He got to where Lazarus was buried, grief had overtaken him. "Jesus began to weep" (John 11:35).

The passage suggests that some of those present thought Jesus was weeping because of Lazarus, but others in the crowd wisely disagreed. Jesus would not have wept for the person he was about to resuscitate. However, Jesus might easily have wept in empathy for those where were hurting, experiencing grief and loss. We are all susceptible to the impact of grief, and certainly, if that was true for Jesus, we shouldn't consider ourselves to be above that same response to grief.

In his letter to the house churches in Rome, Paul spoke to what it means to live in the Spirit of Christ and for that same spirit to live within the life and breath of the follower of Christ. Within that context, we hear the not-really-so-faint call to face the challenges inherent in following Jesus with confidence in God's love.

Today we face one of the most natural and common struggles that human beings regularly are compelled to face: death. Someone we have loved and have personally invested in is no longer available to answer the phone or receive emails or texts. We will never again meet them for coffee or late-night snacks. Perhaps the words Paul offered to his friends in Rome might help us move through our grief with a little more confidence. Let's look at three things Paul wrote in Romans 8:26-39.

God is in all things working toward the good of all.

During those times in life when we painfully ask why things happen the way they do; or when we feel as though we have poured out our hearts to God in prayer only to feel ignored, as though our prayers are left dangling in the rafters of our own despair; sometimes it is then that we hear the inner leanings from God speaking to us in the form of a loving embrace. One has to wonder whether maybe the Apostle Paul had those same musings:

> Likewise the Spirit helps us in our weakness, for we do not know how to pray as we ought, but that very Spirit intercedes with groanings too deep for words. And God, who searches hearts, knows what is the mind of the Spirit, because the Spirit intercedes for the saints according to the will of God.

> We know that all things work together for good for those who love God, who are called according to his purpose (Romans 8:26-28, NRSV).

Isn't love the very essence of who God is? Doesn't it make sense that the Spirit of God who dwells within would grab the imagination of all who are tuned in to that inner voice, and would serve as a navigator through the rocky waters of grief? Even when words cannot give adequate expression, the Spirit of God communicates our pain directly to God's loving heart.

Can we even imagine that God is disinterested in our pain? Of course we can. Yet God, whose voice spoke at the beginning of time and all that had been was formed into all that is, is that same God who is infinitely invested in the well-being of all of creation. Certainly that same God has the capacity to ultimately love all who grieve, including you and me.

Can we further imagine that as we sit in our grief, that God sits with us in the muck of our pain and loss? God is not too dignified to get his clothes messy in that muck. God sees the pain and is drawn toward the person experiencing that pain. And God who loves perfectly does not step in to stop the root cause of the pain, but will invite all who are broken by life and grief to join in the re-creation of life that can be lived hand in hand with God and others.

This is how God loves those who are in pain. God searches human experience and human hearts for an opportunity to impress and imprint upon those who are listening a sense of what might render the greatest outcome toward the good of all. God is speaking and when we listen and participate with God, the greatest possible good will result for that moment. God's Spirit moves our heart's cry into the heart of God, and God speaks.

God is always advocating optimistically for all.

As we have just stated, God is always working toward the very best outcome and sense of well-being for all. But notice how Paul further presses this point.

> What then are we to say about these things? If God is for us, who is against us? He who did not withhold his own Son but gave him up for all of us, how will he not with him also give us everything else? Who will bring any charge against God's elect? It is God who justifies. Who is to condemn? It is Christ who died, or rather, who was raised, who is also at the right hand of God, who also intercedes for us. Who will separate us from the love of Christ? Will affliction or distress or persecution or famine or nakedness or peril or sword? (Romans 8:31-35, NRSV)

Paul here is writing of a very optimistic act on God's part. God "gave him up for all of us." God, the divine parent, gave up Jesus in the hope that God's created race of humans would receive that gift in love. That seems like a risk, don't you think? The optimism of God's grace and love give testimony to the extent of God's investment in creation.

God is that invested in each of us and in our experience of pain and loss, and God is confident in his aim for our well-being. But not just ours, God is equally invested in the eternal well-being of those for whom we grieve. God does not ever give up on the human will to choose life according to God's purposes or aim. As long as we exist in the eternal scheme of things, God impresses the human will toward the greater inclinations of God's dream for creation. I believe that even extends beyond this life. God never gives up.

God is always loving, and nothing can erase that love.

It is not unusual in grief settings to hear persons express the pain of guilt, implying that certainly they have not been good enough to find favor with God. Or perhaps their life choices have placed them in a space where they might face condemnation rather than grace for eternity. Paul seems to take such thinking and feelings on in the last part of this chapter.

> For I am convinced that neither death, nor life, nor angels, nor rulers, nor things present, nor things to come, nor powers, nor height, nor depth, nor anything else in all creation will be able to separate us from the love of God in Christ Jesus our Lord. (Romans 8:38-39, NRSV)

For God to offer an eternal existence for us to spend with God, it makes sense that God desires that shared experience with all. Wouldn't you expect that from a God whose essence is love? It should follow that God would hold that hope for everyone. Therefore, Paul reminds us that God's love is more powerful than any opposing force or influence; even death. With a touch of literary drama, Paul declares that there is nothing we could imagine that could possibly get between God and the objects of divine love.

Perhaps you live in the fear that your loved one is at risk of facing an eternity outside of God's grace. Consider Paul's words "neither death, nor life." Are we any stronger than "angels or rulers"? Paul seems to cover all the bases. From Paul's perspective, there isn't much chance that God's love might be sidestepped. This is not some form of legal or legalistic formula, it is simply the depth of God's desire that all should have eternal life. That sounds just like a God whose essence is love. A lesser god might set restrictions on love and on those who might have access to that love.

As we pause to give expression to our grief today, might we reflect on the character of God whose very nature is expressed in the forward movement of love working for the greatest good for all. Also reflecting, if you will, on the timeless optimism of that love which never gives up on the human will. And finally, let us reflect on the endurance of God's love which nothing can breach. Nor can anything or anyone create separation between that love and the objects of that love, that is, human hearts, even broken ones.

Tracy L. Tucker currently serves as a Chaplain for Community Hospice and Palliative Care in Jacksonville, Florida, following 30 years in full-time parish ministry. He earned his M.Div. from Nazarene Theological Seminary and is currently working on his DThM through Northwind Theological Seminary. Tracy is a Board-Certified Chaplain through the Association of Professional Chaplains and has a Certification in Thanatology through the Association for Death Education and Counseling.

The Wedding at Cana Got Almost Upended!

ANAND VEERARAJ

Wedding banquets are occasions for fun, music, dance, feasting, and wining; but the wedding at Cana got almost upended. Somebody dropped the ball!

Scripture lesson: John 2:1-11
A homily delivered at the wedding of a family member, Chicago, IL, December 16, 2023

Rachel and Matthew! We are delighted and honored to be part of the most important milestone of your life. With parents, families, and every one present here, we wish you God's richest blessings and peace as you begin your journey.

My talk is based on the wedding in Cana (John 2:1-11). The title of this homily is *"The Wedding at Cana got almost upended!"* Don't be misled by the title. If I may offer you an iconic motif for your life, it would be the word "banquet." As husband and wife, we wish your life to be like a banquet—*A Perpetual Wedding Banquet*. Wedding banquets are occasions for celebration of love and life. Even if you cannot remember my homily, I want you to remember one thing. Your life together should be an *Open, Inclusive and Welcoming Banquet.* Wedding banquets are filled with laughter, music, dance, feasting, and of course, good wine. It should not be a one-time event, but an ongoing process throughout your life.

Life is primarily about happiness and self-fulfillment. It is a new way of imagining life, transforming our mundane human grind into creative adventure, novelty, and hospitality. The life and ministry of Jesus reflected a banquet. Jesus said, "I have come that they may have life, and that they may have it more abundantly" (John 10:10 NKJV).

Banquets and table fellowships were hallmarks of Jesus's life and mission. It was a sign of God's kingdom on earth. Jesus ate and drank with all sorts of people, especially marginalized folks and social outcasts. By doing so, he introduced a novel iconic paradigm shift in human odyssey, existence, and survival.

The philosophy of an Open Banquet or table fellowships is simple and plain. When I invite you to my table-fellowship, you may gladly accept and come in. I will spread before you a sumptuous dinner. I would also count this as an opportunity to fellowship and get to know you better so that I may continue to invest in your flourishing. The question is, "How do we follow in the footsteps of Jesus and transform our lives to be an open banquet?"

The First thing to remember—Rachel and Matt—you getting married today is no accident. We are all products of our past. What we are today is due to the past events of our lives. God knew you even before you were born and fashioned you before the foundations of the world. (Jeremiah 1:4; Ephesians 1:4-6). *You are not an accident*; neither am I, nor anyone present here. Not everything from our past, however, has been good for our well-being and flourishing. Yes, we have had our share of disappointments, sadness, painful experiences; but we have successfully overcome all hurdles, hardships, and handicaps. I'm sure you know Led Zeppelin's song, *"Good Times, Bad Times."* And here we are, intact and in one piece. That awareness alone should instill within us awe and wonder, and a sense of utter humility for all that has been invested in our lives—by our parents, families, friends, forebears, society, and the whole cosmos. The cosmos? Yes. The great astrophysicist Carl Sagan famously said, "We are all made of stardust."

That does not mean God gives you a blueprint for your present and the future. No! *You are not an automaton, neither are you a robot.* What is the difference between a robot and a human being? Robots do not have a destiny. Humans do! Robots do not have a life, nor do they think on their own. They are mere gadgets, programmed to perform in accordance with their internal digital logic in response to external stimuli. We humans do not respond mechanistically to situations, influences, or inducements. In each moment, God offers us the best possibilities for moving toward goodness, beauty, love, and flourishing. Yet, God invests us with powers to make choices, draw resources from within and without, to create our own brave new world for ourselves and for others. We have within us the moral and ethical compasses to guide us in our choices. Yes, we perform most mundane actions instinctively, without much thought. On the other hand, we are also empowered to think and act creatively outside the box, to keep the banquet alive. Robots won't do that even in these days of AI Chatbots.

Yes, we are alive, moment by moment. We feel pain and pleasure. "Being Present (*mit-sein*) means," says Fr. Kurian Kachappilly, Dharmaram College, Bangalore, India, "staying receptive to each moment as it comes, immersing ourselves fully in the here and now, without clinging to the past or being preoccupied with the future. A mission of Christian presence is a life of engagement in and with the world around us as *alter Christus*" ("Christmas 2023, A Mission of Presence").

I remember attending a wedding in India. Nothing unusual about the wedding service. After the Wedding March was over, the guests walked over to the banquet hall to await the arrival of the newly married couple. We waited for almost two hours; a few guests became tired and started to leave. After much delay, the master of the ceremony walked in sheepishly and announced that the couple were unable to join the celebrations and went on to invite the guests to join in the wedding dinner. A cloud of gloom fell over the crowd. Slowly, the news started to leak. Eventually, we came to know that the groom grew cold feet and drove off, leaving his newly married wife in tears. Sadly, for this couple, the wine had run out even before their marriage got started.

The Wedding in Cana gives us a peek into how we may keep the banquet advancing with little fanfare in spite of unexpected turns of events. Somebody dropped the ball. Whoever it was, he did not plan for unexpected exigencies. Mary, with her maternal instincts, was keenly aware of the impending calamity. Anxiously rushing to Jesus's side, she whispered, *"They have run out of wine."*

Initially, Jesus was reluctant to get involved. You could almost hear him yell at Mary, "I am not responsible for this calamity. Close the shop and tell the guests to go home." Obviously, Jesus was visibly annoyed and offensively rude to Mary, addressing her as "woman." Undeterred, Mary surreptitiously put together a team of accomplices. Because she knew very well what Jesus was capable of. When Jesus found out about the scheme, it was too late. Something had to be done swiftly before the crisis got out of hand. This was a moment that called for Jesus to think outside the box, summon the divine salve, and turn the water into wine. Only a handful of people at the banquet working behind the scenes knew what had happened. Completely oblivious, the guests continued with their merry making, wining, dining, and dancing.

You may wonder who deterred the catastrophe? Jesus or Mary? I come back to what Mary said to Jesus, "They have run out of wine." Think about this statement for a moment! You may never, ever, ever want to hear this statement from your spouse. A wedding sermon like this is not just for the couple to be married, but for all of us who are present here. So, I exhort you, 'Listen to your spouse in your life!' That is what we always do; and we have been married for over fifty-two years!

In closing, may I draw your attention to what Apostle Paul writes, "*You are not your own; you are bought with a price. Therefore, honor God with your bodies.*" (1 Corinthians 6:19-20 NIV). We do not merely survive for our own happiness and fulfillment. As Christians, we are called to give our lives in service of those in need. We applaud Matthew and Rachel! You both have opted for noble professions—Healthcare vocations. Healthcare is all about our Common Humanity. Throughout his ministry, Jesus healed all manner of sickness, without expecting anything in return (Matthew 4:23-25). By your professions, you both express your Christian witness in the service of those who are physically, mentally, emotionally, and spiritually in need. In so doing, you follow in the footsteps of Jesus, striving toward making this world a better place.

Rachel and Matt! You both are about to make solemn promises to one another and pledge sacred vows before God and this congregation. The words of the vows are taken from the 1999 version of the Anglican Book of Common Prayer, which reads, *"With this ring, I thee wed, with my body I thee worship, and with my worldly goods I thee endow."* Of course, this is Victorian English. Here, you would recite the vows in Modern English. Unfortunately, in the modernized version, the word "honor" replaces "worship," diluting the original impetus. Some liturgists and theologians thought that the word "worship" should be reserved exclusively for the adoration of God, our creator. Applying the term for reverence to our spouses would be sacrilegious. I beg to differ. The act of worship is the highest form of human adoration and devotion we can render to anyone, either divine or human. I strongly believe that your spouse is worthy of worshipful reverence and adoration, second only to God. If you remember to observe this faithfully, day in and day out, let me assure you, your wine will never run out.

"Let your light so shine before men, that they may see your good works and glorify your Father in heaven." (Matthew 5:16 NKJV). God be with you. Amen.

Anand Veeraraj is an ordained minister in the Church of South India and serves as the Pastor-emeritus of the New Jersey Indian Church/Trinity Community Church at Princeton, New Jersey. He is the author of the book, *Green History of Religion* [Bangalore, India: CFCC, 2006] and other books and articles. He earned a Ph.D. in Religion and Ecology from Claremont University, California. He lives with his wife in Warminster, Pennsylvania, USA. He may be reached at: veerarajanand@gmail.com; Phone: 609-516-7696.

Does God Have a Plan?

JEFF WELLS

God lures us on the endless adventure of creation transformation and becoming—but there is no predetermined plan or roadmap.

A sermon preached at the Church of the Village, August 23, 2020
Reading: Jeremiah 29:11-14 (recommended: *NRSV* and *The Message*)

Does God have a plan for your life? For mine? For our church? For these trees or the river behind me? For the whole universe? That seems to be what the prophet Jeremiah has God saying: "I know the plans I have for you." In Jeremiah, God was addressing not an individual, but the community of the Israelites in exile in Babylon. From Jeremiah's perspective, God promised to bring them back home.

Jeremiah understood God to have that kind of power—the power to make plans and then make them happen. There's an aphorism about "plans" that I'm sure most of you have heard. It says, "We make plans and God laughs." That implies that whatever plans we come up with, God can overrule them. Yet, two weeks ago, we talked about process theology, we learned that God exercises power through persuasion and not coercion. So, God lures us. God invites us. God offers us a range of possibilities in each moment. And God desires to influence our decisions and actions. God wants us to choose well, but God does not coerce or control. Instead, God is in a beautiful and mutual relationship with us. It's an amazing ongoing creative process of becoming—our becoming and God's own becoming.

So, if God cannot impose "God's will," is there still value in the image of God Jeremiah offers? Can we reinterpret Jeremiah's words and re-envision the Israelites' God for our own time? Can we reimagine the meaning of "plan"?

God cannot have a *specific* plan for you or me or for our community or species or world in the way people so often conceive of it. God can't have a plan in that sense because God doesn't coerce *and* God does not know the future. While God knows everything that has ever happened and knows all the possibilities that might occur or choices we might make, God does not know what *will* occur until it actually happens. *God does not know the future.* In any given moment, God offers us a range of possibilities. Then, in the split second of our choosing, we get to surprise God! God does not like all the outcomes, but I think God thrives on being surprised!

So, God doesn't have "a plan," but God *does have* an intention, a desire, an ethos, a set of guiding principles grounded in love and justice. God is love and we could say that God is always dreaming about what could be. So, in each moment of our lives, God sees what choice or action or failure to act is going to move us, individually and collectively, in a worse or a better direction. That means in every event, every choice, God's intention and desire are part of the process. As we choose and change and the universe changes, God changes too. We have an impact on God.

Let's think about this another way. God does not have plans, but God sees and offers many possible pathways, for you and me and our community and the environment and for the stars and planets—possibilities for our becoming, our growth, our transformation, our fulfillment. God can handle whatever we throw at her. She is capable of offering a new set of possibilities for every move we make—or fail to make. I suspect you can recognize that pattern in your own life experience—in your own behavior. Has your own "plan" or "vision" for your life remained static? For me, it has been a process in which there were a lot of roadblocks, detours, disappointments, and also unanticipated joys, successes, and surprises.

My own understanding of who I am and the purpose or direction of my life has changed many times in my 63 years. Isn't that true for you? As I prepared this message, I thought, especially, about how my vocational calling has evolved.

First, I thought about my call to "preach." I used to think that God had a plan. I thought God really meant for me to become a pastor and preacher. I bought into the idea that this was "God's will" all along, but that I had ignored or run away from "God's plan." In my mind, I was Jonah, trying to go in the opposite direction and get as far away as possible. But, now I believe God offered me the idea of "preaching" as one of several possible good avenues *at that moment in my life*. I don't believe God was saying, "This is my sole plan for your life—you must do this." Also, that morning in 1999 when I was meditating in my kitchen, all I heard from God was the word "preach." I could have taken that in a number of directions. God did not say, "go to seminary, learn to preach, and be ordained in the United Methodist Church." God invited me to consider "preaching," in the broad sense, as one among many possible directions. And God desired that I would continue to listen to God's leading and co-create a future.

Also, "preaching" was not my first vocation. I did not sense the call to preach until I was 43 years old. I did sense from a young age that I wanted to contribute to making the world a better place, but I did not know what I wanted to "be." In college, I majored in history only because that's the area I had the most credits in when I was forced to declare a major. In the early 1970s, I became attracted to the ideas and practices of Marxism. I didn't *plan* to become a Trotskyist, but that's the direction my life took and, for many years, it became a way for me to grow in and express my passion for social justice. After I went to seminary and got ordained, I used to look back on that period of my life and think it was just a diversion from the real purpose of my life. But the more I have reflected on it, the more I think that God may have actually participated in luring me to radical politics. Now, it seems to me quite possible that God's message—that I did not register consciously at the time—was, "I see this passion in you. This is one possible positive direction for you to pursue. You may learn valuable lessons from doing this. Go be a communist!"

Think about how our relationship with God actually works. We are not passive creatures waiting for God to give us direction. God interacts with our own evolving understanding, interests, passions, flaws. We participate with God in a fabulously complex interplay of God's luring possibilities and our history, experience, gifts, resources, and relationships. God lures us in our ongoing becoming toward the fullest possible experience of loving and being loved—toward becoming the most fully alive we can be. How awesome is that!

God intends the greatest possible flourishing, not just for individual creatures, but for groups, communities, and for the whole universe. This complex interplay with God occurs intensively within communities. If we look closely, it's easy to see that in the Church of the Village—a community we share in together and know well. I'll just give you a recent example. Many of you will already have read the letter adopted and published this week by our Vision & Ministry Council. Just imagine how the complexity of God's luring in dialogue with the passions, interests, and impulses of all our individual leaders gets magnified as we try to make a decision and take action together! In our letter to the Bishop and other leaders in our New York Annual Conference, we strongly backed the statement of Black Methodists for Church Renewal and offered our strong support for addressing the systemic racism and white privilege that have been, and are still, affecting our Conference.

Our letter arose out of a long history of anti-racist proclamations and actions on the part of church members and clergy in churches that became COTV. Those persons and communities were lured by God and made choices in the historical context that extended from the 1960s through the early 2000s. Now, we encounter the contemporary context of the murders of Ahmaud Arbery, Brionna Taylor, and George Floyd, followed by mass protests. Those who came out to protest were also lured by God in the mix of their own histories and experience. This very present context encouraged and inspired already existing groups of NYAC clergy and laity, including Black Methodist for Church Renewal, to issue statements. So, in early August, when I proposed to the Vision & Ministry Council the idea of endorsing the BMCR statement, it led to a rich and complicated conversation, with plenty of contending ideas, and surely the participation of God in each of us AND in our interplay with each other. Ultimately, we came to a consensus around not endorsing, but supporting the efforts to address racism in the NYAC by writing our own statement and encouraging other congregations to do so. If you have not read it, I encourage you to do so. It is a powerful statement that is already being circulated by others and having an impact. Also, I believe the collaborative process that led to has strengthened our leadership and can be a model for how we handle taking this kind of public stand in the future.

God was with us every step of the way. God was intimately involved in the lives of the members of the churches that became COTV, some of whom are in our Vision & Ministry Council. God has been involved in the relationships we have built with each other and with many throughout the Annual Conference. God was immersed in our deliberations over the past three weeks as we moved together toward creating our statement. In that process, God was with us and is always with us, luring us toward always becoming the most loving, affirming, compassionate, and passionate congregation we can be.

At their best, our lives are beautiful mosaics, adventures in continual *becoming*, through our constant interplay with God's love and luring. God loves to participate in the endless wonder of becoming—endless creativity, spontaneity, change, evolution, transformation, and renewal. How much more powerful and relational that is than the vision of God who is either a controlling puppet-master or a distant hands-off observer. God does not offer a roadmap that our lives, our relationships, or our community must follow. Yet, God can lure us out of exile and help us to get back home. To paraphrase Jeremiah, God has "a deeply loving desire for our welfare and not for harm, to give us a future with hope."

Jeff Wells is the lead pastor of the Church of the Village, a progressive, radically inclusive, and anti-racist community in the New York City. He preaches, practices, and promotes process-relational and open & relational theology. Jeff is an active member of the Alliance for Ecological Civilization. In 2022, he helped found and co-chaired the Living Earth Movement. With John B. Cobb Jr., he co-authored a short book, *Is International Cooperation Possible? A Bold Appeal for a Living Earth* (2022). Website: jeffrywells.love

Striving for Goodness and "Missing the Mark"

JEFF WELLS

God cannot compel us to be good and not sin, but God beckons us in every moment toward goodness, beauty, compassion, and love.

Reading: Psalm 32:1-8, 11 (*The Inclusive Bible*)
Sermon preached at the Church of the Village, February 26, 2023

For our new worship series for Lent, the Worship Vision Team decided to take on the challenging topic of *sin*. That's something, I admit, we have avoided talking about much in worship at the Church of the Village. Instead, we have used words or phrases that are easier to digest, like "falling short" or "missing the mark." The concept of "sin," along with the presumed consequences of sin, have so often been used to shame, control, condemn, punish, and exclude people. But avoiding the word doesn't negate its reality. It affects us personally, institutionally, and systemically. So, in this series, we want to explore, gently and lovingly, the reality of sin through the lenses of ethics, grace, repentance, and love.

Today, I want to offer an alternative to the classical Christian doctrine of "original sin." I will share why I think process-relational theology can help us reclaim the theological category of "sin" as a valuable part of our theology and our way of being in the world.

I don't have time to explore the complicated evolution of the doctrine of "original sin," but I do highly recommend the thorough and fascinating Wikipedia article on the subject. I *know* there are some of you out there who want to sink your teeth into the tasty topic of "hamartiology"—that's the churchy and academic term for the branch of Christian theology that studies sin.

Augustine of Hippo (354-430) was the first Christian theologian to offer a robust conception of "original sin." He taught that the sin of Adam and Eve (although the focus is on Adam) was based on harmful desire and that sin is passed on to every human being at birth, not merely by example. Initially, Augustine believed sin was part of our very nature and this inheritance left our ability to choose good severely weakened.

The majority of mainline Christians and others now view the Adam and Eve story as a mythological tale created to explain human behavior and humanity's relationship with God. I suspect that no one in worship today believes that human infants are sinful by nature. Yet, it seems pretty clear that we are surrounded by sin and that none of us escape it. So, how can we understand how sin continues to infuse human behavior? How should we try to deal with it or live with it?

The impulse to sin is something we learn because we are born into and are inextricably connected to families, communities, organizations, and broader social systems which both exhibit *and teach*—explicitly or implicitly—the whole spectrum of behaviors from evil to goodness and self-giving. And it's not a binary. None of us are perfectly righteous or completely sinful. We are a mix of behaviors that span the spectrum. Just as we learn to be selfish, to harm ourselves and one another, we also have the capacity to learn to do good, to act out of love.

I suspect most Christians still view sin as primarily a personal, individual problem. It doesn't help that so much talk about sin focuses on sexual sin in particular while ignoring or downplaying widespread sins like greed, the perpetuation of poverty and homelessness, gross economic inequity, white supremacy, exploitation, destruction of ecological systems and living species, and so on. We may realize that the ways our political, economic, educational, and religious institutions contribute to grave harm done to people and the planet, yet our impulse remains to see sin in our society as the result of individual, personal failures. Theologian, Marjorie Suchocki, who I had the chance to meet at the Process Studies conference two weeks ago, says, "the individualization of sin is the trivialization of sin" ("Original Sin Revisited," *Process Studies* Vol. 20, Number 4, Winter, 1991).

The truth is that we are caught up in systemic sin and we are impelled to be willing or unwilling participants. So, whether we call it "original" or not, we need an understanding of sin that accounts for our collective human condition. Sin is a social phenomenon in the sense that "each individual sin is only properly understood in relation to the backdrop of sin evidenced by [humanity] as a whole" (Suchocki, "Original Sin Revisited").

Of course, individual human beings engage in harmful, unethical, and immoral behavior and we do bear individual responsibility. Yet, those acts do not arise separately from our social milieu. Individual sin is in a dialectical relationship with the sinful policies, practices, norms, and mores propagated by collective structures and systems that provide the soil for them. The individual and the corporate reinforce one another. When we act against someone else's good, we act against our own good as well. In other words, we are all connected.

Process theology aids our understanding of this reality because it helps us to recognize that God is not all-powerful, yet is *very powerful*—always loving and always luring and inspiring us. "Sin" is the word that names the ways we fail, collectively and individually, to listen to God leading.

God does not merely lure each of us individually and separately. God lures all human beings and every element in the universe toward the greatest good, toward love, truth, and beauty. God's desire is to lead all toward the greatest good for all. Sin gets in the way of God's desire and often in the way of our own best interests.

Therefore, God takes into account each of our individual desires, passions, abilities and weaknesses, and all of our past experiences, as well as the harmful ways we may have been shaped, and abuse and traumas we may have suffered. God also sees all of the ways human beings—especially those with the most power and resources, collude with one another to build and prop up sinful social systems. With all of that knowledge and with God's infinite wisdom, God works in us, individually and collectively, to move us toward the good—toward the best possible outcomes for all.

The expressions of human sin that do the most widespread harm are those that arise from human systems of domination and control that benefit relatively few human beings. As human civilizations became larger and ever more technically advanced, the capacity to exploit and do harm also increased exponentially. That has led us to a situation in which humanity is now on the brink of potentially causing the extinction of our own species and threatening the ability of the ecosphere to sustain any life on Earth.

It doesn't have to go this way. Such social sin is not inevitable. There are really bright people around who know how to run an economy that does not depend on the control of giant corporations and the enrichment of a handful of billionaires. There are lots of people who know how to create regional agricultural systems that do not destroy the soil or kill off birds and pollinating insects. We have a pretty good idea of what needs to be done. As scholar activist, Heather McGee, has written about confronting racism, to the extent white people can learn to work with people of color, we will all reap huge "solidarity dividends" that will benefit everyone.

There are shining examples of the way forward. Millions of individuals and thousands of organizations are working in a myriad of ways to confront the ecological crisis and transform the ways human societies interact with the Earth and its living systems. The nation of Bhutan has rejected "Gross Domestic Product—GDP"—in other words, ever-increasing consumption and accumulation of wealth—as the measure of its "progress." Instead, it used the Gross National Happiness Index to guide its policies around economic and social development and ecological sustainability. There are now Gross National Happiness centers in Thailand and Spain, as well.

God cannot compel us to be good and not sin. God's power is expressed through love and a longing for the common good. Perhaps we can never completely overcome our human tendency to sin, but we surely will not diminish the harm we do to ourselves, one another, and the world without God's luring and also without collective effort and acting in mutual solidarity and love.

We know that we humans have the capacity to act outside of mere self-interest and move toward societies based on inclusive care for all human and beyond human existence. We know because we have seen and continue to see examples of it. Process philosophy and process-relational theology give us the tools to see that all existence, not just humanity, is deeply connected and interwoven in a network of solidarity and mutuality. To the extent we can grasp that fundamental truth and listen deeply for God's luring and leading, we strengthen our ability to resist and uproot our collective human tendency to sin.

Jeff Wells is the lead pastor of the Church of the Village, a progressive, radically inclusive, and anti-racist community in the New York City. He preaches, practices, and promotes process-relational and open & relational theology. Jeff is an active member of the Alliance for Ecological Civilization. In 2022, he helped found and co-chaired the Living Earth Movement. With John B. Cobb Jr., he co-authored a short book, *Is International Cooperation Possible? A Bold Appeal for a Living Earth* (2022). Website: jeffrywells.love

You Give Love a Bad Name

JAMES TRAVIS YOUNG

"Rather than institutions and events, God's dynamic vision for our future involves transformative discipleship powered by relational love through the Spirit."

I have friends and family who, when faced with disappointments or difficult circumstances in life, complain about what is going on, only to shrug their shoulders and close the subject by remarking, "But God is in control."

And then when something good happens, the same people wax poetic about the "providence" of God and how they are wonderfully blessed.

Their outlook regarding our existence seems to be as if we are all helplessly tossed about by every wave in the ocean without a canoe or even a paddle. With such a resigned, fatalistic outlook, it really is no surprise that the faith experiences of so many come down to scheduled services in a building, or using prayer like a magic lamp that might or might not be out of wishes.

But that isn't how God is presented in scripture, and that isn't what a real relationship with God looks like.

"Providence" is actually a perfect way to describe how God interacts with earthly creatures. The word comes from the Latin term *providentia*, which is a combination of *pro*, meaning "ahead," and *vidēre*, meaning "to look." So, providence is linked to the idea of looking ahead, or making provisions for the future.

Rather than a controlling God who knows everything and controls everything, leaving it to us to make excuses for why good or bad things happen, when we recognize that God is providential, we accept that God has a dynamic, loving vision for our future. Not only does our agency and responsiveness play a vital, essential role in our relationship with God, but with every other creature as well—and even our own future.

Ephesians 4 employs the same metaphor I used a moment ago, and says that instead of being like "infants, tossed back and forth by the waves, and blown here and there by every wind of teaching and by the cunning and craftiness of people in their deceitful scheming," we can "grow to become in every respect the mature body of Christ, who is the head…joined and held together by every supporting ligament" (Ephesians 4:14-16a, interpolated).

We are not, and never have been, hapless victims of circumstance—we have a real relationship with God. That means God is responsive to us, and we are to God. We work *together*.

That other metaphor in Ephesians 4, that we are the body connected with Jesus as the head, is a great way to understand this relationship: connected relationally with God and one another, "we work together as one unit, growing and building itself up in love as each part does its work" (Ephesians 4:16, interpolated).

So, God has a vision for the future. God's guidance and influence intersects with our human decisions and the natural world's unfolding processes.

Connected together with one another, we are not only participants in our own future, but when we are powered by love, our lives have a trajectory, a purpose that goes beyond just existing and believing.

Because there are things about the world we live in that are bad—even *evil.*

How can it be loving for Christ-followers to do nothing but play church when people within the reach of our arms are starving? Or when others whose lives are filled with fear and sadness and anger and tragedy feel all alone because we're too busy organizing programs and leaving the rest to prayer?

Is that *really* how it works?

I don't think so. People (and churches) like that give love a bad name.

Jesus voiced radically different plans for the church than people like you and me treating it like a business, or event, or anything that can be managed or institutionalized: "And I tell you that you are Peter, and on this rock I will build my church, and the gates of Hades will not overcome it" (Matthew 16:18, NIV).

There are many who miss the point and argue about the apostle Peter's role and the hierarchal succession of apostles over the centuries, or even the meaning of "church." By the way, Jesus spoke in Aramaic, and the actual word he used most literally means "community." But what is often overlooked in this passage should be the most obvious thing:

Jesus said *he* would build *his* church.

Not only does it *belong* to him—not us—*Jesus* is who builds it.

Over and over throughout his ministry, just like in this verse, Jesus told his disciples that the *community* would replace a temple built of wood and stone as where God's presence is evident. He even spoke several times in no uncertain terms of how the great temple King Herod had built in Jerusalem would one day be destroyed, "not one stone left on another" (Matt 24:1-2; Mark 13:1-2; Luke 21:5-6). Both Matthew and Luke depict Jesus lamenting that Jewish leaders in Jerusalem ignored his message.

Over and over, Jesus communicated that a community of disciples could be indestructible against even the "gates of Hades." That is how he said he is building his church.

So, if we are connected together with Jesus and one another as the body of Christ powered by love, then how should we properly respond? What is our role?

As it turns out, Jesus *did* share with his followers how he builds his church in connection with us: "Then Jesus came to them and said, 'All authority in heaven and on earth has been given to me. Therefore go and make disciples of all nations, baptizing them in the name of the Father and of the Son and of the Holy Spirit, and teaching them to obey everything I have commanded you. And surely I am with you always, to the very end of the age'." (Matthew 28:18-20, NIV). That's how it is supposed to work: he builds his church by his disciples making disciples.

This was not a new instruction. Jesus had previously sent seventy-two (Lk 10:1-17) and the twelve (Mt 10:1-4; Mk 3:13-19; Lk 6:12-17) out in pairs, commissioned to tangibly change the lives of others, and empowered to share the same kingdom message he preached.

This may seem like a tall order for regular folks such as you and me, but it shouldn't be: remember *providence*—God has a vision for the future, for us and for all creatures. And God's relationship with us is fueled by *love*.

That is how Jesus said the disciples would be known. According to the gospel of John, on the night Jesus was betrayed, he gave them a final instruction: "A new command I give you: Love one another. As I have loved you, so you must love one another. By this everyone will know that you are my disciples, if you love one another" (John 13:34-35, NIV).

Relationship is *responsiveness*. Just as God responds to us, we respond to God. When we extend responses that are powered by God's unconditional love to others we find connection with, we make Christlike disciples.

The real question isn't how to make disciples, but how to *love*.

Relationship is the answer. People who feel tossed by the waves don't talk a lot about feeling like they have a lot of people tossed with them, no matter who or how they share their feelings. And so many feel alone and excluded, some even by those who claim to represent the church. Relationships must be more than just programs, meetings, or events to be real love.

So how do we love the world within the reach of our relationships?

Jesus also made this very simple. Here is how scripture says it played out:

> … an expert in the law, tested him with this question: "Teacher, which is the greatest commandment in the Law?" Jesus replied: "'Love the Lord your God with all your heart and with all your soul and with all your mind.' This is the first and greatest commandment. And the second is like it: 'Love your neighbor as yourself.' All the Law and the Prophets hang on these two commandments." (Matthew 22:35-40, NIV)

Loving others is like loving God—with all our heart and all our soul and all our mind. It means we hold nothing back. The same way that we would want to be loved is how we are to love others. Everyone is worthy of all the love we have to give.

It's a beautiful idea. And for some, it is also terrifying. There are people out there we all know who give love a bad name.

I could give you example after example from the Bible, but you probably already know someone who gives love a bad name…and if you don't, it might even be you! But remember, we are not alone in this loving lifestyle—God's relational love is evidenced alongside us by the Spirit.

Jesus promised that the Spirit is how God's love connects us together. The book of Acts actually portrays Jesus describing this loving spiritual connection as *power:* "But you will receive power when the Holy Spirit comes on you; and you will be my witnesses…to the ends of the earth" (Acts 1:8, NIV).

Loving others and making disciples begins with loving them as we are loved, and *responding* to them in relationship—just as how God responds relationally to us. And when that happens, as we share our lives, how God's love has transformed us, with that connection we are sharing the very love of Christ, a Spirit that can universally influence any person, any creature.

Whether it is the guy who feels awful because he just lost his job, or the mom whose kids were taken away, or the person on the street corner without shoes asking for change, or a family who has a normal life but lives it reaching for happiness and finding disappointment by the things they buy or the people they vote for, or even the church they attend, *there is no substitute for relational love.*

Our providential God has a vision of you and me working together loving others, and our connections with one another and God forms a community of love and holy power called the church. Though not made of anything like scheduled services, offering plates, bricks, programs, or even sermons, nothing else is more powerful than we are when we join together in love.

James Travis Young is an ordained minister in the Church of the Nazarene and has served for decades in several active ministry roles. Travis is a columnist for Patheos (www.patheos.com/blogs/sacredoutcasts/) and his writing has been featured in several books and publications. He and his wife Mandie are making Christlike disciples in Galveston, Texas, USA.

Essays on Preaching, Teaching, and Practicing Open, Relational, and Process Theologies

The Most Liberating Aspect of Preaching from a Process Perspective for Me

RONALD J. ALLEN

I have heard about 10,000 sermons in my life, many of which depend on notions of God that are troubling. Preaching from a process perspective frees me to commend a God who is intellectually credible, morally faithful, and existentially compelling.

By rough count, I have heard about 10,000 sermons in my life as a result of participating in the church from birth, studying preaching in school (university, seminary, and graduate work), serving a local congregation, and teaching preaching for 37 years in a theological school where I often heard as many as six or eight sermons in one day. I have no idea how many books about preaching I have read, but when I retired, my wife and I converted the attic of our 100-year-old house into a third-floor library to keep the books. I have written and edited several volumes that deal with preaching and the Bible as well as preaching in different theological families, including the two volume *Preaching the Manifold Grace of God* that discusses preaching in about forty historical and contemporary theological families. By this season of life, I have heard enough sermons to recognize how process approaches are liberating. In this chapter, I concentrate on the aspect of process that is the most important to me: the process notion of God that is intellectually credible, morally faithful, and existentially compelling.

In all theological families, the nature and purpose of God is central. A primary purpose of preaching is to help the congregation discern the nature and purpose of God and to respond appropriately. Many theological families conceive of God and our response in ways that leave the preacher in difficult positions of having to explain complexities that go against logic, or/and that picture God acting in ways that I consider immoral, or/and are disconnected from the lived experience of what I perceive to really happen (or not happen) in the world. Process theology liberates the preacher from these conundrums.

Alfred North Whitehead famously said that three conceptions of God dominate most theological thinking (*Process and Reality,* 342-43):

- Unmoved mover. This God—derived from Aristotle and playing an important role in classical theism—is not moved by people or things that happen in the world but dictates (moves) what happens in the world for reasons known only to the deity.
- Ruling Caesar. The church cast the traits associated with Caesar onto its image of God, attributing to God Caesar's absolute power, sometimes exercised brutally. The church sometimes makes the image of God into an idol that represents our own limited and self-serving values, practices, dreams, and social power.
- Ruthless moralist. Christians sometimes think of God as the cosmic monitor of moral behavior—both individual and social—whose primary work is setting out rules for behavior and then judging the degree to which people live by them.

Today, I would modify Whitehead's taxonomy as it oversimplifies some elements and misrepresents others. For example, while some Christians do identify God as a ruthless moralist, Whitehead unfortunately identified the ruthless moralist with the God of the Hebrew prophets, not recognizing that the covenant-making/covenant keeping God of the prophets is quite different from a ruthless moralist.

Few laypeople in the county seat churches in the Midwest where I have done most of my preaching and teaching would recognize Whitehead's specific language (unmoved mover, ruling Caesar, ruthless moralist), but we encounter shadows of these ideas in comments and questions from every day, real-life people. "How can we say that God is love and yet God sends people to eternal punishment?" "How can we claim that God is love and has all power and can do all things yet refuses to act on behalf of the person who prays desperately for God to intervene to heal a child on the verge of dying?" "How could a loving God allow persons of African origin to endure slavery for two and a half centuries, Jim Crow segregation, and ongoing racist discrimination?" "Why would a loving God with a universal reach choose to be present at some moments but absent at others?" "I hope someday I will learn what God was trying to teach me when that terrible thing happened."

Such questions vex many preachers and lay people. Some people, I have to admit, seem untroubled by such issues. The world is so unsettled and threatening, they like the security of thinking a powerful unmoved mover or ruling Caesar has things under control, even if that control sometimes shows an ugly side. Many people are content to live with contradiction. Others develop a certain Stoic resignation. "God's ways are not our ways." "We humans cannot understand God." Still others conclude that it makes no sense—or no difference—to believe in Gods with these characteristics. Speaking frankly, it would be hard for me, as a preacher, to commend such understandings of God. My family of origin had two businesses—law and dentistry—and I would likely have taken up law rather than pay homage to the God who is put forth in many traditional theological systems.

Because there are so many aspects of process notions of God that are important and appealing, it is hard to know where to begin. But I choose the aspect that is most existentially important for me: the confidence that God is simultaneously ever fully with me and ever fully with the world and everyone and everything in it. God is present every moment of every day in every situation. I grit my teeth just a little when the elder prays in the opening prayer of the service on Sunday, "God, please be with us this morning," as if God might not be present. How much better the opening prayer, "God, in whose presence we already and always stand...." I do know people who feel like God has abandoned them, but there is a decisive difference between *feeling* that way and God actually doing it.

The confidence that God is omni-present raises the question of what God does for individuals and for larger communities, including nature. Here the di-polar nature of God is key. According to the di-polar nature of God, God is made up of two poles of energy rather like a single and unified ellipse with its two focal points. One pole is continuing and stable and offers the security of predictability. The other pole is adaptability: God adapts the specific expression of God's purposes to the particular character of each moment.

God's fundamental purpose, as stated so eloquently by Marjorie Suchocki, a theologian who taught at Claremont for many years, is "inclusive well-being" (Suchocki, *Fall to Violence*, 13, 18-19, 42-44, esp. 66-80, 86, 101-11, 158; Suchocki, *End of Evil*, 122-30, 133). That is, God aims for every particle in the universe to live in situations in which it is free for optimum becoming—to be fully what it can be. That is what God continuously hopes for every situation. But the specific possibilities and expressions of well-being differ from context to context. God always adapts to the specific situation.

The nature and limit of divine power come into play here. According to process thinkers, God cannot simultaneously be altogether loving, altogether just, and altogether powerful. If God is altogether loving and altogether powerful, then God would use God's power to end situations that deny love to particular people or creatures or elements of nature. Process theologians often contrast coercive power with persuasive power. God cannot coerce, but God does invite.

Since God cannot unilaterally change situations, God seeks to work in partnership with humankind and other constituents of the cosmos. God is ever present, offering invitations to human beings and other elements of the universe to act in favor of inclusive well-being. Women and men, and other elements of the creation, are free to accept or reject God's particular invitation. If they accept, they move towards optimum well-being in the immediate moment. If they reject—and this is bottom line stuff for me—God does not turn against them. God does not reject them. God offers an invitation towards as much inclusive well-being as their circumstance—now changed by their rejection—will permit.

While God does not have infinite power to muscle people and things around, God does have more power than any other entity. That power is the infinite capacity to offer invitations to inclusive well-being. As a colleague of mine once said, "God never gives up." In every moment of every circumstance God seeks the well-being of all.

The emphasis on God seeking to work through partnership with human beings and other elements of creation means that what people do matters. At one level, human attitudes and actions matter because they affect other human beings and the world itself. Process theologians, then, sometimes say that we are co-creators with God. On the one hand, this designation elevates my sense of agency and responsibility. What I do matters. On the other hand, it is easy to let this designation go to my head so that I have an inflated sense of self-importance. I need to remember that I have opportunities to act for well-being because these invitations come as gifts of grace from God.

At another level, and I emphasize this point: attitudes and actions are also important because they matter to God. Another colleague once said, "What we do matters ultimately because it matters to the one who is ultimate." What we think and do makes a difference to God in that God feels all things and thereby takes them into Godself. We can add to the life of God in a positive way by responding positively to opportunities to well-being or we can grieve God by refusing opportunities for inclusive well-being and thinking and acting, instead, in ways that are self-serving and that undercut the well-being of others.

To be sure, the process notion of God troubles many people. Someone recently said to me, "With the process God, it sounds like life just goes on the way it is already going. When I am lying alone in a bed in critical care in the hospital with a terminal illness, and nothing can be done except for me to squeeze the button that releases morphine into my system, what difference does the process God make to me?" I have not been in this situation myself, and as far as I know, have no immediate prospects of being there, though I know I will one day look mortality in the eye. But the process notion of God suggests a possibility for well-being that is appropriate and realistic to the situation. The patient may feel alone, but God is present. Whitehead speaks of God as a fellow-sufferer and a companion (Whitehead, *Process and Reality,* 347-348). God shares in the suffering of the world, so God feels our suffering in all its painful detail. As companion, God goes with us step by step, moment by moment, so that we are not alone. It is unlikely that the unmoved mover, the ruling Caesar, or the ruthless moralist is going to change the circumstances. I think it can make a significant difference to face into the present and future with a sense of divine embrace.

Ronald J. Allen is Professor of Preaching, and Gospels and Letters (Emeritus), having served for 37 years at Christian Theological Seminary. He recently published You Never Step into the Same Pulpit Twice: Preaching from a Perspective of Process Theology (Eugene, OR: Cascade Books, 2022) along with many other books on biblical interpretation and theology in preaching.

What's in a Name?

GABRIE'L J. ATCHISON

Here, I discuss the possibility of creating a Name Change Liturgy for transgender and nonbinary members of our congregations.

In my mid-thirties, I moved back home to New York City to be near my family. At the time, my sister was attending Union Theological Seminary. Because I had a strong desire to reconnect with a church community, she told me about the Unity Fellowship Church Movement (UFCM), an LGBTQ+-affirming denomination with roots in the African American worship tradition. There were several UFCM congregations across the country, and the one closest to us was in Brooklyn, New York.

UFCM was founded in Los Angeles in 1979 by a charismatic, spiritual leader named Carl Bean. Bean actually started his career as a performer. He had a hit Disco song called, "I Was Born This Way!" Recognizing that African American gay men needed affirming spaces to heal from the devastation of HIV/AIDS and from the rejection of the church, Bean started his ministry. His simple message was, "God is love, and love is for everyone!" The message and the ministry spread to many predominately African American cities throughout the U.S. By the time I came on the scene in the early 2000s, UFCM was an established denomination and community, unique in its ability to raise up LGBTQ+ clergy.

UFCM services include the affirmation from 1 John 4:20, which says, "Whoever claims to love God yet hates a brother or sister is a liar. For whoever does not love their brother and sister, whom they have seen, cannot love God, whom they have not seen" (NIV). Participating in UFCM created within me a desire to help mainstream, Protestant congregations become more inclusive of LGBTQ+ Christians. Decades later, I found Open and Relational Theology to be a helpful methodology for my work.

Open And Relational Theology as a Path to Transgender and Nonbinary Inclusion

Because "transgender" and "nonbinary" may be terms with which many are not familiar, I want to take a moment to provide definitions and to explain why naming oneself is so important to members of these communities. Transgender is an umbrella term that describes one specific aspect of a person's identity. We now understand that sex, which is based on biology, is different from gender, which has more to do with culture, society, and norms. Most of us are assigned one of two sexes at birth based on our genitalia. Someone is defined as transgender when the sex assigned at birth does not match their gender or their gender identity.

Transgender people often say they knew something was different very early on in life. Not everyone has the resources, flexibility, or safety to "come out" or "transition" in physical ways—through hormones or surgery. And not everyone feels comfortable enough to dress or express themselves on the outside, in ways that reflect who they really are on the inside.

Allies of transgender people have begun to refer to ourselves as cisgender. Cisgender simply means that our biological sex and our gender identity match. Identifying as cisgender interrupts the tendency to consider one category "normal" and transgender abnormal. Finally, even though we include a "T" in "LGBTQ+," transgender is not a sexuality. A person who is transgender can also be heterosexual, lesbian or gay, or bisexual. It is important not to assume you know anything about a person just because they identify as transgender. When in doubt, ask. But be respectful.

Nonbinary (also *genderqueer, gender non-conforming (GNC), or fluid*) refers to people who do not identify as one or the other gender. Being neither male/man nor female/woman in our society can be very challenging. Like the idea of identifying as cisgender, allies to nonbinary people profess our preferred names and gender pronouns. This action signals our openness to a nonbinary person who can then let us know to use "they," "they, he" or "they, she" or any other combination of pronouns. By including our own pronouns, we reduce the stigma for nonbinary people.

Queer Theology is burgeoning collection of theories or "ways of thinking about God" that fit well under the umbrella of Open and Relational Theology. Queer Theology deemphasizes the divisions between humankind based on gender binaries and other forms of separation as well as the division between humankind and God while making central the interdependence of God, all living things, and the earth. Queer Theology, like Relational Theology, emphasizes our equal value to God and that who we are as creative beings matters to God. God is the energy that is created when we choose to show love to each other. We create God-energy by restoring dignity, meeting people's basic needs, and listening without judgment. The "open" part of Open and Relational Theology emphasizes that we work in co-creation with God to produce better future possibilities. Open and Relational Theology provides the flexibility to look beyond traditionally held beliefs about sexuality and gender and creates a space for Transgender, Nonbinary, and Queer Christian inclusion.

Finally, our teens and young adults are increasingly identifying as nonbinary or transgender. We also know that heterosexual young adults are turned off by the perceived or real anti-gay stance of the church. Therefore, we must come to terms with expanding definitions of gender if we want the church to survive. There will be many who will want to argue about homosexuality as sin, and we need to respect their beliefs; however, I truly believe that we are at a real crossroads at this time.

The Importance of Name Change

For transgender and nonbinary people, changing one's name is an empowering process and an essential step towards wholeness. Transgender people are given a name which matches the gender they were assigned at birth. For nonbinary people, a gendered name given at birth can lead to a lot of frustration and misgendering throughout one's lifetime. The process of being able to choose one's name is exciting, but can also be a bit intimidating. Another challenging step in the name change process is getting one's name changed legally. I will provide some resources at the end of the essay with organizations that help with the legal aspects of name change. Being able to change one's name legally to match one's gender relates to safety and security in public spaces.

Those who publicly change their names often have a ceremony or ritual designed to mark and celebrate the occasion. My dream is that we can create a space for these celebrations within our own church services. The service will be one more way the community can make transgender and nonbinary people feel connected. The rationale for building a name change liturgy for transgender and nonbinary members of our community is that the process will expand our capacity to demonstrate God's love for all creation. For people who may not have the full support of their families or feel safe or welcome in society, we can create communities of care right in our own congregations.

The United Church of Christ adopted the phrase, "God is still speaking!", and I see this as an example of Open and Relational Theology. As we learn more about the diversity of human experience, God expands with us. What remains constant is our directive to love others. Belonging and inclusion in a church context involves breaking free of rigid ideas and imagining a Christian experience that is big enough for us all.

That said, as faith leaders, we recognize that change is almost never welcomed by church folks. In my search to find inspiration, I began to reflect on the concept of *metanoia*. Metanoia is a Greek word that recurs often in the Gospels, especially in the words attributed to Jesus himself. The two parts of the word, "meta" (beyond) and "noos" (mind) could easily be translated as *changing your mind* or *begin to understand things beyond your own mind*. We often miss this challenge to transform our minds, because in most translations of the Bible, metanoia is translated from the Greek as "repent." And repent has a very different connotation. By translating metanoia as "change your mind" or "expand your mind," we are being asked to change in order to embrace the fullness of God.

The concept of metanoia is a touchstone for the clergyperson or congregation working to design a liturgy for name-change. If we are in community with a person who is transgender, they are not experiencing a metanoia, we are.

Building Blocks for a Name Change Liturgy

As a person we love embraces who they are, the deepest act of love we can offer is to welcome that person and celebrate their new name. For faith traditions that centralize the baptism experience, a transgender or nonbinary person can be baptized as a sibling in Christ under their new name. For other traditions, there may be space to have a separate special ceremony for an individual. There are two annual dates created for transgender awareness and celebration—Transgender Week of Awareness, held from November 13 to November 19 and Trans Visibility Day held on March 31—which may serve as guideposts for scheduling the service. Or a Name Change service may be included as part of a Pride Month celebration held in June.

The following are some ideas for scripture and music which can be used during the service.

Scripture

- **The Image of God—**There are two versions of the origin story for humankind. We are often more familiar with the story in Genesis 2, when Eve is formed from the rib of Adam; however, in Genesis 1, the origin story involves the creation of both male and female. More interesting to me, is that in Genesis 1:26, God says, "Let us make man (humankind, "Adam") in our image," opening the possibility of God as a plurality. And at the very least creating room for the possibility that all of humankind reflects God, with no exceptions (Genesis 1:26-28).

- **The Baptism of Jesus—**In this passage, the baptism of Jesus opens the heavens. God proclaims, "This is my Son, whom I love; with him I am well pleased." (NIV) Through baptism, we may all see ourselves as God's children with whom God is well pleased (Matthew 3: 13-17).
- **Psalm 139—**In Psalm 139, David celebrates a God who knew him in the womb and loves and accepts him unconditionally.
- **Philip and the Ethiopian Eunuch—**Eunuchs show up in the Bible in many settings, and some see them as examples of gender nonconformity or variance. The story of Philip and the Ethiopian Eunuch represents the inclusivity of Christianity. Belief is the only requirement for inclusion (Acts 8:16-40).
- **Children of God—**In Galatians, Paul explains that we are neither male nor female in Christ, all belong (Galatians 3:23-28).
- **The New Covenant—**This scripture speaks to not hiding who we are in Christ (2 Corinthians 3:12-18).

Music

- Traditional Hymns
  - *Amazing Grace* (John Newton, 1779) Amazing Grace is a beautiful hymn which goes along with our theme of change and transformation. It is also a good hymn to use because it will be familiar even to those who do not attend church services regularly. Other traditional hymns include, *And They'll Know We Are Christian by Our Love* (Peter Scholtes, *Blessed Assurance* (Frances J. Crosby, 1873) *Here I Am Lord* (Dan Schutte, 1981), *Great is Thy Faithfulness* (Thomas Chisholm, 1923) or *In Christ There is No East or West* (John Oxenham, 1908).
- Contemporary Gospel
  - *I Told Jesus to Change My Name* (James Cleveland, 1974) James Cleveland's song celebrates the transformation that happens in one's life when embracing Christianity but would work well with the themes we are considering. Other contemporary gospel songs include, *Changed* (Walter Hawkins, 1975), *Imagine Me* (Kirk Franklin, 2005), or *Open my Heart* (Yolanda Adams, 1999).

One Last Note

We need to begin to consider Transgender and Nonbinary Christians as members of the body of Christ who need even more love and acceptance from us—because they will be scorned and vilified by society and even rejected by their own families. I want open and affirming congregations to have the tools they need to support and love all our brothers, sisters, and siblings.

Name Change Resources for Transgender People

- Transgender Name Change Project, Transgender Legal Defense and Education Fund, TLDEF - https://transgenderlegal.org/our-work/name-change-project/
- Trans Lifeline - https://translifeline.org/
- National Center for Transgender Equity - https://transequality.org/

Gabrie'l J. Atchison earned her M.A. in Religion from Yale Divinity School. She is the author of *Are You the Unchurched?: How to Develop an Authentic Relationship with God Inside or Outside of Church* (Wipf & Stock, 2022). Her blog, "The Introvert Coffeehouse" is hosted on Substack (https://gabrieljatchison.substack.com/). She lives in Buffalo NY with her rescue dog, Jack.

Preaching as Relationship

TIM BOWMAN

Preaching without notes reminds us that a sermon is a relationship between the preacher, the text, the congregation, and God.

"You were expecting a bloke? Beard; Bible; bad breath?"

"Yes, that sort of thing."

"And, instead, you got a babe with a bob cut and a magnificent bosom."

Fresh from seminary and excessively female, *The Vicar of Dibley's* Geraldine Granger receives a cold welcome in the quirky but conservative parish of Dibley. The show is hilarious, but also a good lesson for any would-be preacher who thinks preaching begins and ends with a skillful lecture on the content and context of Scripture.

Female, racialized, and LGBTQ2S+ clergy quickly discover that preaching is relationship. Who you are, and who your audience is, matters. Straight white guys like me eventually discover this as well. Geraldine eventually wins them all over, even the stuffy David Horton. She does not do so with brilliant, well-researched sermons. Instead, she shows up every day, is present to their crises and insanities, and lets them glimpse a few of her own. She builds relationships.

Ministry is a relationship; preaching is a relationship. Process-relational theology takes relationship seriously. In this essay, I reflect upon the ways in which preaching is a relationship between the preacher, the Scripture, the congregation, and God. I also explore the ways in which preaching without notes can highlight and heighten this relationship.

Process-relational theology is the idea that God and the world are, at the core of their being, about relationship. Because relationships involve give-and-take, this necessarily means that both God and the world continue to change and be influenced by one another: they are in process.

Consider, for example, a rock. Rocks seem pretty stable. The rock exists from moment to moment and, in each moment, it may remain where it is; roll away; melt or fly apart; or even fly away. Over many years, it may do all of these things. It has very little choice in the matter: its choices are fully limited and determined by its past and its environment. If it is on the hillside one moment, it cannot be on the bottom of the sea the next moment—though if someone comes along and tosses it into the surf, the bottom of the sea may be in its future.

On the other hand, consider me, sitting at my keyboard. Like the rock, if I am in New Westminster now, I cannot choose to be in London at the next moment. Neither can I choose to sprout wings and fly away. I can, however, choose to remain focused on this essay, to get up and go for a walk, or to give my cat the food he is demanding. My choice among all these options will be influenced by my history, health, state of mind, and so on. It is also influenced by my friends', family's, and neighbors' actions, reactions, and expectations. My choice will influence not only my future options, but also the options of those I come in contact with, in the same way that a stone thrown into a pond creates ripples that expand and then diminish into the distance. Our actions have consequences for ourselves and for the world, and in that light, we can judge some as better or worse than others.

This is where God comes in. God has a dream, an intention, for each one of us. God continually invites us, lures us, draws us on to possibilities that develop our potential for beauty and complexity. God's invitation and the possibilities She opens up, increase the options available to us at any moment. Like my neighbors and my family, God influences my choices: God is in relationship with me, and with you. Just as God influences me, I influence God: God, at the very least, experiences and understands the suffering—and the joy—of everything in the world. God is unlike you or me or a rock; God is directly in relationship with everything, at all times and in all places. In this process, all of us are becoming something new, every moment.

This inescapable fact of our mutual influence means that every sermon is in some sense, a conversation. Despite the splendid isolation implied by the magnificent elevated pulpits in some churches, the best preachers will recognize this.

Archbishop Melissa Skelton therefore suggested in a preaching class that we should not say "Amen" at the end of our sermons. This advice confused me. Doesn't "amen" simply mean, "Hey, the prayer or sermon is over now"? No. "Amen" suggests that you have delivered the definitive interpretation of the Word of God. It closes down your audience's engagement with the Scripture text, defeating the very purpose of the sermon. Biblical practice would seem to agree: "Amen" is a Hebrew word expressing certainty, agreement, and truthfulness. On Jesus' lips, it is the first word, not the last, in any discourse ("Truly I say to you…"). In both Testaments, it is a response *made by a gathered people.* "Amen" is not ours to pronounce; the audience may choose to affirm our words—or not. In preaching, we enter into a relationship of give and take.

We also recognize this in worship via the Prayer for Illumination: the congregation asks for the Spirit's aid in understanding the text. During the COVID pandemic, several of our United Church congregations came together for worship in order to share livestreaming expertise and equipment. This meant that we clergy collaborated on the service and rotated the task of preaching. One Sunday, after a particularly hard week topped off by technical difficulties with the equipment, my colleague asked one of us to pray for him before he preached. Someone else prayed for him the next week, and it became our regular practice. Although most of our congregation were remote, via technology, this brought the preacher into closer relationship with them. Instead of appearing alone in having a direct line to God, he was visibly struggling along with the rest of us to receive a blessing from the text. Such a practice recalls the apostle Paul's description of the Gospel as a treasure "in clay jars": the words and their power ultimately belong not to the preacher, but to God.

Ronald J. Allen affirms with other Process thinkers that "God is present in all stages of the sermon." God is with the preacher as she struggles to put her insights into words, there again as the preacher seeks a connection with the audience in her delivery, and with the audience as they consider and (perhaps) appropriate the preacher's words as their own. God continues to be present and visible as the audience lives out the sermon in the world, thereby bringing the preacher and the Word into contact with those far beyond the walls of the sanctuary.

In remembering that the final meaning of a text is not ours to pronounce, and in preaching a sermon that respects the audience and engages them in conversation, we enter into the mode of our God who invites rather than compels. If the sermon, as it is finally experienced, is a collaboration between God, the text, the preacher, and the congregation, then the method of delivery is also important. Allen claims that to make this encounter happen, "The sermon…needs to have the quality of living speech. The preacher should be as fully as possible present to the community. This feeling of presence *has less to do with whether the preacher uses notes, an outline, or a complete manuscript,* and more to do with the character of the moment of preaching."

Is it really true that the presence or absence of a manuscript is fairly irrelevant to shaping the preaching encounter? I am not so sure. Just as no battle plan survives contact with the enemy, Allen also says that "A sermon is not fully a sermon until it is spoken in the presence of the congregation." Anyone who has ever preached a sermon knows this to be true: preaching in the silence of one's head during the writing process, or to a webcam in an empty room, or to an apathetic crowd are different and more difficult than preaching to an engaged audience. The audience's engagement with the sermon is part of the sermon.

That being the case, why not test Allen's claim? Try preaching without notes. I find that such sermons become a collaboration between the preacher's memory, the preacher's habits of thought and speech, and verbal and nonverbal cues from the audience. If a preacher knows his material well enough, he can even adapt his sermon depending on his audience's engagement. This may make the preacher more present to the audience, and vice versa, meaning that the sermon takes shape between them. On the other hand, I have known preachers, myself sometimes among them, who, in the absence of notes, go around and around in circles while the audience tunes out. Such a delivery repels the audience rather than engaging them.

I do not often preach without notes. On my five-point charge in rural Newfoundland, I would often preach three times on a Sunday. The first time, apprehension lent nervous energy to my delivery, but kept me fairly close to the words printed on the page. The second time felt flat, because it was the second service in rapid succession, and projecting confidence, empathy, and wisdom is draining for an introvert. The third time, however, felt like flying! The manuscript was more of a security blanket than a straitjacket at this point; I rarely needed to refer to it because I had mostly internalized the words. The point is not that I could now parrot the script without thinking, but rather that I had confidence and familiarity with my message.

Sometimes, however, I preached without notes by necessity. I realized halfway to the next church that I had left them behind at the previous one, twenty minutes away on winding, moose-haunted roads. I was forced, then, to outline the sermon in my head, noting its primary moves and, by necessity, pare the sermon down to a few key points and to its core idea. This tends to improve the sermon and its retention by the audience. Advertising copywriters are encouraged to focus on one simple, core message for a reason. Manuscript-less preachers who fail to do so tend to wander aimlessly in search of their main point; perhaps preaching without notes can help you discover whether in fact you have one!

Process, open, and relational theologies understand God as in relationship with humanity and all Creation. It follows that the encounter with the Word of God—that is to say, preaching—is also an encounter with God, the preacher, and the audience. Those who wish to embrace and convey this truth may choose to marry the medium to the message and dispense with a manuscript from time to time.

Tim Bowman is ordained in the United Church of Canada, serving in the Fraser Valley of British Columbia. He graduated from the Vancouver School of Theology with an M.Div. in 2007 and is currently exploring Process Theology via VST's ThM program. Tim belongs to two cats, and to his wife and child, Jennifer and Zoë.

Collective Responsibility for the Common Good

JOSEPH A. BRACKEN, S.J.

The interaction of the three divine persons tells us something crucial about the interactions of life

Whether or not we are aware of it, we human beings live in two different worlds. There is the unseen world of quantum mechanics, namely, a web of dynamically interrelated energy-events and pre-existing fields of activity in which these events take place. But there is also the world of common sense experience in which the things that happen seem to be governed by the law of cause and effect. How are these different approaches to physical reality related to one another? Since the world of quantum mechanics represents physical reality at its initial level of existence and activity, it makes sense that the world of common sense experience would be somehow based on the world of quantum reality. Thus far, however, scientists do not agree on the laws common to these two different worlds. So, the majority of people alive and well today simply ignore the existence and activity of the mysterious world of quantum mechanics.

But what one knows nothing about may in fact be an impediment to one's overall freedom of thought and behavior. For example, most people are limited in their personal freedom by the various economic, political, cultural and racial systems at work in contemporary society. Naturally, these systems can be changed over time by people working together to make these changes. Yet many people feel reluctant to join with others to make personal sacrifices for the sake of the common good. They need the inspiration of a leader to redefine the common good as a matter of personal achievement. As President John F. Kennedy stated so memorably in his inaugural address, "My fellow Americans, ask not what your country can do for you, ask what you can do for your country." The deeper issue, however, is not simply having a charismatic leader but the execution of a deliberate plan to improve the common good within the shortest time possible.

Given the limitations of this article, I offer no master plan to revise the notion of the common good. But I do offer the understanding of a key term here, namely, the notion of society. A society involves the rights of individual members of a society in dealing with one another. But it also involves the rights of the society as an institution vis-à-vis its constituent members and the broader community at the time. My principal resource here will be the notion of society in the philosophy of Alfred North Whitehead. Whitehead was personally convinced that the world of Nature is on a feeling level alive even though most of his colleagues in the natural sciences believed instead that the ultimate constituents of physical reality are lifeless entities; tiny bits of matter (electrons and protons) whirling about aimlessly in an all-encompassing field of activity. Instead, Whitehead proposed that these allegedly non-living bits of natter are instead "drops of subjective experience" that somehow combine with one another to produce all the living and non-living things of this world from moment to moment. Admittedly, Whitehead did not further reflect on how something intrinsically alive, these drops of subjective experience in rapid succession, can produce something totally different: namely, subatomic particles (electrons, protons, and neutrons) that have no self-awareness and thus no impulse to engage with any other entity. Instead, he attempted to solve that problem by distinguishing between two kinds of socially constituted entities: a nexus and a society. A nexus or collection of non-living entities occurs by chance with no connection with any other non-living entity apart from the present moment. A society, however, endures over an extended time because it integrates both living and non-living entities into an organic unity with multiple subdivisions. Admittedly, this more complex type of intersubjective unity is not apparent in more primitive life (e.g., plant life and lower forms of animal life). But it is clearly present in human beings and more advanced forms of animal life whose members regularly make decisions in terms of their individual well-being and survival.

Studying the relation between mind and body at all the various levels of existence and activity within the cosmic process, one realizes that the connection between mind and body is much more complicated in a process-or systems-oriented metaphysical scheme than in classical Aristotelian-Thomistic metaphysics. In Thomistic metaphysics, the "soul" or mind of a human being is an immaterial reality, but the body is strictly material, The soul, accordingly, exercises control over the body in this life and is destined to live apart from the body at the moment of death and thereafter. Whitehead's understanding of the mind-body relation, however, focuses on a more this-worldly causal relation between mind and body. As a result, while the relation between mind and body in Thomistic metaphysics is determined in advance by God or a human craftsman, in Whitehead's scheme the mind-body relation is self-determined by its constituents (successive subjects of experience)according to an internal pattern of development. Through their interaction with one another and the external environment, they grow in size and complexity. On reflection, then. Aristotelian metaphysics is grounded in a purely logical format that predetermines the abstract pattern of existence and activity among its components. But in a process-or systems-oriented metaphysics, the opposite is true. A process-oriented metaphysics based on change or evolution focuses on interrelated groups of entities that seem to evolve on their own into a larger group that is more capable of growth in size and complexity (e.g., a family, a local community, national and even international communities) each with the ability to enforce rules and regulations on its members.

Along the same lines, one can also imagine two different kinds of cosmic order, the one grounded in the decision of God and the other in the *de facto* unfolding of a historical process. The first alternative is grounded in God, who is self-existent and thus is the ultimate source of existence and activity for everything else that exists; first, angels or other immaterial entities, then human beings, other animals, and various species of plant and microbial life, even the invisible world of atomic and subatomic reality. With the second alternative, one starts with two or more finite entities engaged in intersubjective relations, then something like a primitive community that gradually develops into a bigger and bigger community, each one with its power to impose restrictions on the personal freedom of its members,

At this point, one can see better the differences between a logical system based on the notion of Being and an empirical system based on the principle of Becoming. A system based on the notion of Being is purely conceptual. That is, it is the first principle in a rationally ordered set of constituents that could exist but still needs to be empirically verified. The classic example, of course, is the metaphysics of Aristotle, which Thomas Aquinas and other medieval scholastic thinkers applied to the Biblical understanding of the God-World relationship. It worked quite well except for the Christian concept of God. It is not one person but tri-personal, an ongoing unity of dynamically interrelated parts or members. At the same time, if one stipulates that the divine persons always act together, then they equivalently exercise the agency of a single person. All three divine persons would thus be involved in the act of Creation, in the salvation of the world through the Incarnation, and in the ultimate integration of the God-World relationship at the end of the cosmic process.

A system based on the principle of Becoming, however, inevitably begins with a plurality of entities not only in this life but in eternal life. As noted above, the three divine persons act together to constitute a perfect community. Hence, when one prays to the Father, one also is praying to the Son and the Spirit. If one prays to Jesus as the Redeemer of the human race, one also prays to the Father and the Spirit at the same time. Finally, if one prays to the Holy Spirit, one feels the presence of the other divine persons at the same time. The advantages in thinking of God in this way. i.e., in terms of a plurality of divine persons as opposed to a single divine entity, are twofold. First of all, if God is an individual entity, then the question arises: whose understanding of God is right or at least more right than the other deities? Secondly. If one expresses one's belief in a multiplicity of religious communities, then one learns from the other religious communities patterns of existence and behavior that could be quite useful for adoption into their own communities. Unity among communities, then, whether religiously oriented or not, is a precious value. But the search for unity among communities always begins with a sense of plurality.

Joseph A. Bracken, S.J. is an American philosopher and Catholic theologian. Bracken is a proponent of process philosophy and process theology of Alfred North Whitehead and Charles Hartshorne. Much of his work is devoted to a synthesis of revealed religion and Christian trinitarian doctrines with a revised process theology. Bracken introduced a field theoretic approach to process metaphysics.

An Immanent God for our Immanent Frame

VINCE BRACKETT

Can a process-relational vision of God save people in the Secular West from the "Malaise of Modernity"?

The Canadian philosopher Charles Taylor, in his book *A Secular Age,* tells the story of the last 500 years in the West (the story of Modernity) as, among other things, a move from a "Transcendent Frame" to an "Immanent Frame." Before Modernity, everyone believed in God (or gods), and the real truth of life was what was going on beyond what we could see: the enchanted, the heavens, the transcendent. But today, the real truth of life is what is right in front of us or within us, what is here and now, what is immanent. We understand the world, above all, on natural, material, and cultural terms. Hence, our secular age, in which belief in God is a contested state.

This move, Taylor argues, is not a *subtraction* story, as though belief in God was removed somewhere along the line, but more of an *addition* story. Compared to ages past, the modern person in the West trying to live a full life now has so many more immanent matters to attend to (their vocation, their inner sense of self, their property, their insurance policies, their hobbies, their image online, etc.), that the door to transcendence has been blocked. 500 years ago, everyone in search of fullness walked through the door instinctively, but no longer.

Like all shifts in culture, the results of the Immanent Frame are a mix of positive and negative. With the door to transcendence blocked, there's a freedom in the fact that our existential concerns are less populated by fears of supernatural evils or wrathful divine consequences. And a turn toward the immanent has meant technology and medicine and science have advanced at an unprecedented pace, decreasing human suffering and lengthening life expectancy.

But the tradeoff for transcendence being closed out, Taylor observes, is a constant, low- grade, background malaise in modern minds: an emptiness, a felt flatness, a lack of connectedness to something larger. He calls this the "Malaise of Modernity." The day-in, day-out of modern life seems so thoroughly emptied of any consideration of divine involvement that apathy and despondency can threaten to bury us. Spirituality can feel like a trite response to our world's great ills, and even if we personally have a strong identification as a believer today, spirituality rarely feels *necessary* to a full life. It's more of a nice supplement.

And yet, Taylor also highlights that even within our Immanent Frame, echoes of our ancestor's unquestionably enchanted past might call to people in the modern world. We find ourselves drawn to horror movies about hauntings, or to the hero's journeys of fantasy and sci-fi fiction, or to coming of age TV shows and movies where characters discover life beyond themselves. We might wonder sometimes, "is there more to life beyond just what my senses can perceive?" Somehow, even with transcendence closed out, the draw to the ineffable, the unexplainable, the spiritual lives on inside the Immanent Frame's walls.

Taylor describes so well my setting in Chicago. I am pastoring people who epitomize the Immanent Frame: running around like chickens with their heads cut off trying to meet the many demands of Modern Life, *sometimes* having experiences they can't explain that call to them about God or purpose or connection or justice or meaning, but a bit embarrassed to admit that or unsure how to talk about it, and *mostly* just feeling that malaise.

My best pastoring moments are trying to get curious about those "*sometimes* experiences" that call to folks. And what I find incredibly revealing and important is that the way people within our Immanent Frame default to describing the occasional unexplainable experiences they have is the way process-relational thinkers describe spirituality, just without technical or theological language.

One person told me once, "The child I lost came to me in a dream, and it was so comforting." I thought of process-relational thinkers suggesting that, because God is the great Fellow Experiencer of all, all live on after death in the memory of God, offering a beautiful interpretation of the phenomenon of our lost loved ones coming to us in dreams or visions.

Or I regularly hear things like, "Once I was able to get quiet, I found that, somehow, I knew within me what to do." And I think of process-relational thinkers painting a picture of the God who moment to moment is presenting us with innumerable possibilities for the open, never pre-determined future (beyond just the limited possibilities we see on our own)—of the God who is always luring us toward the most beautiful, most creative, most loving of those possibilities, if we stop to listen for that God's guidance.

I hear all the time things like, "I was so moved by that song (or poem or show or movie), I couldn't stop crying, and I wanted to talk about it with everyone I know." And I think of process-relational thinkers explaining a panentheistic view of God's relation to the world—in which God is in the world and the world is in God, like a Venn Diagram—capturing so well our intuitions of feeling close to God when we are overcome by beauty or connection or a feeling of alignment.

In my own life, my first ever unexplainable experiences were, in the midst of grief after losing my mom to cancer, feeling an overwhelming love and peace and an assurance that I am not crushed. Those experiences continue to fuel me today. It is a process-relational picture of the God who is with us in suffering that helped me make sense of that closeness and empathy I felt.

Mapping these examples onto Taylor's assessment of our Immanent Frame, I've realized: It makes complete sense that our descriptions seem to verge on process-relational! The process-relational vision doesn't rely on a classically *transcendent* God, who is separate from the world and omnipotent, who sometimes mysteriously intervenes with all-controlling power (but frustratingly not always), and who feels harder and harder to take seriously for people formed by modern natural and social sciences. The process-relational vision—of an always-present, loving, guiding God, who is experiencing the flow of time with us, and who is not the exception to the laws of nature but the exemplification of them—is a profoundly *immanent* vision of God, that therefore holds up inside our Immanent Frame. It makes sense that people whose lives are no longer framed by transcendence would stumble into process-relational concepts searching for ways to describe their unexplainable experiences on immanent terms.

Unfortunately, in popular belief, transcendence is often assumed the moment we're talking about God or spirituality, and most of our churches accept this premise and reinforce it when we teach or unthinkingly pass on classical "transcendence" views of God's relation to the world: when we talk about a "supernatural" God "intervening," or when we speak of miracles as God "breaking" the laws of nature because "a sovereign God can do whatever a sovereign God wants," or when we fail to balance the discussion of God's "holiness" or "otherness" with a discussion of God's incarnation in Jesus, or when we position God "victorious," "high up in the sky," as a Greek or Roman god, rather than as the Great Fellow Experiencer, alongside those suffering in solidarity and self-emptying love.

Is it any wonder that prayer and experience of God fade into the background for modern people, when our lives are no longer framed by transcendence, but most of the concepts and language modeled for us by churches to encourage prayer and experience of God rely on transcendence? It's like trying to install an out-of-date operating system on a modern device. They're not compatible. Eventually, people in churches are willing to talk about the ethics of Jesus, but embarrassed to talk about the Living Jesus. Is it any wonder, then, that the malaise of an exclusively material immanence begins to press in on us?

Much of church liturgies and worship music and preaching fails to help honest people within our Immanent Frame who are open to spiritual experience but just can't un-see that the door to transcendence is blocked. People in my church are always happy to be led in prayer by someone else who is confident praying, but can lack a confidence to pray on their own. Parents in my church want their children to develop relationships with God, but can feel uncomfortable leading group prayer themselves around the dinner table or at bedtime because they don't want to do so inauthentically.

The problem is NOT that people in our secular age are entirely closed to an involved, Living God; the problem is that we're mostly only taught the concepts and language of transcendence to paint a picture of such a God, and those don't work for the modern mindset.

What an opportunity for ministers and churches to teach and model process-relational concepts and language that point to an Immanent God! We modern people are primed for them! We just need help to hear how they might sound coming out of our mouths.

Here are some examples of things we repeat regularly in preaching, prayers, and liturgies at Brown Line Church in Chicago:

> God, you are our Fellow Experiencer.
>
> God, in all things beautiful and wonderful and meaningful, all around us, you are present—calling to us, drawing us to you; we open ourselves to that; we commit to paying attention.
>
> God, you are with us in solidarity in our suffering or grief or hopelessness. You showed us, in Jesus, you know what it is like to despair, to be betrayed, to suffer. You are not removed from the human experience. You know it intimately.
>
> God, we join you in solidarity with [this person / the world]. We join you in working to bring about new, good, even miraculous possibilities.
>
> God, you are not high up in the sky like a puppet master, or out in the future laying out a finish line saying, "Good luck humanity." You are here with us, in the present. Guide us, speak to us.

> God, you are infinitely creative as you look into the uncertain future with us; you see possibilities we cannot; help us to see.
>
> God, you are present to all people, to all things, influencing our world for good, but, as Jesus taught, your will is not always done. Bring about renewal after loss, resurrection after death.

If our worship services can form the prayer lives of people in our communities with process-relational language, confidence can grow to claim more of our unexplainable experiences within our Immanent Frame as interaction with a Living God. The malaise loosens its hold; people feel more deeply and fully alive. Existence is not so flat and empty. It's shot through with the influence of an involved God.

Taylor's description of the "Malaise of Modernity" strikes me as one of the spiritual crises of our time. If the world feels exclusively material and modern people are doomed to a flat emptiness devoid of spiritual significance, what will save us from the dehumanizing cycles of the global economy's endless demands for production and consumption? And what will call us to the higher values necessary to address systemic injustices, poverty, and a climate on the brink of catastrophe? As a pastor, I'm convinced that nurturing people's confidence to claim personal experiences of an involved, Living God can fight the malaise, so we can rise to meet these great tasks of our time with hope and purpose and possibilities. In facilitating such personal spiritual experiences for people, we don't have to rely on beliefs in transcendence that feel increasingly unbelievable or embarrassing to modern people. With process-relational concepts and language, we can paint an accessible picture of an Immanent God for our Immanent Frame—the God in whom we live and move and have our being.

Vince Brackett pastors Brown Line Church, a progressive Christian community with a healthy sense of humor and humility, named for Chicago's Northside "L" train. His background is in education and his interests include basketball, pop culture, theology, and audio/visual technology. He and his wife (and their four kids) have enjoyed living communally with housemates for the last 12 years.

Open Table, Open God

BRANDON BROWN

An open and relational God invites all in radical hospitality to the table. If we avoid fences, the path is easier.

She heard the call of the minister to come forward and receive communion. Yet, once again, she did not respond and stayed in her seat. She knew Paul had warned about receiving communion while being unworthy. If there was anyone who was unworthy, it was her. Years of guilt, shame, and anger swirled within her, and gave certainty of her unworthiness before a sovereign God. God had taken her child. That was the only explanation because "God is in control." Because of her fear, she sat. She did not go forward to receive this grace because she felt God would take her, just like God had taken her child. After all, Paul wrote that some had died in Corinth after he warned about receiving when unworthy. So she sat—as others went forward. She almost thought the minister was looking at her with sadness.

This is a story that ministers hear all too often. The main character here is not an actual person, but is based upon actual people I have encountered during my time in ministry. If we were in a room, face to face, I would ask for a show of hands of who had heard warnings about receiving communion unworthily. The raised hands would probably be a large majority of the people in the room. Why is that? I believe it begins with a wrong idea of God, which allows us to read scripture within that idea.

The warning our group would point to is found in 1 Corinthians chapter 11, verses 27-32. It is a frightening warning. If we eat unworthily, we are answerable for the body and blood of Jesus. There is also judgment for us if we do not examine ourselves. Paul even mentions that several are sick or have died because of the unworthy manner of receiving the meal. That is a frightening warning, but who or what is the target of this warning? It has been used to present a closed communion table. The idea is that any unworthy partaking of communion could lead to spiritual danger. If we have the idea of God as an omnipotent (all-powerful) God who demands proper respect, then we should heed that warning.

If we back up in 1 Corinthians to verse 17, we see what Paul's warning is about. Paul has learned that the Corinthian church has factions and divisions. But beyond the division, Paul mentions that the church is not coming together for the Lord's Supper. Instead, they bring food for themselves and while some get drunk and eat rich food, others go hungry. This is what Paul is referring to in verses 27-32 about being unworthy. If we understand God as a God who is not out to get us, but a God who is with us, this is an easy shift to make. This shift also changes how we view the warnings.

Those who do not love others as fully as God loves us receive Paul's warning. The picture in 1 Corinthians is one of a people whose hearts are closed to the idea that there is hospitality around God's table. Those who are in danger are those who refuse to share and whose hearts are closed. God welcomes the hungry and hurting to God's table. Humans may choose to exclude the hungry, but God does not. Paul tells them that exclusion leads to sickness and death. Can you imagine how excluding someone may lead to their sickness or death? If we see the cause of sickness and death as God, we may imagine that Paul is aiming his comments at those who are not worthy. However, if we see the cause of sickness and death as exclusion from the meal, Paul's comments are not about consequences from God, but about the consequences of the actions of selfish people who were withholding food from the poor among them.

Imagine that Paul is warning those who put fences around the table of the Lord in communion. Are you able to see another side of the directives of the Corinthian church? The contrast here is between human beings who create division, put up fences, and exclude, versus those who welcome everyone to the table. Here is where our view of God becomes important. A closed and unchanging God makes the context of punishment with sickness or death make sense. But if we see an open and relational God involved in the world in radical and self-giving love, the idea that being unworthy leads to sickness is foreign, even nonsensical. To be clear, when we talk about an open and relational God, we are talking about a God whose nature as love does not change. But God may change God's mind, as we see throughout scripture.

Even if we try to place a fence around the table, the gate is out of our control. Jesus tells his disciples in John 10 that he is the gate. As we consider the communion table, Jesus becomes the gate in any fences we might try to create, and he bids all to come. Try as we might, we cannot close that gate. Our words and actions may cause detours and hindrances, but eventually those who hear the shepherd will find the gate despite us. A God who works through relationships does not support our dogmatic fences. I believe God wants us to tear down fences rather than build them. But what does this mean for practical application?

The communion table is a space where helping a community of faith shift to an open and relational view of God can happen. Whether you see communion as a sacrament as I do, or as an ordinance, it is a communal act. Communion is by nature a communal act and it can draw others into community. In this relational reality, we can use language and action to invite into a story that shines a light on God as open and relational.

Communion is an act of worship that invites us to relationship. When received regularly and with intentional language, it will invite people into an open and relational understanding of God and the Church. When considering the language and act of communion in your church, some practical concerns may need to be addressed. These concerns involve the prescribed forms, frequency, and mode of receiving in your context. I will attempt to keep those in mind and remember that any language suggestions should be tweaked for your particular church, denomination, or geographic region.

The invitation to communion is an invitation to a dinner table. While it may not nourish the body completely, it will nourish the soul. This requires language of invitation, meal, and welcome, but we weave those throughout most communion liturgies. The invitation is to a table which does not belong to us or the church, but it belongs to God. Here is where we can use the language of an open and relational God. If we use words like hospitality, feast, and hunger, we can convey the truth of the one whose table we gather around. When I am the "communion pastor" at our local church, I like to speak of the table in terms of one we gather around as friends and family. To put those who may not understand what is happening, we like to give some short remarks about what communion means and how God invites us to God's table. As a church who receives weekly, we also create a rhythm which reinforces the idea of an open table of welcome.

Moving from the initial language of invitation brings us to the point of describing the communion meal. This may be through a formal or informal liturgy. While some ministries have more rigid language requirements, we can still adapt the language in formal liturgy to describe a God who is open and relational. A few practical ideas arise regarding the description of Jesus' institution of the Lord's Supper during the Last Supper. When I am speaking, I like to use the language of giving in selflessness, as Diane Leclerc and Brent Peterson describe in their book *The Back Side of the Cross*. Instead of using the language of betrayal every week, I will use the language of solidarity more often. An example is to say "On the night when Jesus gave himself over in solidarity (standing with) all of us who have been enslaved and harmed by sin…"

Moving on to the last supper, Jesus gathered around a table with both supporters and people who may not have agreed with him. I will mention Judas as a betrayer if it feels appropriate. Your liturgy may not require this, but it is an opportunity to show how God is with all. While transitioning from describing the last supper to inviting the church to receive, we realize the chance to purposefully use welcoming words. The mode of reception can affect how this invitation is delivered. If you pass the elements, it may be an invitation to a metaphorical dinner table encompassing the worship space. If the congregation moves forward in response, it is a welcome to come to the table for all.

This is where we can creatively use our language to describe the open and relational idea we want to convey. Our words may not always be the same, but the general idea we can weave into an invitation is the following. "Church, God loves you and this meal is an invitation to God's grace and mercy expressed through love. You are welcome to this table. Do not fear the table of God unless you harbor evil or would prevent others from coming to this table. God is with us and invites us like any dear friend to this meal. Jesus is present in this meal as we reflect his love toward one another. Come encounter the grace of a God who loves you and is with you working with you to become more loving."

A special way to include children in the response is to find words to speak as they receive, which can explain the purpose of receiving. An example would be to say something like, "As you eat this bread and drink this juice (wine) God wants you to know how much you are loved. Jesus loves you and is glad you have come to eat at his table." Come to think of it, this would not be a bad thing to say to everyone who comes to receive.

The more we speak of a God who welcomes and is with us in relationship, the more they will hear this message. The welcome of a meal at a table is a wonderful example of how an open and relational God acts in the world. When appropriate, events in the life of a church can impact the language. The table is a place where we meet the grieving, the joyful, the sinner, the sinned against, the abandoned, the abused, the comfortable, and the uncomfortable. It is a place of welcome, grace, and love poured out in abundance. It is an unfenceable table because it belongs to God, who has no fences.

The minister invited the congregation to receive and prepared to welcome them to the table. She watched as the congregation moved out from their seats. As was her custom, she glanced at the one she knew was struggling with closed visions of God. Her heart felt heavy for that person, and she prayed she could hear the welcome of God in her heart. The minister glanced back to serve the bread and wine as the congregation came forward. Then, out of the corner of her eye, she saw a movement that caught her heart for a moment. The woman slid slowly from her seat and joined the church as they moved forward. Tears were a real possibility in this moment, but the minister kept her focus on the congregants in front of her. Then the woman approached and held out her hands. "Jesus loves you more than you can ever understand. This is his body, which is broken for you." "Amen" "This is the blood of Jesus poured out in solidarity for you." "Amen." A tear slowly made its way down her cheek as the woman ate and drank with a smile of contentment and relief.

Brandon Brown is an Ordained Elder in the Church of the Nazarene serving as a volunteer Pastor of Discipleship at his local church in Hendersonville, TN. He also works as a Project Engineer for an amazing tech company based in Nashville, TN. Brandon's wife Christi helps to keep him grounded and they currently have a menagerie of cats and dogs at their home in Hendersonville. Brandon is deeply passionate about sharing how our understanding of God and God's relational engagement with our world can welcome us into cooperative practice and theology. His general approach to theology is an improvisational style within a Wesleyan-Holiness context reaching out to other voices in imaginative discourse.

Praying and Singing in the Language of Love

GAYLE HANSEN BROWNE

Open and relational thinking offers transformational ideas about the way in which we pray and sing our prayers.

I recently participated in a weekend spiritual retreat, focused on spirituality in the Celtic Christian tradition. The Celtic Christian tradition is a tradition that emphasizes open and relational thinking. The retreat leader began the morning with these words: "This is the message we have heard from the beginning that we should love one another. … God is love, and those who live in love live in God and God lives in them." (From 1 John: 3 and 4, as paraphrased by J. Philip Newell in *Celtic Treasure*).

Love is the message we have heard from the beginning. Love is also the message that flows through the life-changing ideas of open and relational theology. Three specific ideas come to mind as especially influential when praying in the language of love:

1. God is love. God is present and steadfastly loving with and within everything, everywhere, at all times. Prayer needs to awaken us to the divine love already dwelling with and within us and the universe. God's love is extravagantly expansive, radically inclusive, and seeks to nudge both the human and the non-human world towards actions that promote the well-being of all. The words and imagery we use in prayer need to nurture the expansive and inclusive love that well-being requires.

2. God is relational. We know our experience of God affects us and the non-human world. However, God's experience of us and the rest of the world also

affects God. What hurts one hurts all, God included. What helps one helps all, God included. This suggests two considerations for prayer. First, prayer needs to awaken us to this interconnected web of divine-human-cosmic relationship. Second, prayer also needs to encourage our sense of responsibility to act for the well-being of the whole. Therefore, words and imagery need to awaken us to the wholeness as they call us to action.

3. The future is open. The past has already happened, and God knows everything there is to know about the past. The present is in process, and God knows all the possibilities that exist to be known in the present. God also knows the probable outcomes each possibility could likely have. However, God's aim for the future is always at risk of not being recognized. Creaturely free agency may not choose the best way forward for the well-being of all. To mitigate that risk, prayer needs to open avenues of communication through which the divine wisdom of past realities, present possibilities, and future potentialities can flow. The words and imagery we pray need to help open space in our minds and hearts to receive this wisdom in ways that help us discern the choices we make and the actions we take.

Praying in the language of love fosters expansive/inclusive love, encourages actions for the well-being of the whole, and gives attention to discernment. Congregational singing and spoken prayer provide two gentle ways to introduce such language within the context of public worship.

Congregational Singing

I do not remember where I was when I had this experience. I think it may have been at an ecumenical service focused on justice. The service came to an end. The minister gave the benediction. Then, the musicians began the introduction to the closing hymn. I had not yet picked up the service booklet, but I recognized the tune. It was the tune to *Come Thou Fount of Every Blessing*—one of my favorite hymns. However, when I opened my booklet to sing, the words were different. At first, the difference in words was a shock. But it didn't take long for me to hear and sing them with joy. With lyrics written by Martin Willet, set to the tune called *Nettleton*, which is the same tune used for *Come Thou Fount of Every Blessing*, the first verse sends forth the congregation to be the justice we seek:

Go be justice to God's people;
Teach the hardened heart to learn.

Break the bread of true communion,
Pour the cup of true concern.
Feed the hungry, house the homeless,
Catch the tyrants in their lies;
Be the Lord's anointed servant
So God's justice never dies.

The second and third verses continue in the same vein, sending the congregation to "be healing" and to "be mercy."

Since then, I have enjoyed other experiences of new words set to familiar tunes. For example, David Weiss (theologian, writer, poet, and hymnist) and Sara Kay (singer-songwriter) collaborated to produce the CD, *To the Tune of a Welcoming God.* Kay sings Weiss's original hymn texts, set to familiar hymn tunes. The texts focus on themes friendly to open and relational thinking. In one text, written by Weiss, set to the tune used for *Shall We Gather at the River,* Weiss uses the word "kin-dom"—a word coined several years ago to represent the "kingdom of God" in a more expansive and inclusive way:

Shall we hearken to the kin-dom, we who have in darkness trod?
There is light so brightly shining, leading to the home of God.

Refrain:
Yes, we'll hearken to the Kin-dom, the widening, the welcoming Kin-dom
Hearken with our lives to the Kin-dom that leads to the home of God.

The second and third verses speak to various healings of those who were viewed as outcasts in the Gospel—the lame, the mute, the deaf, the blind, the possessed. The verses celebrate the good news that Jesus came to save "the least." Weiss's website, www.davidrweiss.com offers a link to order the CD, as well as access to hymn texts for worship.

Another hymnist doing similar work is Jann Aldredge-Clanton. Aldredge-Clanton offers texts inclusive of feminine images in reference to God, as well as hymns inclusive of all creation—human and non-human. For example, here is the first verse of an Aldredge-Clanton hymn text, set to the tune *Lauda Anima,* better known as the tune for *Praise My Soul, the King of Heaven.* The Aldredge-Clanton text (found in her book, *Earth Transformed with Music),* begins:

Praise the source of every blessing,
bringing goodness to the Earth,

loving every living being
filling all with sacred worth.
Alleluia! Alleluia!
Radiant life She brings to birth.

The second verse praises God as "the Holy Way of justice," asking God to "lead us to work for right." The third verse praises God as "the Well of Holy Wisdom," asking God to "guide us to save creation." The final verse praises God as "the Great Creative Spirit, birthing beauty everywhere."

Congregational singing has tremendous influence on what takes root in the mind and heart of those who sing. St. Augustine wrote: "The one who sings prays twice." In the act of singing, there is an intense experience of body, mind, and heart acting in concert and focus. As such, congregational singing holds vast potential for shaping what a community believes. Setting new texts to familiar tunes provides a gentle way to introduce open and relational thinking into familiar worship experiences.

Spoken Prayer

One thing all Christian worship traditions hold in common is a place in worship for spoken prayer. However, how and when such praying takes place varies from tradition to tradition.

For example, some worship traditions expect clergy or prayer leaders to pray extemporaneously. For some, extemporaneous also means spontaneous—in the moment, as moved by the spirit. For others, extemporaneous includes prayers written prior to the service by the one who will pray the prayer in worship—much like a preacher prepares a sermon before preaching it.

Other worship traditions pray according to fixed prayers of liturgy drawn from generations of Christian prayer tradition. However, even those with fixed liturgies usually still hold space at different points in the service for optional choices. Frequently, there are choices about opening prayers. Sometimes there are choices involving prayers of praise, confession, thanksgiving, intercession, and blessing. Sometimes there are prayers created by worship leaders and prayer teams.

The following prayer illustrates words and imagery that encourage open and relational thinking:

God of Blessing, you call all creation to new and abundant life.
By your Spirit, the earth and all living things flourish—

plants and trees, birds, beasts, insects, reptiles, fish, people,
and every other living organism.

We pray for the well-being of all your creation—
Understanding of our diversity and difference.
Peace in our communities,
With our neighbors and with those of different faiths.
Hope and healing for indigenous peoples,
And reconciliation in the wider community.

Keep us mindful of the mistakes of the past,
And help us not to repeat them. Amen.

("Opening Prayer for Unity and Mindfulness," George Hermonson, United Church of Canada. "Appendix 1: Communal Prayers," *Divine Echoes,* Mark Gregory Karris)

This brief prayer engages all three points highlighted earlier as ways to bring open and relational thinking into the prayers we speak. The prayer serves as a model for including similar language in extemporaneous prayer. It also provides an example of what to look for in selecting prayers written by others.

First, the prayer focuses minds and hearts on the extravagantly expansive, radically inclusive love of God, whose aim is the well-being of all. For example:

1. The prayer addresses God as "God of Blessing," focusing attention on God's expansive desire for the well-being of the world.
2. The prayer also makes clear that God's desire for well-being is radically inclusive. Blessings are to flow out upon the entirety of creation—all living organisms of every kind.

Second, the words and imagery suggest the wholeness of creation and call us to action. God's desire for blessing all that is requires our attention, rather than God's alone. For example:

1. We pray for humankind to bring understanding to the differences and diversity of all that is.

2. We pray for humankind to make peace in our communities, with our neighbors, and with people of different faiths.
3. We pray for humankind to communicate hope, to commit acts of healing, and to do the hard work of reconciliation.

These calls to action awaken us to the need God has, moment by moment, for us to discern God's aim for the well-being of all and to act on what we discern.

The final words and imagery confront us with our need to open ourselves to the influence of God's wisdom. We need God's wisdom if we are to discern what actions best contribute to the well-being of all. The prayer prays for God's help. However, the way we pray clarifies what the giving and receiving of help looks like. For example:

1. We do not pray for God to rescue us by accomplishing the aim for well-being single-handedly. Instead, we pray for wisdom in discerning what choices to make and actions to take.
2. We pray for God to open our eyes and ears, as well as our hearts and minds, to what the mistakes of the past can teach.
3. We pray for God to open our eyes and ears to the possibilities the present offers.
4. We pray for God to open our eyes and ears to the implications our actions and interactions might have for the future well-being of all.

The work of spoken prayer in public worship is a work of opening. It is also a guide to what inviting and welcoming God's influence involves. Whether we speak our prayers in our own words or in the words and images of others, we can still make choices that help us pray in the language of love.

Concluding Prayer

At the end of the retreat, the leader invited participants to light a candle for love. Soon, all the votive candles on the altar were burning brightly. Then, she prayed:

> You have shown us love, O Christ.
> You have shown us God.
> Show us also our true face
> and the true face of every human being.

Show us the desire for love
and the strength to give ourselves in love …
For we are made in the image of love, O Christ.
We are made in the image of God. (*Celtic Treasure*, J. Philip Newell)

Gayle Hansen Browne is an Episcopal priest, spiritual director, and retreat leader. She earned her M.A. degree in Theology from the School of Theology, University of the South. Browne retired from full-time parish ministry in 2016. She now serves part-time as Priest Associate for Liturgy at St. Luke's Episcopal Church, a small historically black parish in Knoxville, Tennessee.

Meeting Jesus at the Open Table[1]

BOB CORNWALL

Jesus welcomed everyone to his Table, so shouldn't our communion tables be open to all?

Tables are relational entities. It might be a dinner table in a home or a booth at a restaurant or café. If we are sharing the table with others, whether family, friends, or clients, most likely we engage in conversation. The nature of these conversations will depend on the context, but whatever the context, when we eat with others, the food becomes secondary to the relationships present at the Table. When we read the Gospels, we find numerous stories where Jesus sits down for meals. While our thoughts may first go to the Last Supper, Jesus ate with all kinds of people. They might be religious leaders or tax collectors. Sometimes, such as the meal Jesus shared with Zacchaeus, these meals could be life-changing (Luke 19:1-10).

Churches have been known to gather at tables. It might be a potluck dinner, which tends to be a time of fellowship featuring all kinds of comfort foods. We tend not to think of these meals as sacred moments, but perhaps we should. After all, the early Christians celebrated what we call the Lord's Supper/Eucharist/Holy Communion as part of a full meal. That meal included a lot more food and drink than the small piece of bread/wafer and a thimble full of juice or wine that is generally served on a Sunday

---

1. This essay is rooted in a larger project currently titled *Eating with Jesus: Reflections on Divine Encounters at the Open Eucharistic Table.*

morning. As Mike Graves comments, "A small bite of bread and two ounces of Welch's grape juice does not constitute a meal."[2]

We might not be ready to return regularly to the ancient church's practice of sharing the bread and cup as part of a full meal, but perhaps it's time that we begin recognizing that what Jesus shared with his disciples on the night of his betrayal was more nutritious than what we partake of in our communion services. My purpose here is not to suggest ways to expand the meal, though connecting the Eucharist with the potluck, along with prayers and teaching, is worth contemplating.[3] This does seem to be the early Christian practice as revealed in several places in the Book of Acts, as well as in 1 Corinthians 10-11. We're told that soon after the Day of Pentecost, the followers of Jesus "devoted themselves to the apostles' teaching and fellowship, to the *breaking of bread* and the prayers" (Acts 2:42 NRSVUE, emphasis mine). Later in Acts, we read the story of Paul's visit to Troas, where "on the first day of the week, when we met to *break bread,* Paul was holding a discussion with them" (Acts 20:7 NRSVUE, emphasis mine). In 1 Corinthians, Paul addresses abuses of the meal but does not lay out prerequisites other than behavioral ones.

The Christian Church in its many forms will at least occasionally gather at the Lord's Table to share in what is called the Lord's Supper, Eucharist, Mass, or Holy Communion. It usually features a small piece of bread, or its facsimile, along with a sip or two of wine/grape juice. While the person serving the elements might say something to the recipient, very little conversation takes place. Unlike the potluck dinner that may follow the worship service, the presider may inform those gathered in the sanctuary that not everyone is welcome to participate. In other words, they will acknowledge the fences that have been erected since early in Christian history. It might be baptism or belief in Jesus as savior or a disagreement as to the nature of the meal. The meal itself might not only be formal, but it might also be rather somber as in a funeral meal.

While there are important advocates for returning our Eucharistic fellowships to a full meal, it is possible to keep the current format but enliven it. After all, if, as I believe is true, Jesus is alive and present with us through the Spirit when we gather at the Table. It also means that Jesus' dining habits during his earthly journey should have some influence on the way we approach the Table. Since I am an ordained minister within the Christian Church (Disciples of Christ), which practices weekly (if not more frequent) communion, I recommend more frequent gatherings at the Table of the Lord. If we are going to gather frequently, then we must affirm that Jesus is alive and not dead. If that's

---

2. Mike Graves, *Table Talk: Rethinking Communion and Community,* (Eugene, OR: Cascade Books, 2017),

3. For a full description of what that might look like see Mike Graves' book *Table Talk.*

true, then there must be room for joy when we gather at the Table, since this meal, which some call an Agape meal, is an opportunity to connect with Jesus.

I recognize that denominational traditions approach their gatherings at the Table differently. Some are more formal than others. Some Eucharistic traditions teach that Jesus' body and blood are present in or with the elements of bread and wine/juice. Others believe that Jesus is present with the gathered community through the Spirit. We may gather at the Table weekly, monthly, or even less frequently. The people who preside and distribute the elements might be ordained clergy or they may be lay persons (my denomination does not require that an ordained person preside). Again, when it comes to who is invited, the question is, should we fence the Table or take them down? If the latter is true, then it is likely that someone who is not baptized or even sees themselves as followers of Jesus might join us at the Table. If this is true, might they have the opportunity to encounter Jesus at the Table? Might that encounter, like the one Sarah Miles described in her book *Take This Bread*, lead to what she refers to as a radical conversion? As for me, when I preside at the Table, I invite everyone who desires to share in the meal to do so. They may choose not to partake. That is their prerogative. However, they may choose to do so. They might even be part of another religious tradition.

I am one who, again, when I preside, invites everyone present, should they desire to share the meal, to come to the Table. In part, this is a question of hospitality. I believe the hospitality Abraham and Sarah showed the three strangers is an important witness to the power of Table fellowship. It's important to note here that the account in Genesis tells us that "the LORD appeared to Abraham by the oaks of Mamre" in the form of the three strangers (Gen. 18:1-15, NRSVUE). So, you never know who might be present at the Lord's Table. It could be angels in disguise. Additionally, I don't want to limit a person's opportunities to encounter Jesus at the Table.

If we are to understand our Table fellowship in relational terms, it is appropriate to start by contemplating the Triune nature of God. To confess that God is Triune is to confess that God's self is relational. As Catherine Mowry LaCugna writes: "The doctrine of the Trinity affirms that the 'essence' of God is relational, other-ward, that God exists as diverse persons united in a communion of freedom, love, and knowledge."[4] As for the connection between the Trinity and the Eucharistic gathering, she reminds us that "the trinitarian [sic] structure of the Eucharist is a constant reminder that God is not generically or abstractly God, but is the loving God who comes to us in Jesus

---

4. Catherine Mowry LaCugna, *God for Us: The Trinity and Christian Life,* (San Francisco, CA: Harper One, 1991), 243.

Christ by the power of the Holy Spirit."[5] It is this relational God whom we encounter at the Table. If we take the idea seriously that when we gather at the Table and share this meal, even if the elements are symbolic of a more robust banquet, we encounter Jesus then this is a good reason for the followers of Jesus to gather frequently at the Table. After all, as Sarah Miles describes in her book *Take This Bread,* it is even possible for us to have unexpected life-changing experiences as we encounter the living Christ at the Lord's Table.

I have been a proponent of removing every fence that would prevent seekers after God, even if they are not yet believers in Jesus, from gathering at the Table. Throughout the ages, the church (I am using this term broadly) has placed obstacles in the way of people approaching the Table. These fences include prerequisites such as baptism or belief in Jesus as savior. When we erect fences, we tell those present but who are not yet within the circle of the faithful that they are outsiders and therefore are not welcome guests.

When it comes to fences around the Table, they come in many forms. Some are higher than others. They might be behavioral. For example, some churches bar those who are divorced or take positions contrary to the prevailing policies and doctrines of that church. Sometimes it's race/ethnicity or sexual orientation. Maybe it's a requirement that you endorse the church's doctrinal statement. The presence of these fences raises an important question regarding the role Jesus' own practices of Table fellowship influence our practices. In other words, who did Jesus eat with? How did those meals turn out?

Think again for a moment about what happened when Jesus accepted Zacchaeus's dinner invitation. What happened to him when he shared that meal with Jesus? While some people grumbled at Jesus' willingness to dine at Zacchaeus' house, it proved to be life-changing. Zacchaeus "said to the Lord, 'Look, half of my possessions, Lord, I will give to the poor, and if I have defrauded anyone of anything, I will pay back four times as much.'." Jesus responded to his declaration by proclaiming that salvation had "come to this house, because he, too, is a son of Abraham," and because "the Son of Man came to seek out and to save the lost" (Luke 19:1-10, NRSVUE).

While Jesus' eating practices should, in my view, play a central role in our theology of the Table, we might want to go further back in time to the encounter Abraham and Sarah had with the three strangers. Might the hospitality offered by Abraham and Sarah to the three strangers prove to be foundational to our experiences, such that not only might a person, like Zacchaeus or Sarah Miles have life-changing experiences when they respond positively to the invitation to dine with Jesus, but in the case of Abraham and Sarah, their offer of hospitality proved life-changing for them (Gen. 18:1-15), since

5. Ibid, 405.

as we are told in Hebrews, it is possible that when we show hospitality to strangers, we might be entertaining angels unawares (Heb. 13:2).

One of the concerns that gets raised when fences are removed has to do with what the *Baptism, Eucharist, and Ministry* document calls the "Communion of the Faithful." The *Baptism, Eucharist, and Ministry* document, which most Mainline Protestant denominations have affirmed, speaks of "the eucharistic [sic] communion with Christ who nourishes the life of the Church," which "is at the same time communion with the body of Christ which is the Church. The sharing in one bread and the common cup in a given place demonstrates and effects the oneness of the sharers with Christ and with their fellow sharers in all times and places. It is in the eucharist [sic] that the community of God's people is fully manifested."[6] If the Eucharist is the means through which the community is united with Christ and with one another, then if those who are not believing members of that community partake of the elements, does that not break down the unity of the body? I understand the concern, but might the Spirit not use these moments to speak to the hearts of those who participate in the Eucharist? They might not convert, but they might have an encounter with the living Christ.

By practicing the Open Table, we defer to Jesus, who is the host. We follow his lead, following the ways he practiced Table Fellowship. As for people who do not share the Christian faith, the hospitality might speak to them of God's love. One expression of this kind of openness is laid out in an essay by John Paul Sydnor that describes an exchange of worship experiences between a Jewish synagogue and a Christian congregation. When the two communities shared in Christian worship, the pastor of Grace Community Boston chose the Eucharist, and everyone, following the congregation's practice, was invited to the Table, no matter who they were, since they understood that Jesus excluded no one. Therefore, he writes:

> For us, an exclusive ritual cannot express the universal love of God. So, we have opened the ritual; we have changed our practice. By adopting the new practice, we have invited the new ritual to offer us new knowledge—embodied, experiential, communal, ritual knowledge—and, in this case, interreligious knowledge. We weren't just inviting our Jewish guests to watch us take communion. In a constitutive expression of our open theology, we were inviting our Jewish guests to participate in communion with us.[7]

---

6. *Baptism, Eucharist, and Ministry: Faith and Order Paper No. 111,* (Geneva, Switzerland: World Council of Churches, 1982), 23.

7. Jon Paul Sydnor, "Blessed Transgression: On Serving Communion to Jews," *Journal of Interreligious Studies,* 22 (April 2018), 7.

In doing this, they recognized the risks, including misunderstanding, and the belief on the part of the Jewish participants in the exchange that the Christian community was attempting to convert them. Or, it might be perceived as a clumsy attempt by liberals to demonstrate their openness. These and other concerns are valid. In a situation like this, great preparation is necessary. However, if we believe that Jesus welcomed everyone to his Table, should we not do the same? Besides, if we wouldn't exclude someone from the potluck, why would we exclude them from this expression of Christ's love for all?

If we believe in a relational God who is present to us at the Table of the Lord through the presence of the Holy Spirit, then how might we practice Table fellowship? Who is invited? How do we share the meal?

Robert D. Cornwall is a retired Disciples of Christ minister with a Ph.D. in historical theology from Fuller Theological Seminary. In retirement, he continues to write, preach, and serve the church in various capacities, including serving as Board Chair of the Disciples Christian Unity and Interfaith Ministries and as the Disciples of Christ co-chair of the Evangelical Lutheran Church of America-Disciples of Christ Bilateral Dialog.

Small Deeds, Great Changes: Embracing the Hobbit Spirit

ULRICK DAM

Drawing inspiration from Tolkien's Hobbits, I explore transformative ways to revitalize church liturgy and theology for today's world.

"The world is changed..."

I don't know about you, but I am a massive Tolkien fan. His whole universe never ceases to amaze me. From the short children's book, *The Hobbit*, to the magnificent opus-trilogy, *The Lord of the Rings,* to the impressive backstory of *The Silmarillion.*

So, what has that to do with the practices of process-relational theology and church liturgy?

Bear with me here. It will all make sense soon.

Like in Tolkien's work, it is often the smallest of creatures that creates the biggest of change. I believe that is also true for the Church.

Galadriel's prologue states that the world **is** changed. And looking at our world today, that also fits for us in the present day. The past decades have seen an immense change in communication technology, the internet, social media, AI, etc. But has our church managed to follow along in that change?

Yes, our church must change! I am often confronted by conservative Christians telling me that the church must never change, and will forever remain the same. Usually, I point these people back to the roots of our contemporary church. Most of our liturgy and theology about worship are no more than a couple hundred years old. Sure, we can go back to Calvin or Luther, but even then, it only means that the contemporary church is 500 years old. The truth is, that much of our ecclesiology and liturgy is no more than 100 years old. The Church always changes, molds, and works to the relevant in present-day society.

Yet nowadays, the mainstream movement is to update the visual impression of the church. Bring in the smoke machines and LED screens. But the theology, the liturgy, the stuff that actually matters, very few care about updating or making relevant.

And what does that result in?

Church attendance all over the world is declining. We try to use fancier visual aids and louder music, yet it doesn't really work. We place our services in the evening and install a bar. Great! Yet, it doesn't work either.

How can we update the stuff that matters to people today? The liturgy, the theology, the words we use?

I truly believe that process-relational theology could be the spark that ignites a new Spring for Christianity. It could be the start of a reinvigoration and a new relevance for churches today.

If only we let it…

So back to Tolkien. What saves middle-earth is not the great battles or the mighty lords who come up with clever plans. The salvation comes from two small insignificant Hobbits, trotting along, loyal to each other and set on going as far as possible, by taking one step at a time. At the Council of the Ring, before the Fellowship sets out, Elrond—the high elf lord—says it so well: "The road must be trod, but it will be very hard. And neither strength nor wisdom will carry us far upon it. This quest may be attempted by the weak with as much hope as the strong. **Yet such is oft the course of deeds that move the wheels of the world: small hands do them because they must, while the eyes of the great are elsewhere."**

Small hands do the seemingly small deeds because they must.

The road to a reinvigoration of the Church and the liturgy must be trod by rethinking and clarifying why we do, and say, and we do. If we can't theologically make sense of your words or liturgy, maybe we should scrap it?

If we want to see a future for the Church, it is not about grand schemes and strategies. It is about simply starting to make sense of what we actually do today.

In my work as a pastor and leader, I've seen much of our liturgy or church lingo, which we all do or say, but seldom reflect on.

Let me give you an example: Way too often, pastors will quote Jeremiah 29:11: *"For I know the plans I have for you," declares the Lord, "plans to prosper you and not to harm you, plans to give you hope and a future."* (NIV) Whether it is to explain why my best friend just died from cancer or to guide me in my discipleship, this quote is a favorite catch-all filter for many pastors. 'Well, it might not make sense now, but God has a plan and God will use all for good.'

Alright, so I can just lean back and let Jesus take the wheel. All will fall into place because the omnipotent God has every little detail planned and will force creation to follow it with His mighty hands.

But that is not at all what this quote talks about. Not at all.

A pressing matter for me as a pastor has been to redefine what we mean by God's plan and clarify the phrase from a Process-Relational viewpoint.

First of all, the quote is from a letter where Jeremiah prophesies God to the Israelites in exile in Babylon. And what is in the lines just before this one?

Build houses and settle down; plant gardens and eat what they produce. Marry and have sons and daughters [...] Also, ***seek the peace and prosperity of the city to which I have carried you into*** *exile.* (Jer. 29:5-7 NIV)

Seek the peace and prosperity of the city, which I have carried you into…?

Wait, so Jeremiah 29:11 is not just a get-well-soon-card that tells me to relax, lean back and let Jesus take the wheel?

On the contrary, it is a call to action. To actively co-create the Kingdom of God. God inspires, lures, and pulls us into all different kinds of places because that is where we can work to create divine peace and prosperity, because that is where there is work for us.

We need to do these small deeds of clarifying our language within the theologically sound and biblically true framework we find in process-relational theology. So much of what we do and say in the Church—our liturgy, our theology—has lost its connection to the roots. Our small task is to reconnect it.

Another example. We often hear a sermon that says: 'God never changes! God will forever and ever be the same!'

How many of our worship songs say something like that?

And yes, there is something to it, but just not like that. Not so black and white. The issue is that the bible tells us time and time again that God changes, repents, goes back and rethinks decisions, etc. I could easily name: Genesis 6:6, Genesis 6:7, Exodus 32:12-14, Deuteronomy 32:36, Judges 2:18, 1 Samuel 15:11, 1 Samuel 15:35, 2 Samuel 24:16; 1 Chronicles 21:15; Psalms 90:13, Psalms 106:45, Psalms 135:14, Jeremiah 18:8, Jeremiah 26:3, 13, 19, Jeremiah 42:10, Joel 2:13-14; Amos 7:3, 6; Jonah 3:9-10; 4:2, but if you have gone through all those, you're probably getting the point by now.

We need theological sound, biblically true, clarification of what it means, that God remains the same.

For example, let's look at the story of Jonah, whom God tells to go to Nineveh and preach to them so they will turn from their evil ways. At first, Jonah runs away, and we have the "big fish" incident. Jonah finally arrives and preaches. Then, the Ninevites repent, and God "saw what they did and how they turned from their evil ways, he relented and did not bring on them the destruction he had threatened." God changes plans due to creaturely actions. This does not go down well with Jonah, who is angry about why he needed to take that entire journey just for God to show mercy. God tells Jonah off for being more interested in seeing their destruction than redemption: "Should I not have concern for the great city of Nineveh, in which there are more than a hundred and twenty thousand people who cannot tell their right hand from their left."

The story shows a God who truly cares for creation and wants to be in relationship with creatures. It shows us that God willingly changes plans due to creaturely actions. Nineveh has shut out God, turned its back on God, and does not want the relationship. Jonah goes to open up this relationship to show God wants to draw them close again and make the Ninevites turn to God again. Jonah's task was to proclaim the destruction of Nineveh, but instead, he opened the Ninevites to a new relationship with God. And we see a God that relents on the destruction, changes plans, and truly cares about creatures. God changes the plan.

Another of my favorite stories of God repenting is from 2 Kings 20, where Hezekiah falls ill. Isaiah comes to him and tells him that he surely will perish soon and needs to get his house ready for his passing away. Hezekiah is distraught, pleads, and begs God to let him live on: "I beg You, O Lord, remember how I have walked before You in truth and with a whole heart. I have done what is good in Your eyes." Even before Isaiah reaches the exit of the room, God comes to him and tells him that the plans have changed. Isaiah says to Hezekiah, "This is what the Lord, the God of your father David, says, "I have heard your prayer. I have seen your tears. See, I will heal you. On the third day, you must go up to the house of the Lord. And I will add fifteen years to your life." God changes the plan after Hezekiah pleads for his life. Hezekiah does not change his ways, but simply lets God remember the good he has done, praying and supplying God with information. That is enough to make God repent and let Hezekiah live on.

When we say that God is everlastingly the same, we should start to clarify what we mean by that. Yes, God's essence of uncontrolling Love will forever be the same (if in doubt about what this means, ask Thomas Oord) but God's actions or plans are moldable and not set in stone. God changes His mind, not His essence.

It makes sense to talk about God as Love forever being the same, but not about God's plans being unchangeable. The latter is just not biblical.

Step one of making the Church relevant today is to clarify our liturgy and language. Why do we do, and say, as we do? If we cannot answer that simple question, we should stop.

That exercise is something we, as pastors or leaders, should perform every day. Constantly making our language and liturgy more sensible, more theologically sound, and our congregations more well-reflected.

Like the small Hobbits. No big revolution. No eyes of the great are on us. We're simply trotting along, whilst making sure our liturgy and theology actually make sense and that it is relevant.

And whilst we're on Hobbits: At one point later in the story, Frodo is about to give up. All is too dark and heavy. Frodo is almost unable to take that small next step. Like a well-burned-out pastor thinking about how to make it through all the nativity scenes of December. Then Sam steps in, with his glorious speech (Tolkien nerds, you know this one by heart). Sam tells Frodo, he knows all is messed up. The two small figures of them shouldn't even be there, not in that country, not in that story. But they must press on. And to press on, they must have something to hold on to.

Frodo, deep in his self-pity, asks: "What are we holding on to, Sam?" to which Sam promptly replies: "That there's some good in this world, Mr. Frodo. And it's worth fighting for."

I want to paraphrase Samwise here: There is some good in **the Church** and it is worth fighting for!

The world **has** changed, but the answer is not to throw all the old away. To withdraw from the Church, tear it all down and try to build something new.

The answer lies in rephrasing, reinventing, and reinvigorating the Church, through clarifying our language, our liturgy, and our traditions, so they become theologically sound and biblically true.

We need a solid foundation that is true to the biblical narrative, as we find in process-relational theology, and through that make the Church relevant again, moving it into the 22nd century!

Ulrick Dam is a Danish theologian and author, renowned for his book *Building the Basileia: Moving the Church into the 22nd Century.* Known for integrating modern challenges with theological insights, he advises churches and corporations on fostering empathetic, relationship-driven cultures. His work offers a fresh perspective on revitalizing church liturgy and theology for the contemporary world.

I Invented Process Theology

RUSS DEAN

In twenty years of preaching, I developed a theology that turns out to be Process Theology—I should have just read Teilhard!

I invented Process Theology. If I sound like Al Gore, inventing the internet, just stay with me. Here's how it happened.

In a 1989 lecture in "Systematic Theology," at Southern Seminary in Louisville, KY, Dr. Frank Tupper said (a little too casually), "God always does everything God can do." The class erupted. "What do you mean '...*can* do'? God can do anything, anytime. God is *God*!" For thirty-five years, that conversation has been in my head. Sometimes it rages. Sometimes it is like that background radiation across the universe, a constant reminder of a really big bang.

In 2000, my wife and I became the co-pastors of a theologically progressive congregation in Charlotte, NC. They said they wanted to be challenged, "theologically, intellectually, socially." It was the right pulpit, the right people—and 23 years later, the challenge is still on.

Given the privilege and responsibility of our pulpit—speaking honestly to real people, dealing with real struggles—the platitudes of faith which are part of Southern culture felt even more hollow. I could not stand in this pulpit and offer clichés, feed people on a diet of the God who *can*, but mostly does *not*.

My commitment to speak a real word, based on the God I understand through Jesus, led me back to Tupper's classroom, again and again, and through my pulpit discipline I came to claim his idea as my own theology: there are some things God cannot do. Any friend who could, would. Any parent who could, would. Surely a God who could, would, too. Always.

With that conviction as the basis of my journey, I started inventing Process Theology. It would have been easier just to read Teilhard and Whitehead and Hartshorne, but that would only come much later! Struggling with the realities of the world, reading of the discoveries of science, and standing in an open pulpit, I began creating Process, one sermon at a time.

In 2004 I read on "roadsideamerica.com" about Maria Rubio, who was rolling up a breakfast burrito when she noticed a thumb-sized skillet burn resembling Jesus—a miracle! The Holy Tortilla's fame spread, and within two years, 35,000 pilgrims had come, bringing flowers and photos of sick loved ones. Mrs. Rubio quit her job to attend the "Shrine of the Holy Tortilla," constructed in her home.

Aghast at such superstition, I preached, "Finding God: A Natural Revelation." "I do not intend to demean Mrs. Rubio," I began, "but I find the world-wide clamor for supernatural phenomena amusing. I also find it troubling. What human longing—and what fear—is revealed by such groping for *sensational* proof of the divine?"

Developing my argument, I said, "We are right to challenge the superstition passing for 'supernaturalism,'—we are right to challenge these claims of divine intervention. We are right to question such piety, because in a world which knows better, such claims can only fail to convey the true reality and actual presence of God."

I concluded by establishing in my own preaching the foundation of Process thought—which had been established by Whitehead and Teilhard decades ago: "I do not believe God is 'out there,' to be manipulated by the right posturing, intervening for us. I do not believe God is 'supernatural' at all—though we need *not* feel alone in the world with a non-supernatural God. Quite the opposite: The reality of God is the heart of all that is."

Years later, I read, "the world is not God and God is not the world, yet God is the unlimited depth of love, the center, of all that is: a love that overflows onto new life. God is not a supernatural being hovering above Earth but the supra-personal whole, the Omega, who exists in all and through all. 'Only a God who is functionally and totally 'Omega,' the absolute, ultimate whole, 'can satisfy us'." (Ilia Delio in *From Teilhard to Omega*, quoting Teilhard de Chardin).

For a preaching series in 2005, someone asked about evil, and I preached "Grasping at Silk: Everlasting Arms and the Problem of Pain:"

> I cannot reckon in my mind the answers of a theology that needs to maintain the 'omnipotence' of God, when such answers leave so many without comfort, hating themselves for being unworthy—or angrily turning from a God who *could*, but just didn't. I cannot reckon in my mind a 'big picture,' big enough to justify all the pain, or a next life that excuses all the suffering.

I quoted Charles Hartshorne: "...brute power...has to be reckoned with. The one thing we need not... to do is—to worship it!" Then I concluded by saying:

> I believe God is *not* all-powerful—but I have come to believe that if God is that brooding spirit, still bringing order from chaos, light from darkness (Genesis 1), if God is that inner voice of comfort and challenge (1 Kings 19), if God sounds like a Galilean peasant calling us to love our enemies (who really are our neighbors), if God is one Spirit, "above all and through all and in all," (Ephesians 4.6), if God is "the energy in all things, working to bring good" (Romans 8.28, my translation), if "God is love" (1 John 4.8), then God is the only *real* power there is.

Years later I read, "Someday, after mastering the winds, the waves, the tides and gravity, we shall harness for God the energies of love, and then, for a second time in the history of the world, [we] will have discovered fire," (Pierre Teilhard de Chardin, in *Toward the Future)*.

I read, again, about Evangelicals rejecting the truth of evolution and preached "t=0 and Counting: Lessons Along this Darkened Path." Arguing the need to take evolution as seriously as our faith, I defended the science:

> We cannot pick and choose what science we will believe (electricity, computer technology, open-heart surgery) and what we will not, *just* because the science seems to challenge a stagnant and defiant idea about God. If 'evolution' challenges our notion of God, it will not be the first, nor last time, that science shook the Church, but it is high time the Church stopped sticking its head in the sand of dogma and opened itself to the light of an ever-evolving God.

Having defended evolution, I then challenged the notion some scientists hold, that the random chance driving evolution nullifies meaning or purpose, denies any "*telos*" in the world, and I concluded with a story: "If you are still having trouble with the idea that there *can* be *purpose* in the world, even if God did not plan you from the beginning," consider:

> She was three years old when the doctor said there was nothing more he could do. He advised the parents to take her home and love her, enjoy whatever time they had left. They did, but when that little light went out, the last thing these parents wanted was another child. So...they did not plan another daughter, premeditate her birth. They did not seek to create her life out of nothing. They

will tell you, because of their recent pain, that pregnancy, quite unplanned—an 'accident' as it were—greeted them with more dread than joy.

But, cooing at a mother's breast, toddling into a father's excited hands, growing into a woman and carrying their name into another generation… in that emerging grace, light shined, 'and the darkness could not put it' out (John 1.5). As a daughter and sister, a wife and mother, as a pastor and friend, God's light, God's *purpose*, shines.

You see, my wife, little Amy Adair Jacks, was not planned. But neither is she a big mistake! May God light our darkened path, through Christ our Lord. May it be so. Amen!

Years later, I read,

> It simply cannot be unremarkable that the universe eventually abandoned the relative simplicity of its earliest moments and flowered, over the course of billions of years, into an astounding array of complexity and diversity, including human consciousness and moral aspiration. This aesthetic directionality was enough finally to convince the great philosopher Alfred North Whitehead that there is indeed a point to the universe. Purpose means the "realizing of value," and to Whitehead, beauty was the queen of all values. (John Haught, "Science can question the idea of cosmic purpose.")

When I read in 2010 that the world's leading physicist, Stephen Hawking, had published *The Grand Design*, saying, "Spontaneous creation is the reason there is something rather than nothing, why the universe exists… It is not necessary to invoke God to… set the universe going," given my commitments to faith *and* science, I began wondering what this meant for the future of faith, the future of God. After some late-night pondering, I preached, "On Needing the Unnecessary God."

> So, what do we do when science says God is no longer necessary?—because that is where we are. We could let such evidence destroy faith, let a lack of empirical proof disprove God (though God never claims to be empirical). Such is the fate of too many. Science has taken their God. The second, maybe more popular choice, is the position of the Church in many former episodes… denying scientific truth and engaging in battle. Today's fundamentalism is the result of such a position. It is fearful. Defensive. Back-ward looking… and nearly always wrong. The future is forward. Clinging to ideas built on the past will never lead us to God.

Bringing the sermon home, I said:

> It occurred to me that it's not really the *necessary* things in life that make life worth living, is it? Take breathing: it's necessary—but because of science, there are many human beings today who are *breathing*, who can hardly be considered to be *living*—certainly not living the abundant life Jesus promises (John 10.10). Machines can breathe for us. Only God can fill that breath with a Spirit of life…all the best things in life are really not *necessary* at all. Life is one thing…eternal life, abundant living, is an entirely different. So, I'm willing to grant that God may not be "necessary," as physicists measure necessity, but such a truth makes me no less able to proclaim—it may, in fact, make me more excited to proclaim the world's *need* for this Unnecessary God. To breathing, God gives *spirit*. To rules, God gives *relationships*. To all the necessary laws of the universe, natural and civic, God adds… Grace. Who among us could live without Grace? And who would want to?

Long after I wrote this sermon, I read, "The idea of *self*-transcendence indicates that at the empirical level, the emergence of the new is completely open to explanation in scientific terms. But at a deeper, theological and metaphysical level, it is the immanent presence of the divine being that enables creation to become more than it is in itself," (Denis Edwards, citing Karl Rahner in *From Teilhard to Omega*).

A decade ago, I started writing this story in a book, now entitled, *The Power of the God Who Can't: God Always Does Everything God Can Do.* When I got the manuscript to a publisher in 2023, after years of nibbling around the edges, I decided to finally read some Process Theology. I had quoted Whitehead, Teilhard, and Hartshorne in many sermons and in my book, but these were quotes I had collected, not the result of any honest study.

Wow! I don't know whether to be embarrassed that the convictions I discovered—on my own—have been part of Process thought for almost a century, or just to be grateful that after three decades I have finally discovered the real thing! In reading theologians and thinkers who express the convictions of Process Theology, I'm learning so much that deepens my understanding. I'm meeting so many new friends who share my convictions.

It's been a long time coming, but in the *process*, I have gained more genuine excitement about God, more hope for the future of Christianity, and more confidence in the role faith can play in a spiritual revival that is so desperately needed.

I hope the Church won't take as long as I did. Maybe this book will help people discover the rich world of Process thought, so other Christians will not also have to make it up on their own!

Russ Dean is co-pastor, with Amy Jacks Dean, of Park Road Baptist Church. Author of two books: *Finding a New Way Home: The Unlikely Path of a Reluctant Baptist Renegade* and *The Power of the God Who Can't: God Always Does Everything God Can Do*, Russ is the father of Jackson (wife, Madison and grandson, Walker) and Bennett, and loves barefoot and slalom waterskiing, playing music, and woodworking.

That'll Preach: Preaching the Process and Open and Relational Perspective

BRUCE G. EPPERLY

Process and open and relational theology can be preached with vigor and insight. Lively and life-transforming preaching joins the spiritual life of the preacher with the spiritual life of their congregation and presents possibilities for transforming individuals, congregations, and the planet.

Often when I am working on a project, or reading a colleague's text, I say to myself, "That'll preach." While I don't assume lively and understandable preaching is the criterion for theological reflection, inspiring and transformative theological reflection should be able to address the experiences of laypersons of all ages, including children and teens. I have often described my own approach to writing with the maxim, "If lay people can understand it, so can academics!"

Process and open and relational theology need to be preached—with vigor and insight. Process theology needs to be articulated in ways that illuminate everyday experiences of parenting, decision-making, citizenship and politics, human rights, and care for the planet. Communicating process theology in a way that inspires, energizes, and enlightens is not optional: it may have a role in saving progressive Christianity to save the world.

Process Affirmations for Preachers and Their Congregants. Process-relational theology has an open-spirited and relational understanding of revelation and inspiration that can transform the preacher and their preaching. I will briefly outline the heart of process and open and relational thought from my perspective and then apply it to the life of the preacher. Theology is best learned using affirmations that transform our minds and ways of looking at the world. Some key affirmations of process and open and relational theology include the following:

- *We live in a lively universe, joining the permanent whitewater of change with the stability of Creative Wisdom.* Tradition matters, and the fidelity of God matters, and together they are "new every morning."
- *We live in an interdependent universe in which our relationships limit and inspire and our actions shape the contours of the future.* As Southern African wisdom affirms, *Ubuntu,* "I am because of you. We are because of one another."
- *We live in a God-filled universe in which God calls to us in every encounter and experience.* The world around us is ambiguous, and our congregations are ambiguous, but the world and our congregants are constantly touched by God. They experience the Holy even if they are unaware of it. There is a "ladder of angels" everywhere—a "thin place" of inspiration for those whose doors of perception have been opened.
- *Every experience and encounter can be a medium of revelation.* God comes to us in every encounter. There is something to be learned from every experience. Children are sages and so are those defined as neurodivergent. The heavens declare the glory of God and so does the houseless person sitting outside the church.
- *Life is a dynamic "call and response" in which God calls, we respond, and then God calls again, adapting to our responses.* Revelation is always personal. God's vision is for a particular moment in the life of a particular person—or particular congregation—related to past decisions and histories and aiming at future possibilities. God's call is always the "best for that impasse" and the vision of the "best"—the highest contextual aspiration for us and the world—and this call is revised moment by moment in relationship to the concrete situation.
- *We matter to God and can choose to be God's companions in healing the Earth.* God is the "fellow sufferer who understands" (Alfred North Whitehead) and the joyful companion who celebrates. As companions in healing the earth (*tikkun olam*), we make a difference to God. Our actions add to or subtract from the array of possibilities for planetary and personal transformation. Knowing that "God can't" heal the Earth without us, let us aspire to "do something beautiful for God," as Mother (Saint) Teresa counsels.

Preaching and the Spiritual Formation of the Preacher. I believe that good theology involves the interplay of vision, promise, and practice. This same dynamic and interdependent trinity is at the heart of solid and dynamic preaching and spiritual formation.

- *Vision*—how we view the universe and God's presence in the world, and how this shapes, for example, our understanding of ourselves, the nature of salvation, the process of revelation, and our political and ethical decisions.
- *Promise*—the affirmation that we can experience what we believe and, in that experience, we encounter the Holiness of Life reflective of the Holy Adventure we call God.
- *Practices*—joining the "inner" and "outer" journeys, practices enable us to experience and encounter the Holy Adventure in our lives and align with God's vision for Shalom in the world. Practices involve discovering—by the interplay of contemplation and action—"God in all things" and "All things in God."

The process and open and relational preacher must, in the dynamic trinity of vision, promise, and practice, cultivate a theological imagination grounded in their theological beliefs and worldview. Preach what you believe, not what others tell you to believe or what you feel you must say to avoid "rocking the boat." Preaching what you believe adds zest, excitement, delight, energy, and engagement to your preaching and communication *with* the congregation.

Recently, I was invited to be a "bridge minister" for a progressive congregation on the eastern seaboard. The congregation had suffered from what I perceived as lackluster disconnected preaching and often scolding from the pulpit. In my three-month stint, I decided to change the medium and the message. Prior to worship, I wandered about the congregation, engaging the congregants, building relationships, and discovering a sense of their perceptions of why they were attending, despite a season of disengaged preaching and leadership. After church, instead of standing at the door to bid adieu, I returned to the congregation to reach out to the congregants, listening for their stories and hopes for the church. Relationship is everything in preaching. Knowing leads to communication. Intimacy, even at a surface level, gives birth to call and response and communication.

During this bridge time, I chose to preach process and open and relational theology, grounded in my awareness of the congregation's situation and its need to experience the power of affirmative faith. I preached what I believe: God is with us; we matter to God; what we do makes a difference in the world; everyone belongs; healing is possible; the past sets us free for an open future; God loves diversity; our calling is to heal ourselves, our communities, and the planet in companionship with God who needs us to transform the world. The result was immediate and, by the end of my three-month stint, the congregants were alive and lively, looking forward to their congregation's future, and ready to welcome their new pastor.

Practices for Preaching. Recognizing that preaching joins the "journey inward" and "journey outward," to quote a theme from Washington D.C.'s Church of the Saviour, I will lift up a few process and open and relational practices for preaching.

- *Bring Spirit to Preaching.* Preaching is a creative and dynamic practice, joining the imagination, theological reflection, and spiritual formation of preacher and congregants. Preachers cultivate their spiritual lives by daily practices of prayer and meditation. If God is speaking within us each moment of our lives, we need to pause to listen to divine revelation in the events of our lives. Daily centering along with praying the hours—in this case, taking a moment several times a day—to notice your spiritual state and the world around—opens us to divine guidance appropriate to our setting.
- *Be all sense.* North African Desert Parent wisdom says that the monk is "all eye." I would expand this to mean, the monk or, in this case, the preacher, is "all sense," training their whole being to be aware of the world around and within themselves. This can mean many things: having the Bible in one hand and the *New York Times* in the other; noticing the faces of people on the street, in your family, and your congregation; bathing your senses in the beauty of the environment. In being "all sense," we open to the contours of divine energy constantly flowing in and through our lives and attune ourselves to God's vision for the world where we preach, pastor, and live.
- *Be concrete in your spirituality.* Abstractions, whether in ethics, politics, and religion, freeze the world around us. Abstractions, unrelated to the concreteness of experience, live in the past, put us and others in straitjackets, and exclude those who fail to fit into the abstract. Concreteness, living in a congregation's real world, in spirituality, theology, and preaching, gives life, energy, zest, and inspiration for our setting, enabling us to respond to the world that exists, not a made-up abstract world, joining actuality with possibility to transform the world.
- *Open to the eternal and everlasting.* Plunge into the now of the world and your congregation. Preach to the congregation you have, not an ideal congregation,

remembering that the limitations of your congregation are also the womb of possibility.

- *Let your unconscious go to work in your preaching.* A writing practice I have used for decades involves the following: at bedtime, I think about what I will write tomorrow or read a few sentences related to my writing or sermonizing; I commit my thoughts to God and ask that God be present in my sleeping, guiding and inspiring me; and when I awaken, I take some time for spiritual centering and then start writing. Virtually without fail, creative ideas come to me, including a whole sermon or chapter within the first fifteen minutes. You need to do your homework, studying the text and reading the commentaries, but these are a prelude to awakening to the alignment of your creativity with God's.

- *Practice Lectio Divina or Holy Reading.* In preparing for virtually every sermon, I take time for a period of Benedictine *lectio divina* in which I read the scripture twice after a time of silence and then open to the congruence of God's wisdom and my own inner wisdom in anticipation that I will experience guidance, insight, and direction. In *lectio divina*, often a word or image emerges that becomes the kernel of your sermon.

- *Take your sermon for a walk.* In the dynamic nature of divine call and human response, when we move, the Spirit moves along with us. Movement unblocks our imagination. As Jimmy Buffett says, "changes in latitudes, changes in attitudes" and this applies to sermon preparation. In taking my sermon on an intentional "preaching walk," words, images, ideas, and visualizations of people in my congregation arise. I often see myself with Jesus as my companion, sharing with Jesus my insights and letting Jesus speak to me. In movement, there is process, growth, and an "adventure of ideas," that will be addressed to the congregation.

- *Pray for the congregation, visualizing people who will be at church.* Living in an open-spirited and relational universe, process and open and relational preachers recognize the power of prayer to change our lives and bring new insights and energies to our environment, including our congregation. I recall Leslie Weatherhead's comment, "When I pray, coincidences happen. When I don't, they don't." I believe prayer creates a field of force around those for whom we pray and adds to the energy of love motivating our congregations. Prayer, which opens the door for greater influx of divine possibility and energy, is a necessity for the preacher. During my sermon preparation, I take time to pray for the congregation, identifying certain persons as "icons" of God's presence in the church. When I step into the sanctuary, usually 20 minutes before the service, I say a prayer for guidance and compassion, that we be one in spirit and love, and that my words bring healing, hope, and action.

A Final Word. Process and open and relational preaching are transformational, and our congregations need transformation so they can be agents of healing, reconciliation, justice, and welcome and inspire social activism to repair our world and promote human rights. Our churches are a counterforce, a firewall, to the destructive influence of Christian nationalism and, more than that, a place of welcome for seekers, persons traumatized by traditional Christianity, and a place where the marginalized can find affirmation and a home. Spirit-centered process and open and relational preaching can be a catalyst for the Shalom we seek. And, "that'll preach!"

Bruce Epperly has joined seminary and university teaching and administration and congregational and university ministry for over forty years. Ordained in the United Church of Christ and the Christian Church (Disciples of Christ), he is the author of over eighty books in theology, spirituality, ministerial wellbeing and excellence, healing and wholeness, scripture, and spirituality of politics, including *The Elephant is Running: Process and Open and Relational Theology and Religious Pluralism*; *Jesus: Mystic, Healer, and Prophet*; *Process Theology: A Guide for the Perplexed*; and *Process Theology and the Revival We Need.* In "retirement," he continues to write, teach, and preach, along with grandparenting and adventures with his wife of 45 years, Kate.

Spiral of Time: The Christian Year from a Process and Open and Relational Perspective

BRUCE G. EPPERLY

The seasons of the Christian year remind us of God's presence in all the seasons of life. Each moment, day, and season of life can be a theophany, or thin place, where time and eternity meet and where we find direction in our vocation of becoming God's companions in healing the world.

Plato (428-348 BCE) described time as the moving image of eternity. The philosopher believed that the passage of time joins the infinite and the finite, and the eternal and the temporal. Time is not, according to Plato, an illusion. Rather, it is the embodiment of Divine Artistry in a world of change. It is God's vision incarnate in the world of change. Eternal patterns and creative wisdom give birth to the contours of time and the ordered movements of the planets and stars.

Perhaps two year hundred years earlier, the Jewish author of Lamentations reflected on God's presence during the Babylonian Captivity. Despite the chaos of captivity and national destruction, the author described, amid his laments about the state of his nation, God's faithfulness in history and human experience as everlasting, ever changing, and eternal. God is active in the historical and nature process, ensuring order and novelty in a world of accident, change, and tragedy.

The steadfast love of the LORD never ceases,
his mercies never come to an end;

> they are new every morning;
> great is your faithfulness.
> "The LORD is my portion," says my soul,
> "therefore I will hope in him." (Lamentations 3:22-24, NRSV)

God is present in sunrise and sunset, seedtime and harvest, and summer and winter. God is alive in the never changing and the ever-changing. To awaken to God in the seasons of life is to live hopefully despite the challenges of history.

As we consider the passage of time and the character of the Christian liturgical year from a process and open and relational perspective, we begin with the observation that life is dynamic. The process is reality for God and us. You can't step into the same waters twice, as the Pre-Socratic philosopher Heraclitus of Ephesus (circa 500 BCE) asserted. Nor can you step into the same pulpit or sanctuary twice. Time is flowing, and yet there is an order and purpose in the permanent whitewater and perpetually perishing nature of history and our lives. With the coming of each new week and the beginning of each Sunday morning service, the world changes, the preacher changes, and the congregation changes, despite the appearance of stability. God is changing, yet there is a consistent moral and spiritual arc through history.

Many Christian theologians have understood time to be an arrow, moving with divinely ordained purpose from beginning to end. They believe that linear time is the arena of history in which each moment brings something new into the world. God has a plan and will bring it to fruition. These theologians contrast the linear time of Judaism and Christianity with the circularity and repetitive nature of time, described by indigenous peoples and practitioners of Earth-based spirituality, today referred to as Paganism. In their deprecation and misunderstanding of indigenous and Pagan wisdom, and its presence in our own Christian spiritual cycles, they miss the incarnation in the non-human world and order of nature.

I believe that while nuances exist between the Jewish-Christian and Indigenous-Pagan understandings of time, the Christian liturgical calendar brings together both the linear and circular in an ever-expanding spiral of time, in which order and repetition of nature is joined with the novelty of divine and creaturely creativity. Life is moving forward and yet the forward aim of life occurs within the circling seasons.

The Christian seasons of the year celebrate the cycles of Jesus' life as a contemporary experience. But each yearly celebration is unique as history moves forward in novel ways. In the unfolding of human and cosmic history, God is the source of both order and novelty. "The steadfast love of God never ceases." Yet, "God's mercies are new every morning." God's great faithfulness is the revealed in the ever-new and ever-dependable movements of grace in our lives. What appears to be a straight line is an arc and what appears to be a circle is a spiral in the yearly unfolding of the Christian year and the days and season of our lives.

The seasons of the Christian year invite us to experience the open-ended and yet dependable movements of God in our lives. God is embedded in history. The Word and Wisdom of God are made flesh, and God's light enlightens all people (see John 1:1-9). The all-loving, "amipotent," as Thomas Oord asserts, is present in novel and loving ways in the creative process, the life of Jesus, and God's aim at healing and wholeness in the lives of persons and the planet. Seasons spiral forward with no predetermined outcome. The open-endedness of the seasons of the year and our lives allows us to claim our role as companions with God in celebration and agency in all life's changes. God is in history and must adapt to the process that God has shaped in a lively call and response between God and the world, and our own creativity comes in response to God's moment-by-moment and long-term initiatives.

I see the seasons of the Christian year as an opportunity to walk with Jesus and consecrate our daily lives and our own growth from birth to death. Each season in its joining of order and novelty moves us closer to incarnating God's Spirit in our lives and communities. Our relationship with God is dependable and new every morning.

In the next few paragraphs, I will outline a process and open and relational vision of the Christian year, which I believe will deepen the spirituality of many formerly evangelical Christians who have joined the open and relational movement. It will also enhance the spiritual practices of many process-relational Christians, whose mainline and progressive churches often give scant attention to the liturgical year, except for Advent, Christmas, Holy Week, and Easter, and Good Friday Services. The spiral of sacred time involves the following seasons:

- *Advent*—The season of opening to the not-yet and unfinished. Advent is the time of spiritual restlessness as we await the birth of Jesus of Nazareth and the realization of God's vision in history, "on earth as it is in heaven." The coming of Jesus and the fulfillment of history is open-ended, calling us to stay awake to novel revelations of God's presence in our lives and history. Attempts to chart a pre-determined Second Coming of Jesus miss the point in their: 1) elimination of human freedom and agency, 2) binary understanding of salvation separating humankind into saved and damned, and 3) cultivation of irresponsible attitudes toward issues of justice and earth care (If we can do nothing to change the future, dictated by God, why do anything? Only heaven and how to get there matters.) Advent proclaims that the "coming of Christ" occurs moment-by-moment, is many faceted, and is neither predictable nor final.

- *Christmas*—God's incarnation in Jesus and the cosmos. The Word and Wisdom present in Jesus Christ are cosmic and global, as well as historical and personal. In the Christmas season, we affirm that the word lives by the incarnation of God and we recognize that history is open-ended and revelation is universal and constantly unfolding. The celebration of incarnation cannot eliminate the tragedies of life, often the result of human freedom. For example, "the massacre of infants," remembered on December 28 in Western Christianity and December 29 in Eastern Christianity. In the Christmas season, the twelve days between the celebration of Jesus' birth and the eve of Epiphany, we embrace the tragic beauty of life. Christ is born in a world where children are murdered in opposition to God's incarnational love.

- *Epiphany*—The affirmation of God's universal revelation beyond Christianity, the church, and the sacraments. There is salvation outside the church. The Persian magi recognize the Christ Child while the guardians of the faith deny God's presence among the marginalized and oppressed. Saints and mystics may be found in every tradition, reflecting God's ubiquitous and universal presence in the ongoing human adventure.

- *Lent*—The season of simplicity in which we journey with the Habiru people and Jesus in the wilderness, facing temptation and seeking wisdom in the healthy use of freedom. In Lent, we strive toward simplicity of life, discarding everything that stands between us and God's call to relationship. Freedom is real, and we must choose to cure or kill, heal, or harm, further or block God's vision in our personal and corporate lives.

- *Holy Week*—If any week demonstrates the ambiguity of freedom, it is Holy Week. In the roller coaster from Palm Sunday to Holy Saturday, we experience the interplay of God's love and human waywardness. God has a vision, but the realization of God's vision depends on human decisions. Our choices lead to fidelity or disobedience. Despite the tradition of seeing Holy Week as predestined and the Cross as a requirement for God's forgiveness of sinful humankind, Holy Week reveals a very different theology: God must adapt to human freedom; God's Beloved Child is at the mercy of forces beyond Jesus' will; Jesus freely chooses the Cross although other choices are available to him; and perhaps more poignant, God feels the pain of the Cross. The Cross is not predestined, but in the cross, God feels the pain of life and seeks to transform suffering into service and growth. God is the ultimate empath and not an aloof observer of a history unfolding to a predestined plan. Holy Week is open-ended and so is our history as companions of the suffering God.

- *Easter*—Easter is the season of novelty and surprise. A burst of energy, an unexpected quantum leap in experience, overcomes the powers of death and destruction. Christ is risen. The "fellow sufferer who understands" (Alfred North Whitehead) is also the intimate companion who heals and transforms. "Nothing can separate us from the love of God," not even suffering and death.
- *Pentecost*—Pentecost is the season of divine giftedness. The Spirit is in us, with us, and through us. Miracle and wonder are built into the fabric of reality. What appears to be ordinary time is filled with divine possibility. The presence of divine possibility inspires us to respond to God's call with acts of power to transform the world.
- *Creation Season*—Typically celebrated between September 1 and October 4, the Feast of St. Francis, creation season awakens us to God's generous love for all creation. God loves the world—human and non-human alike. The heavens declare the glory of God and so do the cells of our bodies. In creation season, we commit to "reverence for life" by becoming agents of planetary healing.

The world lives by the incarnation of God and God's incarnation is revealed in the times and places of our lives. Abraham Joshua Heschel once referred to the Sabbath as the "sanctuary of time," and affirmed that this day of rest is sacred. Yet, every day and season is sacred. In following the seasons of the year, we consecrate each day and the totality of our lives. In the spirit of process and open and relational theology, the seasons reveal a generous, intimate, freedom-loving God whose power is revealed in healing and love. Not predetermined, the seasons spiral forward, awakening us to the unfolding of our lives and the world in the dance of God's call and our response.

Bruce Epperly has joined seminary and university teaching and administration and congregational and university ministry for over forty years. Ordained in the United Church of Christ and the Christian Church (Disciples of Christ), he is the author of over seventy books in theology, spirituality, ministerial wellbeing and excellence, healing and wholeness, scripture, and spirituality of politics, including *The Elephant is Running: Process and Open and Relational Theology and Religious Pluralism*; *Jesus: Mystic, Healer, and Prophet*; *Process Theology: A Guide for the Perplexed*; and *Process Theology and the Revival We Need*. In "retirement," he continues to write, teach, and preach, along with grandparenting and adventures with his wife of 45 years, Kate.

My Spiritual Journey Is Like a Music Crescendo

AL GEPHART

Players in a world-wide jazz combo, we improvise with God on the theme of love.

I grew up in a conservative, fundamentalist Christian home. I am grateful for the sense of God's Presence that I experienced there, my introduction to the Bible, and to Jesus. At the same time, even as a teenager, I began to have many questions—questions about the Bible and evolution, about Jesus being God, and about Christianity as the only way of salvation. What about my friends who were not Christian? Or those who chose to attend more liberal churches? Were they all wrong?

Music was an integral, important part of my life, almost from the beginning. It was music more than anything that conveyed and lodged in my heart my early Christian faith. I loved to sing the hymns and choruses I learned at church. Hymns like "The Old Rugged Cross," "How Great Thou Art," "Blessed Assurance, Jesus is Mine," and choruses like "Safe Am I in the Hollow of His Hand."

One chorus I learned at summer camp summarized my early faith, challenged me to live as God desired, and encouraged me to share Jesus with others.

> "Let's be true to Jesus, tho' a thousand voices from the world may call;
> 'Twas He who died to save us, and demands our life, our loyalty, our all.
> Since we'll walk and talk with Him when our life on earth is o'er,
> Let us labor now to point the sinner to the open door.
> Let's be true to Jesus, and we'll reap eternal blessing by and by."

I say that my spiritual journey is like a music crescendo. I don't mean what that means to a musician, that I've gradually gotten louder and louder over the years. No, I see the crescendo symbol turned on its side. And I imagine it as outstretched arms, reaching out in an increasingly more open and more inclusive embrace.

As I encountered my world as a young adult, questions, new learning, life-affecting experiences continued to stretch those arms and shape who I was becoming.

Often, I needed to let go of earlier perceptions to embrace what now made more sense. It was not an easy process. The hold of fundamentalism is strong. There is a fear that letting go may jeopardize your relationship with God. It may also mean that you find yourself out of sync with your family and friends. That was true for me.

My first year in college, I helped organize a group of classmates who met weekly to explore the Bible, to share what was happening in their lives, and to pray together. It was called Lawrence Christian Fellowship (LCF). We took turns leading our discussions. We became good friends. It was liberating to be in a safe space where we openly discussed doubts and questions. We sang the hymn "Great Is Thy Faithfulness" at almost every gathering.

> Pardon for sin and a peace that endureth,
> Thine own dear presence to cheer and to guide;
> strength for today and bright hope for tomorrow:
> blessings all mine, with ten thousand beside!
> Great is Thy faithfulness, Great is Thy faithfulness, Lord unto me.

My faith perspective broadened and became less fundamentalistic; more evangelical.

I went to seminary, not thinking I would become a minister, but wanting to continue my exploration of unanswered, haunting questions. I tell people that Fuller Seminary was a liberalizing influence on my life.

In the first fall, I took a class in Old Testament theology. I learned more about the Jewish roots of Christianity. It challenged me to see continuity rather than division between the Old and New Testaments. For Christmas that year, I went to a kosher Jewish store in Beverly Hills and bought presents for my parents. My mom always enjoyed the Shabbat tray I gave her, displaying it prominently in her dining room hutch.

Seminary gave me tools for understanding the origin and development of Christianity. I was able to study the Bible using Greek, and to some extent, Hebrew. I learned about some of the great Christian theologians—Augustine, Luther, Calvin, Barth, Brunner, and Niebuhr. By the time I graduated, I resonated with a contemporary expression of the theology of the Reformers, known as Neo-orthodoxy. I became a

Presbyterian, appreciating that denomination's thoughtful approach to faith and social issues.

Still, I had not yet decided to become a minister. I pursued a Master of Music degree in church and choral music, thinking I might teach music or direct choirs in a university setting. However, something deep inside kept nudging me to consider focusing on church ministry.

In 1970, I was ordained as a Presbyterian minister at the Whitworth Community Presbyterian Church in Spokane, Washington. My job description included the education, music, and youth programs of the church. My crescendo arms had opened a great deal during those preparation years; much more was yet to come!

One year I helped plan a city-wide interfaith Thanksgiving service. I got to know the rabbi at Temple Beth Shalom. I called him afterward to see if he would be open to teaching a class at our church. "What would you like me to teach?" he asked. "Perhaps something about the Old Testament," I replied. There was a significant pause. Then he said, "The 'Old' Testament?" It suddenly came to me that Jews do not recognize their holy scriptures as "old" in contrast to the "new" writings of the Christian Bible. It was a stretching moment. I have had difficulty referring to the "Old" Testament ever since.

Social justice was not a topic preached or talked about in church when I was growing up. One day, Robert McAfee Brown, a Presbyterian seminary professor, gave a lecture at Whitworth College, which was right next to the church I served. I went to hear him.

In his talk, he said that "God takes sides" and "God has a preference for the poor." It stunned me. How could God prefer anyone? Why the poor? His address challenged me to look for references to God's concern for the poor in the Bible. There they were.

> "Is not this what I require…to loose the fetters of injustice…sharing your food with the hungry, taking the homeless poor into your home, clothing the naked…"

> "The Spirit is upon me because he has anointed me to preach good news to the poor…release to the captives…sight to the blind…and to set at liberty those who are oppressed."

> "In as much as you do it to the least of these, you do it to me."

A few years later, I read Brown's book, Theology in a New Key. Brown too had a music background. The book focused on the themes of liberation theology. It is a bottom-up social view that focuses primary consideration on the plight of the poor and the oppressed. Jesus' own life is an example of this focus. This was the beginning of my concern for social justice.

It was a new challenge for me to look at life through the eyes of the marginalized. I began to recognize God's concern for the well-being of people here and now. For a Kingdom of peace and love to come today, on earth, as Jesus invited us to pray. Salvation wasn't just about what happens to us when we die. This was a huge stretching point that significantly changed my faith orientation.

Roman Catholic theologian Hans Kung authored a book, *On Being a Christian* in which he wrote, "God's purpose is man's wellbeing." What? I had always thought my purpose was God's wellbeing. I imagined God is only pleased when I completely obey and live the way he wants me to. "Trust and obey," the hymn said, "for there's no other way to be happy in Jesus, but to trust and obey."

I heard Kung saying that God was on my side, even when I wasn't entirely on God's side and didn't do everything right. God wanted my joy and happiness in life and purposely sought to help me have the most fulfilling life that I could. That was a 180-degree perspective change. Less about divine requirement and judgment; more about God's love and desire for my wellbeing.

Presbyterians initiated a consideration of affirming gay and lesbian persons in the late '70s. I concluded that homosexuality was not a choice and became an advocate for change in the denomination. The corporate decision did not happen until 2014, five years after I retired. Little did I realize early on that in 2011 our own daughter would come out to our family as a transgender person, and that I would be on an entirely new, even more widening inclusive journey.

In the 1990s Marcus Borg began to write about an "emerging paradigm." Something new in Christianity was seeking to be born. It is the product, he wrote,

> "of Christianity's encounter with the modern and postmodern world, including science, historical scholarship, religious pluralism, and cultural diversity."

He highlighted how Christianity has contributed to racism, sexism, nationalism, and exclusivism. His writings got my attention as they were scratching where I was still itching, addressing yet unanswered questions.

Borg's books humanized the Bible for me. *Meeting Jesus Again for the First Time* and *The Heart of Christianity* helped me let go of the out-of-this-world view of Jesus I still carried. The traditional understanding proclaims Jesus as a member of the Divine Trinity, purposely sent to die on the cross to atone for the sins of the world.

The view Borg presented was that Jesus was a person, like each of us, a product of a particular time and place. He was a Jewish mystic deeply influenced by Israel's prophetic tradition. And he was a healer, a teacher of wisdom, a social prophet, and the initiator of a movement. Following his tragic death, Borg said, his followers spoke of him as "the Messiah / Christ."

The cross for Borg was the cost of love fully expressed. Jesus' life and teaching challenged powerful, unjust, and oppressive systems. He became a threat to those in leadership positions. As a result, powerful people conspired to kill with him, thinking he would no longer influence the nation.

However, Jesus rose again in the witness of those who felt his presence with them. They continued to follow his Way, attracting others to join with them. Borg's books significantly contributed to my taking a huge, broadening step in my understanding about Jesus.

In 2003, then serving a church in Tempe, Arizona, we focused for a month on the relationship of religion and science. Our theme was "An Unavoidable Challenge: The Church in an Age of Science and Technology." Throughout history, there are many ways that the church and science communities have been antagonistic to each other.

I learned during that month that those who sought to integrate science and religion did so through the lens of process theology, which arose after the discoveries of evolution and quantum physics. This approach intrigued me and I began to explore it vigorously. Surely, I thought, truth is truth, whether found in science or religion. We need both for a comprehensive world and life perspective.

The more I read, the more I resonated with the process perspective. Over and over, it answered long-held questions. It resonated with how I experienced life. Though it challenged earlier orthodox views, its perspectives on God, Jesus, creation, and salvation made great sense. **I found myself saying, "Yes."**

"Yes" to a different view of God's relationship with creation

Process theology espouses life as an ongoing series of events, each related to and influenced by the past. Each moment is also freely, creatively determined by each entity. In an inter-connected universe, we are influenced by all that has gone on before. The process approach resonated with Martin Luther King's words:

> "It really boils down to this: that all life is interrelated. We are all caught in an inescapable network of mutuality, tied into a single garment of destiny. Whatever affects one directly, affects all indirectly."

This view challenged my Sky-God, omnipotent perspective that imagined God residing in heaven somewhere, sitting like Lincoln in his big chair in the Lincoln Memorial. With absolute, almighty power God looks out on creation and intervenes in human affairs to answer people's prayers and to accomplish the divine will. Above, beyond, and distant, it pictures God separate from me, and only now and then present. Such Presence depends on the depth of my faith and my obedience.

How different to perceive God ubiquitously present and part of each moment of your life, not as a controlling power, but as a Presence of Love luring you to make choices freely that lead to greater wholeness and fullness of life. It is a view that understands God as incarnated in all of life, in all human and non-human entities. In fact, there would no life outside of the Presence of God. Only a chaotic universe of elements. Process theology sees the world not as a collection of objects, but as a community of inter-relating subjects, each with the potential for relationship.

Brian McLaren notes:

> "I do still dare to believe there is a *You* to address in the universe, a Presence, a Love that loves through all loves, a radiant and holy mystery, the Spirit of life and creativity, the Wisdom woven into the pattern of the universe, the 'still small voice' that beckons creation, including me, toward love and maturity.
>
> I can't help but see that *You* shining through in the face of Jesus...and through the lives of holy, compassionate, and wise people I meet everywhere. That *You* that I encounter in life is far better than the *He* many of us were taught in church." (Brian McLaren, *Do I Stay Christian: A Guide for the Doubters, the Disappointed, and the Disillusioned*)

"Yes" to a different view of Jesus:

Traditional Christian beliefs are based on a substance understanding of the universe. Jesus, I learned early, was made of two different substances—human and divine. It is a zero-sum perspective; the more you have of one the less you have of the other. Most of my life I espoused a more divine than human Jesus.

Process theology is built on a relational view of the universe. Creation at its deepest level is not matter; it is inter-relating energy. It is possible, in this perspective, for different energies to exist together, at the same time. It may even be true that the more you have of one the more you have of the other. For example, the more open you are to the Presence of God within you the more human you become.

This is how I began to understand Jesus. As he "grew in wisdom" (Luke 2:40, 52), he responded to the lure and call of God in ways each of us can do. The "Light that enlightens everyone" illuminated him. Similarly, it seeks to illuminate us. And as the Word/Logos became flesh in him, it seeks to become flesh in us.

In other words, Jesus was not a two-substance freak from outer space; rather, he was a human being just like me, who grew in love and increasingly gave himself to the Lure he heard. Perhaps his experience was not too different from my own. I also experienced a sense of call, even as a young person, that I just couldn't shake, even when other voices sought my attention.

John Cobb writes in *Christ in a Pluralistic Age*, that Jesus surrendered himself to the Divine Lure to the extent that his own ego became one with it. He was one with God. What is most significant to me is that potential lies within each of us (John 17:20ff). Jesus is not different in kind from us; only perhaps different in degree, and the context in which he lived out his call.

Anna Case-Winters notes about Jesus (*God Will Be All and in All*):

> "If we do not see 'true human being' in him, then his life cannot serve as a model for our own. If God's presence in him is ontologically different from God's presence in the rest of us, then we cannot be expected to be like him."

Finally, a view of Jesus that made sense to me.

"Yes" to a different view of salvation

In earlier years, I viewed salvation in transactional terms. It went something like this: I am a sinner, powerless ultimately to save myself. God sent Jesus to live a sinless life. His death on the cross would be the perfect sacrifice God required to atone for my sins. He would be my substitute. If I believed in him, which is the required transaction, God would forgive me and accept me into heaven when I die.

To be honest, I believed this dogma for many years, but often wondered—How could this be the way of a God of love? It is the thrust of many hymns that speak of Jesus' death on the cross. It remains the central view of salvation of most Christian churches.

Process theology helped me move from a transactional view to a relational perspective. It understands salvation as an ongoing journey of moments of transformation. God is present in my life as a Lure toward truth, goodness, beauty, and love. I am transformed into the image of Christ and "saved" as I give myself to that Lure. I continuously become a new person, "born again" not just once and for all, but again and again and again. (2 Cor 3:18f) I too, to an increasing degree, become Christ, incarnated Presence of God in the world. As regards heaven, I have decided simply to entrust myself into the Love of God, whatever that may mean beyond this life.

"Yes" to a different mission for my life

For many years, a major life-focus for me was seeking to convert others and to help them become Christians. Jesus was, after all, the one and only Way to God, to truth and to life, and ultimately, to heaven.

How freeing to see God present in all people and no longer objects for conversion. I gradually moved from Christian exclusivity to greater inclusion of all faith traditions. I looked for the gifts others offered out of the diversity of their faith traditions. There is, I believe, that Lure to truth, goodness, beauty, and love in the depths of every person. Interfaith dialogue has become an important part of my life.

I don't accept everything others espouse. In some, the Divine Light seems almost entirely extinguished. Scripture notes, however, that the darkness never completely overcomes it. And God, like a tracking "Hound of Heaven," continues to pursue us all and never tires or gives up. God leads me to join, with an ever broader, more inclusive community of others, to become co-creators with God in an evolving, more loving, and more whole world.

As I journeyed more into process theology, I began to look for those outside of the process community who held similar views, but who didn't speak of process theology explicitly. For example, I discovered John Philip Newell, a fellow Presbyterian in the Church of Scotland, and a scholar of Celtic spirituality. I started using his prayers for personal meditation and in worship. Prayers like:

> You are above us, O God, you are within.
> You are in all things
> yet contained by no thing.
> Teach us to seek you in all that has life that we may see you as the Light of life.
> Teach us to search for you in our own depths
> that we may find you in every living soul. (*Sounds of the Eternal: A Celtic Psalter*, 2012)

"Yes" to seeing beauty in the world

Last, process theology has helped me to look for beauty in the world. There's the beauty of nature; the beauty of a well-executed basketball play; the beauty of a small helicopter flying around the surface of Mars; the beauty of compassion shown to a stranger in need; the beauty of negotiations for peace. I look for it as I take walks and as I read the daily paper.

Mary Oliver writes:

It doesn't have to be the blue iris,
it could be weeds in a vacant lot, or a few
small stones; just
pay attention, then patch

a few words together and don't try
to make them elaborate, this isn't
a contest but the doorway

into thanks, and a silence in which
another voice may speak.

Phyllis Tickle held that "Every five hundred years or so religion undergoes a significant paradigm shift." Evolution, quantum physics, and new technology has made the pluralism of our world more evident and has put Christianity into shift mode. Something is certainly happening. Change is in the air.

Process philosophy and theology has helped me to deal with these changes. It has offered a third option between blindly going on with an earlier perspective I don't really believe as I once did or entirely throwing out my faith in God and my trust in the Way of Jesus, as many have done. The process perspective allows me to feel secure in the Love of God while letting go of orthodox tenets that no longer make sense.

Behind my questions and my doubts is the Lure of God drawing me forward to a broader, more inclusive worldview. What I hold to today is open to review tomorrow, for life is an ongoing process. It is a never completed, life-time adventurous journey of discovery with God. There is no doubt still more arm-stretching to be done.

The church of Christ in every age Beset by change, but Spirit led,
Must test and claim its heritage, and keep on rising from the dead.
(Hymn: "The Church of Christ in Every Age")

At this point in the journey, I find myself in resonance with these words of Ilia Delio :

"I believe in one God, one human family, one planetary community, one body, one love, uniting all in beauty, for God's infinite love is infinite, fecund, and beautiful. I believe I am entangled with all earth life and all living creatures, I believe this future is the relational unity of all things in God, I believe this earth has a future entangled with God, I believe the heart of God is love.

Beliefs guide us, faith strengthens us, but love—well, love is the core energy of life. Where there is love, there is no death, only future. Love raised Jesus from the dead; love heals and makes whole. It is time to stop talking about the risen Christ and begin loving in a radically new way. The power in our midst of reimagining a new world is love." (*The Not-Yet God*, 2023)

Al Gephart is an ordained minister in the Presbyterian Church (USA). He holds master's degrees in theology and church and choral music. He served congregations in Washington State, and Tempe, AZ. He chairs the Interfaith Dialogue Committee of the Arizona Faith Network, and the Christian Path of the Process and Faith program. He is married to Betsy Wells-Gephart, a retired lactation consultant.

The Scandal and Celebration of Ecumenical Worship

DORAL HAYES

What can we learn from worshiping alongside those from other Christian traditions?

I was raised in an interchurch family and so Christian unity is almost part of my DNA. Each week we attended two churches as a family, a conservative evangelical free church and the local parish church, part of the Church of England. As a family, we worshipped at and contributed to the life of both churches, but never, to my memory, did these two congregations come together in worship or prayer. The only time I remember seeing the minister of one church in the other's building was at my dad's funeral. Sadly, in the church, disunity was, and often still is, more common than unity. This is sometimes described as a scandal.

The week of prayer for Christian unity started in 1908, it was conceived by Fr. Paul Wattson from the Franciscan Friars of Atonement in Greymoor, New York. Following the formation of the World Council of Churches in 1948, the week of prayer for Christian unity has been celebrated in many countries and by many churches around the world each year in January. Even if the importance of ecumenism, or Christian unity, is not ever mentioned at any other time of the year, this is one time when ecumenical prayer and worship is sometimes considered, discussed, and even sometimes practiced. January in England is usually a deary time; everyone has returned to work after the Christmas break. There are grey days with less daylight and cold damp nights. As such, the celebrations of this special week of prayer are often muted due to its association with sitting in draughty churches on cold winter nights. Additionally, few are energised to think about and pray for Christian unity when there are so many challenges within their own churches. When faced with reduced numbers, crumbling buildings, let alone safeguarding concerns, and toxic internal disagreements, it is easy to see why worship, prayer, and greater connection with those from other denominations—those who see things differently—seems less of a priority and perhaps even a cause of concern. But as Christians, we seek to respond to the call of Christ and this call includes the prayer in John 17 v 21, "that they may all be one … so that the world may believe." When we consider the damage done to Christian witness and to the wider world by Christian disunity, we are right to feel ashamed and ask ourselves why more people are not compelled to pray for greater Christian unity and why are we reluctant to worship together?

The ecumenical scene in England has become increasingly diverse with the national ecumenical instrument, Churches Together in England having over fifty national member churches. Having worked for over a decade within local, regional, and national ecumenical organisations in England, I believe that both openness and relationality are key to furthering Christian unity. The ideas and voices from within Open and Relational theology can therefore offer fresh energy to this work.

Being open to know more of God

One of the defining characteristics of Open and Relational theology is that the future is not fixed, that it is open. Another is that any understanding vision and understanding of God is also limited. Both of these characteristics point to the importance of having an open perspective as we seek to worship and know more of God.

What does it mean to really be open to know more of God? There are attitudes of heart and mind that we need to cultivate in order to come to God in prayer and worship with an openness to learn something new and to be challenged and changed. Please know that I do not always get this right myself; for all of us, there will be preferences, places of pain, blind spots and prejudice that can restrict our worship and understanding of God. This is where an open and relational approach can help—with God, the focus of our worship, and Christ, our model for behavior—demonstrating both openness and being affected by the other. Being open to know more of God requires a humility to acknowledge that we do not know everything, that our vision is incomplete, our experience limited, and that we may not have grasped the whole picture. A respectful acknowledgement that we can learn from another's experience of God is critical, and this includes those who may think differently from us and whose worship takes a different form.

I have been privileged to be invited into the worship spaces of many traditions through my work, and I can honestly say that my own relationship with God has been deepened through each tradition. I have been reminded of the consistency and beauty of God in Orthodox worship, of the joy and freedom that can be found in God through

Pentecostal worship, and of the importance of listening deeply to God in a Quaker meeting. I have been challenged by the call for action and greater social justice by the Salvation Army, by the deep forgiveness that can be experienced in the ongoing practice of Roman Catholics and by the diverse liturgy, focus on the scriptures and breadth of worship style freely available in the Church of England. Each interaction with my fellow Christians helps me become open to the many diverse expressions of the transformational love of God and to the variety of enriching ways in which I can meet God and share God's love with others.

I spend much of my time in meetings with church leaders from across the denominations, creating spaces where people can come together in prayer, worship, to learn together, and to consider shared issues for the country and the church. Where the most effective work takes place is where there is a real sense of humility, respect, and shared faith and worship, not a desire to control or convert others to their way. It is when those in the room are present with a mind and heart open to God and to what the future might hold, as well as seeing God in each other, that we can most effectively work and worship together.

Being in relationship together

The other defining characteristic of open and relational theology is that God is relational. Relationality is a two-way process. God is in relationship with humanity and humans have the choice to relate to God. As such, God affects humanity, and perhaps more controversially human beings have the capacity to affect God.

An act of worship is also relational, a connection with and adoration of God that has an impact on both God and the worshipper. In the Bible, the Old Testament accounts do not speak of a distant God but one who is affected by the worship of believers and offended by, even jealous of, the worship of other things. In the New Testament, we read of Jesus, the Son in relationship with the Father through prayer and of the richness of Jesus's human relationships with his friends, family, and followers. Jesus is the model for our behavior; having lived as a human, he knows what it is to live in relationships with all their joy and pain. As such, when Christians come together in praise and worship, we can be sure that God is affected, as are the worshiping people both individually and in community together.

When considering ecumenical work and worship through this lens, it is clear to see how important it is that those involved, that the worshiping people, are in relationship together. Where good relationships are present, trust develops, and people are more open to each other and to receive from God. An example of this can be seen in the experience of couples in interchurch marriages (where each partner comes from a different Christian denomination). Couples in this situation often worship together in more than one church and, over time, there is a growing sense of shared faith and practice across the two traditions. From the foundation of their relationship a trust develops that, despite the inevitable challenges of family life, allows each partner to discern, through the others tradition, something more of God. Their regular shared worship together becomes more diverse; they are able to encounter God in new ways and learn through each other's traditions.

I have had the privilege of being part of the English and Welsh Anglican and Roman Catholic Committee for five years. This is an ecumenical dialogue group set up by the national churches that has been in place for over twenty-five years. Throughout this time, whilst being an Anglican, I have grown in my own understanding of and relationship with the Roman Catholic tradition. When I first joined the committee, our meetings and worship were more tentative, reserved, and formal. Through the relationships with each other over a five-year period, through conversations, personal sharing, disagreements, and prayer together our worship became more authentic. Differences became less marked and the sense of coming together to meet God became more tangible. My final meeting with this committee was particularly memorable as we visited the shrine of St Alban, the first English martyr, and prayed together. Standing in what has been a place of prayer for many centuries, the painful divisions of history faded as we met God in prayer together. This five-year period of ecumenical dialogue and worship changed me. I am now more able to meet God in another worship space and this change in me affects my own relationships, work, prayer, and worship.

Conclusion

Sometimes disunity itself is described as a scandal; in other spaces, it might also be considered scandalous to worship together. I would argue that ecumenical worship is not a scandal but a celebration. We do not have to agree on every aspect of theology to come together in worship and I can honestly say that worshiping with those from other Christian traditions has been an unexpected privilege in my life. It has brought a profound sense of joy and peace and challenged me to think more deeply about how I approach worship and relate to God.

As Paul and Timothy wrote in Philippians 2 v 1-5,

> "therefore if you have any encouragement from being united with Christ, if any comfort from his love, if any common sharing in the Spirit, if any tenderness and compassion, then make my joy complete by being like-minded, having the same love, being one in spirit and of one mind. Do nothing out of

selfish ambition or vain conceit. Rather, in humility value others above yourselves, not looking to your own interests but each of you to the interests of the others. In your relationships with one another, have the same mindset as Christ Jesus" (New International Version).

In seeking the mind of Christ, I not only look to the interests of others but to the worship of others, especially those who are different to me, with an open mind and heart to receive from God. In seeking to further Christian unity, I do not desire uniformity. Instead, I wish to understand more of the richness of God's diversity, asking what can I learn, and how can more of God's transformational love be seen in creation.

Doral Hayes is the Principal Officer for Ecumenical Development and Relations at Churches Together in England (www.cte.org.uk) and is a Licensed Lay Minister in the Oxford Diocese of the Church of England. Doral holds a MA in Contemporary Christian Theology from Newman University, Birmingham and is currently undertaking doctoral research at the University of Roehampton, London.

Christ's Cosmic Table

THOMAS G. HERMANS-WEBSTER

Christian process theology provides a vibrant framework to articulate how Christians experience and participate in God's loving activity for planetary well-being through the Eucharist.

Part I

Process theology about the church begins by recognizing that the Church is always already influencing the world by its participation in God's love through Christ. When process theologians approach theology of the sacraments, then, we do not have to begin with figuring out where, when, and how Christ is present in the Body and Blood that are on the Table as if the world and Christ's presence therein is a mechanical system of inputs and outputs. In baptism, we do not have to seek the exact moment of the Holy Spirit's descent upon and into the waters of the font in order to justify our faith. Rather, we focus on the organic and organismic enrichment of the Church's influence in the world through loving life-in-Christ together. This chapter specifically focuses on the Eucharist, and I hope that other people offer theological reflections on baptism in conversation with this chapter in the future.

I am convinced that process theology can and ought to be primarily *constructive* for the world in which God's loving, planetary shalom is revealed and enacted in the Eucharist. While deconstructing harmful or inadequate theologies is important, our task as liturgical theologians is to faithfully participate with and critically reflect upon God's creation of a world that more and more faithfully reveals and enacts God's love. Rather than offering a point-by-point engagement with traditional, substance-based theologies of the sacraments, I begin away from their static notions of presence.

Church is and becomes a society that experiences the world, offers its local embodiment of our interrelated world to God, and receives that offering—and more—back from God through the indwelling of the Holy Spirit in the new moment of creative advance. The pulsing pattern of offering and receiving in our life-in-Christ together embodies our faith in the goodness of life and creation. We have a real relationship with God, in which we, as living members of the Body of Christ, offer the world to God and receive the world from God, redeemed in creative and transformative love.

Christian process theology reframes our relationships with the world in which we live and reorients in our sacramental celebrations toward holiness in those relationships. I call this a "natural sacramentalism" because it focuses our life-in-Christ together on the world in which we live, the world that has been called "good" by God and been loved through each new creative moment in history. Eucharistic worship becomes a structure for recognizing, proclaiming, being grateful for, and participating in the ways that the God of all creation and the God of the oppressed has partnered with all creatures to bring forth, sustain, restore, and beautify the world through Love-in-action. Neither God nor the rest of the cosmos need bread and wine to be transformed into the actual human flesh and blood of Jesus of Nazareth in order to make Christ present in the world, for Christ is present to each becoming event, even to the most trivial puff in far out space. Our life-in-Christ together, our life as Church, is characterized by how we participate in revealing and enacting the love of God for the life of the world.

In Eucharistic worship, Christians remember in faith, make present through love, and order our lives in hope for fuller participation in Christ's own incarnating Love-in-action for planetary wellbeing. Eucharistic worship nourishes our becoming by cultivating a humble attention to how other humans, other-than-human creatures, and Holy Spirit bear witness to Christ's presence and make the influential experience of Christ possible for each of us now. Participating in Eucharistic worship, the en-Christed community experiences conviction and forgiveness of our own failures to love through the grace of Christ who unleashes Love into our midst. Forgiveness of sins within the context of this meal frees Christians for joyful participation in God's holy relationships and reorients Christians to recognize how all meals reveal and enact a vivifying and joyful love for the world. Eucharistic worship orders life's intensity and freedom to make it possible for the world to experience and flourish in a greater intensity of Love over time than we currently experience. Regular celebration of the Eucharist meal structures life-in-Christ for planetary well-being because the holy meal ceaselessly exposes us to the love of God by making Christ influential through the power of the Holy Spirit.

The Eucharist meal reveals God's loving activity gracing the world beyond, with, and through our lives to transform, transfigure, and reorient the present into the divine Reign of Love. "The liturgy helps us to see that we do not need to 'go out of this world' to know God," Norman Pittenger writes. As Karen Baker-Fletcher reminds us, we cannot abandon the dust of Earth and still experience God's "fulfillment of the Spirit's healing, creating presence." The transfigured world cannot be thought of as far off and remote to the needs, sufferings, passions, desires, and lives encountered in our present meals.

Yet our life-in-Christ together cannot be reduced to mere social change, nor can the gospel be equated with a simple utopic vision of an ordered society. Eucharistic worship is and inspires Christian action in and for the world. The Eucharist meal is a foretaste of the otherwise world that lures church into new patterns of living here and now. When we live more deeply and genuinely into our life-in-Christ as persons and as a people, we must actively cultivate holy habits by sharing meals in solidarity for planetary well-being.

Part II

The Eucharist is a good news event that vividly expresses God's love for the life of the world in the relationships of the creatures of this world. In the Eucharist, we are formed to recognize brokenness in this world, to repent of our participation in breaking the world, and to participate in God's life of tender salvation and restoration of the world in Love. Love and justice do not conflict with one another in process theology. The gospel call to justice is a call to participate in the divine release of love into *this* world for abundant life together in God.

Process theologies that focus on the Eucharist are remarkably poised to foster movements for human and other-than-human well-being by analyzing the consequences of philosophies of stasis and status, making sense of God's relationships with and through the world amid tremendous novelty and change. The Eucharist meal's very materiality suggests that a process theology of the Eucharist must recognize our impact on the material realities of the multifaceted relationships with our present and our past. When we intentionally and faithfully remember the dead, exploited, and despised throughout our world's history, we practice an Eucharistic memory that serves as a powerful countersign to how oppressed persons and peoples in our world are violently devalued, commodified, and forgotten.

Process metaphysics can philosophically account for such a powerfully haunting remembrance. The praxis of this memory must bring us into actual solidarity with the crucified throughout history as we more faithfully become the Body of Christ. As Karen Baker-Fletcher writes, these are the "memories [that] we are called to carry of those who have gone on before us [and that] remind us of who we are and whose we are."

We belong to one another in a solidarity that incarnates God here and now, for the life of the world. From the Eucharist meal, Christian action in the world participates in the struggle for planetary well-being, cultivating communities that strive for God's Reign of Love together. The Eucharist meal is and leads to Christian action for the life of the world because it is the praxis of solidarity among creation as well as in and with God, who is the God of all creation and the God of the oppressed.

Part III

By receiving bread and wine and offering it *as bread and wine* for the Eucharist meal, God includes a common meal within God's own action for the life of the world. God is familiar with meals, with the memories, relationships, and hopes that emerge through meals, and with the various ways that humans and human societies use meals to make sense of the world. God intentionally incorporates the Eucharist in God's own becoming *as a meal* for loving justice through the process of creative advance. Simply put, meals fill the consequent nature of God.

Furthermore, the Eucharist reveals that God chooses to respond to the suffering of the world by *hosting and participating in* opportunities for human and other-than-human kindred to gather with one another to remember, participate in, and con-spire towards the Love that weaves and calls forth cosmos. In the Eucharist, Christians are called to recognize how our en-Christed solidarity makes a world transfigured through Love-in-action possible for all other meals. In the Eucharist, Christians experience the broken, despised, disappeared, exploited, and killed of history as our kindred, and these experiences reorient our individual and interrelated becomings. We become participants in Christ's holy solidarity with them precisely because church happens in the breaking, pouring, and sharing of the bread and wine that make Christ present in Love for the world in our midst.

As Christians recognize and live into Eucharistic solidarity with one another and all our kindred, we experience a living hope, stirring up in us desires to live into worlds that are other than the present schemes. This hope is thickened on the faithful journey with God and our creaturely kin. Because we encounter Love-in-action in the Eucharist meal, becoming Christian for the world must include eating all common meals as a habit that seeks and enacts holy food justice. When we eat attentively, we begin to recognize the many ways that we are entangled in both the devastation of anthropogenic climate change and in the Holy Spirit's healing, creating presence with us, assuring us that the injustice and abuse of the present do not have to be accepted while we wait for some heavenly resolution at the End of Time.

Reorienting the eating church is an intentional commitment to restoring relationships with one another in God's loving justice, participating in Christ's attentiveness to each human and other-than-human person. Approaching the Eucharist through a process perspective helps us understand how we confront a dynamic network of sin and selfishness every time we eat and drink. In this confrontation, our kinship with one another at the table, with the growers, with butchers and grocers, with cooks, and with the food itself becomes a material threat to how social bodies are broken for commodity profit in our present age. In the Eucharist meal, the church learns and teaches how to seek, recognize, and live through creative love with oppressed peoples in our world, including the oppressed peoples in the church.

The Eucharist meal evokes a whole narrative of who matters through the eating as it depends upon God's action with and through the beloved lives of God, Humans, Wheat, Grape, Yeast, Water, Soil, Wind, and Sun. These lives bear witness to the creating, responding, sustaining, adventurous, peaceable, zesty, beautiful Love that gathers in and sends forth the church as a coworker for a transfigured world, from a meal that doesn't end. The meal inhabits our relationships just as the bread and wine inhabit our bodies.

Eucharistic solidarity in all our common meals invites us to appreciate meal preparation as the nurturing of soil, recipe books, and all the preparations that make the meal possible; these preparations lay the table for holy encounters with other-than-human and human people in the life of God. Recognizing the vulnerability of Love, God beckons us into hopes for a world of justice through Love-in-action by travelling alongside us and infusing our meals with assurance that we are not alone, that we belong here. For we have never been alone. Our kindred have fed us, and we are called to love them by feeding one another well.

Thomas G. Hermans-Webster is a pastor, theological educator, and editor. He earned his Ph.D. from Boston University School of Theology. He is on the editorial staff of Orbis Books, teaches at Memphis Theological Seminary and Yale Divinity School, and is the author of "Cooking and Eating with Love: A Whiteheadian Theology of Meals for Planetary Well-being" (*Process Studies*, Spring-Summer 2023).

Bulletin Beauty

LESLIE KING

The church bulletin, perhaps the greatest weekly grinds in ministry, is among the finest catalysts for congregational transformation.

In the last 30 years of ministry, I cannot count how many worship bulletins I have been involved in producing for Sunday worship. Each had only a handful of pages, filled with countless words drawn together. Words drawn together and organized into prayers, selected hymnody, sermon titles, affirmations of faith, and calls to worship in order to guide worship in an orderly way. Within the collections of words, novel and traditional vocabulary find an appropriately provocative alignment. Congregants, for their part over the years, have cut out prayers, take sermon notes and bring important marginalia to those bulletins.

Where do ideas begin? How are words chosen? What is the church's role in shaping language? The ordinary, weekly task of creating the church bulletin begs these questions with a tenacity that could wear a novice or practiced theologian down and have us citing published prayers instead of crafting our own. This essay seeks to celebrate the local theologian and author of church newsletters, missives, and notes of pastoral care. But most especially this essay seeks to honor the mysterious work of creating the church bulletin. Ideas, words and language have never been unimportant in civilized life and that is certainly poignantly true these days. Church bulletins play their part and process theology informs the creation of a church bulletin.

> Excursus: Pastoral theologians have a critical role to play in local communities regarding ideas, words, and language. In fact, local communities are brimming with the raw material that might coalesce in constructive ways for

the greater good in civic life. That raw material does not need an exceptional academic nor an excellent writer. The raw material only needs curiosity of a theologian who seeks to dwell in the adventure of ideas in order to draw them toward shared language. Action follows. Congregations cannot survive well without a local theologian to do this work because the congregation's vitality depends on connections to life beyond itself.

Mainstream theology struggles to inspire the lived adventure. The mainstream theologies specialize in doctrine and tradition for the sake of stability. But mainstream theology does not specialize in a grounded adventure which is critical for forward movement. This is the specialty of process thought. Not only do pastoral theologians have a critical role to play in local communities, process thought has a critical role in feeding the silkworm for pastors who apply themselves to the rigors of language and articulation each week. Grounded in common sense and meticulous attention to the way life actually works, process thought is nothing short of a call to adventure that believes in the profound effects of the micro-adjustments that move ideas to words and words to shared language.

A local theologian may even hear the call to adventure as a still small voice, amid the flurry of weekly storms, that begs thoughtful attention to something as ordinary as a church bulletin. A bulletin not for its own sake but for the sake of a shared language that transforms. Let's look at the bulletin creation process: ideas, words and shared language.

Ideas and Initial Aims

Long before a word is on a page, ideas are dancing around in the head. Or, to be more accurate, dancing in the relational space between minds and hearts of people. Conversations, shared projects and constructive problem solving are just a few ways ideas coalesce. In this way, the church bulletin, if attended by the resident theologian, begins its formation in the direct and indirect relationships of congregants in their various experiences of congregational life. As the local theologian observes, listens and interprets, ideas emerge as uniquely relevant for the congregational consideration.

Thus, the concept of *initial aim* in process thought can be very helpful for the adventure of congregational ideas. The *initial aim* provides creative possibilities for the world. When a local theologian participates on their own creative level, *initial aim* might be likened to a leader's hunch or informed idea about what is most relevant for congregational response and transformation.

For me, and many others, the coalescing of ideas has most often taken the form of sermon series and themes. The sermon theme becomes the taproot of a weekly bulletin from which vocabulary grows in order to select scripture, hymns, and write prayers. Sermon themes can be can be generally categorized as missional, ecclesial, biblical, or topical. With a hunch in mind, the sermon theme is selected and thus begins the emergence of that weekly church bulletin.

For the past 30 years, a sermon topic has required my handwritten work on a legal pad. My father, retired Presbyterian clergy, calls the handwritten pursuit of ideas, chasing rabbits. In this process, hunches get honed. In those hours, dialogue with the scripture becomes a playground of great purpose. A strong game of devil's advocate against my own hunch is part of the handwritten work. Argument with my best understanding further clarifies for the listening experience that is yet to come. Lots of the long-hand notes include questions for myself about what I mean. I am asking myself what they have heard before and if it is necessary to hear it again. In the long-hand scrawl, there are thoughts and concepts that get tired and fall away. There are those that go nowhere meaningful and must be abandoned. There is, after enough work, just one idea that pulses with relevance and vitality. But the way that idea will be presented is still ahead of me. There is no domesticating it to my preferences or preconceived ideas. It is hard to be done with a sermon. It may be important to believe that a sermon is not done until it is spoken. In this seven-day process, key words and concepts begin to intersect and compete. What is emerging is something unexpected, organic, and particular to the local congregation.

Vitality of Vocabulary

Religious language is woefully vulnerable to semantic satiation, in which repeated words are experienced as meaningless sounds. Because we are so tradition-based, novelty and appropriate provocation within language are profoundly important. It is important so that listeners may hear and transformative religious experiences might contribute to our continual becoming.

In my experience, theme-based-planning and hand-written pursuits of focus allow for a practical experience of Alfred North Whitehead's concept of *concrescence*. Concrescence is the act of unifying the past hunch with the future possibilities into greater clarity for the bulletin process. Distinct vocabulary, in some ways anticipated and in other ways surprising, emerges as if to offer itself to the project. There is now a well-spring of words for the writing of prayers, affirmations, and homiletics.

There is always a bit of agony in this assembly of words. Freshly arrived and precious words must then compete with one another for appropriate contrast, intensity, and beauty. The creative process, when lovingly attended, demands an intensity that results in the perishing of some words and thus concepts from the project. There is a winnowing of the words that requires the maturity and confidence of the theologian. Even though really wonderful words or ideas will not make it to the forefront of Sunday morning, they have done their part in the becoming of the bulletin. Hollywood's cutting room floor has nothing on the resident theologian's workspace. There is so much that contributes but will not be drawn to the bulletin's page in materialized syntax.

The determination of what will perish is high stakes for the pastor. On the one hand, there are things that we might let perish, or fall to the cutting floor because their intensity is so great. Topical matters of politics, current events, or psychology are some examples. If too much of this sort of material is cut, relevance of subject matter also perishes. Many a resident theologian has undercut their own work by keeping things so generalized that the bulletin becomes intellectual and emotional pablum. What is imagined as "safe" is actually dangerous for religious and civic life.

On the other hand, there can be a cutting of nuanced language that honors complexity. This bulletin finds itself full of absolutes and overstatements that are less than tenable in the wisdom of a work-a-day world. Ironically, hyperbolic statements often fail to convey intensity. Their accuracy fails and is anemic. Ever so gently, within the mind of the listener, the hyperbolic, is stored in the propaganda archive of commercials and political advertisements. Salvific complexity lies on the cutting room floor. But each week, there is another opportunity in this process.

The vocabulary contest happens for the sake of the congregational experience. How shall we characterize the kind of experience we are going for on any given Sunday morning? How is it possible to establish any expectation for imparting a particular experience to so many people as those gathered on a Sunday morning? Process thought is helpful in its use of the term beauty that is defined as a constructive space of deep satisfaction and inspiration. Beauty is the consequence of harmony and intensity that are brought together. One example is the intersection of traditional/familiar language with language that is more novel. At the intersection, the prism of understanding shifts slightly and there is fresh perspective on a familiar subject or a familiar perspective on a new subject. Striving for beauty from a church bulletin within a worship service sets a stage for beauty carried out and extended. Beauty within a worship service may gently persuade participation in beauty outside the sanctuary.

Initial aims, hunches, and even vocabulary are best held gently, for the sake of responsiveness. After all, response is the entire reason for the existence of a bulletin. The response of individual people and the community is as important as any preceding effort in the project of communal creativity. I'm fortunate to work with a church office staff who are painstaking in the creation of the bulletin for the sake of its provocative effect...the response. A bulletin is never just a worship document. True to its etymology, bulletin is the report of an event for public information. Oh, that the church's bulletins would always be imagined as grounding and provocative information for the public after the Sunday event!

Giving Them Something to Talk About

Relevant and appropriately provocative bulletins are relational. The deployment of the bulletin into the hands or the zoom screens of parishioners means that it is no longer the creative act of the resident theologians and church staff teams. The bulletin moves into the realm of corporate creativity.

How many pastors have, in their receiving lines, been met by the congregant who says, "I loved your sermon and I'm so glad you said [fill in the blank]"? In the exchange, the pastor realizes that their initial hunch was not at all communicated to this person. How can this be? A temptation follows to correct or reassert, but there is not adequate time in a Sunday morning receiving line. What has happened to all the careful work?

Process thought encourages us to do our careful work, to be sure. But process thought does not make false promises that the careful work of one person will land in the territory of another with the first person's initial aim intact. Process thought notes that initial aims surrender to the consequent. The deployment of a church bulletin into the hands of a congregant means that the words of prayers, scriptures, and hymns are intersecting with the very particular past and present of that person. Each individual congregation represents a different intersection and therefore a different consequent meaning is derived.

Process thought, unlike other mainstream theologies, does not deal in "shoulds" but in actualities; as each person draws meaning from the bulletin given their particular past and present. The implication is that, within each person, there is a unique competency that is emerging and becoming. Community can strengthen that emergence and becoming. And so, the conclusion of a sermon or a worship service is only the beginning of understanding how we move forward together, gently persuading one another to shared action. Very often, shared language precedes that.

In this way, the highest calling of a bulletin is to give the congregants something compelling to talk about; engagement with one another on an appropriately provocative subject. Perhaps they joke and laugh. Perhaps they confide and confess. Perhaps they solicit and problem-solve. In the tethering force of community, we are not just constrained to a shared pace of action, we can leverage energy to provide constructive space for a wider community.

The consequent work following the deployment of a bulletin cannot be underestimated. The bulletin, after all, is nothing short of a relational mechanism for a congregation's becoming. Throughout the years, I have come to appreciate Alfred North

Whitehead's understanding of God's purpose as creative advance. The feeling that I am, in some particular way, participating in that creative advance each week staves off ecclesial burnout. Building bulletins keeps me anchored to my tradition but always reforming my own language. All of this is for the sake of my congregation and their matrix-like networks who have heard so much already. Even as they are listening, I believe they have so much more to say.

Leslie King earned her BA from Kansas University, M.Div. from McCormick Theological Seminary and her D.Min. from St. Paul School of Theology. It was there that she was introduced to process thought. She is a yoga instructor with Yoga Alliance at the 500 hour level. She and her husband DJ rescue animals while admiring their three adult children.

Becoming Church: Process-Relational Theology and Worship

JORGE LOCKWARD & KATIE REIMER

Process-relational theology posits that creation is a never-ending journey of becoming. In this spirit, we offer snapshots of an ongoing, long, glorious, and, at times, tortuous process of one congregation's evolving worship life.

"To be is to create oneself and thereby to influence the self-creation of those by whom one is known, including God."
—Charles Hartshorne, "The Development of Process Philosophy," 1970

"Sisters and brothers, I beg you through the mercy of God to offer your bodies as a living sacrifice, holy and acceptable to God—this is your spiritual act of worship. Don't conform yourselves to this age, but be transformed by the renewal of your minds, so that you can judge what God's will is—what is good, pleasing, and perfect."
—Romans 12:2 (*The Inclusive Bible*)

In 2016, the authors of this article opened a new chapter in the proud history of Church of the Village, a progressive United Methodist community on the corner of 7th Avenue and 13th Street in the West Village of New York City. Church of the Village, affectionately known as "COTV," has a long tradition of welcoming marginalized persons, particularly those in the LGBTQIA+ community. COTV celebrates human diversity, welcoming people of every color, nationality, sexual orientation, gender identity and expression, physical and cognitive ability, and economic status. This community has long believed that we flourish with many points of view, opportunities for creativity, and participatory worship. Nonetheless, it struggled to bring these beliefs into practice.

It was in this spirit that Katie Reimer, the Chair of Worship, led a process that resulted in the creation of a Minister of Worship Arts position. Jorge Lockward answered the call to come into this role in 2016, and a new chapter in the history of COTV began.

As part of its theological journey, and prompted by existing and emerging relationships, in 2021, COTV engaged a worship series centered explicitly on process-relational theology. In addition to our resident clergy, Rev. Jeff Wells and Rev. Alexis Lillie, guest preachers during that time included Ignacio Castuera, John Cobb, Catherine Keller, and John Thatamanil. A group in the church studied C. Robert Mesle's book, *Process Theology: A Basic Introduction*. Many of the ideas explored during this season resonated with the ethos of COTV and impacted its worship life.

These formal engagements with process-relational theology were certainly helpful. And yet, we believe that the true measure of a congregation's theological and liturgical engagement is found in the ways that process-relational theology principles are reflected in the common practices and rituals of a congregation. This is what we have chosen to focus on in this article.

We have divided our reflection into three sections. In the first section, "The Ecology of Worship," we explore how engaging a diverse web of voices in worship planning is necessary for a vibrant, incarnate and relevant worship. The second section, "The Ever-Becoming God," reflects on how we have embraced an expansive understanding of the divine. This section grapples with both the challenges and blessings of creating space for multiple understandings of God. The third section offers concrete examples of these principles from selected worship services.

Process-relational theology posits that creation is a never-ending journey. In this spirit, we offer the following snapshots of an ongoing, long, glorious, and, at times, tortuous process of a congregation's evolving worship life. We hope these reflections may inspire us and others in the continual tilling, planting, watering, and harvesting of life's garden that is our joy and responsibility.

THE ECOLOGY OF WORSHIP

"When God's people lift their song and from their hearts sing praise to God, it's time for wonders, amazing wonders."
—Latinx Pentecostal Chorus

Worship planning at its best is an act of the imagination. Deeply rooted in the sacred memory of a community, it seeks to create a hospitality for the living development and continuation of that memory. The related questions of *Who plans for that hospitality?* and *How is the hospitality planned?* are foundational to a process-relational informed worship planning.

Mainline Protestant worship planning processes privilege clergy and music directors as the centripetal axis for imagining worship. It also privileges established guiding elements such as the liturgical seasons of Western Christianity and the Revised Common Lectionary. More often than not, it over-values the way things have been done in the recent past. While the advantages of this approach are many and apparent, its liabilities are often hidden from view.

As corollaries of historic hierarchical-colonizing processes, these pathways, guides, and values tend to center power. Additionally, they are at a constant risk of becoming perpetual tautological justifications of themselves. Their enthronement hinders the principles of universal-ecological creativity that are core to process-relational theology by creating systems forever shackled by "what-has- been" and robbed of the possibilities of "what-could-be."

The gospel stories that narrate the multiplication of the loaves and fishes (Matthew 14:13-21; Mark 6:31-44; Luke 9:12-17; John 6:1-14) illuminate the matter at hand.

A large crowd who had followed Jesus to a remote place is in need of nourishment as the evening comes. Jesus' disciples, bound by past experiences and understandings, declare the situation to be impossible. They ask Jesus to dismiss the crowd so that each may find nourishment for themselves.

In Mark's telling of the story, Jesus asks the disciples, "How many loaves do you have?" They answer "Five—and two fish." Jesus asks the disciples to organize the people in groups of hundreds and fifties. And then, crucially, Jesus *blesses* what is available and gives these resources back to the people. The ensuing miracle results from a refusal to be bound by what previous experience names as "possible," along with blessing what is available and daring to name it as enough. These postures, along with the act of inviting people to join in the new ethos, elicit the miracle of sharing.

Here are some ways that COTV engages these miraculous processes.

Worship Vision Team

The Worship Vision Team is comprised of the Pastors, Chair of Worship, occasional Seminary Interns and is facilitated by the Minister of Worship Arts. The Worship Vision Team is a space where large, overarching ideas about worship can be engaged in an environment that encourages questions, collaboration, and creativity. As much as possible, the conversations in the Worship Vision Team are purposely focused on the theological aspects of worship *before* delving into practical considerations.

One of the primary functions of the Worship Vision Team is to discern themes for worship series. While the pathways towards discerning particular themes are unique, they always arise from open-ended questions engaged over a few meetings or during ad hoc retreats. Some of the questions we ask ourselves are:

- What is happening in the world?
- What is going on within the life of the COTV community?
- What is going on in our own lives?
- Where do we see God's Spirit at work?

These questions have led us to explore themes that are incarnate to our life together (see example).

Beyond the discernment of seasonal themes, the Worship Vision Team explores substantial questions about COTV's ritual life. Here are some recent examples:

- How can our worship center marginalized voices?
- How do we engage Confession and Assurance of Pardon in worship in ways that honor COTV's theological journey?
- How do we engage the Spirit's call to be an onsite and online congregation?

Some of the questions we are currently engaging are:

- How can we continue the journey of engaging worship "beyond words" using gestures, silence, meditation and other non-verbal expressions?
- How can we create hospitality for a contextual understanding of adult baptism that aligns with our theological journey?

- How can we welcome families with children who struggle to come onsite on Sundays?
- How can we continue to develop our Funeral Rites in ways that faithfully reflect our theological journey?

Having a dedicated space for conversation charged with continuous engagement of overarching questions has been instrumental in keeping us "on our toes," dancing ecologically within the blessed spiral of development.

First Imaginings

A First Imagining is a conversation about an upcoming worship service held approximately two weeks in advance of the service. The scheduled preacher provides the impetus for the conversation by sharing their first thoughts about the sermon. A small group of 3-4 persons interact with the preacher, sharing their own perspectives. The meeting's facilitator then asks open-ended questions to elicit further conversations, such as:

- How does our conversation intersect with, and illuminate, the Eucharist/Holy Communion?
- What happens when we put an anti-racist lens to this conversation?
- What visual images come to mind?
- In what ways does this conversation impact your life? What will be different because of it?

A First Imaginings conversation ignites an ecological process. Others who did not participate in the conversation have access to its recorded notes via Google Docs, and are invited to add further comments. As planning for the worship service develops and worship elements such as music, dance, prayers, ritual actions, sermon, etc. are discerned, the First Imaginings conversation becomes an invitation to everyone to engage, contribute and be informed by the conversation.

Reimagining the "Worship Committee" into Teams

Worship Committees can be a mixed blessing in congregations. At their best, they provide space for persons who care deeply about worship to meet, share, coordinate efforts, dream possibilities and discern solutions. At their worst, they can easily devolve into spaces where opinions and complaints are not accompanied by actual engagement and work.

Early in our work at COTV, we found that the persons who would share the most in Worship Committee meetings were not always doing much work. Additionally, we found that some of those who were doing the work had reached a level of exhaustion that sapped any sense of joy or satisfaction from their ministry.

To address these two issues, we decided to engage a new model that evolved from the traditional concept of a Worship Committee into a Teams model. In the Teams model, groups of people take on responsibility for a particular area of worship. The following motto became operational among us: "If it does not give you life…don't do it." It took a long time to identify and nurture leaders for each team, and even longer for the teams to develop a sense of ownership and responsibility, but eventually we ended up with the following:

- Music
- Sacred Dancers
- The Stream Team (Livestream & Zoom)
- The Visuals Team (Image selection and PPT design)
- Altar Design

The Teams model has been crucial in eliciting a wide, connected ecology in COTV's worship life. We are repeatedly surprised by the creative engagement and solutions that Teams develop on their own. The work of supporting and nurturing these Teams, as well as facilitating their connection to each other and to the whole, has been holy and fruitful work. The regular monitoring of Team Leaders to make sure they experience their work as life-giving eventually spread to other areas of the church, especially Nominations. Nowadays, the motto "If it does not give you life…don't do it" is commonplace in the language and ethos of COTV.

THE EVER-BECOMING GOD

"Bring many names, beautiful and good,
celebrate, in parable and story,
holiness in glory,
living, loving God.

Hail and Hosanna! Bring many names!"
Bring Many Names
W: Brian Wren, M: Carlton Young
Words © 1989 Hope Publishing Company

Connecting with the Divine is an essential part of worship. This raises many important questions about the name and nature of God. Who is this One we are connecting with? What names should we use in approaching God? How do we make room for changes in the ways we see, experience, and name God? These questions have high ethical implications because, ultimately, they privilege some realities while disprivileging others. The evolutionary process of signifying and resignifying God is a critical component of worship.

Naming God

Many theological constructs (and their worship praxis counterparts) have a well-intentioned desire to provide stability and coherence. Theologians, clergy and worship leaders feel responsible for providing clear understandings of God to parishioners. However, this strategy generates fundamental tension.

One tension arises from the fact that from the Divine refusal to be owned or contained. As we gain more experience and understanding of God, two things can happen. At best, we may come to realize how vast, awesome, and incomprehensible the Divine really is. At worst, we can make our experience of God normative, slipping quickly into idolatry and pride, assuming that we have mastered God.

Faith communities that avoid the necessary journey of expanding their God language face another tension that arises from the diverse and often radically different understandings of God that their parishioners bring. A faith community that does not honor these differences, or tries to force them all into a common experience, risks doing violence to the soul.

And so, the question of how to gently shepherd a congregation into a shared exploratory journey that honors diverse understandings of God while also eliciting new possibilities is not an easy one to answer. This question is further complicated by how a particular church self-identifies. COTV understands itself to be a progressive theological, social, and political space. We belong to the United Methodist Church and are often in conflict with the tenets and practice of our denomination. We are a Christian church that honors and values non-Christian understandings of the divine.

Here are some examples from the imperfect and glorious journeys we have traveled towards an incarnate and ever-becoming God.

Expansive Language

"But," Moses said, "when I go to the children of Israel and say to them, 'The God of your ancestors has sent me to you,' if they ask me, 'What is this god's name?' What am I to tell them?" God replied, "I AM AS I AM. This is what you will tell the Israelites: 'I AM has sent me to you'."
—Exodus 3:13-14 (*The Inclusive Bible*)

This famous exchange between Moses and God offers clues for the essential task of naming God. When God utters that primordial phrase, "I am as I am" ("I am who I am," "I will be who I will be"), an infinite array of possibilities emerge. God cannot be contained by a single name. God is alive, mysterious, and profound. God's many names emerge in ever-becoming relationships.

This gives rise to COTV's practice of naming God in relation to the moment. Careful consideration is given to ensure concurrence between the ways we name God and the realities of our life at any given moment. "Liberating God" evokes something different than "Refugee God." "Spirit of Life" suggests something different than "God who is with us." "God the Father" brings forth one experience, while "Mother God" or "Creator God" or "Source of our Being" brings forth other experiences.

The construct of the Holy Trinity in the Christian tradition has offered us a rich garden for naming a God whose very being can only exist in community. The Trinity helps us move beyond a fragmented God into One who is in an eternal dance within and beyond itself.

In many Christian spaces, the word "Lord" has become the most common way to address God—a nickname for God, if you will! Unfortunately, the word implies hierarchy and maleness, as well as failing to faithfully represent its original meaning. Among the early Christ followers, calling Jesus "Lord" was a subversive term. Christians risked losing their lives by refusing to name Caesar as "Lord." An additional challenge with the word "Lord" is that it implies a God who wields power over, rather than one who loves and lures. Because of these complexities, we have chosen at COTV to use the word "Lord" sparingly, and only when its original counter-cultural meaning is clear.

Preaching

Preaching can be understood as the intersection of divine intention (God's lure) and human realities, leading to the birthing of new possibilities. In other words, preaching rises from the consequent (what is) opening the door to the primordial (what could be). Because of this, preaching must depart/begin from the lived experiences of both preacher and gathered community, and respond to the movements of the Spirit in both.

The previous section, The Ecology of Worship, explained how COTV's worship planning process insists on connecting human realities with God's lure by asking questions and engaging a wide array of voices. Different people bring diverse experiences and have access to different parts of the divine. By engaging many voices, we believe our community has a richer palette to draw on in experiencing an ever-becoming God.

This process is further enhanced by an intentional engagement of a broad range of preaching voices. In many churches, one or several ordained clergy are frequently expected to be the only sources for preaching. However, this limits the ways any given faith community has for understanding and experiencing God. Since every one of us is made in the image of God, we believe that a diversity of voices, within and beyond the community, is essential for preaching to illuminate and bring forth the movements of God in our midst.

Furthermore, the preaching cycle necessarily involves both speaker and listener. To this end, we have experimented with ways to make room for that cycle. Early in our journey, we held conversations with the preacher after the service where multiple perspectives could be offered around the message. More recently, we have experimented with small groups of 3-4 persons gathered around small circular tables that engage in conversation right after the sermon aided by an open-ended prompt in the form of a question. These forms of conversation have significantly deepened our community into an embodied experience of God. In these models, the preacher becomes just one voice or vehicle for discerning and experiencing the movements of the Spirit.

Eucharist

The Eucharist (Holy Communion) is a defining practice within the Christian tradition. It is meant to be a primary means for understanding and experiencing the Divine. Unfortunately, it has lost much of its meaning and power in many settings. When this worship renewal journey began in 2016, COTV celebrated the Eucharist once a month in a ritual often lacking in energy and vitality. The journey to becoming an engaged Eucharistic community was an early dream that took a number of years to take root. This section will describe that evolution.

At a Worship Vision Team retreat in July 2019, we dedicated much conversation and thought to the Eucharist. We reflected on what communion meant to each of us, and to our community. We talked about the practice of communion in different times and places, and how the ritual has been misinterpreted and co-opted by powers.

We asked ourselves what it means to break bread together, and how this practice intersects with the issues in the world around us.

Eventually, we decided to pursue an entire worship series centered on the Eucharist. We titled the series "Breaking Bread," and dedicated the season to exploring how this ancient practice could transform the way we live and act within and beyond our faith community. As we celebrated Holy Communion each Sunday during the series, we were surprised by the community's affirmative response. We realized that it responded to a thirst in our community. And so, we decided to practice communion every Sunday, a practice that continues to this day.

From the on-site baking of delicious gluten-free bread to the joyful singing of the Sanctus, Holy Communion at COTV is now an engaged, anticipated and grounding ritual for our community. Clergy and Lay share leadership in this living ritual that continues to change and adapt to new inklings, circumstances and movements of the Spirit.

The COVID-19 pandemic brought significant challenges to our Eucharistic journey. After much conversation and prayer, we decided to continue having communion, trying different approaches. The joy of returning to the physicality of partaking communion onsite has been tempered by the disparity in the experience of Communion from our continued online community. We have tried several approaches, including inviting our online siblings to have elements prepared in their homes, and also assigning one of our pastors to be chatting online during the distribution of the elements onsite. However, these measures have not led to the desired sense of true community that we are looking for. Thus, we find ourselves in a difficult place. One of the most significant moments in our worship life—the one that is meant to unite us the most—has become the hardest one to bridge the onsite/online divide. However, we know that this difficulty is a blessing, as we trust that every struggle leads us into new possibilities.

A FEW EXAMPLES

Worship Vision Team

We have worked to connect the themes of our worship series to what is happening in our community at any given moment. Here are a few examples of worship series' themes we have discerned together:

- Dear God… (2017). We realized that many in our congregation were asking questions about God and trying to make sense of how God acts in the world. This led to a worship series built on questions to God elicited by the congregation.

- Dismantling Racism (2018). Although COTV has long been a multi-ethnic congregation, we understood that racism and white supremacy are the waters we swim in in the 21st century United States. Knowing that the journey towards being an anti-racist church was long and ongoing, we pursued this worship series to follow God's prompting into a deeper commitment to these values.
- The Art of Letting Go (2019). We realized that forgiveness was not something we had explored deeply as a community. This was particularly challenging in the divisive political climate of that year. We engaged this series during Lent to grapple with Jesus' call to love our enemies.
- Demystifying the Bible (2020). Different people in our congregation have come from diverse Christian backgrounds, and we realized there were many questions in our midst about how to relate to the Bible. We engaged this worship series as an opportunity for us to explore possibilities for connecting with scripture.
- The Political Community: A Faithful Engagement (2021). The 2020 U.S. presidential election and its aftermath brought many difficult realities to the surface about our country. Emotions were complex and intense as we engaged this series, particularly following the January 6, 2021 insurrection on the capitol building in Washington D.C. We explored the intersections between our faith and our political engagement during this worship series.
- Wade in the Water: The Beauty, Mystery, and Power of Worship (2022). As we shifted from online worship to a hybrid onsite/online service, many questions arose about what exactly we were doing in worship. Exploring these deeper questions was helpful as we engaged the practical and technical questions about how to do hybrid worship. This was also an opportunity to invite our congregation into a more conscious reflection of what we are doing together when we worship.
- Spirit Journeys (2023). A series built from the testimonies/life-experience of particular COTV members). Although we regularly engaged preachers from beyond our community, we realized there was a lot of wisdom within the members of our congregation which we had not yet engaged fully. This worship series was designed to invite COTV members to share their testimonies and experiences of faith along the journey of life.

Eucharist

During the COVID-19 pandemic, we were faced with the challenge of how to engage Holy Communion without being together in the same physical space. This example from April 19, 2020 shows one approach we tried early in the pandemic. We invited the congregation to speak short, strong, and affirming statements. Additionally, we welcomed the mystery of Communion through the use of a Native American flute as the celebrant held up the elements.

WE GATHER AROUND THE TABLE OF GRACE
THE GREAT THANKSGIVING

Celebrant speaks:
Now, friends, it's time to gather around the Table of Grace.
Especially in this Easter season,
we celebrate life and resurrection to new life.
Communion gives us life.
Because, in this sacramental moment,
we remember that on the night Jesus was betrayed,
he gathered his followers
and offered them not just a meal to feed their bodies
but an ongoing way to feed their spirits.

Let's say it together:
Communion feeds our spirits.
Communion feeds our spirits.

Jesus took bread, blessed it, and broke it and said,
"Take and eat, for this is my body,
broken and given for you.
Do this to keep my Spirit alive in you."

Let's say it together:
The Spirit of Christ is alive in us.
The Spirit of Christ is alive in us.

Then, Jesus took a cup and gave thanks to God.
He shared it with all of them and said,

"Drink from this cup,
for this is my blood, the essence of my life,
offered as a new covenant,
a new way of being God's people.
Do this to keep my Spirit alive in you."

Let's say it together:
The Spirit of Christ is alive in us.
The Spirit of Christ is alive in us.

Let's remind ourselves again of the good news that gives us life.

Would you say with me:
Jesus is with us!
Jesus is with us!
God is with us!
God is with us!
The Spirit is with us!
The Spirit is with us!

I invite each of you to extend a hand toward the table, in body or in spirit.
Let us pray.
Loving, Life-giving God, we give you thanks that in Jesus,
you remind us how you walk with us in our suffering,
offering us ways to enter into new life, hope, joy, and love.
Help us to open our eyes and hearts
to experience your presence made real for us,
in this bread and this cup,
and in all of us who are gathered,
so we may experience the fullness of life.
Inspire us to bring the life we've found in worship out into the world,
to transform the people and places that need it most.
We pray, claiming the name
and following the way of Jesus,
Amen.

Celebrant holds up the bread, gesturing towards the camera:

Friends, this is the body of Christ, broken and given for us and for all.

A musician plays a couple of measures on Native American flute, as the celebrant holds the bread. A couple of seconds after the flute melody ends, the Celebrant places down the bread and lifts the cup towards the camera, saying:

"And this is the cup of salvation, poured out for us and for all."

The musician plays a couple of measures on Native American flute as the celebrant holds the cup.

Music

In the Waters

Originally written for a "Water Communion Service" led by Unitarian Universalist seminarians at Union Theological Seminary in New York City, this song quickly became core to COTV's worship life. Here is an iteration of one of its many uses, in this case, as part of a memorial service for Louise Fawcett, a beloved COTV member.

Music starts, a dancer pours water into the baptismal font as a pastor speaks

We gather in solidarity, as a community,
brought together by the shared waters of baptism
to signal and celebrate the bonds of love we share.

all sing

Dancer engages with long blue fabric moving it among the congregation.
Pastor continues underscored by music.

We are gathered, sharing in sorrow and mourning
with all who love Louise Fawcett.
Seeking comfort and sharing compassion.

all sing

In the sorrow we are one ///
we are one ///

We are gathered in thanksgiving for Louise's life
for her spirit of service,
for her resilient witness to justice,
for the healing power of her presence and smile.

all sing

In thanksgiving, we are one ///
we are one ///

We are gathered to tell and retell stories about Louise
so we may be, once more, inspired by her faith,
Touched by her compassion,
nurtured by her love.

all sing

In the journey we are one ///
we are one ///

In the Waters
Words: Jorge Lockward, Music: Nehemiah Luckett

We Are One in the Struggle

This song helped us as we struggled to name apparent contradictions of pain/separation and unity/hope during the COVID-19 pandemic.

We are one in the struggle; we are one in the pain.
We are one in the crying; we are one in the rain.
We're sojourners and dreamers of new possibilities.
We are seed, sign and witness of the dream, of God's dream.
We are seed, sign and witness of the dream.

We will stay in the struggle we won't hide from the pain.
We will cry with each other, offer shelter and space.
joining dreams, sharing visions of new Heaven and Earth.
We are seed, sign and witness of the dream, of God's dream.
We are seed, sign and witness of the dream.

We Are One in the Struggle

W: Jorge Lockward, Katie Reimer, Rebecca Watts

M: Peter Scholtes

Come, Come, Whoever You Are

Many COTV members are actively working to heal shame that has come from many sources. Some carry shame from earlier experiences in other Christian church settings. Others carry shame from the reactions of their families to their coming out as LGBTQIA+. This song has become a powerful invitation to release shame as we come before an infinitely merciful God.

A Sacred Dancer pours water during the intro to the song

Come, come, whoever you are,
worshiper, wanderer, lover of leaving.
Ours is not a caravan of despair.
Though you have broken your vows
a thousand times.
Come, come again, come.

Come, Come, Whoever You Are

W: attr. Jalal ad-Din Rumi, 1207-1273, tr. unknown

M: Jorge Lockward

Prayer

Our ways of naming God in prayer became more expansive during the worship series in 2021, when we explored process-relational theology. Here are a few examples of the prayers we wrote during that journey.

August 8, 2021

God Who Is Beyond Our Naming,
Thank you for this expansive,
ever unfolding life.
Thank you for the infinite possibilities
within us,
around us.

Awaken in us a deeper sense of awe.
Increase our curiosity
so that we may soften into the eternal dance of life.
Amen.

August 29, 2021

God of our Life-Journeys
Incarnate, Living Christ
Indwelling and Ever-present Spirit
We thank you for the ways you search us out,
the ways you meet us where we are
the ways your love finds a way to reach us.
Amen.

September 5, 2021

Creating God,
Incarnate Word,
Living Spirit,
For such a time as this,
with our very own lives at stake,
draw us close to your heartache
and show us...
how to love
this earth.
Amen.

Jorge Lockward served for many years as Director of the Global Praise Program for Global Ministries of The United Methodist Church, where he edited several resources on global music and worship. A respected lecturer and workshop leader, Jorge has lectured at many Theological Schools and worship conferences. He currently serves as Minister of Worship Arts at the Church of the Village in New York City.

Katie Reimer is passionate about creating spaces for connecting to the Divine. She strives to build relationships of messy mutuality across all that divides, nourishing the conditions that allow life to flourish. Katie is a worship leader, theologian, pianist, and teacher. She serves as the Executive Director for the World Day of Prayer International Committee (worlddayofprayer.net), and the Executive and Artistic Director for the Mimesis Ensemble (mimesisensemble.org).

Point to the Blessing

PAUL NANCARROW

The practices of ministry are all about helping people deepen their own experience of co-creativity with God.

A parishioner asked me to pray with her before undergoing surgery. She told me the surgery wasn't "serious," it wasn't life-threatening; but it would involve general anesthesia, and that made her a little nervous. She said she wanted prayer, but she wasn't exactly sure what to pray *for*. She didn't think she needed a "miracle." She didn't expect that God would "do" anything outside the ordinary way medicine works. But she didn't want to leave this "apart" from God, either. She wanted to commend her surgery "into God's hands," as she put it; she wanted to ask God's blessing in her need.

So, I took her hands and prayed. I prayed God would grant wisdom to her surgeon, that God would guide the surgeon's hands. I prayed God would inspire her nurses and all her care staff to compassion and insight in using their skills for her well-being. I prayed God would send healing grace to strengthen her body for healing and recovery and restoration of fullness of health once the surgery was complete. I prayed that God's good will for her would be done.

And in this case, just as important as what we prayed was what we did *not* pray. We did not pray for supernatural miracles. We did not pray for an interruption or intervention in the natural processes of organs and cells and machines and instruments. We did not call for God to "break in" from "outside" the universe to work healing. Our whole shared prayer was about God working *with* natural processes, about God taking up our very human actions and *guiding* them toward good outcomes, about God *weaving* God's aims for well-being into and through the successive moments that would comprise her surgery.

In my efforts to apply process-relational theological principles to the practices of ministry, a central and enduring theme has been *co-creativity*. Process-relational theology has helped me to clarify and express a belief that God is not distant from the universe, that God is not far-removed from the ordinary and everyday occasions of our lives. I do not accept the proposition that God created the universe long ago, intending it to be a closed and self-sustaining system, which God then committed to human management, leaving God to "look in on" the world every so often and work a miracle or send a prophet as needed. There are parables of Jesus that speak of a landowner who plants a vineyard or entrusts money, and then "goes away" for a long time, leaving tenants and servants to work in his absence; I think too many people take those parables as a *literal* description of our present relationship with the creating God.

Instead, I see in process-relational theology a way to speak of God's intimate involvement with the universe, God's creative presence in every moment of becoming. Every active occurrence in the universe, from a quantum interaction to a moment of human awareness and action, begins with an initial aim from God, a creative impulse to enact a divine intention. Creatures receive these aims from God, and weave them together with influences from the world around them—physical forces like gravity and electromagnetism, chemical materials like oxygen and carbon, consequences of past actions and aspirations for future accomplishments—and from this weaving, creatures bring forth moments of their own becoming. Creaturely actions embody God's creative aims more or less completely: some events represent divine intention well, while others fall short of the goodness and well-being and richness of experience God had envisioned. But *all* creaturely actions, *all* moments co-created out of God's aims and creatures' responses, are felt by God, are received into God's experience of the world; and from the particular details of these world-feelings, God fashions new aims for each creature's *next* moment.

In this way, a creature's existence is like a constant and ongoing *dialogue* with God. No creature, no moment, is *separated* from God, but everything that happens in the world and in life is the result of co-creative *combination* of God's activation and our activity. God whispers new possibilities to us moment by moment in our lives, always guiding us toward actions of justice and peace and love, if we will listen.

When our moments come close to achieving God's aim, we add a new good to the world, from which God can then fashion aims toward even greater good. When we fail in our combining of influences into action, and we cause pain or suffering or loss, God receives this also into God's feeling of the world, and forms for us new aims to heal from hurt and grow in good. As Marjorie Suchocki puts it so succinctly and beautifully in her book *In God's Presence* (1996), "God works with the world as it is, in order to bring it to what it can be."

As a priest and a pastor, I have always considered it my calling to help people become more deeply aware of their own dialogue with God, of God's promptings and possibilities in their experience, and of their responsiveness to God in embodying divine aims in their personal and social actions. It has been my intention to engage the practices of ministry in such a way as to help people grow in mindful and intentional and joyful co-creativity with their God.

For that reason, when I preach, my goal is to open a space for congregants to experience divine inspiration and human interpretation, co-creating *in their own minds* an experience of insight and understanding. I do not want simply to reel off my own interpretation of a Gospel passage, as if to say, "Here, now you know what this means." What I want is to guide hearers step by step through an interpretive process, so that an understanding can blossom in their own thinking. I do not want simply to exhort, to pronounce as if from on high, "This is what God wants you to do"; but to lead hearers to an interior openness where they can feel God's aims for them resonating in their own motivation.

In a sermon for a Sunday in the Season of Creation, when the Hebrew Scriptures reading from the Revised Common Lectionary was the parting of the Red Sea, my goal was to help people recognize divine aims at work in natural processes. I wanted to do more than encourage them to be "good stewards" of an environment once created by a distant God, but to be more aware of our vital role as co-creators in natural flourishing. So I highlighted natural elements from the story: a strong east wind blowing all night long to push the waters back from a marshy seacoast; the Israelites on foot being able to walk across exposed mudflats where the heavy Egyptian chariots got bogged down; the water flowing back in the morning, after the wind died down, and the soldiers not being able to make their way through the flooded marsh. I shared my thought that Moses was inspired with extraordinary insight to discern in these natural processes the activity of God to liberate them from slavery, and to call the people to join in that activity by risking the mud crossing. I asked congregants to consider how they themselves might discern the activity of God's liberating will in the natural and personal events of their lives, and how they might co-create with God such good in their world.

That sermon was the expression of a process-relational theology of Creation, even though it did not use any process-theological terminology or technical concepts to make the point. It was an attempt to *demonstrate* process-theological thinking in action, and to invite people into experiencing divine and human co-creation for themselves.

Or again, in the areas of parish outreach and social ministry and mission, the process-relational principle of co-creativity has been an important influence. Process theology holds that God is always and everywhere already active in the world. There is, therefore, no sense in which the work of the Church "brings" God to where God is not, or "does the work of God" where God is not already at work. In organizing parishes for ministry in the community, outside the walls of the church, I encourage people to begin with a process of discernment, looking at the neighborhood and community at hand and asking, "Where do we experience God's aims for right-relationship and well-being as possibilities in this place?" Instead of thinking, "We are the Church, and the Church is supposed to do *x*, so how can we do *x* here?", I encourage parishes to ask, "What is the actual need here, and how do we see God preparing possibilities to meet that need, outside the church as well as in the church, and how can we join in actualizing those possibilities?"

When a parish wanted to develop closer ties to its neighborhood—since most of the parishioners came to that church from homes in other neighborhoods and towns—it began by looking for people who were already aware of the neighborhood's needs and already addressing the neighbors. We found a community center that had feeding and after-school programs already in place, and were in need of money and volunteers to maintain and grow those programs. Instead of trying to reinvent their wheel for ourselves, in the name of our parish, we found ways to partner with the center. We discerned God at work in the work of the community center, and joined with God and with the center to co-create new possibilities for the common good of our neighborhood.

Important to this kind of missional outreach is the core practice of being attentive to our own ongoing dialogue with God in co-creating the events and actions of our lives. As individual persons, and as groups of the faithful together, God is always giving us aims for goodness and truth and beauty, we are always embodying those aims to the degree that we can, we are always offering up our completed actions to be felt by God and the world, and God is always receiving our actions and weaving them into the wholeness of the world and new aims for new occasions. This is as true of discerning opportunities for outreach as it is of feeling deeply transformative movements of the spirit in prayer. The hard hands-on work of justice and peace in the world is also a work of co-creativity with God.

I once shared with a group preparing for ordination that the work of the priest, the *whole* work of the priest, is "to point to the blessing." It is God who activates blessing in giving aims for the best possible well-being in any given situation; but it is the creature who must give of itself to actualize that possibility in the world; therefore blessing is always a co-creation of God and creatures. Within the Christian community, the ministry practices of preaching and mission and worship and prayer all point to the blessing, they all lift into prominence the principle of co-creativity, in order to help people experience in themselves the activation of God's co-creative call.

Paul Nancarrow is an Episcopal priest who has been active in parish ministry for nearly forty years. He is co-author of *The Call of the Spirit: Process Spirituality in a Relational World*, and blogs at "Transfigurations" (paulsnancarrow.wordpress.com). He can often be found on trails and highways in the Midwest, pondering divine and creaturely becoming from the saddle of his bicycle.

"The God Ecosystem": Preaching Process Theology Through the Season of Creation

SANDRA G. NIXON

Use the Season of Creation's "earthiness" to introduce process theology to your congregation in worship.

I was in my 20s and studying at seminary when I discovered I am a mystic. Being exposed for the first time to the writings of Francis of Assisi, Meister Eckhart, Julian of Norwich and others, I came to understand that my lifelong sense of the sacred, God-revealing nature of, well, *nature* is in fact an experience that has a name: Christian mysticism.

I'm also drawn to process-relational thought and theology which, over the years, I have come to realize, is directly connected to my mystic leanings and experience.

What's the connection?

Process theologian Jay McDaniel has said that we "need a vision of the world within which God is working, in order to have a vision of the God of the world."

Mystics experience and directly connect with what theologian Paul Tillich describes as the "depth (God) dimension" of reality embedded in the natural world. From that intuition, we further intuit that, since nature is interconnected, interdependent, and relational, these qualities must also be part of God's nature.

When I look to process-relational theology, I find not just an affirmation of this way of seeing the world, I also find an expansion of it, and a unique way of articulating the reality at the heart of the universe. I feel at home in language such as "natural, relational flow," "inter becoming," and "collective emergence" in which every being participates and has some measure of freedom and creativity.

Process theology has given me theological language for the mystic world of which I am a part. It's also made it challenging to be a congregational pastor! Let me explain.

I am an ordained minister in a progressive protestant denomination with a self-described "big theological tent," which happily affords me a certain latitude when crafting worship services, including language for God in prayers, music, and sermons.

That being said, part of my role is ensuring worship is aligned and in continuity with the historic faith of my tradition. I also feel a responsibility to tread lightly and respectfully amongst the diverse theological perspectives of my parishioners, many of whom were either: (a) raised in the church but haven't been exposed to quality adult faith formation which would give them the opportunity to evolve their faith and theology beyond what they received in Sunday school, or (b) have no church background and are "God curious" but unfamiliar with theological language.

In my experience, for many in the pew, phrases like "we are co-creators with the divine" or language about being co-participants in the "inter-becoming" world with God (and maybe even being co-evolvers of God), need to be introduced not only with care and sensitivity but also in a way that shows how these ideas can be understood to be in "faithful continuity" with our tradition.

However, I also feel a responsibility to the increasingly urgent issues of our times, to which I believe the church must respond, as a Christ-centered community called to seek justice and love kindness in the service of God's initial aim of abundant, flourishing life for all.

If our faith does not provide a grounding for that work, including a trust in God's agency, in and through us, then I am not sure why the church is here!

Integrating Process Theology and the Season of Creation

Over the past number of years, I have tried to subtly include process-relational concepts in my worship and preaching. However, this fall—with care and sensitivity—I decided to overtly introduce process theology to my congregation through a sermon series, using the Season of Creation as the "container," and mysticism as the portal.

With their intimate connection to the natural world, many of the scriptures—in particular the psalms and many of Jesus' parables—make good entrance points for introducing process-relational thought (PRT) and process theology. Given the connection between PRT and the natural world, and the fact that I use these texts in particular during the Season of Creation, this container (the five Sundays in September and early

October, ending with Canadian Thanksgiving) seemed like a good fit for introducing PRT to the congregation.

A Role for Awe

Although the ultimate goal was to introduce PRT concepts, I realized that an essential element would need to be to *cultivate awe*. Albert Einstein famously remarked, "There are only two ways to live your life. One is as though nothing is a miracle. The other is as though everything is." I am a firm believer that awe is the foundation for faith, which connects us to the "depth dimension" and cultivates in us the humility which allows us to grasp our true place in the universe and live with respect in creation.

That sense of awe also needs to be rooted in our understanding of the spiritual and energetic interrelatedness of all things, and thankfully, the natural world gives us plenty of examples! The focus for me was to help the congregation explore how natural processes which, when contemplated, lead us to awe, also point us to the fundamental structure of reality as loving interconnection and inter-becoming, at all levels (physical/spiritual, cosmic/quantum) and in which we can find a faithful "God," of which we humans and our spirituality are a part.

Season of Creation Sermon Series

APPROACH:

Step 1: Identify patterns and phenomena in nature that exemplify what process theology would assert about the nature of the divine, and divine activity in the world.

Step 2: Preach wonder and awe (using identified natural phenomena and patterns)

Step 3: Connect patterns in nature to affirmations of God in scripture & the faith tradition. (We need to create a bridge for people to cross, from current "faithful" beliefs to expanded, new ideas that are accepted as equally "faithful.").

Step 4: Articulate and connect core Process Theology concepts.

OUTLINE:
Week 1: "Pearl of Great Price" (Intro to Season of Creation)
Scripture: Jeremiah 18: 1-10, Psalm 139

Key Ideas:

- Shortcomings of theology rooted in a mechanistic worldview
- God is found in natural patterns and phenomena that demonstrate that we and the universe are divine energies interacting in a field of loving energy/consciousness that continues to emerge towards greater wholeness.
- If we believe that God's self-giving love and image are within us and within all things, we will choose not to play God but to understand and respect our role in the whole, as part of the whole. This frees us to playfully engage our clay-being with the potter's creative, loving energy—and trust that this will produce something good for us and for the world.

Week 2: "Divine Patterns" (Waves)
Scripture: Psalm 104
Key Ideas:

- Exploring wave patterns in nature (water, light, sound, gravity, seismic, consciousness)
- In classical physics, the wave equation describes how water waves ripple the ocean, seismic waves ripple rock, and gravitational waves ripple the fabric of spacetime. In quantum physics, the "wave function" describes the behavior and properties of particles at the quantum scale.

Resources:

- Virginia Woolf: the relationship between consciousness and creativity is "a wave in the mind."
- Song: "Love is the Seventh Wave," (Sting)
- Poem: "Some Thoughts About The Ocean and The Universe," by Rebecca Elson

Week 3: "Holy Networks" (Roots, mycelia and fungi)
Scripture: Psalm 19
Key Ideas:

- Interconnection: Talk about how mycelial, tree root, fungal, and other networks are mutually supporting, communicate and have agency/freedom
- Natural networks help us understand the vast interconnectivity of God's wondrous world, cultivate respect for the intelligence and "being" of all living things, and help us understand ourselves as collective and connected beings

- Like fungi, we are also, in every present occasion, connected to the past and to the future possibilities of our becoming—including of what God's spirit is encouraging us to become.

Resources:

- Book: "Entangled Life: How Fungi Make Our Worlds, Change Our Minds and Shape Our World" by Martin Sheldrake
- Book: "Finding the Mother Tree" by Suzanne Simard

Week 4: "All God's Creatures" (with Blessing of the Animals)
Scripture: Psalm 104
Key Ideas:

- Respect for all beings and for interdependence of all
- Our understanding of "sentient" and of "lower/higher" beings needs to be challenged (or even turned on its head?).
- There are different kinds of perception, communication, agency, and intelligence, including collective intelligence, which spans time.

Week 5: "Divine Growth" (Seeds, soil and harvest—Thanksgiving)
Scripture: Joel 2: 21-25, 27, Mark 4: 30-32
Key Ideas:

- Exploring the relationship between seeds, soil, harvest, mycelial networks
- Full circle: The harvest of grain becomes the seed for next year's crop
- Concept of "naturalizing" (working with what's there, support soil life/biology by adding in enhancers) and connect to process-relational concepts of novelty, possibility, and agency.

Resource:

- Book: "Animal, Soil, Mineral" by Barbara Kingsley

What happened?

The sermon series went over quite well with my folks. It built on a foundation I had already laid, including a couple of sermons delivered in the spring which used the mysticism-infused intro to John's gospel as a springboard to introduce some preliminary process-related concepts.

I received positive feedback from folks who were already part-way there: for example, those who, like me, "find God in nature"—the gardeners, and those who have been drawn to other spiritualities such as Buddhist thought or energy healing. There was also significant receptivity from those who had read other progressive theology, such as the writings of Richard Rohr.

One newcomer in her 30s remarked, "This is just what I'm looking for."

One long-time United Church member told me: "I'm finally hearing in the pulpit what I have personally believed for years but couldn't reconcile with 'the faith'."

Others expressed appreciation for how process theology not only seemed to resonate with contemporary science and their own experience of the world, but provided an ethical framework and imperative for taking action on climate change, racism, and other issues of our day.

Next Steps

I decided to build on the positive reception from this sermon series and subsequently offered a two-week intro to the concept of "Ecological Civilization," based on the recent (process-inspired) book, "What is Ecological Civilization? Crisis, Hope, and the Future of the Planet" by Philip Clayton and WM. Andrew Schwartz. Next, I am planning to take the congregation into a deeper dive of both process theology and the concept of ecological civilization through the formation of a study group which will also explore how the congregation can engage in faithful public witness and action, including a challenge to incorporate process ideas into their mission statement.

Conclusion

In my experience, process-relational ideas do resonate with congregations. Many folks in the pew are receptive to the core concepts at least at a certain level, especially as the reality and effects of climate change begin to touch our daily lives. Most people realize now that what happens to the planet affects us all; that our wellbeing is tied to the well-being of the earth and its ecosystems.

Process theology takes the process-relational concept of the organic, interconnected nature of all things further, asserting the presence of a loving, relational, creative, "prime mover" God at the heart of this reality: a holy, organic, cosmic and spiritual ecosystem. The message that we in this church, in this moment, are nothing less than part of each other's, the world's, and God's own becoming is, I believe, the central affirmation of process theology and one which, if embraced, can transform lives, communities of faith, and in turn, our societies and world.

Perhaps due to the ecological and other crises our world now faces, the time may be ripe for process theology to gain more traction within our churches and propel the "beloved community" to take a more active lead in engaging with the urgent issues of our day. Congregational leaders are uniquely positioned to plant and cultivate those seeds of transformation, with trust that the spirit will nurture those seeds and create the conditions for growth and connection to other networks of love and justice beyond the church walls.

May it be so!

Sandra G. Nixon is an ordained minister in the United Church of Canada. She earned her M.Div. at the Vancouver School of Theology and has been in active congregational ministry for over twenty years. She currently serves as Coordinating Minister with Trinity-Grace United Church (www.tgucvan.com) in Vancouver, Canada. Sandra lives with her family in Richmond, BC and enjoys west coast gardening, cooking, kayaking, and yoga.

Preaching Open and Relational Theology in a Reformed Church

VIKKI RANDALL

Preaching Open and Relational Theology in Reformed or Calvinist settings is challenging, yet possible.

One of the most challenging settings in which one might teach or preach Open and Relational Theology (ORT) is in a Reformed Church. Reformed theology, drawn from the work of John Calvin, is essentially classical theism. Its heavy emphasis on God's sovereignty often presents a barrier to the core concepts of ORT. Yet, there are various reasons someone who aligns with ORT might find themselves in a Reformed church: family or personal history, the appeal of Reformed polity, or the inclusiveness of an affirming denomination. Some may not have been exposed to Open and Relational theology until after they were already established in a Reformed denomination.

I have served for 28 years as a pastor in one such Reformed denomination, the Presbyterian Church USA (PCUSA). I identify with the Open wing of ORT. I will speak primarily from that perspective—your mileage may vary. I hope my experience and process for including Open Theism in my preaching and teaching may be helpful as a starting point, even for those in a different context or coming from a Process or other theological stance.

There are many Reformed denominations—several varieties of Presbyterian, Christian Reformed, and Congregational churches. The Southern Baptist denomination also has become very Calvinist in recent years, as have many evangelicals. Arguably, this might be a factor in some of the abuses we have seen in evangelicalism around authority and hierarchical and authoritarian leadership.

Identifying Obstacles Within Reformed Theology

Often people associate Reformed or Calvinist theology with the Synod of Dort (1618-1619) of the Dutch Reformed Church. The Synod rejected Arminian/Wesleyan theology, affirming instead five key points (TULIP): total depravity, unconditional election, limited atonement, irresistible (or irrevocable) grace, and the perseverance of the saints. But many Reformed denominations do not align with all five points (e.g. "three-point" Calvinists), evidence that Dort is not as defining as is often assumed. The various Reformed denominations vary in how closely they hew to Dort. However, most Reformed denominations stress God's sovereignty as a key distinctive.

In its confessional documents, PCUSA never references the Synod of Dort or the five points of TULIP. Instead, we affirm five "Reformed essentials" (PCUSA Book of Order: F-2.05):

1. The sovereignty of God (majesty, holiness, and providence)
2. The election of the people of God for service and salvation
3. The covenant life of the church
4. Faithful stewardship
5. Working for the transformation of society against the human tendency toward tyranny and idolatry

Most Reformed denominations have one or more confessional statements that help parse, either explicitly or implicitly, the degree to which they align with the five points of Calvinism. Helpfully, PCUSA has ten confessions rather than just one, which can dilute the impact of the more strongly Calvinist ones.

PCUSA's ten confessions can be loosely grouped into three categories, beginning with two ancient, ecumenical creeds: Apostles and Nicene. Most Christians are familiar with these. The language is broadly inclusive and, generally, not problematic for ORT. PCUSA gives these ecumenical creeds the most emphasis and authority, which can provide some leeway to depart from other confessions that are more problematic.

This is followed by five Reformed confessions from the 15th-17th centuries: Scots, Heidelberg, 2nd Helvetic, Westminster Confession, and the Shorter and Longer Westminster catechisms. The view of divine sovereignty in these five documents pose the greatest obstacle to ORT, especially its assertion that God's omnipotence and omniscience is limited. For example, both the Scots and 2nd Helvetic confessions contain multiple references to "God's chosen ones" or "the elect" who are predestined for salvation, contrasted with "the reprobate."

Perhaps the most problematic is the Westminster Confession and its two related catechisms. It contains beautiful language, but with disturbing theological implications. Unfortunately, some Reformed denominations have only this one confession, rather than balancing it with other, more moderate statements, as in PCUSA. The confession describes God as "without passions, immutable, immense, eternal, incomprehensible" (PCUSA Book of Confessions, 6.011) and "most sovereign dominion over them, to do by them, for them, or upon them, whatsoever himself pleaseth.... his knowledge is infinite, infallible, and independent upon the creature, so as nothing is to him contingent or uncertain" (6.012). "By the decree of God, for the manifestation of his glory, some men and angels are predestined unto everlasting life and others foreordained to everlasting death" (6.016-7).

Yet some statements in the Reformed confessions appear to contain contradictions and awkward efforts to avoid the conflict between absolute divine sovereignty and free will: "God from all eternity did by the most wise and holy counsel of his own will freely and unchangeably ordain whatsoever comes to pass, yet so, thereby neither is God the author of sin, nor is violence offered to the will of the creatures, nor is liberty or contingency of second causes taken away" (Westminster, 6.014). Westminster also states that "God alone is Lord of the conscience" (6.109).

The five Reformed confessions were followed by three 20th-century confessions: Barmen, the Confession of 1967, and the Brief Statement of Faith. There is very little in the modern confessions that is problematic from an ORT perspective, and the last two offset many of the errors found in the Reformed confessions. The modern confessions show greater emphasis on free will, and openness to new ideas about faith. It's helpful to emphasize these if facing opposition to introducing ORT concepts. For example, the Confession of 1967 says: "God has created man in a personal relation with himself, that man may respond to the love of God the creator.... Man is free to seek his life within the purpose of God" (C67: 9.17).

Practical Tips for preaching/ teaching ORT in a Reformed Setting

Here are some tips I've found helpful for teaching ORT in a Reformed setting:

1. Prepare in advance for opposition by coming up with your "elevator speech"—your short answer to the question of how you understand sovereignty, omnipotence, and election. My short answer is that the Sovereign God freely chose to

create a world with an open future. They freely chose to self-limit omnipotence and omniscience to allow humanity the freedom to choose love.

2. Avoid specialized terms like Open or Process Theology. Less theologically sophisticated congregants are often distanced by the jargon, while more theologically educated might be aware of the controversy and become pre-emptively defensive.

3. Walter Bruggemann reminds us that people don't change worldviews quickly. Take a gradual approach—develop one idea at a time as building blocks. Take time with each step and use repetition to allow for a paradigm shift.

4. Parse out the principles of ORT in particular passages and verses—let the congregation see it in action. Show how these are not esoteric abstractions, but impact our everyday life in real, practical ways.

5. Be prepared to take on difficult passages like the "hardening of Pharaoh's heart" in Exodus or the predestination language in Romans 8.

6. For less biblically literate congregations, introducing simple biblical hermeneutic tools first is helpful. Rachel Held Evans' book Inspired does this well.

7. Gently point out inconsistencies, but also point out how ORT is the framework from which most of us innately operate (e.g.: we intuitively act as if our choices are free).

8. Be humble and model openness—share a range of views within Christianity, then identify the one you hold.

9. Recognize that often people cling to Calvinism out of habit, family tradition, but most of all, fear. As much as Calvinism fails to answer the hard questions of suffering, it offers a comfortable assurance of divine control in a world that often seems chaotic and unpredictable. Relational theology can be a disruption to that comfort. Be alert to pastoral care issues around that. Stressing the things we can put our faith in—the goodness of God, the love of God, God's desire for all things to be restored—can be reassuring.

10. Remind your congregants of the fruit of classical theism. Adopting a framework like Calvinism that is contrary to our lived experience distances us from God and leads to spiritual complacency and hypocrisy (arguably, this may be why we are seeing shocking abuses within evangelicalism). But adopting a theological framework that is consistent with our lived experience enlivens faith and

opens our eyes and hearts to the movement of God's Spirit. Pastorally, this is why it's important! People can become engaged, excited, and transformed when their faith makes sense.

Logical Progression of ORT Ideas

It is helpful to think of the progression of thought, the building blocks of Open or Relational Theology, and line them out in a logical way. Introduce them one at a time. Keep referring back to the precepts already covered, showing how they form a seamless whole. The progression that works well for me is:

1. Understanding Scripture and the nature of inspiration (again, a short series or Bible study on Rachel Held Evans' Inspired can be helpful here).
2. Introduce a Jesus-centered hermeneutic for difficult passages: looking to Jesus as revealed in Scripture as the best picture we have of God. Interpretations that differ from that picture (e.g., limited atonement) should be suspect.
3. Introduce the idea of inaugurated eschatology—the Kingdom of God as "both now and not yet." This is a helpful preliminary step for understanding issues around theodicy.
4. When speaking of the atonement, emphasize the "Satan-ward theories" (ransom and Christus victor) rather than the "God-ward theories" (substitution, especially penal substitution, and satisfaction). Coupled with inaugurated eschatology this can become the building blocks for a theology of suffering.
5. Use Philippians 2:5-11 to explore the idea of kenosis, and what Jesus' incarnation can tell us about the nature of divinity. Move away from the "omnis" to divinity defined by sacrificial love, as exemplified in Jesus.
6. Talk about free will and the choices we make. Having established that love is the defining characteristic of God, you are ready to talk about how love requires freedom: it must be chosen. God takes a chance on human freedom.
7. Now you can talk about the future as being open to many possibilities. God cannot know which choices will be made by free creatures, but can respond in love as they come. Beyond that, there is a range of views among the ORT community on how to parse limited omniscience. The position I lean toward that seems the "least far" from Reformed thought is: God knows everything exactly as it is—a future possibility, contingent upon our free choices. God can make

promises about their intent in each of these contingent future possibilities—just as humans can make promises about their future intent, even though we cannot predict others' actions.

8. With these building blocks in place, you're ready to talk about the problem of suffering. I draw on Walter Wink and Greg Boyd and their understanding of spiritual warfare.

In summary: teaching and preaching Open and Relational concepts within a Reformed setting is challenging—yet important. Some will respond defensively, for a variety of reasons. Making significant paradigm shifts in our foundational thinking can be uncomfortable and disruptive. Some will respond joyfully, as the new perspectives of ORT begin to name and address deep and troubling conflicts in their Calvinist assumptions. In either case, as pastors and teachers, we can be a "non-anxious presence" that normalizes even the discomfort of considering new paradigms. The payoff is the enlivening of faith that happens when we adopt models that fit with our lived experience of God and the world, allowing us to experience God in new and profound ways. People become engaged, excited, and transformed when their faith makes sense.

Vikki Randall lives in Monrovia CA, and has 28 years of pastoral experience, serving large and small churches, mostly in PCUSA. She received a D.Min. in spiritual formation from Azusa Pacific University and has served there as adjunct faculty in undergrad theology since 2003. She is passionate about transformation and experiencing God's presence.

Gods and Doctors

KATHLEEN REEVES

Who has not been touched by grief? But we can soften the blow with a fresh approach to death and medicine by knowing when to draw the line between what doctors and God can do and what they can't.

"Life doesn't feed on life. Life doesn't nourish life. Death feeds life…. Our deaths can, in every sense the word can be meant, feed life—unless we refuse to die, or fight dying, or curse dying, or spend all our dying time not dying."
—Stephen Jenkinson

Grief Walker

When I was a young child, I would watch Mutual of Omaha's *Wild Kingdom* with my family. This was a nature show that didn't hide death. When the cheetah caught the gazelle, and bit into its neck, I would cry and wish for it to free itself and run. As the cheetah carried the gazelle's lifeless body up into a tree, I would get so angry that it was so unfair! The cheetah was so mean! Why did the gazelle have to die? My father didn't console me. Instead, he told me that this was the way of life and that everything must die at some point. He explained the cheetah would die if it didn't eat and that would be sad too. He explained that there was a balance in nature and that it may seem mean, but there is a beauty in it as well. This was my first lesson about death and dying. Twenty-five years later, I sat at the bedside of my dying father. After a massive heart attack, his damaged heart could no longer sustain his body. Death demands surrender and there was nothing I could do to stop it. Medicine was limited, and God couldn't heal him. Creativity may follow, but death comes despite doctors or gods. Death is a natural part of the cycle and without death, nothing new can emerge.

I learned about the medical conveyer belt and the denial of death, as the severity of my father's illness blindsided my family. The doctors talked over us instead of to us. No one offered us hospice or even prepared us for his death. Death caught us by surprise. The doctors kept offering us hope and when they had given up, not much was said. If death is an inevitability for all life, why do we think it could be overcome? Death came for my father, and it changed me; I learned from his death. We cannot stop death, but we can change how we approach it. God cannot stop death, but God is with the dying and the bereaved during the dying time and always. Whitehead (1979) depicts God as "the great companion—the fellow-sufferer who understands." God is a grief walker. I knew I would teach this to anyone who would listen, and I would try to be a companion to the dying through this sacred time. I became a grief walker. I propose that facing death is not giving up on life, because fighting for life only to buy more time to fight against death is not living at all.

Now, twenty years after his death, I am a hospice chaplain. I sit at the bedside of dying patients every day. What I see most often is the denial of death. As I walk beside these people as they face death, it brings my own death into focus. I am now more aware of my own aging. Even though I have far to go, I am situated in my own timeline with my experiences behind me. All my life has led me to this current place, affecting my future possibilities. This knowledge makes me more aware of my own body, what I eat and how I move. We will all die, but need we fear it? Could we instead make it holy, a sacred moment where we enter through a threshold? This is what I embody in my work with the dying. Grief is normal and holy as well. We must honor our grief instead of hiding it. I currently walk beside my mother as she navigates her terminal illness. I know that her life is ending, and I am preparing. We face the mystery with honesty for what it is. I am her grief walker.

I have often heard the question from hospice patients: *Why is God doing this to me?*

God can't prevent death, nor would I ask for such a thing. Yet nevertheless, again and again the elderly die in emergency rooms after going through the traumatic heroics of bone breaking CPR and invasive breathing machines. Just as we mistakenly believe God can prevent death, we put our faith in medicine. Going to the emergency room does not guarantee that we can be saved from death. Death may come, and medicine is not omnipotent any more than God is. I have walked with hundreds of families through grief because I follow the families of my hospice patients for a year after the death of their loved one. I see the anger at both the omnipotent God who should have saved their loved ones and the doctors who failed them. Medicine is the new God and we put our complete trust in it. Of course, many people can be saved through medicine, but there are limits, and there is a time to let go. There is a point at which the treatments are no longer curative, but tortuous. The exact line may be difficult to discern, but the current trend is to cross far beyond it. I have had patients admitted to hospice and die within hours. This is not the purpose of hospice. Quality over quantity is the goal of hospice and hospice should begin when a patient has about six months to live. Those six months should be as full of life as possible. It should include grandchildren and walks on the beach even if it is from the boardwalk in a wheelchair. This is the time for saying goodbye through family dinners, sorting old photographs, holding hands and saying, "I love you."

Doctors Can't

In 2020, as I faced the death of another family member, I asked process theologian John Cobb about death. I was looking for a new perspective. John spoke of a perpetual perishing of each moment of our lives. But then John also talked of mystery, beauty, and possibilities.

Death is a threshold. It is a sacred moment that so few experience with awe and wonder.

When I received a call that my beloved uncle was dying, I dropped everything and rushed to Palm Springs to be with him. We were at the inevitable point that no one in my family would talk about. I had been lecturing about death and dying for a year before my uncle's illness, yet I still struggled to talk about it when it was with my own family. I knew they didn't want to discuss it. I think this is typical for most Americans. I witnessed this in my work as a hospice chaplain. My personal experiences with the death of a loved one have involved, without exception, the denial of death. We live in a death-phobic and death-illiterate culture. And there I was with no language to break down the barriers.

As I stayed with my uncle in Palm Springs, I took him to a doctor at a cancer center where they seemed ill- equipped to deal with him. He weighed 128 pounds and was too weak to walk. The doctor came in with a whirlwind of medical options that included feeding tube, chemotherapy, and radiation. There was only a barely recognizable statement that he could be dying, "We will see if we can get you stronger in order to have chemotherapy, but if not well, you might have to accept that we can't do chemotherapy."

My uncle didn't hear the last part and I imagine that most patients don't. They hear the hope in the options of a feeding tube and chemo. But often for someone who is already dying, these treatments cause more suffering. Katy Butler wrote about her family's struggle when her father became ill, "When my father was vigorous and lucid, (my mother) regarded medicine as her wily ally in a lifelong campaign to keep old age, sickness, and death at bay. Now ally and foe exchanged masks. Medicine looked more like the enemy, and death the friend." Hope is the most powerful emotion at times like this. Hope magnifies the slimmest possibility and asks the doctor or God for healing. In process thinking we have many possibilities and in cases like these: one of them is death. Death is always one of our possibilities and if we accept it, talk about it and explore what that means, we might live more fully.

I thought we would have more opportunities to speak to the doctor. The doctor never returned our calls, despite my aunt's attempts to contact him. They admitted my uncle to the hospital the same day as our visit to the cancer center. My uncle kept saying, "Just zap this thing" while pointing at his throat. I know that he knew that he was going to die eventually, just like everyone else, but I think he thought he would have more control over his dying and that he could put it off a bit. Stephen Jenkinson wrote, "The bargain for More Time is a gamble for More Life, in oncology, in palliative care, in any foxhole. More Life is the reward of More Time, so the hope goes. But More Life at the end of your life is lived in the distinct, ample, palpable presence of your death… Your More Life, it turns out, includes More Death, a lot More Death than you ever imagined could be in one life."

I have read many books that dive into the problematic relationship between the medical profession and death. It seems that for doctors, there is a disconnect between the whole patient and the body part that is diseased. The patient loses in this fragmented approach to medicine that is in denial of death or treats death as failure. But this is a two-sided proposition. We seek out miracles and doctors feel pressured to provide them. It's a consumerist problem. We believe we can buy our health if only we have enough money to afford the best doctors. But money only takes us so far. Katy Butler wrote in *Knocking on Heaven's Door: The Path to a Better Way of Death*, "When my father was vigorous and lucid, [my mother] regarded medicine as her wily ally in a lifelong campaign to keep old age, sickness, and death at bay. Now ally and foe exchanged masks. Medicine looked more like the enemy, and death the friend."

Yet, with all my knowledge, I still got sucked into the system. How could I be the one to tell my uncle that he was dying when his doctors didn't back me up? I doubted myself and my knowledge of the limits of death and dying. I also did not want to alienate my uncle or my family with talk of death when they still had hope. It would have been as if I was asking them to give up. But the reality was he was already dying. Death is a process, and it takes longer than people think.

Memento Mori

My uncle was admitted to the hospital directly after the cancer center appointment and given intravenous nutrients and hydration. A surgical opening, called a Peg-Tube, was created into his stomach to allow liquid protein feedings to be administered directly to his gastrointestinal track. He was given a port, inserted under his skin and attached to an artery for a chemotherapy treatment that would never happen. I wondered if the doctor actually thought it possible that he could gain enough weight in order to undergo chemotherapy. How could I, as a lay person, know that chemotherapy was impossible when the doctor did not? But I was right, and I should have questioned it because the doctor was just going through the motions. Was this to avoid the conversation that should have occurred? I learned that this is the norm in modern medicine: keep doing stuff until your back is up against the wall. But these procedures are painful.

My uncle wanted them to just zap his esophagus with some radiation so he could eat. He thought it would be that easy. He talked about taking the entire family out to a big dinner. But once he was discharged home, he rapidly deteriorated and in December and January, he refused to have more than two feedings a day through his peg tube because it made him feel bloated and uncomfortable. Sometimes he took only one feeding a day.

We got a nurse practitioner on the phone to explain that they couldn't do chemotherapy or radiation in his weakened state. We never could get his doctor on the phone to tell him this. It wasn't until the last week in January that my uncle opted for hospice. By then, he was so weak from lack of nutrition that he slurred his words and was too exhausted for interaction. Shortly after he went on hospice, I made the hour-long drive to his home in Palm Springs and never got to see him because he was sleeping the entire time. My family lost valuable time with my uncle because by the time he entered hospice, he was so sick and his condition so advanced that he could not have the goodbye conversations that would have been so meaningful.

How did this happen on my watch? I felt guilty for not speaking up. I felt robbed of time to sit and talk with my uncle. I wondered if he was afraid. I'll never know what he thought.

Thresholds of Awe and Wonder

Now, as I care for my mother as she faces a terminal illness, I wonder if I will be successful in overcoming the medical conveyor belt. I have already complained to the doctors that she has too many appointments and blood draws. I asked the doctor if he could not cure her, why not manage her gently? But he must go through the motions. To the doctor, she is reduced to body parts, and she sees a different doctor for each organ. This is counterintuitive to life. Our bodies are systems and beyond that, we are social beings with family and friends. All are affected. I am being robbed of valuable time with my mother as we go through the motions of a medical system that can't cure her. I don't look to God to cure her. I look to God to walk with us and be there as we talk deeply about our lives. I ask that God hold our hands as we face this final year together. I ask that when the time comes, that God would receive my mother into the great "all," and that I could see a little more clearly her impact on the world.

What if doctors incorporated a process relational view of terminal disease? If we begin with God can't, we might accept that doctors can't either. We can look at the possibilities and think creatively. Without death, there is no life. I want to de-medicalize death and return it to a place of sacredness. Birthing and dying are thresholds of wonder.

We complete the cycle when we return to the earth. This is our final gift, our contribution, yet the system is set up to withhold even this. Embalming and cremation harm the environment and the funeral industry is a for-profit consumerist endeavor. They normalized the denial of death. But natural or green burials are on the rise. People are starting to realize that we are part of an ecosystem. We are part of the food chain. Decomposers play a critical role in the flow of energy through an ecosystem. They have evolved to do this work. They break apart dead organisms into simpler inorganic materials, making nutrients available to primary producers.

The denial of death is a has become a fundamental aspect of human existence, rooted in history, psychology, and society. While it serves as a defense mechanism against the existential anxiety caused by mortality, it also hinders our ability to fully embrace life. By acknowledging and confronting our mortality, we have the potential to lead more meaningful, purposeful lives and cultivate a healthier relationship with death, ultimately enriching our human experience. Embracing death as an integral part of life can lead to a more profound understanding of what it means to be human and open us up to the mystery of what is beyond the threshold.

Kathleen Reeves holds a Master of Divinity, and her areas of focus are thanatology and process philosophy. Kathleen is an ordained interfaith minister. She currently works as Director of Chaplaincy, Spiritual Care and Bereavement in hospice and assisted living. She is a Death Midwife, Board Certified Hospice Chaplain, Supervisor Education Fellow in Chaplaincy, and grief counselor. Kathleen is a published poet, often writing about death and loss.

Great News—We Get to Preach Politics!

PETE SHAW

What if there is a way to approach personal and social injustices that unites more than divides, inspires more than disheartens?

"Please, Pastor, talk more about politics!" said no one, ever. "Instead of sharing what we're thankful for this Thanksgiving, let's debate presidential candidates." No thanks. "For Christmas, please get me more streaming subscriptions to 24-hour news services." I'd prefer sharing a bed with the fleas from a thousand camels. Political discourse in church these days is as welcome as a dead fly in a punch bowl.

Conventional wisdom instructs polite society to avoid talking about religion and politics to keep things civil, peaceful. The bummer for Christian pastors is that religion is supposed to be our wheelhouse, and our central character, Jesus, was deeply political! A strong amount of denial is required to avoid touching the third rail of politics. Yet if we are to be faithful to the teaching and example of Jesus, we have no choice. His Sermon on the Mount was full of political commentary, including instruction on nonviolent resistance. Going the extra mile, turning the other cheek, giving the shirt off your back—these were not tips on how to be a nice person—they were nonviolent acts of disruption designed to highlight injustice. His comment on paying taxes unequivocally challenged Rome. His criticism of elite Jewish leaders' greed in the face of poverty spoke into unequal systems of distribution. Jesus centered his life and mission on shalom—the expansive Jewish word that is sometimes understood simply as "peace" yet runs much deeper. It refers to holistic well-being for everyone, healing deep wounds both physical and emotional, a source of everlasting abundance from the heart of God, allowing harmony in and among all aspects of creation. Because Jesus was animated and motivated by shalom, he simply called attention to its absence (or opposite) when he saw it. On one occasion, the light of shalom shone upon a particular short-statured tax collector.

Zacchaeus was a wee little man. A wee little man was he. He climbed up in a sycamore tree for the Lord he wanted to see. And as the Savior came that way He looked up in the tree. And he said, "Zacchaeus, you come down, for I'm going to your house today." How many of you began humming the tune along with these lyrics? This is one of those stories that gets relegated to children's sermons. Yet the story has a much deeper purpose than to highlight a vertically challenged Jewish man. Zacchaeus was a tax collector. Viewed as a traitor to the Roman Empire, he was also known to be a cheat—ripping off his fellow countrymen with the blessing of Caesar, enriching (and isolating) himself each day. He was a Capitalist before the word meant anything—getting away with as much as the market would allow. Which was a lot. Diana Butler Bass, in her excellent book, *Grateful*, notes that he was a climber—not just of trees, but of the social ladder. His livelihood was based on a tit for tat model that was all about getting what you could without regard for others. The ancient world he inhabited assessed people based on their societal position. Zach didn't climb the tree simply because he was short—he was literally maintaining of his position above everyone else.

When Jesus called him to climb down, he was inviting dialogue on level ground, as equals. Further, instead of waiting for Zach to invite him to dinner, which would have set in motion the tit for tat system, the "I blessed you with dinner, so you now owe me a favor because I'm big and you're small" cycle, Jesus invited himself over to dinner, to bless Zach with his presence, which he in no way deserved. This was a deep reversal that would have broken the internet if they had one. Jesus' invitation to dinner was also more than a meal—it was an invitation to operate from a shalom-centered worldview, where decisions and relationships aren't calculated by who can do what for who, but by the unitive vision that positions everyone as equals in the unifying love of God.

And it was, in fact, an invitation, even if it sounds like Jesus was forcing his way into an expensive meal with good wine. Zach could have responded differently by maintaining his position of authority and rank. He could have laughed Jesus off, "In your dreams, preacher-man!", and we would note that a guy with power and money chose to reject Jesus' offer. Zach had the power and freedom to refuse.

But he didn't. Instead, he accepted Jesus' invitation not just to dinner, but to a different way of being, born from grace. According to Bass, his declaration that he was going to repay everyone he ripped off was effectively a resignation from his role as Chief Tax Collector. He was done marching to the beat of Rome and all it represented. He said yes to following the way of shalom.

This story reflects well key principles promoted by Open and Relational Theology (ORT). In contrast to more classic theological renderings where God acts as the ultimate authority, occasionally overriding human choice and demanding God's will be done (or suffer the consequences), we witness a God who, in relationship with these characters, is open to what comes next. In this story, Jesus rolled into town already famous for operating by a different vision, one where God is motivated primarily by love and not power, and where genuine invitation implies real relationship and an open future. Jesus had agency to invite Zach down from the tree, and further agency to invite himself over for dinner as equals, all motivated by love. There was no coercion here. Only loving invitation. Shalom's light shone on everything out of place given the ancient system of reciprocity that kept power in the hands of very few and equality out of reach. Not even God could know for certain how Zach would respond, or, if we push it further, how Jesus would respond to the nudge to start this whole exchange. If Jesus was truly human, even he had the agency to not ask Zach to climb down to level ground and share a narrative-and-table-flipping meal—no Jewish person would blame him for refusing company with such a traitorous thief. But Jesus embraced a shalom-centered vision to see with eyes of love even those believed to be enemies of the state. Jesus said yes to shalom. Zach did, too.

This is how God operates in the world according to ORT—constantly wooing us to recognize where Shalom needs to develop more fully and accept the invitation to say and do something to facilitate its flourishing. It requires risk. It is terrifying as it bucks systems and the powerful people benefitting from them. Sometimes those people conspire to squash such visions of Shalom to maintain their position, even to the point of killing an innocent, poor, nonviolent, anointed prophet-preacher during a Passover festival in Jerusalem. God did not stop such behavior because God is not controlling, but always operates from love, which accommodates individual agency. Yet what beauty blooms when love, grace, and shalom are fully chosen! What generosity flows from such an embrace of love so freely and fully given! Dinner is served! Wine flows! Tax bills shredded! Refunds received! Jesus' and Zach's respective embrace of God's invitation of shalom opened the door to more and more shalom.

Did you catch that this story addressed a contentious political problem? Challenging political issues in this process of invitation and response is displayed throughout the scriptures. This is why the rights and protections for widows, orphans, and refugees/immigrants expanded over time. As people lived and examined their political reality, they recognized shalom required greater protection and provision for the most vulnerable among them. Someone felt the nudge from the source of shalom (God) that was drawing attention to the absence of love and justice. Someone saw the vision and mustered the courage to draw others' attention to the discrepancy, which was welcomed by some, but not all. Sometimes human beings do not behave humanely toward the most vulnerable, sometimes dismissing or denying the reality of injustice because to address it would require change and sacrifice. Sometimes human beings have been known to resist shalom. The Prophets were some of the greatest advocates of shalom in their day, pleading to leaders and the general populace to embrace shalom for the benefit of all. Sometimes their messages were heeded. Sometimes the prophets lost their lives because it can be easier to kill the messenger than to accept the message.

As people of faith in the Christian tradition, and informed by Open and Relational Theology, we recognize that Jesus' teaching and modeling serve as our primary way of seeing and being in the world. That means we are invited to live by the light of shalom as we shine that light wherever we go, illuminating shadowy places. We are invited to risk identifying what doesn't align with shalom, standing for justice and well-being for everyone that will be uncomfortable for the messenger and the receivers. This is a choice to talk about the things that relational, familial, local, and global systems will not entirely appreciate. Yet this is our invitation to embrace should we desire more shalom anywhere and everywhere. This is choosing to talk about the political challenges we face, appealing to a much larger dream than that offered by binary blue or red visions. This is an invitation to receive the cup, even if it means we lose our lives while preserving our being. To drink from that cup is to sip from that everlasting well of living water, or the wine that will pour so prodigiously as envisioned in the eschaton. In this context, to choose pain or suffering or worse is to choose life, to choose love, grace—shalom—come what may.

This process-oriented vision also implies that ethics, laws, attitudes, and policies require continual reexamination and potential revision—the Law isn't as fixed as some proclaim given the evidence of Scripture. Consider Paul, who was once the leading advocate for strict adherence to Jewish Law, only to reverse course completely in favor of grace after encountering the risen Christ. Perhaps process itself is the actual basis of reality as Alfred North Whitehead proposed, requiring us to remain limber as we continually reimagine what shalom is calling for in our ever-changing context. Could this mean that in our contemporary world, shalom may call us to revisit the protections and provisions for the most vulnerable among us today, which still include widows, orphans, and refugees/immigrants and others? Could it also suggest that there may be voices of vulnerability that are only hinted at in ancient scripture? Vulnerabilities related to race, class, economics, climate, and human sexuality come to mind. What is shalom inviting us to see, hear, and do? What needs to change to allow more shalom for all? If we who claim to be animated and motivated by shalom don't stand up and speak out, who will?

At such a time as this, when division feels especially pronounced, may we choose the higher and deeper and wider vision of shalom that invites us and all of creation toward greater well-being. May we be truly encouraged—filled with courage—to lovingly, graciously invite others to a more beautiful vision that is never forced. May we together see more beauty and peace bloom because we have chosen to plant seeds and tend the garden of which we are stewards. May shalom be our means as well as our end, so much so that people may forget to become offended by our political talk because they cannot deny its beauty and would not dare return to its willful absence. May we be known—especially as we engage in political discourse—for embodying the shalom we desire to foster. May we celebrate when invited to usher more shalom into being, because we don't have to do this—we get to do this.

Supporting Songs: Oceans (Hillsong UNITED), Grace (U2), Act Justly Love Mercy Walk Humbly (Pat Barrett), Dwell (Casey Corum), Ever Be (Strand, Greely, Wilson, Heiligenthal), Goodness of God (Johnson, Cash, Ingram, Fielding, Johnson).

Pete Shaw has been Senior Pastor of CrossWalk Community Church (CrossWalkNapa.org) in Napa, CA since 1999, leading it from an Evangelical ethos to one that fully embraces Open and Relational Theology. He loves good wine paired with delicious food and enjoys working off those calories on his road bike. He earned his M.Div. ('95) and D.Min. ('06) from Northern Seminary.

Designing Worship from a Process Perspective

CASEY T. SIGMON

Worship is a powerful ritual shaping belief and action. So, are process ideas reflected in our words and actions?

If you are anything like me, you didn't grow up in a process theology household. My parent's religious category in the 1980s is what we now describe as None, though they may have checked the Catholic box when pressed on a survey. When I first stuck my toe into the waters of organized religion as a teen, I encountered a relationally based evangelical community that consistently articulated Jesus as God with us, for us and loving us despite our sinfulness. Our worship revolved around singing and praying to Jesus—the One who loves outcasts, befriends strangers, and feeds the hungry body so that souls would eventually be drawn to the waters of baptism and experience new life in Christ.

But the language in prayer and song about God and who God is did not resonate as strongly. This was especially the case in 2001. The year of my baptism also was the year a camp co-worker died by suicide, two planes crashed into the Twin Towers, and America began the War on Terror. Along with the emphasis on Jesus' love (yes to this!), there was a constant barrage of metaphors for God's power: *God is good, and God is All-Powerful! Through Christ, we have victory! God gives and takes away, but I will say, Lord, blessed be your name!*

I struggled to mind the gap between the loving solidarity of Jesus and the all-powerful God who could do anything to bring peace and healing but doesn't.

I became a worship leader in 2004, writing prayers, planning worship series, and choosing songs. I could not find the words to address my unease in my local tradition's worship vocabulary. The juxtaposition of bad things happening to good people with worship articulating *God is Good, and in control of it all* led me to seminary. Here comes the flow. A seminary class on "God, Suffering, and Evil" led me to process theology. *A-ha! God is love and ever-loving, and God cannot coerce us to act in loving ways! That's why we see suffering! It's not all God's fault!* My theological vocabulary changed. Now I had to search for worship language that reflected a process understanding.

For the last 15 years of ministry—both as a congregational pastor and professor at a seminary—I've been working to align my process understanding of God with the words spoken, sung, and sermonized on Sunday. It's not an easy task! But it is an important one.

From a process perspective, I believe worship is an event that choreographs a dance of God's body as its words, actions, order, silence, and rituals cultivate openness to the living God and one another. God feels our worship, and we feel God in worship. This mutual feeling impacts our lives (and God's!) in profound ways. In prayer, petitions, and proclamation, worship also opens us to the world's fullness—care and concern for and with those who suffer, including creation beyond humankind.

You probably know the challenge. Many of our liturgies have accumulated metaphors and frameworks for God that contradict process thinking with a focus on God's manipulative power, punishment, control, etc.

When we introduce people to process ideas, worship is a subtle and enduring event to focus our creative and collaborative process energies. When we pay attention, we will quickly notice misalignment from the very first words of the liturgy. For example, I led and participated in liturgies that asked God to be present among us, fill the space, and move in our midst at the start of the service. The underlying assumption is that God will not show up unless we ask God to do so. If we have the right intention and conditions, God will show up in our worship (instead of dwelling…where exactly? On the throne? In the sky?).

Process theology does not operate from this assumption. God is already and always as close to us as our breath. Worship is not setting the appropriate conditions for God to come to us. Instead, worship cultivates our *awareness* of God. We pray away hindrances to our connection to God in our worship as process thinkers. We design and embody a liturgy that heightens our awareness and desire for communion with God. We move into the ordinariness of our days, longing and hungering to maintain that state of relational connection and awareness. This is the flow and aim of worship from a process perspective.

Many of us will not need to throw out our worship ordo entirely to amplify a process understanding of God—who God is and how God is with us. Following are invitations to help the worship leaders design, curate, and create a liturgy consistent with process theology.

Call to Worship

This is the first movement where one can discern whether a liturgy emerges from a process perspective. Fundamentally, God is ever-present and active in a process perspective. So, when a call to worship asks God to present Godself in our gathering, one must assume that they are not operating from a process perspective.

While God is present, we are prone to distraction and inattention to the presence of God. A call to worship is a ritualized moment that gathers our collective focus on the Living God and prepares us to feel and respond to that presence in our ritual.

- No more "If you could just come here, God," petitions
- Recognize and remember the One who is Omnipresent
- Ascribe worth to the vision that flows from God

Congregational Song

Music powerfully shapes our language for God and our understanding of how God is with us. Augustine of Hippo is attributed to the quote: "Singing is praying twice." It has been said that people do not walk away from worship, humming the sermon. Instead, they go into the world humming the congregational songs chosen on Sunday morning. So, music can be one of your first areas of attentiveness as you seek to design worship that amplifies a process understanding of God and creation.

Formal process theology is young, not quite a century old. So, one area of growth for those process thinkers who are musically inclined is to compose congregational songs intentionally. Until we have momentum, the leadership seeking alignment with process thought can be attentive to the following as they look through the lyrics of hymnals and CCLI songs.

- God is not unchanging and unmoved—God changes with and through us, a moving mover.
- God is not far away—God is intimate and infinite.
- Our home is not heaven or some escape plan from creation—we are meant to be at home here and co-conspiring to create more opportunities for flourishing and justice to be experienced for all.

- God is not Almighty, All-powerful, Sovereign over all, and manipulating all to the good—God's power increases or decreases through our interactions, our saying yes to God's possibilities for our communities.
- Christian faith is not in its fullness when we only focus on Jesus and me. Be attentive to the lyrics' balance of I and We and Us (no Them—God holds all and does not excommunicate any bit of creation).

Confession and Pardon

For some, confession is an overlooked or walking on eggshells movement in the Sunday liturgy (we don't want bad vibes here!). The Protestant tradition did not agree on the role of confession in worship once the primary voices of reformation removed the categorization of sacrament from the practice of reconciliation. Some traditions absorbed the practice into the Lord's Supper/Communion as part of the movement to be ready to come to the Table (with a scriptural foundation in 1 Cor. 11).

From a process perspective, confession and reconciliation are vital to forming a community that is alert to the vision of God—who loves and cares for all of creation and who feels everything from every part. With contrition (meaning we feel regret for something we have done or failed to do considering what God seeks for us), confession (naming out loud as a group or in a one-on-one situation what we feel regret for), and absolution (forgiveness). We are individually/collectively attuned to the energy and guidance of God when our consciousness is clear and redirected toward the vision of God.

Every move matters. If we stay in remorse, we slip into shame and may fall into reactivity or passivity instead of collaboration in shalom and justice.

So, what themes could punctuate a confession and pardon in the liturgy from a process perspective? Here are some prompts.

- Sin is a broken relationship and a life-diminishing relationship between any living being, including God.
- Denial of the web of creation in which we are entangled is a sin needing contrition and confession to move toward changed action.
- Denial of self-value is a sin needing contrition and confession to move toward changed action.
- Denial of value within other humans is a sin needing contrition and confession to move toward changed action.

- Absolution/pardon offers us the power to change as those forgiven and loved by God. It should be addressed in conjunction with confession. Otherwise, we will not participate and will dwell on the feelings of pain and shame that do not lead to love.

Communion

Not all traditions offer a weekly meal. I am part of a tradition that gathers around the Table whenever we gather for worship. This physical activity dramatizes our connections to God, creation (from which the bread and contents of the cup come), and one another. Oneness is an aim from God, not that we would all be homogenous but that in our distinctiveness, we still belong to each other and are stronger and more beautiful because of our unity in diversity.

How can our actions align with process theology? Christian traditions of sharing from one loaf and one cup certainly more vividly symbolize connection than individual packages of elements that individuals pick up from a table on their way in and whose trash is dropped in a bin on the way out. When we, who are physically able to, approach the Table together and receive the elements from another human being, we feel more acutely the presence of God in the ritual and the body. And when we notice those whose bodies do not allow them to move easily to the Table and bring the meal to them, we more accurately reflect God's presence with us and the tender care that nothing and no one is lost.

Sending

The Sunday liturgy is only one amplified moment or event in the flow of communal worship, leading to a life of worship for everyone as they leave the assembly. Worship implies a yes with every choice to God's invitations. It also implies a no to competing opportunities that do not reflect the love of God, love of self, love of other humans, and love for creation. This is articulated first in our baptismal vows, whether we affirm them in a believer's baptism or a sponsor/parent says a yes on behalf of an infant or child in the sacrament.

We are sent not with a charge or marching orders but with invitations that should by now be irresistible to the people who've shared this assembly experience:

- To stay open to feeling and action
- To notice God- every response of a yes to God's invitations is a chance to worship God beyond Sunday morning.

- To be loyal to the world and therefore loyal to God
- To seek mutual dependence and care within our circles of community

Language for God

This final invitation continues the ideas shared under musical selections and compositions. As we make more intentional choices in worship design, we start by inspecting the words we use for God and creation in a wordy worship service (unless you are a Quaker).

In all the movements above, be intentional about how you name God. Our handed-down Christian go-to of "All-Knowing, All-Powerful, Almighty, Sovereign Lord…" does not align with the process understanding of God in Community, Holy Three in One.

What can we affirm of who God is and how God is with us in our address to God in prayer, sermon, and song?

- Knower of all possible possibilities…
- Poet of the world…
- Whose persuasive love beckons us…
- Omnicompassionate one…
- Who feels with the world…
- Overflowing fullness…
- One who does not hide…
- Ever-present…

Conclusion

Sunday worship is how we understand ourselves over time, impacting our ethical actions. Worship articulates and enacts the vision in word and action so that we fully and generously love God, neighbor, and self. Over time, we will be more sensitive to the possibilities for ritual words, actions, and patterns that align with process thought, and more resources will specifically be designed to aid us in these efforts. It starts with you!

May you stay open to the Purveyor of Possibilities as you make intentional worship design and leadership choices.

Casey T. Sigmon is an assistant professor of preaching & worship at Saint Paul School of Theology. She earned her M.Div. from McCormick Theological Seminary and her Ph.D. at Vanderbilt University. Sigmon is the author of *Engaging the Gadfly: Moving from Reactive to Reflective Preaching in the Digital Age* (Cascade, 2024) and other articles. She loves theology and pop culture.

God Is Not in Control, Nor Controlling

PAUL SWEARENGIN

A view of a controlling God points us towards controlling, legalistic religion rather than a truly divine partnership.

Let me share three different moments that display the Christian view of a God in control of the world:

"God needed your mother in heaven," my father was told when, at just nine years of age, he lost his mother to cancer. That young version of my dad wondered why God didn't have enough mothers in heaven already and had to take his.

Years ago, I asked a friend to pray that everything would come together in my attempt to buy a business.

"If God wills it, everything will work out," my friend said. Would God really want my deal to fall through as part of some interstellar plan?

I once attended the funeral of an eight-year-old boy who'd died of a rare heart infection.

"This is God's will," said the grieving father as he spoke over his son's casket.

Each of these scenarios make me wonder why an omnipotent, loving god is unable or unwilling to fulfill heavenly plans on earth without the need for killing a child, sinking a business deal, or leaving a kid without a mom. Maybe we've actually accepted a corrupted view of a controlling, unfeeling divine spirit of heaven, because we need simple answers and simple order in the world to avoid pain of our own, and perhaps even more so, to avoid responsibility in sharing the pain of others.

Maybe we need to better learn the meaning of "love god; love your neighbor as yourself."

In nearly two decades of pastoring and well-being coaching, I've constantly needed to help people deconstruct the idea that everything is either God endorsed or God allowed (as free will does all the damage). Christian mantras such as "all things work together for good" are coping mechanisms to force the receiver to mask their hardship so as to not create discomfort for me. This constant brushing off of the pain of others creates a group mindset where any transparent display of emotion is viewed as weakness or tied to a lack of 'faith in God.' An environment of denial and hiding emerges where it becomes impossible to live out Jesus' top commands of living in partnership with the divine spirit of heaven and to be the spirit of god to one another on earth.

Ultimately, such an environment steals a person's humanity and puts its adherents in bondage to man-created religious law. Statistics on American suicide prove this mindset is not serving people or our culture well and is literally deadly. It's time to change the religious Christian narrative of a controlling god in control of the world.

I help people to open up to a different Bible narrative that, start to finish, tells of divine pursuit of partnership with humanity. This partnership was struck with Abraham, lost at Sinai and restored through Jesus. Teaching of a partnering divinity offers heavenly relationship, rather than a punishing religion. This must be a point we emphasize again and again in our teaching, as the human abhorring of change requires theology to be "pried from their cold dead hands."

"Go from your country and your kindred and your father's house to the land that I will show you," the story of Abraham (né Abram) says in Genesis 12 (ESV). Abraham chooses a partnership with heaven not from fear of punishment, but the promise of opportunity. Jesus similarly made this promise in John 14:12 saying followers would do "even greater things" than Jesus. God sealed the deal with Abraham through a traditional covenant ceremony of animals cut in half and the two partners walking together through the blood-soaked path between the parts. God, however, passes through alone. Forever demonstrating that the divine spirit of heaven isn't looking for a relationship with people accountable to heavenly rules, but a priesthood unencumbered by shame and able to spread the goodness of heaven to neighbors… and even enemies.

This requires human beings to let go of the comfort of blaming "God's will" for the problems around us and requires us to accept responsibility to make it "on earth as it is in heaven." Wisdom from the Hebrew book of Jonah tells us, "those who cling to worthless idols, forfeit the opportunity for steadfast love (Jonah 2:8, version)."

I like to use the example of Stanley Kowalski, a character portrayed by Clint Eastwood in the movie *Gran Torino*. Kowalski was a former Korean soldier who'd been trained to see Southeast Asian people as subhuman. Though arguable, Kowalski might say that mindset was beneficial as it helped him survive war and return home. But later, as his neighborhood diversified, Kowalski was confronted with the choice of holding onto that once beneficial mindset of the past, and use it to categorize his Hmong neighbors, or he could lay that mindset down and learn to receive love from these neighbors and even find a greater purpose to his floundering life.

Abraham had to let go of his sources for safety and comfort: his father's lineage. Christians have to lay down our belief that a sinner's prayer makes us OK, no matter how we treat others.

Without the cover of a controlling god, Abraham became responsible for negotiating a standard by which Sodom could be saved or destroyed (I sometimes wonder if Abraham should have kept pushing until he finally just demanded it be saved to preserve Lot and his family.). Abraham brings a curse on an Egyptian king. Abraham has to allow his nephew to choose the best plot of land while Abraham must trust that his partnership with heaven would take care Abraham's own needs. Abraham's actions were "credited to him as righteousness" (Romans 4:3, version) through his friendship with heaven (James 2:21-13) rather than fealty of worship to a controlling being.

As human beings, offered a partnership with a divine spirit, we are responsible for what happens on earth. When things don't go well, we must own the pain and share it with each other (mourn with those who mourn—*Romans 12:15*) as part of the life process. We can't get away with a "God has a plan" platitude and then walking away. We are now the "Paraclete" (Holy Spirit) for one another, responsible to "come alongside" those around us.

Abraham accepted this partnership. At Mount Sinai, the people of Moses did not.

"You shall be to me a kingdom of priests and a holy nation" (*Exodus 19:6, ESV*) God offered. Instead, the people desired a god they could manipulate to grow their crops and kill their enemies. They chose a transactional bargain with the divine, which then required relationship to be measured against a rulebook, rather than in relationship.

"You've heard it said...," Jesus would state, "but I say...." In this statement, Jesus was pointing out how religious rules bring the hypocrisy of using them as bondage for others, while providing wiggle room for ourselves. Jesus then would demonstrate how a higher standard would be that simply avoiding a sexual act with a woman was not enough for righteousness, but always respecting the personhood of a woman, with no desire to sexualize her for our own benefit.

As a pastor, a couple came to me and shared that financial issues, including the woman losing her housing at the end of a lease, had them considering moving in together. They wanted to know if God would be mad at them for doing so. Well, there's a rule in the Bible against adultery ("you've heard it said...") but empathy forced me to lean into understanding their situation. They wanted to be married but wanted to be in a financial position to bring family from the east coast for that occasion. They were committed to one another in their hearts and felt no need for a certificate to affirm that.

The situation and time simply didn't afford them a better option than "living in sin." I gave them my blessing because I believe that is the heart of the goodness of heaven we see displayed in Jesus ("...but I say").

Jesus never claimed his mission was to start a new religion with a new set of "go and sin no more" rules. John 3:17 says the purpose of Jesus was not to condemn the world but to *sozo* it. The word *sozo* is often translated "saved" in the Bible, but actually means experiencing a reconciliation to wholeness and original purpose. Jesus' message was to remind humanity of a relational partnership available with heaven, rather than a punishing religion of control.

Whenever a person comes to me asking for God's will in a life decision, I ask, "what do you want to do?"

When King David decided to build a temple, we see the Bible again relay the narrative of divine partnership.

"I've never thought about putting my name on a city," God told David, "but because it's in your heart, David, I'll partner with your son to build it."

David wasn't asking for God's will, he was asking his partner to give clearance for David's idea. The story shows a divine spirit trusting the whims of a human being, just as the god of the Bible did when allowing Moses to argue against the slaying of all the people, when God honored Elijah's idea for a miracle contest between Yahweh and Baal, when Isaiah went from saying he was unclean to demanding he be the one to share the message of heaven, and when Jesus prayed for Peter not to be sifted as wheat.

"But I want to do what God wants me to do," said a church member, asking me about a life decision.

"Why do you believe God doesn't trust your instincts in this?" I asked. "Maybe God wants you to share responsibility for the decision rather than blaming something mystical if it doesn't work out?"

In the Hebrew book of Jeremiah, it talks about the "testing of the heart." The word translated as heart in that passage is the literal Hebrew word for "kidneys." Why would the divine spirit of heaven want our kidneys to be tested? Because the ancient Hebrew considered the kidneys to be the seat of emotions in a human being, much like today we might call it a "gut feeling." This says to me that checking our emotions--what do we feel in our gut--while asking heaven for wisdom, rather than permission, is a process endorsed by heaven so we can learn trust of ourselves and grow in our ability to make it on earth as it is in heaven.

"Don't be conformed to this age (the groupthink around you), but be transformed by the (ongoing) renewal of your mind," says Romans 12:2 (ESV, use of "age" rather than "world" and asides mine). The word "transformed" in this passage is used only one other time in the Bible, when Christ is "transfigured" on the mountain. That transfiguration was so amazing that Peter wanted to build a shelter and live there as long as possible! Encouraging people to leave behind safe mindsets and echo chambers of the past invites them into the risky opportunity of being transfigured into something breath-taking. Like a caterpillar being broken down in a cocoon in order to emerge a completely changed and beautiful creature.

And why do we want this transformation?

"…So that you can know what is good and right" and some versions say "and the perfect will of God."

The God of the Bible puts the will of heaven into the hands of those willing to be transformed on an on-going basis. That god cannot be controlling. That god cannot have a "do it my way or else" mentality. That god allows for mistakes. That god allows people to make choices without shame. That god raises up a people of "priests" who can share the goodness of heaven with their neighbors and their enemies.

Why would anyone choose a punishing religion in the hands of an angry god, when they can choose partnership and truly impact the world?

Paul Swearengin is a life coach, a professor and one who asks hard questions of the status quo. A former sportscaster and business owner, Paul followed a ministry call into ordination with the Vineyard Association of Churches. You can find Paul's videos on TikTok, YouTube and Instagram under @UnconventionalPastorPaul, and his coaching services and curricula at Pastor-Paul.com.

God Glasses for Process Preaching

BONNIE TARWATER

When you put on these God Glasses for Process Preaching, you may be like me and begin to dance out from behind the pulpit and right out of the church building altogether.

For you, my friend and process preacher, a gift, God Glasses for Process Preaching. These glasses put God into focus, like a modern microscope or telescope. We see all the dynamic interconnected relationships and feelings everywhere. Too often, us modern people tend to see the universe as a static machine. Process theology offers us the most precious gift imaginable. The God of love comes into focus in the new age of physics, someone we can do business with, as we say in Twelve-Step Programs. Hafiz, the Sufi mystic, writes in his poem, *The God Who Only Knows Four Words,* "Come Dance with Me." As soon as your eyes are accustomed to the world of dynamic feelings and relationships, God calls you. "Process Preacher, may I have this dance?" I encourage you, be brave and gracious and intertwine yourself in God's arms. Come, dance. "Thank you, God, I would love to dance." No longer alone, you are beheld by God. God holds your heart in love. You hold God's heart in love. You are one another's beloved and together you dance.

Now I am warning you—when you put on these God Glasses for Process Preaching, you may be like me and begin to dance, like you have never danced before. You may find yourself dancing out from behind the pulpit and then right out of the church building altogether. When your eyes get adjusted to this postmodern God worldview that aligns with the ancient mystical world view, the lyrics to the University culture song, "There is no God, no meaning, no purpose and the universe is a machine," begin to fade away. You begin to dance to a grand diversity of music, a tango, then a waltz, ballet perhaps or even a square dance or rumba. You and God, dance partners down to your cellular level. You feel the vibrations of the universe—God's loving heart beats and keeps tempo. Aww, how magnificent this new relational dance with God. Music and vivid rainbow colors and, lo and behold, God called by many names—Spirit, creator of the universe, Source, Allah, Shekinah, Holy Mama, S/He, Emmanual, the one who is *with us*—is a dancer extraordinaire. God of process relational preaching is the God of the dance for, "There is the music of Heaven in all things." (Hildegard of Bingen)

Our process relational organic world view invites partnership preaching with all aspects of worship and church. Worship dances and is continually becoming an interconnected web of life, just like our common home, Mother Earth and the cosmos. Preaching God's word necessitates deep thinking *and* feeling. As a young woman, I worked in the professional theater and learned that emotions live in the cells of our bodies. Writing sermons on computers and then reading them from the pulpit is way too small. God calls us to use our whole selves, including our bodies and hearts. Everyone is welcome at God's table and it is past time we welcome and include the non-human creatures in worship and church.

Process preachers are transdisciplinary. Coffee hour and church soup suppers are not separate from preaching. Our purpose everywhere is to connect our communities to God in praise and thanksgiving, for prayer and confession, for ecstatic dancing and social justice action. Ministers are intellectual public speakers and also artists, theater directors, musicians, theologians, community builders, mystics, healers, party hosts and hostesses, that hold the vision of radical countercultural communities of passionate love for God and the world.

I had a consciousness-raising experience and awakened to the severity of our earth crisis working on Dr. John B. Cobb Jr.'s Seizing an Alternative Conference in 2015. After the conference, I had several dreams and synchronistic experiences and felt God was calling me to dedicate my life and ministry to the Earth in some way I did not understand. Traditional parish ministry was not working for me anymore. My husband, Dr. Walt Rutherford, and I began a house church dedicated to the Earth, Church for Our Common Home. First, we worshiped in our living room in the San Diego suburbs, just the two of us. We moved out to the back yard and others came. Sometimes we took our worship to the beach. When the local news in San Diego reported that the American Empire was kidnapping children, we went to the Otay Mesa Detention Center to do civil disobedience. We protested with Moslems, Jews and Christians, chanting, "This is what theology looks like!" We were inspired to hold worship on the sidewalk in front of the prison and called out to those inside to join us in spirit. "We shall awaken from our dullness and rise vigorously toward justice. If we fall in love with creation deeper and deeper, we will respond to its endangerment with passion" (Hildegard of Bingen). Now we have relocated to Oregon and are exploring biodynamic farming and worship in the barn with the animals on a five-acre farm we have named the John Cobb Eco Farm.

Dr. Cobb invites us to dance with *God and the World*, a wonderful book with the same title written in 1969. If we are not preaching about the world then we are not preaching about God and vice versa. Whether or not we are conscious, we are living during the destruction of our habitat and the 6th mass extinction of life on earth, the only one created by us humans. Process preaching must tell the truth about what is happening in our world. 150 species are going extinct every day and we are facing the worst existential crisis the human family has ever known with the threat of nuclear war, social injustice, and ecological catastrophe. Like me, you may find yourself not only dancing in front of the pulpit but catapulted right out of the church building altogether as we welcome God into our hearts and bodies and include the non-human creatures in our congregations. Do you hear the cries of the Earth? Preach to her. She needs you. St. Francis of Assisi had a love affair with God and began to "dance," so to speak, with God as he preached to and for the animals outside. I highly recommend these God Glasses but be warned. There is music and dancing in God's universe that may sweep you off your feet. There is an open future luring you into an adventure of possibilities. Mystics fall in love and have our hearts broken when we open our hearts to "God and the World."

Process theology invites us to experience the wonder of an organic ecological world. God calls preachers to share the truth that the Earth is an organic living organism, an interconnected web of life, alive for 4.5 billion years and she is suffering. What we most need to do, to save the earth, "is to hear within us the sound of the earth crying" (Thích Nhất Hạnh). God is merciful. We can handle hearing the cries of the Earth because we also hear the cosmic music of creation. Please stop for a moment and be quiet and listen to God and the cosmos. ".... turn to the animals, and let them teach you; the birds of the air will tell you the truth. Listen to the plants of the earth, and learn from them; let the fish of the sea become your teachers. Who among all these does not know that the hand of YHWH has done this? In God's hand is the soul of every living thing; in God's hand is the breath of all humankind" (Job 12:7-10). Process theology calls us to preach to and for the natural world.

Jesus ministered and partied, danced and had deep feelings for the least of these, the most vulnerable, the poor, the oppressed. God is calling us to minister and party, dance and have deep feelings with the least of these in this historic time. And who is the least of these two thousand years after Jesus lived? The natural world. Yes, we still have plenty of poor and suffering humans to minister to, but God is calling us to stop killing the natural world and invites us to fall in love instead. Our opening invocation and prayer at Church for Our Common Home is a song by Raffi, "Our dear, dear Mother, Daily provider, Earth be your name, the time has come to honor you, to know you and to show our love…."

Dreams are God's forgotten language. It is past time process preachers share their dreams, telepathic and mystical experiences, as well as stories from the other side. Reading process theologian, Dr. David Ray Griffin's book, *Parapsychology, Philosophy, & Spirituality: A Postmodern Exploration*, gave me permission somehow to preach about my own experiences. Modern people are desperate to have mystical experiences affirmed by the church. The teachings of Jesus radically transformed my life during a personal crisis. Sharing personal stories of heartbreak and joy is the way we develop intimate relationships. During the Passing of the Peace at our untraditional church, we always share the Good News of the Gospel and say out loud, "God loves you and there is nothing you can do about it." Our prayers call upon the Christian mystics to join us—Hildegard and Viriditas (life force), Francis and Clare of Assisi, Jesus and Mary Magdalene, please join us from behind the veil. We need you. When I preach at Church for Our Common Home, my biggest concern is how to keep Matthew the goat from eating my sermon. Preaching to our wounded duck Bobo, I know that, "Every creature is a glittering, glistening mirror of Divinity" (Hildegard of Bingen). If Jesus and Mary Magdalene were alive today, they would invite the natural world to God's table.

We read our Twelve Step Program for an Ecological Civilization at the beginning of worship (appended), as we sing, dance, and pray to and with the creatures and God in worship. Our church members include Bugs the Bunny, Matthew and Mark the goats, (Luke died, God rest his soul), chickens, ducks, cats, dogs, and more. Our Interfaith Secret Prayer Garden is a place outside, "the secret inner closet" (Matthew 6:6). We have created twelve altars on twelve trees inviting prayers for creation here and everywhere, a kind of Living Rosary at our Secret Garden Retreat Center.

Joanna Macy reports that people in Chernobyl after the nuclear melt down wanted to dance. After catastrophic experiences, we need to be together and with God of the dance. Sitting in church pews, we may die of a broken heart. We give everyone rainbow dancing ribbons at the end of worship and we dance with the animals and our Zoom friends around the world. Rainbows are the symbol, from the story of Noah's Ark, of God's promise to love all creatures, always. Re-membering God's love and dancing together is our barn church's benediction.

Hey, I have an idea! Let's gather all you process preachers and have a big dance party. I'll bring God Glasses for Process Preaching and dancing rainbow ribbons for everyone. Let's not bring our modern competitive habits, OK? Let's give one another love and support and have an Earth Crisis Support Group and Potluck Party (ECSG). This is my new version of coffee hour or church soup suppers, if you will. We gather in small groups and share our feelings and tell the truth about what is going on in the world. During the potluck party, we plan actions. It's a hybrid of the early church in people's homes who always shared a meal, Twelve-Step Programs, and psychological support groups where we share our common challenge, the earth crisis, and we no longer feel alone. The idea for ECSG's came out of John Cobb's latest book, *Confession*, and his invitation to me to write the last chapter. The Appendix are the guidelines for ECSG—a kind of confessional for modern secular people. Christians have a unique responsibility to welcome and make a place for everyone—Christians, Jews, Muslims, the spiritual but not religious, atheists—everyone welcome at God's table for our new kind of Holy Communion, a secular meal with local neighbors.

Preachers are called by God to create loving local and global community in the noble prophetic tradition of radical truth telling. We are hosts and hostesses of a divine dance party sharing Jesus's vision of the Kingdom of God, called by many process folks an Ecological Civilization. God calls the church to prepare for the famines and ecosystem collapse, as we imagine an ecological civilization, a future of hope. The heart of process preaching is about passionate feelings of love for the teachings of Jesus, God, our human family, the natural world, all of God's creation. I asked John Cobb once, "So Whitehead says that the universe is made up mostly of feelings, like how much—95% feelings?" "Oh no, much more than that." My, oh my, John Cobb, that is a lot of feelings everywhere!

Evangelical Christians have benefited from process theology that gives up the supernatural God for a God of deep intimate feelings who loves everyone. Liberal Christians desperately need process theology to get them out of their heads with a God of deep feelings of passionate love in all creature's bodies, who dances ecstatically with and for the natural world. We are not alone; we are held and are dancing in God's body. Time is short. It is past time to get creative and bold and lead confessional prayers in safe sanctuaries of hope. May we preach from our minds, *and* hearts, *and* bodies about our passionate love affair with God and the world. Imagine that you and God are preaching together and the two of you are like the couple at the planetarian in the Academy Award-winning movie of 2016, *La La Land*. You may begin to levitate into the stars and cosmos together or dance with the angels deep inside the earth. "This little light of mine, I'm gonna let it shine." While dancing with my beloved first born granddaughter Laina, we began spontaneously singing together, "This little dance of mine…Dancing with God all the time."

Twelve-Step Program for Ecological Civilization

The Church For Our Common Home is God centered and guided and dedicated to Mother Earth. We work for an Ecological Civilization with our 12-step program and we:

1. Share the truth that the current 6th extinction of life on Earth, the only one created by humans, is an invitation for transformation as a human species.
2. Share the history and human habits of dominant over relationships and commit to relationships of collaboration, partnership, and co-creativity.
3. Make amends for our alienation and abuse of the natural world and our idolatry of scientism and rationalism using transdisciplinary reconnections of religion, art, psychology, ecology, etc.
4. Explore eco-feminist and process theology, celebrating God and Goddess language, symbols and relationships.
5. Study the teachings of Jesus and Mary Magdalene and their Church of Love highlighting the radical teachings and the way of doing unto the least of these, love of enemies and service to God not money, with newly found gnostic scriptures and the world's ancient wisdom traditions.
6. Offer diverse spiritual practices to develop loving relationships with the natural world, Mother Earth and all creation.
7. Honor the invisible realms of dreams, prayer, intuition, parapsychology, and imagination.
8. Celebrate the visual and performing arts, ritual making, beauty and creativity as divine spiritual practice.
9. Celebrate intergenerational community by intentionally including and honoring the very young and old.
10. Encourage consciousness raising with integration of body, sexuality, mind, spirit, feelings, intuition, and imagination.
11. Work for social justice locally and globally in partnership with other organizations
12. Experiment with nontraditional church in order to create relevant, spirit filled and loving community.

Rev. Bonnie Tarwater served as a parish minister in United Church of Christ and Unitarian Universalist churches and is the founder and minister of Church for Our Common Home, www.churchforourcommonhome.com. She and her husband, Dr. Walt Rutherford, offer counseling services and retreats at The Secret Garden Retreat Center at the John Cobb Eco Farm and are exploring biodynamic farming.

What is Theological Preaching? Thinking with Tillich and Process Theology

JOHN J. THATAMANIL

Amid multiple crises faced by humanity and the living Earth, many people of faith long for a theology and a language of faith that makes sense and speaks to real-life struggles for meaning and purpose.

Every sermon is theological, and yet few sermons are. This apparent contradiction trades on an equivocal use of the word "theological." The first half of the sentence points to an obvious truth; no sermon is empty of theological implications. Some implicit set of theological convictions animates any sermon. Nonetheless, based on personal experience, few sermons have as their *explicit* goal a direct engagement with theological convictions for the sake of explication and, if necessary, reformulation.

Sermons customarily have in mind a range of purposes: exhortation, consolation, spiritual formation, and moral formation among others. In mainline denominations, whatever the preacher's goals, they must be accomplished expediently. Speaking as an Anglican/Episcopalian, I have no more than 12-15 minutes to work with. Given the brevity of that time frame, it is hardly surprising that a direct engagement with theology is an uncommon homiletical task. Still, in an age in which the work of Christian education at the congregational level—particularly for adults—is vanishingly rare, explicitly theological preaching seems more necessary than ever.

My own limited experience at two congregations on opposite ends of North

America, one Canadian Anglican and the other Episcopalian, suggests that there is real eagerness for explicitly theological preaching.[1]

If my own admittedly limited sample size of congregations is any indication, people in the pew want their preachers to reanimate the language and basic categories of Christian faith. It is not just that congregations have a specific set of questions that they need answered, questions perhaps about theodicy or religious diversity. However important these specific questions may be (and they most certainly are), what I sense is something deeper. My experience suggests that there is a *desire for root and branch revivification of Christian discourse*. Their core desire—or at least what seems most satisfying for the congregations I serve—is to have the language of faith make sense. I am tempted to say, "make sense again," but that would be to presume that that language made sense in the first place. After all, even lifers, those who have grown up for their entire lives inside the church, share this longing for intelligibility and meaningfulness. They seek a workable theology, a livable theology, a theology that speaks to real-life struggles for meaning and purpose.

My own mode of theological preaching is correlational in the sense of that term as deployed by Paul Tillich, whose own theological sermons are my primary homiletical inspiration. Readers who know Tillich know that in his theology, questions derived from human experience, as those questions are formulated by culture, are then correlated with answers as they are derived from revelation. In the sermonic moment, this means that the preacher must allot a fair measure of time to the work of laying out some real human and cultural problem before turning to the work of formulating a theological answer.

Tillich and I both believe that *perennial* human questions always take *particular* cultural configuration. The questions asked by 21st century North American communities cannot possibly be the very same ones asked in the 1st century Levant. So, the method of correlation requires from preachers the capacity for two kinds of interpretation, the interpretation of culture as well as the interpretation of scripture. Every preacher must, therefore, also be a theologian of culture.

Of course, this question-answer method need not be woodenly applied. Even an exegetical sermon focused on interpreting a lectionary reading might be correlational insofar as the preacher remembers that we read from our particular here and now. Preacher and congregation alike do not come to the text as blank slates. We come with our worries, anxieties, questions, and broadly speaking—from our cultural moment

---

1. I am an Associate Priest at the Anglican Church of St. John the Divine in Victoria and Associate Priest at St. Mark's Church-in-the-Bowery in New York. Both congregations understand themselves to be progressive justice-seeking communities with deep intellectual curiosity. I've also preached in several other congregations in the Anglican Diocese of Islands and Inlets.

and context. To ignore the situations that we bring with us to church as we begin to preach is to render the sermonic moment irrelevant.

How, for example, can contemporary Christians in North America ignore daily reminders of the climate crisis when in church? How do middle-class Christians whose only source of reliable wealth lies in their own homes reckon with the conundrum that as their home values increase, the more the homelessness crisis expands in their cities as persons are priced out of home ownership and even affordable rentals? How do we confront the ways in which our smartphones keep us online, disengaged, and distracted in the virtual world as the quality of our relationships in the non-virtual world takes a hit? To bypass these issues such as these is an act of evasion.

To fail to bring such questions to the scripture and tradition is also to imply that they lack the resources, vitality, and power to address contemporary questions. Not only are the congregation's needs ignored, but scripture and tradition are deployed to answer questions that no one is now asking. Correlational preaching is rooted in a double confidence that God is not done speaking, and Christian scripture and tradition can speak even into our contemporary moment.

By contrast, when such questions and challenges are explicitly addressed in preaching, there is a palpable sense of alertness in the congregation. Congregants recognize that something of pressing concern is at stake; so, the sermon is not the same old same old. The level of engagement with the sermon is high because theological preaching that addresses such issues is worldly, in the best sense of that term. It reminds congregations that the church and its Gospel exist for the world, not the world for the church.

To be clear, theological preaching in this correlational style is still a far cry from the propositional articulation of a systematic theology. That is not what I have in mind when I speak about "theological preaching." In fact, just what I take "theology" to mean in the preaching context is worth spelling out briefly. As I note in my sermon in this volume, theology is a far more encompassing notion than we have come to think of it in our time. Presently, the term has come to designate an area of academic inquiry—a *wissenschaft* to use the German term. Only the writer of theological books can count as a theologian. Under the spell of this disciplinary sense of theology, I have had theologically gifted preachers and congregants insist vociferously that they are not theologians; only I am. Perhaps this limitation of theology to academic confines is yet another reason for the relative lack of theological preaching. Pulpit pastors have learned, under the spell of disciplinarity, to think of themselves as pastors or priests but not as theologians. Only their seminary professors count, and then too, only those who teach systematic theology.

In my sermon, I note that "theology" is the work of striving to answer Augustine's question, "What do I love when I love my God?" As the question itself makes clear, theology is as much a matter of "truing" the heart as it is "truing" the mind. Theology seeks to repair not just our always inadequate notions about the divine, but it strives also to ensure that our devotion is not given over to unworthy objects of attachment. Theology is intellectual eros—the work of answering Christ's command: "You shall love the Lord your God with all your heart, and with all your soul, and with *all your mind*." It is this full-blooded sense of theology that parishioners seek.

In the sermon I preached just today ("Silence and Resistance: On How to Hear the Divine Voice," January 14, 2024), I took up the question, "Under what conditions might it prove difficult to hear the word of God?" The question was prompted by a crucial verse in our Hebrew Bible reading for the day from 1 Samuel: "The word of the Lord was rare in those days." In a discussion with our congregation's "Sermon Circle"—a group that gathers on Wednesday mornings to read lectionary passages for the coming Sunday, congregants concluded God is always speaking; so, the verse can only mean something like, "The word of the Lord was rarely *heard* in those days."

This observation prompted me to formulate my question—a question derived from the congregation's own engagement with scripture and not just a matter of my personal and idiosyncratic interest. What makes it hard to hear God's voice not just in Samuel's day but in our own? I posited two factors about our present moment. First, we find ourselves in a political, cultural, and economic context of constant clamor, a clamor in which meaningful silence is all but crowded out. Political noise, cultural inundation driven by FOMO, Fear Of Missing Out, and economic pressure all press against us, making time for silence hard to come by. As a result, we find it hard to hear not just God's voice but even our own.

A second factor: we have given up on the possibility that the structural conditions that shape and constrain our lives can really be changed. We have settled into what the eminent political theorist, William Connolly, calls "passive nihilism" (*Facing the Planetary: Entangled Humanism and the Politics of Swarming*, 2017). We may hold in principle to core values, but in our growing despair that we are fated to live with the climate crisis driven by planet consuming capitalism, we deny in practice the values we theoretically affirm. An existentially troubling posture.

The theological trouble is that the God that Jews and Christians confess is the one who proclaims, "I am doing a new thing!" How can Christians possibly hear from a God who lures us into genuine novelty—a core process affirmation—if we have resigned ourselves to maintaining that things will always be as they are now? Deny the possibility of genuine change, and it becomes prohibitively difficult to hear God's invitation to novelty and transformation. How can you hear what you believe to be impossible? Recall the quip attributed to Frederic Jameson, "It is easier to believe in the end of the world than the end of capitalism." Talk about passive nihilism!

I recount just some features of today's sermon (not included in this book) to illustrate what theological preaching in the correlational mode might look like. A careful analysis of a culture in which silence increasingly seems impossible performs the work of a theology of culture. The incessant demands imposed by our politics, our culture, and our economy pose serious obstacles for cultivating the kind of spaciousness in which genuine listening is possible. Mapping this problem and inviting the congregation to struggle with these features of their own lives strikes a chord. In a post-church "Sermon Talkback" conversation, congregants affirmed that this is indeed a struggle for them as well as the struggle of what the Buddhists call "monkey mind"—a mind so crowded with one thought after another that internal silence feels all but impossible. This aspect of the conversation not only touched on theology of culture but also pastoral theology and spiritual formation.

The explicitly theological element of the sermon takes up a core problem: how can you hear the God who lures us toward newness and transformation if you live under circumstances that have led you to believe that nothing really can or will change? This is a profound spiritual predicament but also a head-on engagement with a core feature of Christian proclamation, one that process theology insistently affirms. God is a God who lures us into the future, who presents to us possibilities as yet unrealized. The theological work of the sermon requires reminding congregants that "God is in the transformation business." God is the one who proclaims, "Behold I make all things new" (Rev 21:5).

Culturally induced torpor and resignation to planet-ravaging capitalism dramatically diminishes our capacity to hear that God. The God who makes all things new cannot be heard in a cultural climate that denies the possibility of genuine novelty. So more than silence is necessary if Christian communities are to hear the divine voice. Silence must be wedded to resistance empowered by a radical expectation that the God who does not bless the status quo is still speaking.

These are, of course, searching theological affirmations, but the sermon need not trade in systematic theology. We need not explicitly speak about "a doctrine of God," "a doctrine of revelation," or "soteriology" in order to do theology, though I can assure readers that no harm will come to preachers if they do. Nor did I work up affirmations about God into a process theology or a Pannenbergian theology in which God is resolutely a God of the future. Congregants may or may not be interested in theology at that pitch and disciplinary rigor, but they are most assuredly committed to a thinking faith—"faith seeking understanding" to use Anselm's classic phrase. Surely among the gravest sins of preachers is underestimating their congregations.

Preaching in this way is a source of profound vulnerability and tremendous joy. It is vulnerable work because preachers cannot speak into real cultural vexations without implicating themselves. My struggles are on full display even though I rarely speak in an autobiographical key. When I speak of the constant distractions of mediated life, they know I am speaking about myself. When I speak of the temptations of the market or "passive nihilism" in the face of the climate crisis, they know I am speaking about myself. I cannot accuse for I am thoroughly implicated.

But because these are the concrete struggles that congregants also face, in good theological preaching, they know I am in it with them. And, that also is the source of joy. When congregants and I together discover that scripture and theology can indeed speak to these questions, we recognize that we are on a journey together into the promise of theological life—not just theological thinking. We are doing the work of faithful meaning-making together, and few joys are the equal to this loving work of communally living out what Bishop Michael Curry calls "the Jesus Way."

Some Concluding Words on the Promise of Process Theology for Theological Preaching

While I do not customarily fly "the process theology freak flag" when I preach, the theologically informed listener will catch regular hints of process motifs. Process theology offers an endless cornucopia of resources for those who wish to preach in the correlational mode. For example, few contemporary schools of theology have as much to say about ecotheology as does process. Process thinkers from Whitehead forward sound notes of deep relationality that make it impossible to conceive the human as anything other than earthling. Process relationalism undercuts any and all attempts at escapist theology that denies our creaturely ties to our fragile planet.

Process theologians have noted at length the dead ends to which a theology of omnipotence leads. Congregations not only need ways to think of God beyond omnipotence to escape the theodicy trap—why is there such atrocious evil if God is omnipotent—but they also need theologies that put an end to human passivity. Awaiting a God who will rescue us from our ecological predicament is a sure-fire recipe for doom.

Christians in progressive congregations also need theologies that do not put them at odds with the work of science. A God of the gaps, an interventionist God, a God who interrupts the workings of the natural order—all these accounts of divinity strain credulity and disempower human beings from living in the world as we know it. Process theologies have struggled with and worked to develop intelligent alternatives to all of these dead ends.

The congregations I work with want and need credible theologies. I know no one is brought to faith by intellectual labor alone, the labor that produces credible theologies, but the lack of such theologies does readily lead to faith's atrophy. The sober dawning of awareness on some cold morning—"You know, I don't think I believe any of this anymore; I'm not even sure what any of this means"—that is the risk that we run when preachers and their congregations fail to engage in the adventure of theological ideas.

John J. Thatamanil is Professor of Theology and World Religions at Union Theological Seminary in the City of New York. He is the author of *Circling the Elephant: A Comparative Theology of Religious Diversity* (2020) and *The Immanent Divine: God, Creation, and the Human Predicament; An East-West Conversation*. His areas of research include theologies of religious diversity, comparative theology, and philosophical theology. He is an Anglican but much else besides. Specifically, he studies Advaita Vedanta and Tibetan Buddhist traditions both academically and spiritually. He is a Past President of the North American Paul Tillich Society and the first Chair of the American Academy of Religion's Theological Education Committee. Most recently, John has been ordained as a Priest in the Anglican Diocese of Islands and Inlets where he serves as Volunteer Associate Priest and Diocesan Theologian. He is also an Associate Priest in St. Mark's Church-in-the Bowery in New York.

The Baby and the Bathwater

JASON TRIPP

Open and relational ideas about God and God's interaction with creation offer compelling new pathways for those tempted to throw out the baby with the bathwater.

The massive shift in the North American religious and cultural landscape over the past generation has been well documented. Here in Canada, the percentage of those identifying as having no religious affiliation (the Nones and Dones) has more than doubled over the past 20 years, paralleling similar trends in America. This seismic shift in the North American religious landscape presents unique challenges and opportunities to those of us in vocational ministry tasked with the preaching, guiding, and inspiring of those entrusted to our nurturant care.

For the past 15 years, a significant emphasis of my vocational ministry has been journeying alongside the growing number of those filled with a lingering sense of doubt and dis-ease with the faith they have inherited. For many, their entire belief system is analogous to a carefully constructed house of cards with every occasion of disillusionment and doubt threatening to topple the entire house. Sadly, for the masses who have inherited a religious ideology where one's faith is only as strong as one's certainty of their beliefs, the temptation for many is to throw out the proverbial baby with the bathwater.

The idiom "don't throw out the baby with the bathwater" finds its origin in Germany in the 16th century. It conveys the importance of preserving what is of value, when in the process of disposing what is harmful or undesirable. Without a doubt, much of the "bathwater" of the church has indeed become contaminated. The toxic pollutants of noxious theology, the abuse of power and being co-opted by the rampant consumerism of our Western capitalistic culture, have left many weary and wounded.

The sad irony is that while churches are meant to cultivate personal and communal experiences of refreshment and reinvigoration—paralleling that of a therapeutic bath—the religious experiences of many have been anything but. For many, either jettisoning the faith or embarking on an arduous and lengthy process of religious detox become the painful but necessary last resorts as a means of survival and restored sanity.

For those of us responsible for preaching and preparing worship services, open and relational ideas about God and God's relationship with the world can unlock compelling new and refreshing alternatives for those in our faith communities experiencing great distress.

As I reflect on my own theological deconstruction and my experiences journeying alongside others over the past 15 years in vocational ministry, I've noted some helpful pieces of wisdom conveyed to me and passed along to others.

Fragile: Handle with Care

When I was 12 years old, I vividly recall my parents calling a family meeting with me and my two younger sisters. They informed us that my mother had been diagnosed with breast cancer. I was devastated. My mother was the most pious, loving Jesus-follower I knew. At the time, I could not understand how a loving God who controls all things would allow my God-fearing mother to be afflicted with such a horrible disease. The theological formation I had inherited in my conservative evangelical family and church led me to believe that God was omni controlling and everything was part of God's mysterious plan. This led me to believe that my mother's cancer was either somehow part of God's blueprint, ultimately meant for good, or it was designed to either test her faith or expose hidden sin in her life. After receiving the news, I stormed out of the house where I walked the streets all night while processing this earthquake event in my young life. Through tears and anger, I spent much of the night interrogating God. My safe, protective theological bubble had burst, and the house of cards of my faith began to come crashing down. This was the genesis of my theological deconstruction. I was left feeling fragile and afraid.

This sense of fragility I sensed as things began to shift for me was not unique to my experience. As we find ourselves living in a secular age where belief in God is no longer widespread, nor necessary in the minds of many, a fragility of beliefs (and unbelief) is commonplace. As Andrew Root astutely notes in his work interacting with influential Canadian philosopher Charles Taylor, "We now live in a time where the very idea that God is real and present in our lives is no longer accepted. Indeed, it's widely contested. Belief has been made fragile—for the pastor as much as for those in the pews."

As I look out over the congregation gathered on a Sunday morning, I can no longer assume that those in attendance are comfortable and secure in their beliefs. The vast majority of those in our faith community—both in person and online—are yearning for authentic community where they can come as they are, welcomed to love and be loved, while given permission to wrestle with their doubts and questions of faith. For some, our little Methodist community is the last stop on their way out of the church, a last-ditch effort to hold on to something authentic and beautiful, while healing from the trauma of authoritarian religious dogmatism. For others, it's an on ramp to the beginning of a journey to explore and experience the allure of the God of uncontrolling love.

Being attuned to the widespread fragility of beliefs in this secular age means preachers need to intentionally focus on the nurturing grace of Jesus, while resisting the authoritative rigidity which has wounded many to the point where throwing out the baby with the bathwater becomes a painfully live option on the table.

This Calls for an Intervention

Open and relational theology eschews tired old notions of an interventionist God, whose presence is often understood to be restricted to the individuals deemed righteous and the spaces historically deemed sacred. This was the impetus for my rage filled "God interrogation" upon receiving the news of my mother's cancer diagnosis more than 30 years ago. Holding to a primitive interventionist understanding of God who desires to shower blessing and protection upon the pious, while punishing the wicked, left me with little comfort or clarity to healthily navigate that earthquake event in my young life.

It was only as I began to open my heart and mind to more loving and Christlike ideas about God and God's relationship to creation, that I could gradually, as the Apostle Paul writes, "put an end to childish ways" (1 Corinthians 13:11). As I overcame the fear of engaging with and learning from the rich, vast wisdom beyond my conservative evangelical bubble, I was slowly able to—out of the rubble of my toppled house of cards—reconstruct a new theological house. This ongoing building project has remained sturdy, being built upon the twin foundations of "God is Love" (1 John 4:8) and "God is like Jesus" (Colossians 2:9). In a very real and urgent way, what I needed, and what many others I have the privilege of preaching to and engaging with need, was a loving intervention.

Open and relational thinkers have been instrumental in helping me re-center love as the essence of God's nature and the highest and most beautiful calling of creation to participate with God in bringing flourishing and wholeness to lives, communities and all of creation.

In the greatest sermon ever preached, Jesus repeatedly utters the phrase, "You have heard it said…" after which he offers invitations to those listening to refine their thinking and living to be in harmony with God's loving desire for right relationships rooted in love. In a sense, the entire Christ event serves as a sort of divine intervention, but ironically, not reinforcing ideas about an interventionist God, but to disrupt and display the essence of God's non-violent, self-sacrificial, ever-present love.

In re-centering love, open and relational theology claims, "You have heard it said, God intervenes in the affairs of creation in ways that display God's power and love according to God's mysterious will and purposes for creation...but I say to you, God has been and forever will be invested in and intertwined with all of creation, faithfully present and lovingly luring by and for love in ways that are non-coercive."

Preaching informed by open and relational theology is subversive in the ways it disturbs and disrupts long held ideologies about the nature of God and God's relationship to the world, which can perpetuate fear, trauma and fatigue in those trying to hold on to a faith that is substantive and beautiful.

As open and relational theologian Anna Case-Winters writes in her superb book, *God Will Be All in All: Theology through the Lens of Incarnation*, "Beginning with the Incarnation opens the way to seeing that God is really in the world, though always more than the world. This shifts the discourse for us, revealing the deeper reality of divine presence (incarnation) in all things. If that is the nature of God's relation to the world, then the Incarnation in Jesus of Nazareth is not a contradiction or an exception to God's ordinary way of being. It is rather an exemplification of who God is."

Holding to a robust understanding of God's deep incarnational presence cannot be overstated. Periodically, during our Sunday worship gatherings, I will remind the congregation that my role as pastor is not as much to convince them that I hear from God, but rather, to remind them that they can and do hear from God. This ability to experience the presence and love of God, is surely not limited to time together during Sunday worship, nor the traditional acts of piety we deem sacred (such as prayer and engagement with Scripture) but can be experienced in all our relationships, in nature, in pop culture and even in the mundane monotony of everyday life.

Ad Astra: To the Stars

Perhaps no popular culture experience in recent years has resonated as deeply with me as it relates to the journey of religious deconstruction and reconstruction than the 2019 film Ad Astra. Directed by James Gray and starring Brad Pitt, the film uses the sci-fi genre as a beautiful backdrop to tell a story of an interstellar journey of our protagonist, astronaut Roy McBride, as he travels across our solar system in an effort to save humanity from impending destruction.

At the beginning of the film, we learn that Roy (Pitt) is the son of hero space traveler Clifford McBride, the first astronaut to ever lead a manned mission to the outer reaches of our galaxy. Thought to be long dead while leading the Lima Project as far as Neptune, Roy discovers that his father is not only alive, but is responsible for the continuous electromagnetic pulses threatening the destruction of earth and all of humanity.

As Roy processes this news and embarks on a journey across the galaxy, he discovers horrendous revelations about his valorized father, causing him to become deeply unsettled. Through a series of voiceovers throughout Roy's journey, we get a glimpse at his inner struggle. At one point, Roy remarks, "I don't know if I hope to find him or finally be free of him" and in the penultimate scene, after being reunited with his father, Roy is forced to let go of his father, who has long abandoned him and his mother, prioritizing his mission of discovering intelligent life beyond the stars over investing in the relationships entrusted to him. It's a deeply moving climax in a film which serves as a meditative metaphor for the long and arduous journey of letting go of long-held views of God, which need to be abandoned and healed from.

The film is beautifully bookended by parallel scenes where Roy undergoes regular mandatory psychological evaluations as part of his SpaceCom vocation. At the beginning of the film, the camera is intentionally somewhat out of focus. Roy's demeanor is one of stoicism and pragmatism, lacking authentic human connection. In the final scene, having journeyed across the galaxy and back, enduring hardship, isolation and psychological distress, Roy gives a final stirring psychological evaluation, with both the camera and his life now in much greater focus. The film and the final monologue sum up the beauty of open and relational theology, with a focus on the immanent presence of God and an attentiveness to nurturing authentic loving relationships around us. It serves both as a mirror to the inner life of those undergoing the journey of religious deconstruction, as well as an invitation to preaching which sensitively and empathetically tends to the wounds and needs of those yearning for a more Christlike God and beautiful faith.

"I'm active and engaged. I'm aware of my surroundings and those in my immediate sphere. I'm attentive. I am focused on the essential to the exclusion of all else. I'm unsure of the future, but I'm not concerned. I will rely on those closest to me, and I will share their burdens as they share mine. I will live and love."

Jason Tripp lives in Sudbury, Ontario, where he serves as a pastor and chaplain. He holds an M.Div. from Tyndale Seminary and is working towards his Doctor of Theology Degree in Open and Relational Theology at Northwind Theological Seminary. As a basketball enthusiast and cinephile, he enjoys coaching, refereeing and playing basketball, as well as regular pilgrimages to local movie theaters.

Speaking of God, Death, and Dying

TRACY L. TUCKER

Open and Relational language gives voice to a healthier understanding and more clinically satisfying encounter with people who are grieving.

Half of a decade into my tenure as a hospice chaplain, I discovered what I should have observed already: a necessary tool for the work of supporting the patients I serve was missing. All of the required units of Clinical Pastoral Education (CPE) were behind me now. The requisite clinical hours were completed, and the paperwork was submitted in impressive fashion (at least that is how I remember it). The result was that I then passed the boards and was granted my Board Certification as a Chaplain (BCC). Impressed? I hope not. I still found myself reaching out for something that eluded my clinical grasp.

Leaping forward: I remember sitting in a swing under a tree in the front yard of the house where my wife had grown up. We were visiting her mother. The weather was nice in Tennessee with lots of sun and the wind wisping slightly, the fear of COVID-19 abated for the moment. It was a great place to read the book I had brought from home. As I read, the book began to grab my soul. Sitting in that moment with tears beginning to roll down my cheeks, I remember whispering the words "That's it. That's what I've been looking for." In my hands sat Thomas Jay Oord's, *The Uncontrolling Love of God: An Open and Relational Account of Providence*.

Before returning to the house to rejoin my extended family, I surfed Facebook and quickly located Professor Tom's email address. Trying not to sound as excited as I was, I fired off an email and hoped that sometime in the future I might receive a reply. It didn't take long, and we were in an ongoing dialogue that continues to this day. In my note to Tom, who has become a friend and mentor, I explained that reading through his work I had found something that I have been searching for: language. I had a lot of thinking and learning to do, but inadvertently had bumped into the one key tool I did not already possess: language for communicating what I believe about God, and concepts like death, dying, fate, and love. Open and Relational Theology (ORT) opens for me a channel of expression to say what I'm feeling in my inclinations about God and God's activity in the universe and in the human spirit and experience.

The established parameters of this essay will not allow me to explore in any depth all that I might say about what my newly found language has afforded me. But by highlighting three points of ORT, perhaps I can communicate enough to stir the interest of those reading this essay. We shall consider essential love, freedom, and foreknowledge.

God is First and Essentially Loving

John, the epistle writer, states it clearly this way "God is love" (1 John 4:8). The entire cadence of the New Testament moves to the heartbeat of God expressing love for all: in the life, teachings, and passion of Jesus; and in the development of the church. Even the final sermon where John the revelator imagines God through Jesus as the ultimate portrayal of divine, limitless compassion always reaching out, optimistically inviting all who will to embrace his love. God is love, and for those who lean toward ORT, love is necessarily the starting point of any understanding of God.

I recall at one point in my development I tended to start with God as sovereign, as large and in charge of all things. I felt safe with that point of view. Who wouldn't? If the right person is in charge, calling the shots and possessing the power to control, then the right things will certainly happen, and justice will prevail.

However, that doesn't, and didn't, work for very long. Even as I write this essay, a deadly war is raging between the Palestinians and their Israeli neighbors where families are being brutally destroyed and lives are being snuffed out. In response, Israel, instead of living into the grace of the God of their ancestry, is choosing to retaliate at an accelerated rate to prove they cannot be taken advantage of. Somehow, this simply doesn't sound like a world controlled by a sovereign God of love.

God, as imagined in ORT, is identified by love that is pure—not enabling, but empowering. The God of uncontrolling love is not free to impose a divine will or "plan" upon any part of creation. God values diversity and engages it in the good work of moving all of life toward a sense of well-being and universal peace. This is the essential love of God at work.

In the world of hospice where I spend the bulk of my time, people are looking for peace and well-being, although some have interesting ways of talking about such. The language one employs in the face of loss conveys a great deal about that person's view of God and the relationship God has with the world. I hear it frequently in the whispers of grief and the quietness of unresolved pain. “Where is the God who is supposed to be taking care of things?” “Why is God putting me though this?” “Is God really trying to teach me something in this?”

Sometimes a family member trying to find meaning in the meaninglessness of loss and death gives expression to that loss in thunderous ways, “Why would God let my brother die like this?” or “I don’t get how this could be part of some divine plan!” or “I don’t want anything to do with a god who would let someone suffer so much.” Surely God is in control and has the power to act on that control and surely God could somehow stop the suffering. Couldn’t he?

For ORT thinkers, the response is “no,” God’s love is never controlling and although God is always working toward influencing and prompting creation toward well-being, God’s essential, uncontrolling love simply can’t unilaterally stop evil, intentional or natural. In another of Tom Oord’s books aptly titled, *God Can’t*, he wrote,

> The God capable of control is at least partly to blame for the evils we’ve endured.
> He could have stopped them single-handedly.
> The God who allows evil is guilty.
> A guilty person, by definition, isn’t perfectly good.

I very often hear persons at the bedside of a dying patient use any one of the variations of the statement, “Well, this is part of God’s plan.” Watching my own mother’s journey through the haze of dementia, I found it insulting to hear people speak as though God had some purpose being lived out in the loss of my beloved mother’s personhood. God did not bring about that condition, nor was it part of some plan. And, Hell No! GOD WAS NOT USING THIS TO TEACH SOMEONE A LESSON!!!

God is a God of love and if God was able to single-handedly prevent evil in any form, the God I know, the God of essential love, would do it. God does, however, enlist people to cooperate in the good work of bringing about the end of suffering and evil. Teresa of Avila stated it much better than I:

> Christ has no body now but yours. No hands, no feet on earth but yours. Yours are the eyes through which he looks compassion on this world. Yours are the feet with which he walks to do good. Yours are the hands through which he blesses all the world. Yours are the hands, yours are the feet, yours are the eyes, you are his body. Christ has no body now on earth but yours (Catholic-Link.org).

I have the glorious privilege of working alongside tireless hospice care providers. They are the hands and feet through which God works to bring about healing of heart and spirit. They are the testimony to God's loving presence in the face of pain.

One final thought about the essential loving nature of God is that this loving nature is not justice driven. Rather, many who embrace ORT see God as eternally optimistic that all will ultimately embrace God's loving aim and choose to participate. Most Open and Relational thinkers agree that there really is no judgement leading to an eternal punishment. Persons grieving their loved ones have found solace in that.

Human Freedom is a Thing

Because God cannot control anything unilaterally, it makes sense then to conclude that freedom of human will and action is part of the divine equation. This presents a quagmire for us, because while it means we can choose in large part our own destiny. It also means that necessarily we are responsible for the consequences of those choices. Human freedom is the result, though, of the creative energy of an essentially loving God who does not control.

A person whose lifestyle is marked by the abuse of their body may likely become one of my patients at an early age as a result. A person who chooses to act irresponsibly behind the wheel of a fast-moving vehicle may face the unfortunate reality of injury or death of another or themselves. These are not occasioned by some divine oversight, regardless of the language of insurance companies as "an act of God." Human free will is just that, a choice made by some member of the human race, often apart from the purposes of God.

A patient's wife in a hospice room may wonder why her husband is suffering from alcoholic liver cirrhosis and why God is allowing it. "Why didn't God stop him from drinking and making the past forty years so difficult and creating division within the family?" Just as an essentially loving God cannot control evil, neither can God violate human freedom, which would be another form of control.

But Does God Really Know What's Up?

This is a particularly difficult point for me. I'd prefer to conclude that God foreknows all that will happen before it happens so that in God's perfect timing and loving consideration, I might avoid some of the challenges of living in a world where people regularly choose to hurt other people, pandemics catch us off guard, and emotionally charged crowds suddenly become violent at the outcome of a sports event. But that is not how it works.

I've observed as patients frequently operate from an assumption that "God knew about this long ago. Nothing catches God by surprise." While some of that might be true, ORT suggests that God does not, in fact, possess a crystal ball or have absolute, certain foreknowledge. The fact of human free will precludes such foreknowledge. If I have free will, then I can choose, even at the last minute, a direction that I previously did not even anticipate. Certainly, God, who knows all that can be known, is able to recognize potential outcomes and make predictions based upon prior decisions. However, it is inconsistent with human free will for God to know with absolute certainty the future which is affected by human decision.

Stated plainly, if God foreknew one hundred years ago that I would choose a ham sandwich for lunch today, that implies making that sandwich today was already part of a pre-written history. I will put ham between slices of bread. God knew it to be so and therefore I had no choice. In fact, the choice was made before I was even born. There is no free will in that. God's essential love nature is not controlling and does not have absolute foreknowledge. How could God know with absolute certainty that my loved one would die when, where, and how they did, given the reality of free will? And how can an essentially loving God be the source of that particular death?

Conclusion

The freedom and language of ORT has gifted me with a way of speaking into the experiences of and even the pain of hurting people. With full integrity, I will not attempt to "correct" someone else's thinking. That would not be loving. I will, however, respond to the aching heart cry of a person in grief with the hopefulness of an uncontrolling God who is at all times present in the pain. Because God is not controlling, God is not the author of pain. Because humans are free to choose, we are able to choose well and can be assured that God is doing all that can be done to help us choose well. We don't need to be concerned that what happens has been predetermined. There is always hope for a better day. The language of ORT allows us to say these things with credibility, consistency, and purpose.

Tracy L. Tucker currently serves as a Chaplain for Community Hospice and Palliative Care in Jacksonville, Florida, following 30 years in full-time parish ministry. He earned his M.Div. from Nazarene Theological Seminary and is currently working on his DThM through Northwind Theological Seminary. Tracy is a Board Certified Chaplain through the Association of Professional Chaplains and has a Certification in Thanatology through the Association for Death Education and Counseling.

Effective Evangelism in the Key of Process Theology

JOHN WESSELS

Evangelism becomes effective and faithful in fresh and relevant ways when it embraces the process theology perspective.

Imagine

Imagine church events where people are coming to faith through evangelistic messages proclaimed from a process theology perspective! I am always striving for this nowadays and I am delighted that there has been some fruitfulness. I tell you the story of how I got here and why I think this is an important place to be.

The Process Theology Seed is Sown

I am a South African, 58 years old and have been in full-time ministry here since I was 23. I have been serving in Trinity Methodist Church, Johannesburg, for the past 10 years. I was briefly introduced to process theology during my mid-twenties when studying at Rhodes University in Grahamstown, a university in a historically colonial frontier town in South Africa. It was in the early 1990s and South Africa was on the verge of democracy. I remember being taught that God is at work in every dimension of existence, ensuring progress in life. In writing that sentence, I intentionally did not go back to my notes from all those years ago to check if that was exactly what we were taught—rather I am expressing the memory I have carried of that lesson.

I do not think that Alfred North Whitehead was mentioned in this introduction—rather it was process theology from the natural sciences perspective of Pierre Teilhard de Chardin. As an aside, in South Africa process theology has a very small following, but where it is known, it seems that de Chardin is more widely recognized than Whitehead.

When I heard that introduction to process theology, I remember saying to myself "I like that" and "I don't want to forget that". So, I stored it in the back of my mind in a file marked 'I may need this one day'.

Missing Jesus! Finding the Shepherd I had Lost

It was a somewhat different perspective that really made the lights come on for me at university. Our education was influenced by liberation theology and within that perspective we were asked to read Albert Nolan's *Jesus before Christianity*. That book, accompanied by many of the other things we were learning, suddenly made an impact on me.

I still remember the moment when I was walking up the stairs in the Divinity department when suddenly within, a whole new world opened to me. It was a sudden breakthrough of insight. It felt like a rush of light into me and with it, a whole host of possibilities lit up within me that I had not even seen before. Ever since then, I have looked back on that moment as my "burning bush" experience.

Until that moment, my relationship with Jesus was defined as "spiritual" in a way that excluded all other dimensions of life. In that moment of revelation, I experienced within myself a whole world of doors open up through which Jesus could enter and have lifesaving significance for individuals and society. Suddenly, I saw that Jesus and his kingdom have spiritual, relational, political, social, cultural, personal, psychological, religious, ecological, earthly, heavenly, economic, local, global, and even cosmic significance.

That moment released an enormous amount of energy and inspiration within me—I went into ordained ministry with an unrelenting passion to offer the attraction of Jesus and his kingdom vision. Eventually, after 20 years, I published my disciple-making teaching material in a comprehensive 472 page book with the title *Missing Jesus? Finding the Shepherd we Lost.* As I write this essay, I have just completed a series of 25 videos of me teaching the content of the book.

COVID!

COVID hit five months after I published my book—which was disastrous for sales, but it did drive me to go back to that file in the back of my mind marked "I may need this one day".

As I led the congregation through the COVID-19 storm, I realized that my theological paradigm was insufficient to make sense of God's role in the pandemic. I was dissatisfied with the theological perspectives I was hearing, but I did not have a viewpoint from which I could offer anything better.

You may remember that theological reflection fell into three categories: retributionists—God had angrily sent the virus to punish the ungodliness of the world; restorationists—God has nothing to do with causing the virus but God will use the virus to restore God's kingdom; integrationists—not bothered with the question of God's role or any judgement on humanity, rather focused on integrating efforts of role players in responding to the virus.

It seemed to me that we were being offered options of a monstrous god or deism or atheism/agnosticism. In both deism and the monstrous idea, god is essentially outside of the world—either sending harm from the safe distance of heaven or uninvolved. These options did not seem to me to honor the reality of God. Nor did those options seem to acknowledge our responsibility for our environmental recklessness, nor God's role in the many warning signs we had been ignoring.

I believed in a much more intimate understanding of God's role in the world, whilst at the same time I did not believe that God would unilaterally initiate a deadly virus to punish this world. However, I had no way of coherently articulating this. I was aware I needed a new metaphysical perspective to understand God's relationship with the world.

Thanks to my introduction to process theology at university, I knew that this was where I had to go for a new metaphysics. I started a self-study journey that continues today. I bought and read introduction books, listened to podcasts, and watched YouTube videos. Most resources were from people trained at Claremont School of Theology and so I was now exploring process theology from the heritage of Whitehead's process philosophy.

The questions that COVID evoked have not been easy to answer—but I am grateful for how much I am learning. My worldview has grown, and I am in deep amazement of God's ongoing creating of a deeply interwoven relational process attracting us to greater wholes. I now appreciate God is "the fellow sufferer who understands" (Whitehead). Although God knew that zoonotic viruses could infect humanity, God did not know that COVID was coming and certainly never sent it—rather God is at work in our response injecting possibilities and persuasion into all creatures all the time so that we may become a clearer expression of God's loving genius.

Discussing Life's Big Questions

As this new process theology stream grew, it soon flowed into the river of my vocation of offering the attraction of Jesus and his kingdom vision. A fast-flowing rapid developed in the middle of this river energized by both evangelism and process theology. I had a strong heart for evangelism and disciple making and now I wanted to use process theology to extend that work.

I developed a six-week evangelistic journey in which I gave my faith response to big questions of life such as: "Does God exist?"; "What is the meaning of life?"; "Why is the world so broken and evil?"; "What is hope and is there any?"; "Is Jesus important?"; "Why be a Christian?". In my talk about God's existence, I included a section on "The god not worth believing in" in which I make it clear that I am not asserting the existence of a god who is an abstraction, nor a god who is all-powerful and in control, nor a god of religion.

I have called this journey "Table Talk—Discussing Life's Big Questions." We put people into small groups with facilitators so that each person can share their views on these questions and discuss my presentation. We encourage the members of our congregation to bring non-church-going friends, neighbors, colleagues, and family to join them on the journey. Each week, I give participants the opportunity of following me in prayer to enter relationship with Jesus. I am happy to say that many participants do take that step with me. There is always a portion of the group who say that they were about to give up on the Christian faith before doing the "Table Talk" journey, but have now had their faith restored.

I have also developed a talk "Why is Evolution an essential truth for Christians, Atheists and Agnostics." I presented this talk at a special "Table Talk" event at a restaurant. It was very stimulating and popular.

Picture of God

I never say "The process theology perspective is ….", rather I teach, preach, and pastor from that perspective without attaching a label. Some of the highlights of this in our sermon series have been:

- Drawing your Picture of God: in which I helped people with questions like, "Is God in control," "How does God act in the world," and "What is the Cosmic Christ.".
- The Names of God: one of the names was "El Shaddai" in which I made a strong case against the English translation "Almighty" for that name.
- The Slow Work of God: linking Teilhard's poem of that name with the gradual development of people in John's Gospel.

- Holy Courage—Embracing the Adventure of Discipleship: a series for Lent and Easter based on Bruce Epperly's Holy Adventure: 41 days of Audacious Living. I emphasized that the Bible shows that God invites us to be partners in healing the world and that this requires courage because there remains uncertainty and open-endedness about the future.
- Prayer—It looks like we are doing nothing but …: in which I presented prayer as active engagement in God's work in the world.

I am currently preaching from the lectionary and here I have developed a reading plan for the year so that we as a congregation can spend time with the readings before each Sunday. In this reading plan, I suggest some online resources that I find helpful in reflecting on the readings. These include "processandfaith.org" and Bruce Epperly's "Living a Holy Adventure."

I thoroughly enjoyed the 15-week lectionary journey through the book of Romans during 2023. I used the John B. Cobb and David J. Lull commentary *Romans*, and this set us free from many of the misunderstandings and misrepresentations of Paul's monumental book. One misunderstanding is drawing too sharp of a contrast between faith and works. Paul mostly sees "faith" as "faithfulness." It is better to understand Paul as describing a faith that works—and so I gave the lectionary journey the title "Faith that Works."

In preaching, teaching, leading, and pastoring, we are dealing with people's picture of God all the time and it is enormously helpful to be doing this work from a process and relational perspective. I am constantly helping people to understand the nature of God's power—that it is the power of love, which is the greatest power; it is not controlling but rather persuasive. In this, I have often used Thomas Jay Oord's wonderful word *amipotent* (the power of love) and I believe I was one of the first preachers to do a sermon on it soon after he published it in an ORT Short podcast in September 2021.

I have come to speak of the wonderful phrase from Sheri Kling "The Whole-making Nearness of God" as a synonym for the Holy Spirit. Sheri has written a wonderful song of this name, and our choir has learned and presented that song.

Conclusion

I am enjoying an exciting space of fruitfulness and meaning in ministry from blending my evangelistic heart with my developing process theology mind.

John Wessels is an ordained minister in the Methodist Church of Southern Africa and is the author of a comprehensive disciple-making resource "Missing Jesus? Finding the Shepherd we Lost." Visit www.missingjesus.net He enjoys long-distance trail running and any time he can get in the mountains. John is married to Angela and they have two children, Ashlynn and Luke.

Teaching ORT—Yikes!

DEANNA M. YOUNG

Teaching Open and Relational Theology is risky business—but worth the risk.

Open and Relational Theology (ORT) is foreign to so many people and introducing this theology can be risky business. In my opinion, it is worth the risk of alienating a few so that many can experience the freedom and peace that this theology brings to the understanding of the formerly perplexed. I say, "formerly perplexed" because so many try to make sense of a God of Love that would "cause" or "allow" suffering in this world. To affirm that there is a dissonance helps the hearer to prepare for a potential solution to this problem.

To be sure, there are some who do not acknowledge the dissonance because their theology is such that anything that is attributed to God in scripture—whether it is violence, destruction, or condemnation—is considered right and good because it is of God. This traditional understanding of God is foundational and embedded into their understanding. Challenging the foundation of their faith, in my experience, may feel like a personal attack to them. Before we ever begin to share ORT, we must be aware of the objections that might be offered and be ready to address them.

I'm writing to share my experience of teaching ORT in an established United Methodist Church. Sharing ORT should be done in such a way that it is not perceived as a differing religion, but instead, a different way of thinking about God. If one is to teach ORT, a few guidelines might be helpful.

First, a relationship of trust should already exist. In other words, I would never try to teach this theology to a congregation that I am unfamiliar with or one with which I have not been in relationship. It is imperative to understand the theological mindset which already exists in the people.

Next, I would begin in the classroom with small groups. Create an atmosphere of discovery where questions are encouraged and discussion welcomed. As one student stated, "conversation not confrontation" was expected in class.

I always tell my class members that I will not tell them what to believe. Instead, I will tell them what I believe. Then, I will help them think theologically for themselves and figure out what they believe and how to articulate it.

Be willing to wonder with the people. Be willing to explore and hear their thoughts. Be ready to explain the reasoning behind your thoughts. And be ready for defensive criticism. Allow the criticism to sit in the room before you jump in with a response. Often, others will have a response to that criticism. Ultimately, you can agree or disagree but always allow each person their own opinion. Never get defensive in response to criticism.

With these guidelines in mind, I will write about my experience teaching my book, *Unblaming God: Interpreting the Old Testament Through the Lens of Jesus Christ,* in two classes for approximately 50 people in total. These people have heard me preach over the years and my sermons always point to my belief that God is Love.

I began these classes asking why the participants were taking this class and what were their "why" questions of God. Following are some of the questions presented:

1. God, why are you punishing me?
2. God, why am I still here?
3. God, why did my daughter die first?
4. God, why did you cause my baby to be stillborn?
5. God, why did you give me cancer?
6. God, why didn't you heal me?
7. God, why are people born with disabilities?
8. God, why do you still love us?
9. God, why did I get my miracle, but the other didn't?
10. God, why do you ignore me?
11. God, why do you allow things to happen?

After I recorded all the questions, I pointed out that most of these "why" questions imply that the ones asking the questions believe God is in control.

Next, I divided the whiteboard into two sections: "God is" on one side and "Jesus is" on the other. First, I invited the class to tell me how they would complete the "God is" statement. Of course, I got all the typical classical descriptions, including omnipotent, omnipresent, omniscient, immutable, impassible, and timeless as well as love, mighty, creator, good, forgiving and many other positive adjectives. They also said vengeful, demanding, holds a grudge, and angry.

Then, we moved on to the "Jesus is" statement. All of the responses were positive such as: savior, teacher, love, kind, forgiving, patient, friend, bold, firm, gentle, radical, courageous, generous, obedient, omniscient, healer, servant, open, miracle worker, scholar, riddler, human, divine, table flipper, son of man, carpenter, humble, compassionate, redeemer, understanding, holy, relational, The Word, eternal, full of grace, and truth.

There was some crossover between the two. However, I pointed out how different the descriptions were and asked "Why?" Since Jesus is God made flesh, shouldn't they be the same?

I asked, "How many of you would agree with the statement that God is Love?" Everyone agreed. I pointed out that we can see love in the description of Jesus without fail. However, there were characteristics in the "God is" category that did not depict a loving God.

I then asked how they would define love. Usually, when I ask this question, the participants use 1 Corinthians 13:4-8 to describe love. "Love is patient, love is kind. It does not envy, it does not boast, it is not proud. It does not dishonor others, it is not self-seeking, it is not easily angered, it keeps no record of wrongs. Love does not delight in evil but rejoices with the truth. It always protects, always trusts, always hopes, always perseveres. Love never fails." I asked if this definition of love applied to the description of God they gave. The answer was no.

I defined the ORT definition of love which is "love always promotes the well-being of God's creatures and creation." I worked from this definition throughout teaching the book.

Next, we looked at all the classical theological descriptions of God—omnipotent, omniscient, immutable, impassible, and timeless. We defined them as they are typically used and reframed them using ORT. As we moved on throughout the book, we applied these reframed definitions to the Old Testament stories covered.

Another critical step in this process is teaching about God's essential kenosis and that everything God has done, is doing, and will do emanates from God's love. God cannot do anything that is contrary to that love. This love means that God does not control and will not overpower our free will, power, and agency.

Once this foundation had been established, I then proceeded to teach my book. In the first two chapters of the book, I continue to lay the foundation of ORT and explain why it matters not only in our lives but also in the interpretation of scripture.

Then we worked our way through four disturbing stories in the Old Testament that portray God as a violent, manipulative dictator. Using what had been learned about ORT and God's love, we pointed out where the stories were inconsistent with our new understanding. Then, we reframed each story using ORT. We discussed the new interpretation, the value and relevance of the story for us today.

What I noticed during the classes was that some participants began reframing on their own as they asked about possible interpretations of other Old Testament stories. In the beginning of the class, I told them I wanted each of them to figure out what they believe, why, and how to articulate their belief. This began to happen in these classes—success!

As we concluded the book and class, I asked participants to provide feedback on both. Here are a few of the responses:

"It makes you think and wonder."

"It opens your mind. May open your mind to other things."

"It gave me peace."

"It's been a mind expanding for me."

"It takes courage to consider."

"Your book was quite a weight off of my shoulders! It is very helpful to look at the bible in a less literal way, and to view God as loving, and not punishing or causing terrible things to happen to certain people."

"Deanna's book demystifies the contradictions of God's character in the Old Testament and shows us how God is always love. She walks through several stories of the Old Testament and breaks them down. She brings a historical, practical, and faith-based approach to her theology always remembering that if it doesn't read like God is love, then there's something else going on in the text. I left the book feeing comforted, empowered, and hopeful. Read it on your own, read it in a group; read it, ask the big questions, and watch your faith strengthen."

"I absolutely adored this book. If you're even remotely on the fence about reading it, give it a go. The book is rooted on the foundation of love and may have a huge impact on your personal relationship with God—specifically on how you give and receive love to God and, therefore, yourself and others. If more people knew, believed, and practiced the theology of this book, our world would look, and feel, drastically different."

"You've helped me find my way and what I believe without being told what to believe and for that I'm eternally grateful. My response to someone who's contemplating reading your book would be, allow your heart and your mind to be open to a God of love. Allow yourself to question, for no one has all the answers, but this is a good place to start."

To be sure, not everyone was in total agreement with ORT. I would say out of the 50, one person was oppositional to ORT. Even so, his questions and comments fostered great discussion around the points that the literalist would present. As stated earlier, we must allow space for these discussions—conversation but not confrontation.

In the end, the people who took the classes want more of studies like this. Two students are beginning a Sunday school class that will only study ORT books. The seed has been planted. I can't wait to see it grow.

Deanna M. Young is an Elder in the United Methodist Church. She earned her doctorate from Northwind Seminary in Open and Relational Theology and her Master of Divinity degree from Perkins School of Theology at SMU. Young has authored two books: *Unblaming God: Interpreting the Old Testament Through the Lens of Jesus Christ* and *Connecting the Dots: Connecting Everyday Life Experiences to Spiritual Truths.*

Worship Elements Expressing Open, Relational, and Process Theologies

For additional examples of worship elements from a process-relational perspective, see the essays "Praying and Singing in the Language of Love by Gayle Hansen Browne, page 289, and "Becoming Church" by Jorge Lockward and Katie Reimer, page 355.

Worship in Process: An Offering of Prayers and Hymns

JOHN BALLENGER

When I received the invitation to contribute to this book, it intrigued me. The editors expressed the desire to balance sermons and essays with elements of worship informed by process-relational theology. So, I am grateful for the opportunity to offer these prayers and hymn lyrics as models for incorporating the hopes, values, and affirmations of this perspective in worship. All prayer texts and hymn lyrics are used by permission of John Ballenger.

Prayers for the Church

God, Your church throughout its history has
and continues to let You down.
But it is also full of the most wonderful people on earth I know.
It is sometimes small-minded,
but it is also home to some of the most creative geniuses
the world has ever known.
Sometimes cruel, also nurturing some of the great kindnesses.
Sometimes judgmental and exclusive,
sometimes modeling grace and inclusiveness.
Your church often lets You down
often surprises the world with a glimpse of and into You—
which is to say, it's just like the people who make it up.
And so we know You love Your church—
for those moments when we get it—get You,
and in those moments we fall short.

We grieve those who reject You because of us.
We confess to being an impediment to faith for far too many—
even as we celebrate those who have found You in and through us.
May we humbly never assume ourselves to be any better than we are—
any better than anyone else.
May we not project self-righteousness or arrogance.
May we focus on doing more and more of what is best
and less and less of what is not.
May we listen more than we proclaim
and let our proclamation flow from our listening to You.
May we hold the highest of expectations
but in kindness with the assurance of love.
May we confront cruelty, meanness, lies, injustice—
with the kindness and truth, the wonder and beauty
of the faithful life we know.
May we not seek and plan to impose on others,
but commit to serve others—
even others we don't understand or even like.
This we pray in Jesus' name, amen.

Our God, we pray for Your church—
for the ways it has undermined itself in our world
by being too much like the world and not enough like You.
We remind ourselves, though, it's never too late—
that whenever we reclaim being like You—even some—just a little,
there is still the surprise
of amazing, wonderworking, transformative power to be found.

So remind us we are not here to give people answers,
but to live as witnesses to the importance of the best questions.
We are not here to impose our values and choices on others,
but to live as witnesses to the richness and wonder of life
shaped by the values we choose.
Remind us, then, that our challenge
is not a lack of power, but of conviction
and our dream not one of control, but of love.
Remind us that our model way of being
is not one of victory, but of commitment.

Amidst prayers for Your church, God, we pray for ours, too.
For those dreaming our future and for those working our present.
For those who are us and for those who need us.
For creativity and generosity and commitment.
For hope and peace and joy and love.
We pray for what we believe Woodbrook offers
so critical to our culture and community,
even as we pray for our own integrity and humility
and all that Woodbrook needs.
And all of this we pray in Jesus' name and presence, amen.

We begin a new year.
You have seen a lot of those, God!
Over two thousand within the life of the church.
Another two thousand years
within the brilliance of the Jewish stories of faith.
Four and a half billion years since the earth was formed.
You have seen so many new years,
seeing new has surely become old to You!
And yet, You continue making all things new.
You continue to offer new life—rebirth.
You continue to extend hope and name possibility.
May we, as those who follow You, cultivate the discipline of always asking,
what does it mean to love today—in our times—our circumstances?
May we embrace the newness that requires,
even as we claim the ancient continuity that grounds it—
the consistency that is God and good
amidst an ever-changing world.
We live in the uncertainty of how to do church
in the coming year and coming years.
We live with the grief of how much is different—
how much has changed—how much is challenging.
But we live in the uncertainties of what and how to do church
with the certainty of who we are as church—
a local community reflection
of the truth of God as best we understand that.
So whatever the year (and years) bring,

may we seek to ever be more of who we know God to be
(which always has to do with love, right? With justice—
accepting responsibility for the vulnerable—
stewarding our world toward hope in Jesus' name, amen.

God, daffodils have come.
They're not gone yet, but they're going.
Forsythia's popping. Tulips are showing.
The cherry blossoms in DC peaked last week.
We were down in the Carolinas this past week
and saw azaleas and dogwood, yellow jasmine,
a ruby falls red bud.
Spring is a burgeoning blooming chaos of growth and color ...,
and if the church is an angry or boring
monochromatic, monotone—
mono-anything, really,
we have fallen so far short of what we could be—
who we could be.
So fill us with different colors.
Singing different songs with rich harmonies.
With different shapes and sizes.
Offering different insights and making different affirmations.
Seeing Jesus and naming God in different ways
and enjoying and celebrating the differences.
Not afraid of anyone's truth,
but anticipating the growth
that only occurs when your own truth
is confronted by someone else's.
This we pray in a culture increasingly invested in conformity
and monochromatic, monotone
in the name of the colorful God of diversity,
amen.

When I think, my God, about what I want the church to be—
how I want the church to be known,
it's as a community of people telling a different story

and trying the best they can to live into that different story.
I would love the church to be thought of
as a place where people are loved—
where people are safe.
I want people not so much to be impressed
with a sanctuary that a church has,
as much as the sanctuary a church offers.
I want the church to be associated with justice and anti-racism.
I want the church to be associated with support for laws and policies
that protect our children—
and not making up support they don't need.
not "protecting" them from books and ideas
and people who are different and the truth of our own history,
but protecting them from guns and from hunger,
from ignorance, shortsightedness, and judgmental rejection.
I would love for the church to be identified with relentless creativity
and timely relevance.
I want people, when they think of church, to think well that's something that matters.
I want the church to be thought of as those seeking to be good stewards of creation,
working for peace, rejecting violence,
confronting selfishness and lies and those who exploit fear
and exploit others.
I'd love for the church to be a place where people know
you can ask big questions
not just where you're told the ultimate answer.
That's not so much how people see the church in our culture,
but it is how I would love for them to.
That's my hope—my goal—
a mission statement, I guess,
in Jesus' name, amen.

We pray for Your church, our God,
which too much seems to get backed up and locked into
defending You and details of stories about You—
with stating absolutely and explaining
rather than celebrating You and Your way of being
and asking and exploring and wondering

through both the sacred stories and our own lived experience.
As church, we too often come across as defensive, we know,
than as wonderfully (and non-anxiously) intrigued—
more invested in telling others what they need to do
because of how angry God is,
than figuring out together what it is we want to do
to express the love we find at the heart of it all.
So reorient us, God, toward wonder and joy
and ongoing discovery in Jesus' name, amen.

Hymns

Long, Our God, We've Been Waiting
My God, we are weary and troubled.
No hope in the chaos we find.
And life is too much overwhelming.
The cost of Your love we've declined.
Long, our God, we've been waiting
for life to be as You first dreamed,
but the fears of this world dim light divine,
and the faith that with wild hopes once teemed.

Our world is a mess of confusion,
and lies and crass violence reign,
and means become ends that are selfish,
and too many Christians are mean.
Long our God we've been waiting
for life to be as we have prayed,
but the world spins on and our lives don't change.
We deny in whose image we're made.

My God, it feels like we're regressing—
rejecting great love for control
and choosing to value more power,
thus turning our back on Your soul.
Long our God we've been waiting
for dreams that transcend status quo—

that invite us into a deeper life
in which always Your presence we know.

Our God how Your stories still gift us
keeps embers alive in the dust—
keeps our own eyes focused on living—
on signs of Your work we still trust.
Long our God, we'll keep waiting
for love that will overcome fear
for the faith and hope to sustain us now
that our lives to Your grace would adhere.

The meter is 9.8.9.8. with refrain and works with LEMMEL the tune to which we sing "Turn Your Eyes Upon Jesus."

Genesis Rings (Echoes Re-sound)
Genesis rings with what was heard,
echoing God's creative word:
"Now let there be!" (Let there be!)
And we see (and we see)
ever new possibility (ever new possibility).

Music resounds, yet sweet and strong
echoing angel's joyful song.
For born today (born today),
we still say (we still say),
God's truth's made flesh to show the way
(God's truth's made flesh to show the way).

The divine story echoes too,
ever attuned to what's most true—
that love will win (love will win)
and begin (and begin)
working redemption deep within
(working redemption deep within).

Truth does re-sound for ears that hear
echoing boldly far and near
"Now let there be!" (Let there be!)
And we see (and we see)
ever new possibility (ever new possibility).

The meter is 8.8.4.3.3.3.8.8. and works with JÜNGST,
the tune to which we sing "How Great Our Joy."

God Always Does Everything
The first and seventh verses are sung as that melody is written.
The second through the sixth verses, though, are transposed
into the minor key. If, when our major faith affirmations are confronted
by the minor keys of life, we faithfully, thoughtfully and honestly
sing into and through the discomfort, we can end up—can—
back with our major faith affirmation—revised probably, yet affirmed.

We doggedly sing the faith we confess,
that comfort does bring, and relevance profess.
In spite of the wondering, the doubting what's true,
it leaves us believing and hoping anew.

The living that's stress, the fear that clings tight,
dark days that depress, the absence of light,
we look to our faith, and we look for our God—
and find very little beyond the facade.

When death and dis-ease and tragedy strike,
and no one at all knows what you feel like,
no easy God answers do justify pain,
and simplistic thinking fails us as inane.

Traditional words no longer hold weight.
The stories we heard no meaning create.
The strong affirmations that once we believed—
the old celebrations now all seem naïve.

We no more accept the stories as told—
the idolatry of God in our mold.
Our distrust of power we honor as wise,
and knit back together a faith we revise.

We're facing the truth without any fear.
We no longer rue the view through our tears,
but honor our reason and science's claims
and thus find grounds legion to ponder God's aims.

God-with-us as love transforms every now—
not pow'r from above, but presence below.
God always does everything that God can do—
the song that we sing that we treasure as true.

The meter is 10.10.11.11. which works with LYONS,
the tune to which we sing "O Worship the King."

Hold Onto God Loosely

Land on God's names lightly. Learn to let them go.
If they're free to leave you, more of God they'll show.
Every name revealing veils as much, you see.
Hold onto God loosely. Love the mystery.
Hold onto God loosely with the words you choose.
Let the truth be bigger than language you use.

Breathe in God-talk gently. Let it fill you whole.
Yet to try and hold it will exact a toll.
Inhale inspiration. Exhale what grows stale.
Never knowing fully's the best way to fail.
Hold onto God loosely with the words you choose.
Let the truth be bigger than language you use.

Claim ideas gently. Let them share their truths.
Treat them as suggestions, never as hard proofs.
Walk with God but humbly, as the prophet says.
Sometimes knowing more means that you're claiming less.

Hold onto God loosely with the words you choose.
Let the truth be bigger than language you use.

The meter is 6.5.6.5.D. with Refrain and works with WYE VALLEY, the tune to which we sing "Like a River Glorious."

I Love to Ask the Questions

I love to ask the questions
of all that we assume—
amidst our declarations
revealing, we presume.
I love to ask the questions
that strengthen and renew
the energy of wonder
as all good questions do.
I love to ask the questions
that start investigations
into faith affirmations
of God and steadfast love.

I love to ask the questions
that deepen what we think—
provoking contemplations
so certainty might blink.
I love to keep retelling
the tales we think we know
that with more humble spirits
we'll see where all they go.
I love to ask the questions
that help with navigations
of farther explorations
of God and steadfast love.

I love to ask the questions
that widen into more,
exceeding limitations,
expanding what's adored,

reframing faith's traditions,
revising what's most true—
love asking congregations
to let the grace break through.
I love to ask the questions
that offer new directions
while making new connections
with God and steadfast love.

The meter is 7.6.7.6.D. with Refrain which works with HANKEY, the tune to which we sing "I Love to Tell the Story."

I, Wondering and Stumbling

I wonder as I wander out under the sky, *
why God in God's wisdom for our love does vie.
As poor ordinary people like you and like me, *
I wonder as I wander, * what in us God sees.

For Jesus came to us God's story to tell—
to draw truth and grace from that deepest of wells—
to heal us and love us, our great fears to quell,
that we might know God's hope and live it out well.

We grow into faith, and we grow into praise,
and more of God finds us if more's what we chase.
For less is an option, obscuring God's face,
but faith that is healthy needs always more space.

We grow into stories that have enough room
to call and surprise us within all our tombs—
to welcome and nurture in narrative wombs,
and guide us to morrow where more options loom.

I, wondering and stumbling, fall onto God's road—
for sinners and saints a most welcome abode.
It's narrow and hard, but the good seed is sowed—
a welcome extended as we all share the load.

From certainty's fold I will gratefully stray
into the embrace of the dawning new day.
To joyfully risk the unknown, I now pray,
for God will be with me as we find the way.

My heart, when it's true, is God's imprint on me.
To follow its leanings is God's will to see.
But twisted and warped by the world it can be.
My heart is my struggle for identity.

God's story, if I claim it, makes its claims on me.
My living must show it for integrity.
Lip service won't cut it, God's will for to see.
Discipleship does need my own honesty.

My story is built on foundations so strong—
on God's presence with us—with us all along.
Life's storms we will weather. With God we be long.
That is now my story; that is now my song.

** John Jacob Niles. The meter is irregular but works with APPALACHIAN CAROL, the tune to which we sing "I Wonder as I Wander."*

Restory Us Anew
When the story that was made flesh
is retold in careless ways,
as it's retold, can be untold
and to idols give God's praise.
Can You restore us our story
and restory us anew?
For we suffer the distortions
that the sacred truths undo.

When the militant aggressors
represent the prince of peace,
and the lies and overt cruelty
one who came as truth and grace—

when some claim God's justifying
all the sin of hierarchy
and the righteousness of violence,
we have lost integrity.

If we limit to the measure
of our minds the God of all,
what we value is our pleasure.
It's the story of the fall—
the denial of our trusting
the rejection of true hope
to the lesser we're adjusting
minimizing God's true scope.

Yes, we're shaped by what we're fearing,
what we want and what we see—
by the claim that we're adhering
to the way "it's supposed to be."
Yet the story as it's retold
still unfolds relentlessly
into grace and truth and wonder
in God's presence joyfully.

The meter is 8.7.8.7.D. and works with NETTLETON
the tune to which we sing "Come, Thou Fount of Every Blessing."

The Shock of Grace
The shock of life's most ruthless days
undoes what I believe,
and daunting questions it does raise
from which there's no reprieve.

Then in the midst of all that's hard,
when love's still manifest,
I find with faith for life I'm scarred
and do believe that's best.

The shock of grace exposing lies
with wonder, faith rebuilds—
with fewer answers, more surprise
as love trust risked fulfills.

The meter is 8.6.8.6.C.M. which works with NEW BRITAIN, the tune to which we sing "Amazing Grace."

We Only Know Transcendence
In what we see, creation all around us,
in what we love, in that which leaves us awed,
unique to all, the details that astound us,
that we will praise and joyfully applaud,
creation sings the music of what's real
that's blessed by God—that's blessed by God.
Creation sings the music of what's real:
it all is good. It is all good.

In words we read, the stories, songs and teachings,
the brilliance of imagination's gift,
what we name well the Holy Spirit's reachings,
that both inspire and do our souls uplift,
holy texts sing the music of what's true:
our God creates; our God redeems.
Holy texts sing the music of what's true:
our God hears us; our God is here.

In Word made flesh, the life and times of Jesus,
the shocking love that always grace extends,
the Word's own words still full of truths that seize us,
and testify that love the broken mends,
our history sings the music of our God
in what seems small that is immense.
Our history sings the music of our God:
the harmony of God with us.

In loves we know that make of life sweet wonder,
a lover's touch, a baby's wordless squeeze,
the friend of years, from who we can't be sundered,
the antidote to our world's great dis-ease,
for love will sing the music of what heals:
in what I know is all I need.
And love will sing the music of what heals:
there is someone who cares for me.

We only know transcendence immanently,
inferred from life in what all God reveals,
but with intent we see reverently,
and know the truth appearance can conceal.
Then my life sings the music that we know:
God is with us. God is with us.
And my life sings the music that we know:
Immanuel. Immanuel.

The meter is 11.10.11.10. with Refrain and works with O STORE GUD, the tune to which we sing "How Great Thou Art."

John Ballenger is a graduate of the University of Virginia (BA), the Southern Baptist Theological Seminary (M.Div.), and Brite Divinity School (D.Min.). John has served Woodbrook Baptist Church in Baltimore, Maryland for the past 20 years, having served churches in Georgia and Texas before that. He grew up a preacher's kid, a missionaries' kid (in central Europe), and has been described as a relentlessly creative lover of the Word—always reading, writing, thinking and rethinking. There's little he loves more than chasing an idea that might offer a different perspective.

Queers and Dears, Liturgies just for US

MONICA CORSARO

It's time for the faith community to be OUT. These liturgies are written unapologetically to celebrate being Queer, being in love with the Divine and the Divine being in love with us in an open relational way. To use doing Pride Month or anytime. Love is love after all, all the time.

Pride Month Liturgies

First Week of June

Call to Worship:

One: Welcome to this House of God, where all are loved and deemed fabulous in the name of the One. God says we are glad you are in the House at this moment and especially as we begin the season of Pride!

Many: We come from many places, many faith traditions, but it is in the seeking of loving together as family we all find unity.

One: Like Abraham and Sarah, Ruth and Naomi, Hagar and Ishmael before you, they were people who loved God, but also at times were pushed to the fringes, isolated alone and they struggled. God knew their struggle, God knows who have struggled and it might seem you will be asked the impossible, living your faith openly, but do not think of it that way. Look around. Others are with you, support you, love you, and are community with you, so let us together we say, **"we are family**."

Many: We admit we ponder: it might be too much.

One: Have no fear, authentic relationship takes risk but is so worth it: fly a flag, walk in a parade, say yes when asked to volunteer with your time in your faith community, welcome the stranger. All these acts, great and small, answer God's call. And God lets us know, God is with us.

Many: God is with us.

Centering Prayer:

Divine Love of the universe, you invite us to hold the needs of our siblings as dear to us as our own needs. Asking us to love our neighbors as ourselves, today, tomorrow, the next day and…in this moment, may we make it so.

Second Week of June

Call to Worship:

One: This is a day of new beginnings, where love is in abundance.

Many: We are grateful, like those called before us, to follow Jesus.

One: Jesus invited tax collectors, fishers, the forgotten, the haughty, the proud, the queer and dear. Jesus invites you on this day too, to be here to sing, to pray, to make a joyful noise unto the Divine!

Many: And while at times we may waiver or not feel confident, we can find comfort and confidence knowing the God of many names, will protect us, relishes in all of us, as we are, in our many identities, and colors of the rainbow, and calls it fabulous.

One: Have no fear, authentic relationship with each other and with God is all God hopes for, longs for. God calls you beloved and invites you to be in relationship as you are. And you are so good! God is with us.

Many: God is with us.

Centering Prayer:

Universal Love, thank you for sending us Jesus, our Teacher and Messiah, to model for us the way of love to ourselves, our neighbors- human and non-human, and to be grateful for the precious planet we call home. We offer these prayers of rainbow love on behalf of ourselves and our neighbors, on behalf of your creation and our fellow creatures.

Third Week of June

Call to Worship:

One: Welcome to this place, of grace and love, joy and dance. This moment will never come again, so be in this moment and welcome the non-binary God of love into your heart, mind, and body.

Many: We come before you with many thoughts in our minds, many intentions in our hearts. May we stop all the thoughts and just live into the intentions, and may our words say it is so.

One: Jesus teaches us, whatever may be on our minds, may it be expressed in words of truth, like the prophets who lived and spoke before us: Harvey Milk, Marsha P. Johnson, James Baldwin, Bayard Rustin, Frida Kahlo, Dr. Renee Richards, Lorraine Hainsbury. Let's take a moment of silence…you fill in the blank. Because of them, God continues to be with us in our open and vibrant community today.

One: Like the daughter, like the son, like the mom, the dad, the child, the grandparent, and evil systems of the world. All need God's macro and micro love. So together we can heal and can be healing agents for others. Let us come out of the faith closet and share the justice-seeking, intimate-loving God who is within, with us and everywhere! God is with us.

Many: God is with us.

Centering Prayer:

Creator God,
You call us to love passionately and compassionately. Loving God,
you call us to serve you with all that we that we have, with our inquiring mind,
our weary and energetic bodies and our fire spirit!
You teach us when loving your creation, our sisters, brothers and siblings then,
we are like you.
Open our hearts to the possibilities of what can be in this moment, and the
moments to come as we walk with each other on this journey of
universal and dynamic love.
May it be so.

Fourth Week of June

Call to Worship:

One: Welcome Fabulous! Beloved! Community of the Creating and Creative whom today we will call Ms. Divine.
Many: We come today, this month, every month and every year full of rainbow Pride. May we be able to share this love and pride for all those who do not know it yet, because when we say all are welcome to God's grace we mean ALL are welcome.

One: Fabulous ones, know that the Jesus of the past, the Christ of today and the God of tomorrow are part of the universal love that embraces you in this moment. All you have to do if you choose is to receive, receive, receive.
Many: We come and celebrate in this moment our authentic selves and let us say it again we are fabulous. We the queers and dears of Ms. Divine.

One: Love each other in confidence community. God is here, there, and everywhere. God is with us.
Many: God is with us.

Centering Prayer:

Creator and Creating God,
We celebrate our bodies. We celebrate our minds; we celebrate our orientations; we celebrate our identities. And because we know we are loved fully for who we are, we want to share this love with others. May it be so.
May we with all our body, mind, and spirit
love your creation, our sisters, brothers, and siblings.
May we keep our hearts open in compassion.
And may we be the healers in a hurting world
Amen and amen.

Monica Corsaro is the Senior Pastor at Fairview Community Church in Costa Mesa, California. The church is affiliated both with the American Baptist Church and the Congregational Church, United Church of Christ. Fairview Community has happily been open and affirming since the late 1990s. Monica received her D.Min. from Wesley Theological Seminary and her M.Div. from the Iliff School of Theology. Monica has been a lifelong activist: first chaplain ever to Planned Parenthood Federation of America, taking on the Boy Scouts of America for their anti LGBTQI polices and winning. Her writings have been in the form of op-ed pieces in *Time, Washington Post, Seattle Times*, just to name a few. You may spot her in Southern California trying to find that good cup of coffee.

Prayers

BETH HAYWARD

Giver of night visions,
You rouse us from sleep with invitations to unlikely places:
You lure us to the unfamiliar edge,
where our good senses would never have us travel.
We hear the echo of your whisper in sighs too deep for words.
We long to embrace your call, even to places that seem all wrong.
We ache to trust that a whisper might hold a call as convicting as a shout.
As we are startled from sleep with bold, unsettling plans:
May our grip on illusions be loosened,
may our settled ways be shaken,
may our path be forged in humble hospitality.
You rouse us from sleep,
relentless, persistent, giver of visions:
We open to your will and your way. Amen.

Into the heart of Divine Love we are called:
Called to: come and see, touch and know the wondrous blessing of your love.
The invitation is ordinary and awesome:
a soft whisper breathed into a tired heart,
an open hand gently waiting to be clasped.
With every breath we seek to open to the invitation.
Knowing that it leads to places:
unexpected, unsettling and uplifting beyond compare.
May we hear and know the promise of your love. Amen

Lured

This prayer calls us into the season of Lent. The wilderness is a key metaphor for this season and one that is particularly congruent with an open and relational interpretation.

We gather, seeking a path of Holy Wonder:
reluctant to enter the persuasive allurement of the wilderness,
fearful of the hard truths that may land at our feet.

To the wilderness we bring our secrets, our losses,
our temptations and frustrations.
To the wilderness we bring our tentative hopes,
our joyful praise and seeds that seek nourishment.
To the wilderness we bring all that we are
as we seek to be all that we are to become.

Even as we are pulled in all directions,
we find our centre in Love.
Even as we enter the deep,
we are buoyed by the embrace of Love.
Even as the way remains unclear, we are lured by Love.

May this wilderness path lead to the
places we are called to pursue. Amen.

Born this Night

This is a prayer for Christmas Eve, a bringing together of the particular of the birth of Jesus with the universal birth of the Christ into every moment of our living.

From the edge of deep darkness we arise:
opening to the radiant light of the mystery of this night.
Lured by the embrace of your divine love:
love incarnate, love in radiant human form,
love first made known in the birthing of a universe,
love fully realized in the birthing of a babe,
love fully possible in the birthing of our hearts.

The wonder of this night seeps into our souls
like light in winter darkness,
filling each one with a promise of divine possibility.
The love born this night lights our way and opens our hearts:
filling each one with abundant Bethlehem possibility.

Night Visions

This prayer is rooted in Acts 16:6-9, where Paul and his disciples are being called to travel from Asia to Europe for the first time. They didn't expect this calling. It's a moment of novelty and they, like us, must choose if they will respond to the lure of the Holy One.

Giver of night visions,
You rouse us from sleep with invitations to unlikely places:

You lure us to the unfamiliar edge,
where our good senses would never have us travel.
We hear the echo of your whisper in sighs too deep for words.
We long to embrace your call, even to places that seem all wrong.
We ache to trust that a whisper might hold a call as convicting as a shout.

As we are startled from sleep with bold, unsettling plans:
May our grip on illusions be loosened,
may our settled ways be shaken,
may our path be forged in humble hospitality.

You rouse us from sleep,
relentless, persistent, giver of visions:
We open to your will and your way. Amen.

Called

This prayer arises from the open and relational notion that each moment is one in which we are becoming. It seeks in invoke our receptivity to the divine lure present in each moment.

Into the heart of Divine Love we are called:
Called to: come and see, touch and know the wondrous blessing of your love.

The invitation is ordinary and awesome:
  a soft whisper breathed into a tired heart,
  an open hand gently waiting to be clasped.
With every breath we seek to open to the invitation.
Knowing that it leads to places:
  unexpected, unsettling and uplifting beyond compare.
May we hear and know the promise of your love. Amen

Beth Hayward is an ordained minister in the United Church of Canada. She has over twenty years of experience serving congregations. Beth writes and speaks about the practice of ministry from an open and relational perspective. She hosts a podcast called Souls in Soles, https://soulsinsoles.podbean.com/. You can connect with her through her website at http://bethhayward.org

Re-tuning Religion in a Process-Relational Key

SHERI D. KLING

The hymns we sing drive the theology we believe and share. Much of that theology no longer seems life-giving. Isn't it time for our religious hymnody to be "re-tuned" to a process-relational key?

Striking New Chords

Music is undeniably powerful.

I'll never forget my visit to an Alzheimer's facility years ago. As I sat as a volunteer in the common room where five or six patients were gathered, each seemed quite alone in their silent interior. Not one of these elders seemed conscious of the others nor of the images blinking from the corner television. But when the movie scene shifted to a church congregation singing a much-beloved hymn, one of the patients began heartily singing along. Just as quickly, when the music stopped, so did the woman's engagement with her surroundings. She retreated again to her inner world.

As a student at the Lutheran School of Theology at Chicago and the Claremont School of Theology, I was exposed to contemporary movements that have been flourishing for decades, including feminist theology, liberation theology and process-relational theology. All express ideas of God, humans, and the rest of creation that differ significantly from classical Christian theology, especially regarding the power of God, the equivalence of the *imago dei* in men and women, the present goodness of the world, the relationality of all things, and the radical incarnation of God or Christ in creation. Yet, if we asked the proverbial "man on the street," my guess is that a large percentage would be unaware of the way these ideas have shaped current theology since the early 20th century.

One reason for this, I believe, is that churchgoing Christians internalize the theology we sing. If our hymns continue to only express classical theology, then our church members will continue to only believe classical theology as well. In response to this reality, I've been moved as a theologian and songwriter to synthesize significant themes from process-relational, eco-feminist, and liberation theologies into hymns for congregational singing. Two of those are "We All Are Related" and "Love is Perfect Power."

We All are Related

Drawing from the work of such thinkers as Sallie McFague, Rosemary Radford Ruether, John Cobb, and Pierre Teilhard de Chardin, "We All are Related" begins with a science-inspired choral chant of our beginnings.

Fiery brilliance, cooling gas, condensing gravity
Atoms forming stars and carbon-fueled diversity
Earth with sky and oceans, molecules then multiply
Stardust is the mater of the cosmos and all life.

In these introductory lines, I have harmonized the vast scope of everything from the Big Bang to life on Earth. The final line nods toward John Polkinghorn's claim that "We are all made of the ashes of dead stars." This takes us directly into the first stanza, where I establish the central theme of interconnected relatedness throughout the matrix of life.

We all are related, woven as threads in earth's tapestry.
A kinship creation, depending on all in deep harmony.
Internally formed by each other, creative and free,
We all are related, wholly and actively.

If everything that exists began, primordially, in the earliest traces of hydrogen and has been constructed out of elements that were first birthed in stars, then we are all made up of the same *mater* (the Latin root of our words "matter," "mother," and "matrix") and born from that same "womb." We are therefore "related" and kin to each other. But we are not just *externally* related, according to Alfred North Whitehead's philosophy of organism. We are actually "internally formed" by our relationships of the past world. Yet, if it were only the past that formed us, life would be an endless "earworm" of the same melody repeated *ad nauseum*. No, in a world of novel becomings, process theology imagines God as calling us forward from a future of creative possibility.

The world is becoming, the future of God is luring us there.
Grace within chaos, the pow'r of the new, holiness bare.
The Singer is singing the Song we are yearning to share.
The world is becoming, process is everywhere.

While all of this "becoming" is a beautiful thing, for those of us in the midst of upheavals and changes, life can feel quite chaotic, random, and difficult. Yet it has always been my sense that there is a certain grace within the chaos of life because the Divine is at work at its very heart. When order trembles with something new, we witness an ineffable holiness that is raw and powerful. Yet, we can also tune our ears to hear the strains of the Song that the Divine Singer is singing, which I believe is the song that our hearts yearn to sing as well.

Sallie McFague describes creation as the body of God, and our third stanza relates this claim. Here God incarnates in *every* thing, not only in one human born in Bethlehem. Here, God is the *anima mundi*, or "soul of the world."

God is embodied, Word become flesh, in all that we see.
Deeply incarnate in every bird, in every tree.
In the heartbeat of billions of bodies just wanting to be.
God is embodied, soul of the world, breathing in me.

If God is embodied in all things, then all things have value. A reason Whitehead's philosophy is considered deeply ecological is because he recognizes all things at all levels as subjects with their own internal *experience* and inherent *value*.

All things have value, all the way up and all the way down.
God is redeeming the lowliest stone and the glorious crown.
Christ is the pattern in every atom around.
All things have value, whispering Spirit Sound.

Here I riff on the idea of humans as being thought of as the "crown of creation." Crowns often include jewels, minerals or "stones," that, though "lowly," possess their own beauty.

Seeing Christ as "the pattern in every atom around," is rooted in the Gospel of Thomas, where it's written that Jesus claimed to be the source of all things and found at the center of the split piece of wood or of every stone. Cobb, Griffin, and others have also described the *Logos* or Christ as a pattern of wholeness in all things. It follows, then, that God is interested in the redemption of all things, not just of humans. And all things whisper the same "Spirit Sound" that is sung by the Singer in the second stanza.

If technologically driven and consuming humans are ever to have more life-giving relationships with each other and the natural world, then we need to be liberated from the grip of dualism that sees matter as "dead," as merely stuff that gets pushed around by external forces. We need a new way of seeing, and this is what we cry out for in our final stanza.

We need liberation from seeing our world as dead-matter machines.
All creatures as neighbors, a healing embrace, so held we are free.
Entraining our rhythms to the heartbeat of Life consciously,
We all are related, in a world that's becoming,
Where God is embodied, And all things have value,
We are liberated, affirming the world we see.

Love is Perfect Power

Another hymn, "Love is Perfect Power," emerged from a class at Claremont with Dr. Frank Rogers on Compassion-based Methods of Social Healing and Reconciliation. In this composition, I weave in tones of people like Paulo Freire, Dr. Martin Luther King, Jr., and Frank Rogers, as well as process thinkers. Here we sing harmonies of communal transformation, nonviolent direct action, God's incarnational presence in the world, all beings' inherent relationality with God and each other, God's adventurous seeking of novelty as well as order, and, finally, that God acts in the world through love and persuasive power. I hope that in singing my growing catalog of process-friendly hymns, congregations can begin to internalize new ways of seeing the world.

I've intentionally set these themes to the traditional Irish tune of the beloved hymn, "The King of Love My Shepherd Is." Just as nonviolent action destabilizes societal expectations, singing about God's power as persuasive rather than coercive within the melody of a familiar hymn based on a caring yet kingly image of Jesus can subtly overturn expectations of that tune. We begin with a refrain set to an original tune that simply states the core idea.

Love is perfect, perfect power,
Perfect, perfect power is love.

A foundational idea in process-relational theology is that God's power is persuasive and not coercive. Whitehead writes that God "is the lure for feeling, the eternal urge of desire." Even within the world of corporate training, the idea that the most effective force in nature is a "pull" force rather than a "push" force has been taught by Kenneth Meyer, a former client and president and CEO of Pull Thinking.

As in the first hymn, our communal interconnectedness, inter-responsibility, and divine origins are stressed in the first verse of this one.

In community we all belong;
We are formed through incarnation.
So when the powers press the weak,
We call for liberation.

But we hold no Pollyannish views of the world. We know all too well how much suffering and destruction are born from the misuse of power. As Whitehead reminds us, "The glorification of power has broken more hearts than it has healed."

This world is full of fear and rage;
Domination steals all choices.
Compassion, boldness, hope, and strength
Empower silent voices.

The only way to counter such destructive forces is to empower those who have been silenced and to align ourselves with the direction in which God's Spirit lures us. That movement toward abundant life seeks the enjoyment of *all*.

God's Spirit moves toward abundant life,
So that all who live may flourish.
Injustice threatens everyone;
Rise up, so all are nourished.

Stanza four returns to the theme of persuasive love that John B. Cobb, Jr. and David Ray Griffin argue is the "divine way of doing things." In a world where entities have real freedom and creative agency, God relies on influence, not domination.

Our God does not dominate the world;
We choose each realization.
For perfect love seeks not control,
God's power is persuasion.

King reminded his readers that a preference for order was a "stumbling block" to freedom. Process theology agrees that novelty is as much a value of God as is stability. Imagination and adventure are necessarily part of the melody of life.

We now must turn from the ordered past,
Seeking God's imagination.
Divine adventure brings new risks,
for wholeness and salvation.

Again, it is King who recognizes that meeting hate with hate, force with force, and violence with violence only serves to increase evil. Therefore, nonviolent resistance uses the "creative weapon of love" to change the hearts of oppressors. To meet hate with love, we must nurture a compassionate presence within. Then, Rogers teaches, if we can engage compassionately with that which is aching within ourselves and others, we can begin to plant seeds of transformation.

So we stand and meet all force with love,
Tending seeds of transformation.
We bring the power that can redeem;
God's reconciliation.

God takes in everything the world does, redeems it, transforms it, and returns it with whatever value may be preserved. Therefore, in the kingdom of God, evil is not isolated from good; it is overcome by good.

Conclusion

If sung in congregations, will these two hymns speak to those who yearn for a Powerful Father God or Benevolent Cop in the Sky who will come with fire in the end times to destroy death and God's enemies? Will it comfort those who see embodied existence as a "world of woe" and a "veil of tears," and who seek their salvation only in a pain-free, distant Heaven with golden streets? Probably not.

But I believe there are many of us who ache for what Joseph Campbell described in *The Power of Myth* as "the rapture of the experience of being alive"; people who, like me, can sometimes glimpse the Oneness of a grace-filled Reality that exults in embodiment, even with its heart-rending sorrows. I believe there are those who seek to align themselves with the sacred flow of healing love, dynamism, and adventurous creativity that can bring relationship, reconciliation, transformation, and abundant life to all. Let us now sing those hopes into being.

Sheri D. Kling, Ph.D., is the director of Process & Faith with the Center for Process Studies and interim minister of Redeemer Lutheran Church in Bradenton, FL. Sheri earned her Ph.D. in Religion: Process Studies from Claremont School of Theology. She is a theologian, songwriter, and spiritual companion, as well as a faculty member of the Haden Institute, adjunct faculty with Claremont School of Theology, and the author of *A Process Spirituality: Christian and Transreligious Resources for Transformation*. She regularly delivers dynamic "Music & Message" presentations to groups, and offers courses, concerts, and spiritual retreats. She may be found online at sherikling.com.

Editors

Jeff Wells is the lead pastor of the Church of the Village, a progressive, radically inclusive, and anti-racist community in the New York City. He preaches, practices, and promotes process-relational and open & relational theology. Jeff is an active member of the Alliance for Ecological Civilization. In 2022, he helped found and co-chaired the Living Earth Movement. With John B. Cobb Jr., he co-authored a short book, *Is International Cooperation Possible? A Bold Appeal for a Living Earth* (2022). Website: jeffrywells.love

Vikki Randall lives in Monrovia CA, and has 28 years of pastoral experience, serving large and small churches, mostly in PCUSA. She received a D.Min. in spiritual formation from Azusa Pacific Seminary and has served there as adjunct faculty in undergrad theology since 2003. She is passionate about transformation and experiencing God's presence.

Nichole Torbitzky is an Associate Professor of Religion and University Chaplain at Lindenwood University. She earned her M.Div. from Pittsburgh Theological Seminary and her Ph.D. from Claremont Graduate University. She serves as the editor for the Process and Faith lectionary series (https://processandfaith.org/lectionaries/#gsc.tab=0) and is working on a book about Process thought and atonement theory.

Thomas Jay Oord, Ph.D., is a theologian, philosopher, and scholar of multi-disciplinary studies. Oord directs the Center for Open and Relational Theology and the Open and Relational Theology doctoral program at Northwind Theological Seminary. He is an award-winning author and has written or edited over thirty books. A gifted speaker, Oord lectures at universities, conferences, churches, and institutions. Website: thomasjayoord.com

Video recordings of many of the sermons included in this book are available on our YouTube channel: @PreachingUncontrollingLove.

If you would like to submit a sermon for consideration, please email Uncontrolling.Love.of.God@gmail.com.